Post-conflict Eritrea:

Prospects for
reconstruction
and development

The War-torn Societies Project aims to assist the international donor community, international organizations, NGOs and local authorities and organizations to better understand and respond to the complex challenges of post-conflict periods. Once fighting has stopped, a fragile ceasefire must be transformed into a lasting political settlement, emergency relief provided, and a process of political, economic, social and psychological rebuilding initiated to lay the basis for future sustainable development. These are gigantic tasks; they are interrelated, with progress in one depending on progress in the others and they must, therefore, be tackled simultaneously.

The War-torn Societies Project was jointly initiated by the United Nations Research Institute for Social Development and the Programme for Strategic and International Security Studies of the Graduate Institute of International Studies in Geneva, in response to a widely recognized need for systemic analysis of present experience and practice. It aims to contribute to a better integration of different forms of international assistance – humanitarian, economic, political and military – within a coherent policy framework, to encourage a better alignment of external assistance with local efforts and thus to bring about a more efficient and effective use of local and international resources.

UNRISD is an autonomous United Nations research organization, focusing on the most pressing problems of social development. The Institute emphasizes a holistic, ivmultidisciplinary and political economy approach in its work.

PSIS is a centre for training, research, documentation and consultation on questions of international and regional conflict and security, arms control and disarmament. It is part of the Graduate Institute of International Studies in Geneva, Switzerland, and is financed by public and private contributions.

Post-conflict Eritrea:

Prospects for reconstruction and development

Edited by

Martin Doornbos and Alemseged Tesfai

The Red Sea Press, Inc.
Publishers & Distributors of Third World Books

11-D Princess Road  P. O. Box 48
Lawrenceville, NJ 08648 Asmara, ERITREA

The Red Sea Press, Inc.
Publishers & Distributors of Third World Books

11-D Princess Road   P. O. Box 48
Lawrenceville, NJ 08648   Asmara, ERITREA

Copyright © 1999 UNRISD

First Printing 1999

Library of Congress Cataloging-in-Publication Data

Post-conflict Eritrea : prospects for reconstruction and development
    edited by Alemseged Tesfai & Martin Doornbos.
      p.   cm.
   Includes bibliographical references.
   ISBN 1-56902-108-2 (HB). – ISBN 1-56902-109-0 (PB)
    1. Eritrea–Economic conditions. 2. Eritrea–Economic policy.
3. Eritrea–History–Revolution, 1962-1993–Economic aspects.
I. Alemseged Tesfai. II. Doornbos, Martin.
HC847.P67 1999
338.9635–dc21   98-55215
                                 CIP

TABLE OF CONTENTS

LIST OF TABLES

CHAPTER 7

LIST OF ACRONYMS

ADB	African Development Bank
AHP	Animal Health Programme
ARP	Agricultural Rehabilitation Programme
CCU	Central Co-ordination Unit of WSP
CERA	Commission for Eritrean Refugee Affairs
CFW	cash-for-work
CIDA	Canadian International Development Agency
CORRA	Commission for Relief and Refugee Affairs
DPA	Department of Public Administration
ECDFU	Eritrean Community Development Fund
ECRFU	Eritrean Community Rehabilitation Fund
EEA	Eritrean Electricity Authority
EGB	Eritrean Grain Board
ELF	Eritrean Liberation Front
EPLA	Eritrean People's Liberation Army
EPLF	Eritrean People's Liberation Front
ERA	Eritrean Relief Association
ERRA	Eritrean Rehabilitation and Relief Agency
ERREC	Eritrean Relief and Refugee Commission
EU	European Union
EW&FIS	Early Warning and Food Information System
EWDFA	Eritrean War Disabled Fighters Association
FAO	Food and Agriculture Organization of the United Nations
FFW	food-for-work
GDP	gross domestic product
GER	Gross Enrolment Rate
GSE	Government of the State of Eritrea
GTZ	Gesellschaft Technische Zusammenarbeit
HPC	Horticulture Producers Co-operative
HRD	human resource development
ICS	interconnected system
IEG	Imperial Ethiopian Government
IFSP	Integrated Food Security Programme
IGAD	Intergovernmental Authority for Development
IMF	International Monetary Fund
ISNAR	International Service for National Agricultural Research
MAU	mass administration unit
MLG	Minister of Local Government
MSMEs	micro, small and medium enterprises
NCEW	National Confederation of Eritrean Workers

NGO	non-governmental organization
NORAD	Norwegian Agency for Development Cooperation
NSP	National Service Programme
NUEW	National Union of Eritrean Women
NUEYS	National Union of Eritrean Youth and Students
OBS	Otto Benecke Stiftung
PAR	participatory action research
PCE	Petroleum Corporation of Eritrea
PFDJ	People's Front for Democracy and Justice
PGE	Provisional Government of Eritrea
PPR	*peste de petits ruminants*
PRA	participatory rapid appraisal
PROFERI	Programme for the Repatriation and Reintegration of Refugees
PSIS	Programme for Strategic and International Security Studies
PTSA	Postal and Telecommunication Services Authority
QIP	quick impact project
RET	renewable energy technology
RICE	Research and Information Centre on Eritrea
RRPE	Recovery and Rehabilitation Programme of Eritrea
SAH-ARP	Seraye, Akeleguzay and Hamasien ARP
SASEBA-ARP	Sahel, Senhit, Semhar and Barka ARP
SCS	self-contained system
SIDA	Swedish International Development Agency
TLU	Tropical Livestock Unit
TPLF	Tigrayan People's Liberation Front
TSE	Telecommunication Services of Eritrea
UNDP	United Nations Development Programme
UNFPA	United Nations Population Fund
UNHCR	Office of the United Nations High Commissioner for Refugees
UNICEF	United Nations Children's Fund
UNRISD	United Nations Research Institute for Social Development
UNV	United Nations Volunteers
USAID	United States Agency for International Development
WFP	World Food Programme
WHO	World Health Organization
WSP	War-torn Societies Project

PREFACE

MATTHIAS STIEFEL, DIRECTOR, WAR-TORN SOCIETIES PROJECT

The War-torn Societies Project (WSP) was born in 1994. The early nineties had seen the end of the Cold War and great expectations that a new era of peace was upon us, when the development efforts of the international assistance community might bear fruit in a climate of stability and growth. This was not to be. The new times had instead brought conflict and suffering on a scale not seen since the wars of half a century before. Billions of dollars spent in countries such as Somalia, Cambodia and Angola had delivered no sustainable peace. The international community seemed unable to cope with such failures and was searching for new forms and approaches to external assistance.

It was in this climate that the War-torn Societies Project was set up by the United Nations Research Institute for Social Development (UNRISD) and the Programme for Strategic and International Security Studies (PSIS) of the Graduate Institute of International Studies in Geneva, and with the support of 28 bilateral and multilateral donors. In four countries emerging from conflict and beginning the task of rebuilding — Eritrea, Mozambique, Guatemala and Somalia – the project aimed to pilot innovative methods of participatory action-research to explore the challenges involved in post-conflict rebuilding and to begin to define where and on what terms external assistance might usefully complement local and national efforts in reconstruction in a way that would contribute to sustainable peace.

WSP set out to create a 'neutral space' in each country where the many actors involved in post-conflict rebuilding – both national and international – could come together to explore and debate the conflicting tasks facing the country as it set out on the road to peaceful development.

This debate was focused around a number of themes that the participants had themselves chosen and that formed the basis of interactive research carried out by a team of local researchers. The results of this research, carried out in five working groups in Eritrea, form the main body of this volume. The research, however, was not static: as the debate progressed, the participants called for more investigation, raised questions, reoriented conclusions and became both the instigators and the receivers of the research findings. Thus research became process, and it is this that makes WSP an unusual, potentially unique tool for rebuilding.

Eritrea was of special significance to WSP as the first of the four country projects and the place where many of the early lessons of WSP were learned. When we began work in Eritrea, we were looking essentially to learn about the potential role of the external assistance community – an issue of particular importance in Eritrea, which had developed over the years of struggle a fierce sense of independence from foreign aid and intervention – but we soon learned that we were learning as much about the internal dynamics of rebuilding, about the complex mixes of actors and issues that must be juggled if reconstruction is to succeed, and about the hundred and one nitty-gritty issues that can arise in setting up a collaborative project like WSP and that have to be understood, negotiated and carefully managed. We found our way through this complexity with the invaluable help and support of our country team in Eritrea, the many participants in the WSP process at all levels, and with a small but dedicated band of people at the central level in Geneva.

WSP's first Coordinator in Eritrea, Narayo Techlemichael, had been at the meeting which first gave birth to the War-torn Societies Project in 1994 in Cartigny, Switzerland, and was a staunch supporter from the outset. His replacement, Tesfai Ghermazien, then Minister of Agriculture in the Eritrean Government, similarly gave wholehearted support to WSP's work. As WSP came to a close in Eritrea, Arefaine Berhe, his successor as Minister of Agriculture, became the project's third Coordinator and rounded off the work so ably begun by his predecessors. To these colleagues, and to the teams of researchers and administrative staff that they led, we owe a huge debt of gratitude.

Throughout the project's time in Eritrea, it was honoured with the cooperation and participation of the Eritrean Government and President Isaias Afwerki. The understanding and support of national authorities is obviously vital to a process that looks to the heart of policy-setting and peace-building, and we are pleased and grateful for the fruitful collaboration of the Eritrean Government.

Thanks also go to Martin Doornbos, WSP's International Researcher and a key player in helping the Geneva coordination team to support WSP Eritrea effectively, and to the other members of the Central Coordination Unit who have contributed to the success of all four WSP country projects. Most of all, however, we thank the many people who participated in the WSP experience in Eritrea, who committed their time and energy to the project and who will continue the vital task of rebuilding Eritrea and helping it travel on the path to peaceful and sustainable development.

1

THE WAR-TORN SOCIETIES PROJECT IN ERITREA: AN INTRODUCTION

Martin Doornbos

W hen a country emerges from a liberation struggle, prolonged civil war, or other similarly profound conflict, what are the first steps it needs to take? Numerous tasks in rehabilitation and reconstruction are waiting to be taken up, each calling for urgent attention, each constituting a priority concern to both the political leadership and the people at large. But how do such tasks relate to each another, and how should they be prioritized? One of the first tasks must be to inventory what needs doing, for example to identify the most critical challenges in post-conflict rebuilding and take preliminary stock of the available tools. In line with overall strategies, the key challenge becomes that of determining which policy instruments should be developed to launch the long and arduous process of post-conflict reconstruction and development. There are crucial research tasks to be fulfilled in this connection, focusing specifically on the identification of policy options and requirements. Equally important is the need to devise mechanisms which can help generate clarity and understanding of the interconnections between various policies and actions in the areas of rebuilding and development.

This volume addresses key areas and issues of post-war reconstruction in a country that is emerging from prolonged and profound conflict: Eritrea. The book comprises the core of the research carried out by the War-torn Societies Project (WSP) in Eritrea, launched in July 1995 to contribute to the clarification and discussion of policy priorities in Eritrean development. It presents the findings of the main themes researched in the course of this project, all of which were focused on broad priority areas in post-conflict rehabilitation, rebuilding and development: the challenge of social reintegration, infrastructure development, food security, human resource development, and basic questions of governance. Each of these themes has been the subject of extensive discussion and debate by Working Groups established as part of the project. In these Working Groups, researchers and other actors with a direct interest in the topic met regularly to discuss preliminary research results, deliberate on additional questions to be asked, and reflect on the relevance of the research for the role and agenda of various agencies on the Eritrean development front. Thus, the results of this work can be largely seen as a collective product. As these research findings are expected to be of interest and relevance to much wider circles concerned with Eritrean reconstruction and development, both within and outside the country, they are now brought together in this revised format.

In mid-1998 the world was shocked to learn that Eritrea had once again become engaged in armed conflict, and again with Ethiopia. Saddening as this is for a country and people still trying to overcome a legacy of conflict, it does not necessarily alter the basic contours sketched in this volume with respect to the issues of reconstruction and development faced in Eritrea today. Although, in several respects one must fear that the existing issues have already become aggravated. Aside from the immediate casualties – thousands of newly displaced people are joining the large number of others already in need of support and rehabilitation – the war is taking a toll in terms of new infrastructure devastation, and food security has become threatened for many more people than those most recently displaced and affected. Activities in other areas of reconstruction have inevitably slowed down, and may halt altogether.

While it is too early to assess the extent to which the renewed conflict will affect or delay the prospects for rebuilding, there is no doubt that the characteristic Eritrean determination to carry on with the agenda for reconstruction and development will remain strong, or indeed strengthen. The dispute itself has rapidly evolved into one about more than borders alone. Indeed, its economic and political-symbolic dimensions tend to heavily overshadow the immediate question of correct boundary demarcations. One early interpretation that briefly circulated internationally suggested that the confrontation typically reflected Eritrea's youthful, militant nationalism. However, another view of the renewed Ethiopian/Eritrean conflict would be to see it as a signal that the former dominant power, Ethiopia, appears determined to set limits on accepting newly independent Eritrea developing national policies and institutions, beginning with its own currency. On the Eritrean side, the long-term commitment remains one in which reconstruction and development, on Eritrean terms, are still the overriding principles. Hopefully, the momentum that had gathered can soon be regained. In this context, this volume's discussion of priorities and issues in key policy areas concerned with reconstruction and development may be expected to fully retain its relevance. It is with this perspective in mind that the title originally designated for this book, **Post-conflict Eritrea: prospects for reconstruction and development**, has been deliberately retained.

The chapters that follow are devoted to the issues identified as key themes in post-conflict rebuilding and development: social reintegration, infrastructure, food security, human resource development, and governance. The chapters are preceded by a general overview of post-conflict reconstruction in Eritrea, and followed by an analysis of substantive and conceptual issues raised in the course of this particular research effort.

The introduction first looks at the basic components of WSP, then provides a conceptual background, specifically relating and contrasting WSP research to earlier modes of participatory action research (PAR). Subsequently, it briefly sketches the Eritrean historico-political context within which WSP was launched, before presenting a more detailed discussion and analysis of the WSP Eritrea experience through a review of some key phases and dimensions of the project.

THE WAR-TORN SOCIETIES PROJECT: BACKGROUND AND BASIC COMPONENTS

WSP's premise is that post-conflict rehabilitation typically involves a wide range of actors, internal and external, but that it is often hampered by the actors' lack of understanding of the links between some of the basic issues and priorities concerned. This is due to an insufficient exchange of information about the various actors' policy agendas and, last but not least, by the limitations and lack of flexibility resulting from several external actors' own terms of reference. In that light, WSP proposed to initiate action research projects in selected war-torn societies, to facilitate jointly sponsored research activities in priority areas of social and economic reconstruction, and to promote policy dialogue and synchronization among the main actors involved. In this context, research and policy action are viewed as potentially interrelated in multiple ways. Research intends to help identify priorities for policy involvement and adjustment, at the same time mapping out the programmes in which various actors are already engaged. In turn, actors are expected to not only respond to research findings, but to also call for new areas of enquiry, collectively steering research in new directions. In the process, dialogue among actors – government and other national agencies, multilateral and bilateral aid agencies, and non-governmental organizations (NGOs) – about research priorities and findings and their respective policy agendas, is expected to be of intrinsic value.

WSP's approach was laid down in a project document which was accepted as a basis for action at a 1994 seminar in Cartigny, Switzerland. The document outlined a number of crucial steps to be followed and elements to be included in each country project. In terms of organizational structure and staffing, this involved the selection of a national Project Director who would have overall responsibility for the project and liaison with key government and external agencies. The director would furthermore be responsible for the formation of a Project Group which would assume collective "ownership" of the project and which would consist of representatives of the main internal and external actors in post-conflict rebuilding. The director would also recruit a Research Co-ordinator, other core researchers, administrative support staff, and logistical support.

In terms of operations, the first task for the core research team would be to prepare a Country Note, a substantive paper discussing the key social, economic and political conditions and requirements of the country in the post-conflict situation, with attention to the interconnection of various issues. The Country Note would serve as a basis for discussion in the Project Group and for the selection of key themes or Entry Points, usually not more than five, for research that could highlight policy issues engaged in by different actors.

For each of these themes, a Working Group would be constituted, comprising actor representatives with a particular interest or engagement in the policy area concerned. Then the members of the Working Groups would confer among themselves and with the relevant researcher(s) on setting the priority level of various issues, and the manner of implementation. They would also be expected to direct the research and feedback based on preliminary findings. In the research activities and in Working Group deliberations, a special effort was made to ensure a meaningful "policy mix", as well as an "actor mix". WSP projects would have an expected duration of approximately one-and-a-half years, the period considered necessary and sufficient to initiate a process that might become self-sustaining. Throughout the projects' duration, a central co-ordinating unit (CCU) in Geneva would provide close monitoring and backstopping of research activities, and arrange logistical support.

Based on this general framework, WSP was launched in Eritrea in July 1995, followed by Mozambique in the same year, Guatemala in August 1996, and Somalia in January 1997, the latter after a prolonged preparatory period. The Eritrean project concluded in December 1996 with a final workshop, and was followed by an extension until May 1997 to allow for the preparation of a successor arrangement.

WSP AND PARTICIPATORY ACTION RESEARCH IN COMPARATIVE PERSPECTIVE

WSP experience and its particular Entry Point into the research-policy nexus can be looked at in various ways: its potential as a forum for policy dialogue; its capacity to generate policy-relevant research data; and its comparative advantage as a tool in problem identification and solving, to name but a few. Each of these angles highlights a particular aspect of what, in most WSP contexts to date, quickly became a complex set of processes and interactions, involving researchers, policy makers and other interested parties.

Each of these angles, by implication, also adds an element to thinking more generally about the possible links between research and policy. These links occur in multiple forms in different contexts. They have also often been hampered by a lack of adequate feedback mechanisms. It is a common refrain that sound policy preparation requires reliable research back-up (and feedback), but the search for solid and relevant connections between policy and research is a continuous struggle being waged on many fronts. WSP has come to represent a significant effort toward making such connections, specifically in situations of post-conflict reconstruction and reconciliation.

One interesting way to look at the WSP experience and to understand its rationale and objectives, or at least some dimensions therein, is to place it in the context of the development of participatory approaches toward problem-oriented and problem-solving social research. Some of WSP's roots can be traced back to innovative forms of PAR, which became prominent in the late 1960s and 1970s when it was developed particularly for application in micro-contexts such as small rural communities.

Anthropologists and other researchers would associate themselves with, for example, small groups of peasant farmers, and through extensive discussion with them would try to identify the needs and aspirations of local communities and help them conceive of what local people could contribute to these ends. Conscientiousness and awareness-raising about the key problems facing social groups and the strategies to overcome them were central to this approach.

On the research side, the problem-orientation and participatory dimensions of this new approach stood in stark contrast to "classic" anthropological research in which the researcher strives to observe and accurately record social interactions within the study community while trying to stay outside the process. On the policy side, the basic assumption of this new participatory approach was that it might allow for a more accurate identification of needs and problem-solving options than solutions and programmes devised elsewhere and handed down to passive recipients.

Both of these new aspects, problem-orientation and participatory dimensions, demanded entirely novel roles and skills on the part of the researcher. Beyond observation and analysis, which were by no means to be superseded but were assigned a more preparatory and supportive role, the researcher would essentially act as a facilitator, providing a venue (at least symbolically) and guiding the interactions and collective thinking of participants in the "project". Instead of striving for "scientific objectivity", which at roughly the same time came under heavy fire as ultimately unattainable anyway, researchers were expected to empathize and identify with the local community's self-examination and quest for ways to improve their conditions. Nonetheless, this new role posed its own professional requirements, including codes of conduct, which in due course would become the subject of a good deal of discussion and elaboration.

PAR was developed in the 1960s and 1970s in Latin America and other Third World regions, in the wake of liberation theology and as a supplement to conventional research methods. While it soon gained a place in the repertoire of social science research strategies and methodologies, there was also ample opportunity to tone down the somewhat exaggerated expectations it initially aroused. Elements of PAR can currently be found in various problem-solving strategies.

Conceptually, WSP was directly derived from some of the basic ideas governing PAR. In particular, its stress on common reconnaissance of issues and policy priorities and on dialogue to better appreciate different actors' perspectives, owes a great deal to the PAR premises. What makes WSP different and unique, however, is that it represents what may be called a quantum leap in participatory research methods. What was first developed as a research methodology at the micro level was lifted to the macro level, both in terms of addressing broad national issues and in terms of the participation of a variety of actors, internal and external, playing key roles. Here, the participants are representatives of various major agencies rather than a community of peasant farmers, and the facilitators are a WSP Project Director with a research team rather than an individual researcher. Also, while PAR researchers were generally (though not necessarily) outsiders, the WSP researchers are invariably insiders, who are widely recognized as interested parties in the process. Nevertheless, the basic idea of researchers guiding and supporting a collective research engagement and dialogue to identify policy solutions for key issues in reconstruction remains the same.

However, there is a further difference. Micro-level PAR not only addressed the local level, but also sought to empower participants such as small farmers in their dealings with powerful agents such as landlords or the state. Therefore, in confrontational situations, its role was essentially conflictual. WSP, on the other hand, not only focuses on the macro level, but strives to create bridges for dialogue and communication. Its role is thus basically consensual.

WSP's basic assumption was that post-conflict situations have an acute need for broadly based dialogue and communication, as well as for the generation and sharing of sound information as to the requirements and priorities for reconstruction. Post-conflict situations are potentially characterized by a lack of clarity, by confusion and/or overlap regarding which actors – government branches, private organizations, international agencies – are doing what, and what policy responses they are developing to immediate and long-term needs. Also, there is usually little, if any, opportunity for regular communication among key actors in the field. Therefore, WSP's premise is that mapping key issues and key policy initiatives through jointly-initiated research, and using the research results as a basis for dialogue toward an improved understanding of different policy approaches and possible co-ordination, may help fill important gaps.

Does it indeed do so? Definitive answers can be given with confidence only when the WSP pilot projects are completed and the processes and results more fully analysed. Nonetheless, several striking experiences already stand out. In the first two countries where WSP projects were launched, Eritrea and Mozambique, the dynamics of the projects worked out quite differently, as could have been expected in different contexts. However, the common element was that in both countries participants reflecting on their involvement in WSP Working Groups singled out the element of dialogue as having been of foremost significance in contributing to a better understanding of different actors' positions and policies. Representatives of NGOs and multilateral agencies, for example, remarked that it was through WSP that they had attained a better appreciation of the rationale of government policies, while participants from government or political organizations observed that WSP had provided a much-needed forum for sharing some of their policy considerations with other actors engaged in reconstruction. Beyond this, it was reiterated from virtually all quarters that the involvement in WSP had indeed been a shared learning experience, which in a number of instances had helped to indicate viable solutions to common issues.

In terms of providing a forum for creative dialogue and generating a common sense of direction, the initial country experiences suggest that WSP may be credited for succeeding in transferring some basic elements of PAR from the micro context to the macro level. But if this seems to hold significant promise for national and international engagement in reconstruction efforts, what can be said about the possible limits to participatory problem-oriented research – beyond dialogue as it were – under the auspices of WSP? Again, the particular context in which WSP-style action research is being undertaken appears to be of crucial importance in determining both the needs and the possible scope for its engagement.

In this connection it will be useful to recall a basic assumption underlying the WSP concept, namely that PAR at the macro level will be especially relevant in post-conflict situations with marked uncertainty of the actors involved and the policy objectives they are pursuing, and with a clear need to arrive at a broader consensus. However, if governments are wary of involving others in the policy process and insist on controlling the agenda for national reconstruction, it is likely that they will not be in favour of participatory policy research going beyond dialogue. Dialogue may still be considered useful in this context, and of potential service to the government in office, but the latter will be more prone to ensure that any policy dialogue which it did not initiate itself will not encroach on its prerogative to (re-)set national policy priorities.

In fact, there may be some ambivalence in governmental responses to WSP's role and approach. On the one hand, a government may acknowledge its potential value in facilitating dialogue among different actors (possibly including some former rivals) and so have an almost natural interest in making use of the opportunity it offers as an additional forum to get its messages across. On the other hand, governments may be concerned that policy dialogue thus enacted might follow a largely autonomous course and become a new locus for policy initiatives. These are delicate questions and may not always be explicit, but they constitute real issues and deserve to be acknowledged by all parties concerned. In principle, respecting the limitations they impose, WSP's particular approach to action research has the potential to make strategic contributions to rethinking key issues in post-conflict reconstruction.

ERITREA: THE CONTEXT

Before assessing the role that WSP has come to play in Eritrea, there is a need to properly understand the Eritrean context. Several aspects of this context are of major importance as they strongly influence the nature and style of policy interactions: the background of the liberation struggle, the orientation of the political leadership that emerged from it, its present role and position vis-à-vis Eritrean society, the style and mechanisms of policy making, and the overall strategies and objectives of government policies.

The continued importance of the liberation struggle against Ethiopian annexation to the composition and orientation of Eritrea's political leadership can hardly be overestimated. The duration, nature and intensity of this conflict have had profound effects. The 30-year war that came to an end in 1991 was intense and required an extraordinary degree of adaptation and improvisation. These factors weighed all the more heavily because, more than almost any other war in recent times, it was fought in isolation. And adding to the physical and social scars was a costly war within the war, as the Eritrean People's Liberation Front (EPLF), ultimately victorious, for some years engaged in a fierce struggle for hegemony with the Eritrean Liberation Front (ELF), from which it had earlier split.

On the Eritrean side the war was not fought by a regular army, using regular divisions and hierarchies, but by flexible units with a common background in a movement-based type of engagement. This attracted a spectrum of young men and women from many walks of life, urban and rural, who after the war derived a sense of pride, and a certain privilege, from their status as ex-fighters. Over the years, social life within the front developed its own codes and ethos, which many members of the leadership and rank and file continue to live by.

On delivering ultimate victory and political independence to Eritrea, the EPLF took up political leadership as a matter of course, replacing the controlling Ethiopian administration. From the commanding heights of government the People's Front for Democracy and Justice (PFDJ), the new name assumed by the EPLF, continues to view a unified front as a necessary condition for confronting the challenges of post-war reconstruction and development. Moreover, those within the front tend to believe that the means by which the challenges of war were successfully tackled can now be put to use to meet the challenges of peace. Whereas one side of this ethos stresses learning by doing, and addressing issues as they are encountered, another side emphasizes maintaining unified policy positions vis-à-vis internal and external actors.

This unified yet flexible front culture has several implications for the style of government in Eritrea. For example, there is a continued reliance on informal lines of communication among front members, and on *ad hoc* decision-making and policy readjustments as issues and situations demand. Also, there are as yet few written, "general" policy statements being issued, and very few fixed positions of government responsibility. Instead, government is regularly reshuffled, to the extent that not only will every minister be expected to change seats, but many senior officers are similarly exchanging positions, very often to fields that are entirely new to them. One implication is that neither attachments to any particular government office, nor authority derived from any specific expertise, are likely to develop. Overall unity and command are thus more easily maintained.

This pattern has many ramifications and can be interpreted in a variety of ways, though they all imply a particular emphasis on the unity principle. Vis-à-vis the external world, at any rate, what counts is the Eritreans' determination not to let the war-born sense of self-sufficiency and independence get lost in the maze of international aid agreements, policy packages or their attached conditionalities. As the youngest of independent African states, Eritrea appears determined not to become a donor-driven country like so many others in Africa, and if this implies foregoing potentially attractive propositions, it seems prepared to pay the price. There is a "take it or leave it" attitude vis-à-vis foreign donors, who are welcome to support projects or programmes that have received the government's approval, but whose own propositions for involvement in different sectors carry little weight, if any. Instead, the government is determined to do things its own way, even if it means taking unorthodox steps, making internationally unconventional decisions or saying it is not ready to adopt a particular policy. One popular Eritrean motto that is sometimes cited in this connection is "Never kneel down." The initiative remains firmly in Eritrean hands.

External agencies – bilateral, multilateral or non-governmental – are generally not accustomed to this. Elsewhere, they have often found willing partners listening to their proposals, partners who were *a priori* prepared to accept externally-devised policy packages and the conditions that come with them. Thus, UNDP compounds, together with representatives of USAID, EU and the World Bank, have come to constitute nerve centres in more than a few African countries, at times having more detailed or up-to-date information on certain policy issues than the government. For many external agencies, the Eritrean stance is a novel experience, which takes some effort getting used to. Aside from the *a priori* restricted scope of their activities, what probably concerns the external actors most is the relative lack of communication from the government with respect to various policy fields, the relative lack of predictability of their own operations, and the consequent difficulties of budgeting and planning.

There is an implicit dialogue of sorts underlying this pattern of internal/external relations in Eritrea. Multilateral and bilateral agencies and NGOs would expect the Eritreans to get their act together and to develop "normal" working relationships with the outside world and its representatives. The web of international arrangements and agreements to which all independent states are party is growing increasingly intricate, and the international "system", even though it is not monolithic, expects the Eritreans to assume their role with all the rights and obligations it implies. Furthermore, with globalization and worldwide economic transitions accelerating, it is sometimes argued – and some Eritreans might agree – that if Eritrea does not engage in this wider movement and catch up, it will be left behind.

Eritreans for their part seem unconvinced that such "normal" relationships are an absolute must, and would rather take their time to develop them their own way, and preferably on their own terms. This is not a matter of intransigence. Part of the thinking is the analogy that during the 30-year liberation struggle fighters on the front were left to their own devices, with few if any outside powers coming to their aid. So there is some doubt as to whether or why these arrangements should be rushed into now. Additionally, it appears that the ex-fighters still largely in command are determined to retain overall control of the strategies for post-war development, in possible opposition to returnees from exile who might be more inclined to engage in collaborative international links. Finally, in much the same vein, it is feared that Eritrea unconditionally joining "the system" might inevitably mean being relegated to a kind of junior status in many of its external relations, which it is felt is definitely to be avoided. Clearly, there is still a strong nationalist sentiment at play: a "fought" independence is to be consummated, not dissipated.

It was in this context and climate that WSP Eritrea was launched. In retrospect, it appears that the responses and interactions it has generated were in many ways predictable, though when the venture set out it seemed to start out for entirely uncharted waters.

Preparing for Research

Eritrea was a candidate for a WSP project as it appeared to be representative of a particular type of post-conflict situation, namely one with a clear political structure and a strong and legitimate governmental authority. Also in this respect, the Eritrean context differed radically from that of, for example, Guatemala or Mozambique, where the post-conflict situation was characterized by the primary need for ongoing reconciliation among former adversaries. In these areas Eritrea seemed to be a relatively "easy" case, and potentially suitable to start with. Eritrea certainly fulfilled the WSP criteria of a country whose infrastructure was severely damaged and where rebuilding and rehabilitation efforts were high on the agenda in a whole range of areas. However, as would become clear in the course of the project, Eritrea was not or did not see itself as "war-torn" in the sense of having to cope with serious internal social and political divisions. Nor would it, in the end, turn out to be an "easy" case. In fact, when WSP chose Eritrea as the first case for implementation in early 1995, it was probably not aware of how special and unique a case Eritrea would be with respect to the external/internal actor equation.

Nonetheless, during several preparatory visits to Eritrea by WSP representatives in 1995, expectations of what the project might constitute in the Eritrean context were discussed and compared with key members of the Eritrean government and other potentially interested actors. During these discussions it became clear that WSP Geneva and the Eritrean government had some different expectations about the potential outcomes of the project. However, it also appeared that the respective expectations did not really involve opposed agendas.

Thus, accepting that the endeavour would necessarily be experimental, Eritrea became WSP's first country project. Dr. Nerayo Teclemichael, then head of the Eritrean Rehabilitation and Relief Agency (ERRA), became the first Project Director. Dr. Berhane Woldemichael, a former representative of the Research and Information Centre on Eritrea (RICE) in London, became the full-time Research Co-ordinator.

Setting up the project was a learning exercise in many ways. For lack of any blueprints or scenarios as to how to go about the task, it appears to have been approached in the time-honoured learning-by-doing fashion. In many cases this involved clarifying – or skipping – a fundamental question, such as who should be making the decisions to begin with. Indeed, a cluster of questions soon announced themselves concerning priorities and initiatives in WSP operations, the extent of autonomy in decision making and, ultimately, the project's ownership.

The logistics of setting up WSP in the Eritrean city of Asmara became even more complex as a result of the basic choice made to establish it as a distinct entity, so as to provide for a neutral physical space where actors could meet. Therefore, affiliation with or location on the premises of existing institutions was not sought, but instead a villa was rented to serve as the administrative cum documentation centre and a venue for Working Group meetings.

Following the initial preparatory steps, the WSP Eritrea research team set about the task of drafting a Country Note which was to serve as a point of departure for the selection of a number of Entry Points, broad policy themes on which WSP research efforts would subsequently concentrate. This took some time and effort, but once completed the Country Note provided a broad overview of issues central to Eritrean reconstruction and development. Main sections of the note were devoted to the legacies of the Eritrean conflict, positive as well as negative, and to the challenges that lay ahead. Post-conflict experiences of reconstruction were discussed – the process of political rebuilding, issues affecting rehabilitation and social reconstruction, the reintegration of war-affected populations, the role of food aid and economic rebuilding – along with local initiatives and the role of external actors in Eritrean rebuilding. The document, which is reproduced in a slightly revised form as Chapter 2 of this volume, was presented in February 1996 at the first meeting of the Project Group, the broadly representative body of external and internal actors invited to take part in the WSP project, serve as its forum, and initiate its next steps. The meeting itself constituted an important and unprecedented event: assembling all relevant external actors and a large number of relevant internal actors for a full day of relatively open discussion was no minor achievement and appeared to break new ground in Eritrea.

At the Project Group meeting, as previously noted, the themes chosen as Entry Points for further research were food security, social reintegration, human resource development, infrastructure and governance. Other themes were suggested, notably gender issues and the plight of pastoral communities and environmental security, but after some discussion these were not selected as separate Entry Points. Similarly, the role of international assistance *per se* had been proposed as an Entry Point, but again this was felt to be a topic already closely related to several of the main themes and that it might naturally come up for discussion within each specific context, which it did. In the end, it was agreed that gender issues, the role of private business, and local initiatives should be given special attention as cross-cutting themes within each of the Entry Points chosen. In the course of the research, as will be shown, this attempt was only partly successful.

In the discussion of Entry Points, a certain distinction emerged between the ways in which internal and external actors dealt with questions of international assistance. External actors tended to propose more direct relief and conflict-related issues, and to look at issues more in a short-term perspective, while Eritrean members of the Project Group preferred to focus on long-term concerns, or to look at the same issues in a long-term developmental perspective. Such was the case with: food aid, which the Eritrean members chose to consider from the angle of food security; reintegration of refugees and ex-combatants, which the Eritreans preferred to consider within the context of the wider subject of reintegrating marginal or excluded communities into society; and government/external actor relations, which the Eritreans preferred to handle under the much broader category of "governance". Similarly, human resource development and infrastructure development were themes deliberately chosen by the Eritreans with a long-term perspective in mind. The same trend occurred when more generally discussing the role of international assistance. The Eritrean position was not to focus primarily on aid when looking at their relations with the international community, but rather on questions of their integration and position in a wider economic and political context, regionally and globally. These reactions were of course perfectly consistent with the determination, shared quite generally among Eritrean policy-makers, to avoid becoming a donor-driven country and entering into aid-determined external relations.

Following the selection of the main Entry Points, Working Groups were convened around each theme and Project Group members were invited to indicate in which Working Group they would like to participate. Meanwhile, core researchers were to be recruited for the research tasks to be undertaken, in dialogue with the new Working Groups, on each of the designated themes. At this point, the new Project Director, Dr. Tesfai Ghermazien, then Eritrean Minister of Agriculture, who replaced Dr. Nerayo Teclemichael (who had been appointed to a senior position with WHO's regional office in Brazzaville, Congo), assured Geneva that the recruitment of suitable researchers would best be handled by WSP Eritrea. Because recruiting qualified researchers would be no easy task in Eritrea, given the scarcity of highly-trained people, WSP Geneva, it seems, was relieved by the Project Director's reassurance that the Eritrean office would carry out this task.

However, when the Eritrean researchers were selected, it turned out that all five candidates were high government officers, most of whom were working closely with the respective government departments dealing with the issues they would be researching. Thus, the head of the planning department in the Ministry of Agriculture, Haile Awalom, was assigned the research on food security; the principal project officer engaged in the resettlement of refugees with ERRA, Teclemichael W/Giorgis (Rosso), was to take on research on social integration; and the Acting Land Commissioner, Alemseged Tesfai, was given the theme of governance to analyse. In addition, the Director of the Housing Bank, Araia Tseggai, a macroeconomist by training, took on the theme of human resource development, while another senior government economist, Dr. Tekeste Ghebray, was invited to take up the theme of infrastructure development. Responsibility for finalizing the report on infrastructure development was given to Dr. Berhane Woldemichael following Dr. Ghebray's departure to become Executive Secretary of the Intergovernmental Authority for Development (IGAD) in Djibouti. In all cases, the idea was that the research would be conducted on a part-time basis, and in principle with the help of research assistants for fieldwork.

The rationale offered for recruiting professionals within the government as part-time WSP researchers was that it would be extremely difficult to find alternative suitable candidates in Eritrea. It was also reasoned that the researchers concerned would have the double advantage of considerable familiarity with the problem areas concerned and direct access to most of the available documentary data in the country. No doubt there was a great deal of validity to these arguments, even though in the diaspora there would have been many qualified Eritreans capable of, and probably interested in taking on the research tasks concerned. However, recruiting Eritreans from the diaspora would probably have been cost-prohibitive. Alternatively, other suitable candidates might possibly have been found in Eritrea, though this would almost certainly have required a good deal more effort.

Nonetheless, the arrangement also had the effect, if not the intention, that no independent researchers would be making enquiries into policy areas that might possibly be considered sensitive, and also that what would be presented as WSP research findings would be assured of the implicit approval and co-operation of the Eritrean government. The bottom line was that, politically speaking, it would hardly have been feasible to do anything else, if WSP wanted to have any role and influence at all. Meanwhile, one important implication of the choice of working with senior government officers was that it would give a particular slant and direction to the discussions within the various Working Groups, namely that of an 'informative' dialogue on government policy between government and external actors. In this connection, it was important that all Working Groups had come to comprise a good mix of internal and external members.

WORKING GROUPS AND ENTRY POINTS

From all accounts given by participants at the time and in retrospect, it is evident that the WSP Eritrea Working Groups soon developed into the project's key locus and focus of activities. If until this point establishing WSP in Eritrea had seemed an uncertain venture into new territory, strewn with all the obstacles this might involve, the project now clearly had its own momentum. From the start, the various Working Groups were highly animated discussion groups, generally made up of members with a "vested" interest in the topics concerned on account of their professional engagement with external aid agencies or Eritrean government departments.

The Working Groups' first task was to further define the scope and boundaries of the research to be undertaken under the specific heading of each group. To this end, the core researchers associated with each Working Group prepared preliminary outlines of the research, which were discussed at the first meeting of each group and subsequently modified in the light of members' comments. Due in part to the multiple reconnaissance of interests that was taking place, most of these meetings elicited lively discussion: the reconnaissance included an initial exploration of the ground to be covered, with ample arguments for and against broader or more narrowly conceived parameters. Members became familiar with each other's individual involvement and preoccupation and where these converged with their own concerns. Also, members often gave meaningful advice on methodology and research approaches, and offered to make relevant data available to the researchers concerned. Many participants in the Working Group meetings found them to be a useful learning exercise.

The other main and continuing reason for the keen interest in these meetings on the part of many Working Group members was the fact that for the first time a channel was opened up for substantive communication between the Eritrean government and non-governmental, mostly external actors. All sides acknowledged and appreciated the value of this communication, though the rationale tended to differ. External actors emphasized the enhanced understanding they gained of the government's policy on a number of fronts, and of the rationale behind various measures. However, some wondered whether the converse – government gaining a better understanding of the perspective of external actors – was also true. For their part, government members said they had come to appreciate the value of a communication channel like WSP for better putting the government's position across, sometimes adding that they realized the Eritrean government had not been particularly strong in communicating its policies to the outside world. When thus speaking about WSP as a new "channel" for communication between government and external actors, some also pointed to the need to recognize that the channel, rather than serving purely as a conduit, actually "forced" participants to clearly think through and articulate their position. There was general recognition and reaffirmation that "policy" was a matter for the Eritrean government, and that the informative exchanges taking place under the auspices of WSP were not and should not be influencing policy.

Clearly, the Working Groups emerged as the core of WSP activities, and not the Project Group, which was too large a body for effective communication and which met less frequently. An important role of the Project Group was to give visibility to the project and draw a great deal of initial attention to it. The Project Group also represented the thematic unity of WSP engagements. From its initiation the Project Group functioned as an overall umbrella for WSP activities and formally sanctioned new steps within the project; in principle the Project Group figured as the nominal "owner" of WSP Eritrea. It will be important to reflect further on the meaning of this in connection with basic questions about symbolic "ownership" of WSP that have come to command much attention in the course of the project.

While the Working Groups seemed to take off quite naturally as meaningful focuses of dialogue and research activity in the Eritrean case, it may be instructive to look closely at the factors that appeared to facilitate this, and also at the strengths and weaknesses of the Working Group format. First, there is no doubt that the informality possible in a group of 10 to 15 participants contributed strongly to the effectiveness and positive atmosphere of the meetings. Second, part of the credit is probably due to the manner in which the Project Director and Research Co-ordinator convened and led Working Group meetings. As they both chaired many of the group meetings, a homogenous approach emerged and, by raising issues and questions from a relatively independent perspective, they often succeeded in stimulating a substantive dialogue and meeting ground between researchers and other internal and external actors. A third source of strength of the Working Group format was the common interest in the subject matter. Apparently, the WSP venue also was significant for Working Group members who on occasion met officially on matters of common concern, but without the informality that stimulated discussion. In sum, the Working Group format appears to have developed into quite an effective venue for researcher/actor interactions.

Closely connected to the questions of Working Group format and role of the Project Group already referred to, is the scope of the selected themes. In all five themes chosen in Eritrea, this scope was broad indeed. The reasons for this may have ranged from a deliberate attempt to cover broad, interrelated problem areas, to the practical constraint at the Project Group level to formulate more clearly defined areas for inquiry, or possibly a combination of both. At any rate, it should be observed that a broad body like the Project Group, with 60 to 70 participants present for at most one day, cannot effectively delineate research themes in an ultimately satisfactory manner. At most it can, through votes in favour of key words, point to certain areas it would like to see taken up for closer examination. From there it becomes necessary to either develop more specific research questions on selected issues within the areas, or assume that priority must be given to the broad mapping of problems and prospects, possibly to be followed by detailed investigation at a later stage. In the Eritrean case, basically the latter course was pursued.

THE RESEARCH THEMES

In Eritrea, a country having recently emerged from a prolonged war, there had not been much chance for conventional policy research to develop as a regular activity. Though overall strategies were clear and well enough understood, policy-making in the field needed to be largely based on continuous experimentation, improvisation and adaptation. This is not to say that research was non-existent during the days of the EPLF. In fact, a good deal of field and desk research was conducted during the struggle, mostly by the departments of Public Administration, Health, Education, and Political and Cultural Affairs. Moreover, starting from an entirely different concept of research, the Eritrean struggle may well claim to have pioneered various important forms of research in action – "action research" of a kind – such as the development and testing of new practices and techniques in medicine and communications, behind the front line. Today, the *prima facie* impressive reconstruction project of the Massawa railway line provides an example of this learning-by-doing approach in "front-line" research and action, and serves as a reminder of the ethos characteristic of the years of struggle.

However, in "normal" circumstances policy-oriented research inevitably involves a whole range of desk tasks and the drafting of research reports, all in preparation for making basic policy choices or assessing policy performance in various fields. In this sense, it may be said that Eritrea for a long time lacked an involvement in research during the years of the struggle. What is more, there may be a certain "cultural" dimension to it. A non-research orientation is not readily replaced by a disposition to have policies prepared by research with the aim of, for example, critically scrutinizing requirements, options and outcomes before final policy choices are made. When moving in such a direction, which may be prompted by the growing complexity and changing nature of issues requiring decision-making, many adaptations and re-orientations are called for both at the "receiving end" of policy-makers and at the "offering" researchers' end. In fact, moving toward an optimal research/policy relationship is likely to involve a step-by-step process of many mutual adjustments of expectations among policy-makers and policy researchers.

With this background of an extensive gap in policy research, WSP proposed an action research project starting from broadly defined Entry Points at the macro level. There was a certain logic underlying the decision made by researchers and Working Groups to first map the field in terms of basic assets and liabilities in the current Eritrean situation. An attempt was also made in each case to take stock of what needed doing and what basic requirements to begin with, followed by the formulation of relatively large numbers of recommendations. Thus the various research projects were less devoted to weighing the pros and cons of a specific policy issue, but more represented a kind of broad baseline survey of the main issues and challenges. These might be followed at a later stage by specific and sharply focused inquiries. An exception was the governance report which, although still general in scope and coverage, focused on government measures and initiatives toward establishing a new political-administrative framework in Eritrea.

Thus, the WSP report on the challenge of reintegrating returnees and ex-combatants, prepared by Teclemichael W/Giorgis (Rosso) and included as Chapter 3 of this volume, gives an initial overview of this focus area: "the challenges and problems created by the process of social reintegration in post-conflict Eritrea, more particularly the situation regarding returnees and ex-combatants". In terms of experience and access to data, the author, as previously noted, was very well placed to prepare the report, as he had for years been one of the principal officers responsible for the government's reintegration programmes. The chapter surveys the issues and reports on the results of case studies of four settlement sites. It opens with a discussion of the definition of reintegration and the scope of research, which concentrated on specific problems encountered in the reintegration of returnees and demobilized combatants. Subsequently, it outlines the magnitude of social disintegration in Eritrea, detailing the need for social reintegration of both refugees and fighters, before discussing various dimensions of the reintegration process. The author discusses the policy framework and specific programmes which were adopted, namely the Programme for the Repatriation and Reintegration of Refugees (PROFERI) in the case of Eritrean returnees from Sudan, and the Department of Reintegration of Demobilized Fighters (Mitias) for demobilized combatants. The chapter further includes an analysis of existing policies and programmes, discussing issues of food aid, agriculture, land and shelter, and makes several pertinent observations, notably that in refugee resettlement it will be more useful to develop flexible packages of assistance rather than uniform, fixed-site allocations.

The chapter continues with a detailed account of experiences and findings in Alebu, Ali-Ghider, Fanko and Gahtelai, discussing the extent of social reintegration, aspirations and achievements, environmental issues, gender and vulnerability issues, and the provision of social services. On the basis of these studies, the author calls attention to the need for special support for the elderly and households headed by women, saying that as "no fewer than one-third of the households concerned fall into this category and there are real physical and social limitations to their participation in agricultural activities, it becomes essential to identify ways of helping them find alternative sources of income". In addition, he argues in favour of greater flexibility and recipient participation in the provision of shelter.

In a similar vein, the report on the state of infrastructure development, prepared by Dr. Berhane Woldemichael and presented as Chapter 4, surveys a number of key areas of infrastructure development, including road construction, ports and port management, the railway system, the energy sector and telecommunications. The current state of affairs of each area is reviewed and key requirements and priorities are discussed. This is followed by a description of the institutional and management capacity for the sector concerned and some of the specific projects and policies that have been launched or are being considered. In several of the areas, possible alternative policy approaches are discussed. As well as using official documentation, the chapter is based on interviews with selected officials and potential users and investors, particularly with regard to the functioning of the port of Massawa. Therefore, the chapter generally represents a useful preliminary reconnaissance of the state of infrastructure development in Eritrea.

The report on the problem of food security in Eritrea, prepared by Haile Awalom and included in this volume in revised and abridged form as Chapter 5, by all accounts constitutes the most elaborate and detailed of all. Containing a general overview and an extensive discussion of issues of food security and agricultural policy in the Gash-Barka region, the original report totalled 162 pages, including numerous tables and graphs. The author brought together a wide range of available data on the state of Eritrean agriculture and agricultural policy, with the objective of providing a basis for an informed assessment of the extent and prospects of food security in the country. The chapter, after sketching the chronic lack of food security in post-conflict Eritrea, takes up broad aspects of agricultural, livestock and fisheries production in relation to food security, then discusses policies and programmes to promote agriculture and food security in general terms. This is followed by a description of agricultural production and land use systems, paying particular attention to matters such as cropping systems, with specific reference to Gash-Barka. The latter includes a discussion on the pros and cons of promoting cash crop and subsistence agriculture to address food security, livestock production systems and their constraints, agro-industrial development with a number of examples, natural resource conservation measures to improve food security, and the role of agricultural research in increased crop and animal production, as well as the contribution of agricultural credit and marketing policies to sustaining food security. The chapter concludes with an analysis of options for achieving food security.

The report on the development of human resources for national construction, prepared by Araia Tseggai and reproduced here in revised form as Chapter 6, takes a different approach in its attempt to identify the current state of affairs and requirements. In principle, taking stock of human resources may start from either the supply side or the demand side. A supply-side approach might start with the availability and employment needs of refugees and ex-combatants, and of other categories of skilled and unskilled labour in search of adequate employment opportunities, exploring ways to give each category a meaningful role in the process of political rebuilding and economic recovery. In contrast, the present inquiry has opted for a demand-side point of departure. Recognizing that demand can be broken down into long-term and short-term, and can be further differentiated with respect to either the formal or informal sector, the research has concentrated on the category which is both short-term and formal so as to arrive at a baseline picture of formal sector human resource requirements. Thus, the chapter reports on an extensive questionnaire-based survey of human resource requirements and training needs in Eritrea, conducted among selected policy-makers, employers (government and corporate) and training programme administrators.

Roughly at the time that the report on the development of human resources for national reconstruction was finalized, a broad-based discussion on the need and elaboration of human resource development strategies took off in and outside government circles in Eritrea. As an outcome of these discussions, human resource development was adopted as one of the key strategies for Eritrean national development. The report presumably has played a useful preliminary role in these discussions.

Among the various Entry Point reports prepared in the context of WSP Eritrea, none appears to have aroused as much interest and discussion in and outside WSP circles as the report on governance by Alemseged Tesfai, included here as Chapter 7. There are probably several explanations for this. First, it discusses a wide range of dimensions of governance in Eritrea, past and present, in an informative and readily accessible manner. Thus, after some preliminary discussion of the concept of governance, the chapter gives an interesting historical account of aspects of governance during the Italian, British and Ethiopian periods of government, before coming to the years of the struggle and the period since Independence. Subsequently, it delves into a number of specific areas and issues that have recently attracted attention and been the subject of much discussion, notably changing structures for local administration and communication, purposes of the land proclamation, the question of popular participation, the role of the National Union of Eritrean Women (NUEW) and the National Union of Eritrean Youths and Students (NUEYS), and the scope of the private sector in the light of the government's macro policy. All these are discussed in a manner which highlights the issues and policy choices while explaining the rationale of the instruments adopted. Finally, the chapter addresses the question of international economic co-operation and the Eritrean approach to the relationships involved. Instead of accepting a donor/recipient relationship characteristic of many countries in Africa and elsewhere, Eritrea developed the concept of partnership in development, predicated on equality of involvement, from which it seeks to engage in international economic co-operation. The chapter suggests that WSP's phrase "war-torn society" may actually be a misnomer in the Eritrean case because, aside from the physical destruction caused by the war, it is felt that the country emerged from the struggle as socially unified as practically possible.

The governance report drew wide attention among external and internal WSP participants in Eritrea because it was the first time that a range of recent government initiatives and measures had been explained and put in broad perspective before a body of external actors. Due in part to this particular theme and the focus on the Eritrean government's recent policy initiatives in administrative and political restructuring, but also on account of some basic questions it raised about the relations between the government and external actors, the premise of international assistance, the governance report provoked a good deal of interest and discussion. WSP Working Group discussions on governance were reported to be among the liveliest and most intensive. Interest aroused by the report can be largely credited to WSP, as it was the challenge they conveyed and represented which led to the effort to comprehensively articulate the Eritrean position on a series of governance issues.

Several of the points raised in the governance report were subsequently elaborated by Alemseged Tesfai in a general analysis of WSP in Eritrea. This report, **Eritrea: Post-War Challenges of Development: Analysis of**

WSP Eritrea Research, was prepared for the final National Workshop held in Asmara in December 1996 and appears in this volume as Chapter 8. In this concluding chapter, the author presents a review of each of the Working Groups. Furthermore, the chapter presents a thoughtful discussion on the links among the different research themes, placing them in the context of the "policy mix" and the policy unity pursued during successive phases of reconstruction by the Eritrean government. Again, in taking up the international factor in this connection, the chapter questions the relevance of conventional donor-recipient relations for Africa in general and for Eritrea in particular, outlining instead the elements for alternative forms of partnership based on a recognition of mutual respect. Precisely because it spells out these alternatives at some length, the chapter is also relevant to WSP. Initiating a WSP project in a context such as that of Eritrea means abandoning assumptions about "ordinary", (for example, common dependency-based) relations between internal and external agencies.

THE QUESTION OF NATIONAL OWNERSHIP

The Eritrean WSP experience raised important questions about "national ownership", several aspects of which are worth considering more closely. In order for WSP to have a chance of attaining long-term sustainability in any of the countries concerned, recognition of the need for some form or sense of "national ownership" is essential. At the final workshop of the Eritrean project in December 1996, President Isaias Afwerki made a point of raising that question. His cautious warning was echoed in June 1997 by the Mozambican minister responsible for governmental reform, who similarly implied that, while WSP had been making an interesting and valuable contribution, it should take care not to become involved in the determination of policy, which was the government's own job. It is quite possible that similar words of caution will be articulated in other contexts where WSP might be seen as addressing policy agendas.

Starting from the opposite side, without clear national support WSP's potential role and impact is likely to remain marginal, amounting at best to a kind of playground for external actors. However, with national ownership being reaffirmed, a question that is likely to emerge is whether space will still be provided for meaningful dialogue and exploration of policy alternatives that external (and possibly some internal) actors might be interested in. Putting it even more plainly: would firm national ownership make WSP a less interesting proposition, particularly for external actors? The short answer appears to be that even, or particularly, in the political context of a government determined to emphasize national ownership, external actors remain keen to participate in a forum such as that offered by WSP because it represents one of the few channels available to them for receiving background to government thinking. Even though this was not the exact intention to begin with, the circumstance indeed gave WSP a prominent and useful role in Eritrea.

Ultimately, the question is a fundamental one, related to the question of power and control over policy processes. In reality, "national ownership" means government involvement or control, which can be given various forms and therefore does not necessarily require final, precise definition. The question implies a dilemma for both sides. For externals, as already suggested, the weighing is of opportunity costs, and is likely to be entered into as long as a net advantage in terms of receiving relevant information can be realized. For their part, as the Eritrean experience appears to illustrate, national governments are likely to be interested in the potential of the communicative dimensions of WSP for their own purposes, namely if it can help strengthen their overall co-ordination and command of national policy processes. However, they are likely to become more reserved and critical of a project that would seem to shift the locus of policy debate outside their reach, or even reduce the government to just another player in its proceedings. To the extent that hosting a WSP project means sharing or diluting this control in favour of stronger external influence, national governments are naturally unlikely to be in favour of it. In this sense, the dilemma is basically not resolvable. Both sides need to contemplate the dilemma and establish to what extent they are prepared to make the concessions necessary for worthwhile participation.

As already noted, at an operational level the question of national ownership is also related to the roles of the Project Director and Research Co-ordinator and the status of the research team, as well as to the way their roles are perceived in the specific national context. Thus, in the Eritrean case, the decision to have a cabinet minister as Project Director and to recruit most researchers from among the ranks of top government officials seems to illustrate a keen awareness of this question on the part of the government. Within its limited parameters, WSP Eritrea became closely tied with the government, though nonetheless providing a welcome venue for communication with external actors. To the extent that the prospect of diluting control over the policy process might be perceived as a potential threat, there may be grounds for crediting the Eritreans with having ingeniously constructed a strategy of averting this danger, namely by effectively "nationalizing" the core research establishment involved in the project.

In conclusion, several significant points stand out. Most importantly, Eritrea was the first country context in which WSP launched its relatively complex interactive action research programme. Therefore, Eritrea provided the context in which, with a good deal of trial and error, a WSP process was brought to life and in which, through numerous on-the-spot adjustments, the basic contours that would be followed elsewhere were established. It was in Eritrea that WSP learned its first important lessons, not entirely without cost, on how to maintain its role as a suitable forum for interactive policy dialogue. Similarly, Eritrea provided WSP with its first exposure to the meaning and implications of "national ownership" in the context of WSP projects, and how WSP might best come to grips with it.

Beyond these lessons, which no doubt have contributed to improvements in the approach adopted elsewhere, a broader implication of the Eritrean experience stands out. This is the fact that the Eritrean case has come to represent a fundamental qualification of the premise on which WSP was based, namely that it should be a sophisticated tool for improved donor communication and co-ordination in post-conflict rebuilding activities. The principal lesson the Eritrean experience taught WSP was that its main added value would lie not in improving donor co-ordination but in its role as a facilitator and forum for dialogue among external and internal actors on issues of post-conflict reconstruction. Once this lesson was learned, it soon turned out that WSP could, and did in turn, help Eritrea to reflect on the value of overcoming crucial communication gaps in policy preparation, and of engaging in broader informal dialogue on issues of shared policy interest.

Finally, a WSP contribution not to be underestimated is the wide range of data and analysis it has generated on the themes taken up for closer scrutiny. It is to be hoped that the material brought together in this volume will be of relevance to Eritrean policy-makers and to many others concerned with the prospects for reconstruction and development in post-conflict societies.

REFERENCES

Rebuilding War-torn Societies: Problems of International Assistance in Conflict and Post-Conflict Situations, UNRISD/PSIS, Geneva, November 1994.

2
RECONSTRUCTION AND DEVELOPMENT IN ERITREA: AN OVERVIEW

BERHANE WOLDEMICHAEL AND RUTH IYOB

The legacy of the 30-year conflict in Eritrea can be understood in terms of its positive accomplishments, its negative impacts, and the challenges that lie ahead. The war, although bloody and destructive, was not without positive consequences. Liberation was achieved in Eritrea against all odds, by a small country defeating an African military power. Military victory could not have been achieved without the slow and painful experience of developing a people-centred movement and a self-reliant structure (political, social and economic). Nevertheless, the negative consequences of the conflict permeate life in Eritrea. The World Bank considers Eritrea one of the most underdeveloped countries in the world. Thus, Eritrea is confronted with many challenges whose resolution depends on a clear understanding of both the positive and negative experiences of the past.

POSITIVE CONSEQUENCES OF THE CONFLICT

One positive trade-off of the Eritrean conflict is that it created, more than ever, a strong solidarity among its people. No section of Eritrean society avoided the struggle or escaped the effects of the Ethiopian occupation. In the fight against a common enemy, a great deal of social

---

This chapter is a revised version of the Eritrea Country Note prepared in January 1996 by the same authors with the assistance of Patricia Weiss-Fagen.

interaction took place which helped the various groups understand and appreciate each other's cultural distinctiveness and values. This social interaction became the foundation for self-help and local initiative throughout the country after Independence.

While this action was taking place spontaneously among the Eritrean population, another type of social transformation, which transcended ethnic, religious, class and gender differences, was being introduced by EPLF to its members. During the struggle, the organization sought to include all ethnic and religious groups and to transcend divisions based on social class. Equally important was the progress made relating to the protection of women's rights. Despite deeply rooted cultural obstacles, EPLF confronted the problem head-on by declaring and seeking to implement women's rights in areas such as marriage and resource allocation. Women made up some 30 per cent of EPLF, indicating the extent of its commitment.

EPLF was involved in virtually all aspects – predominantly education and healthcare – of Eritrean life in the regions under its control. A distinguishing feature of the education system developed by EPLF was the integration of theory and practice. The first model school was opened in 1976 and named Zero School. Throughout the struggle it served as a teaching laboratory where methods were tested and refined before being implemented in other EPLF schools. At one stage, EPLF ran more than 150 schools for almost 50,000 students.

EPLF's health service was equally impressive. Its famous barefoot doctors not only treated common diseases and provided health education, they also taught self-defence and survival strategies. EPLF's largest hospital, in Orota, attracted patients from as far afield as Sudan.

EPLF never fell into the trap of theorizing without practice and action. In military as well as political, social and economic concerns, theory was firmly rooted in Eritrean reality. EPLF emphasized self-reliance not only for political reasons, but because there was no choice. EPLF learned through early, hard-won experience that survival primarily depended on its own meagre resources. During the struggle, every possible item was ingeniously used and reused. External purchases were limited to absolutely necessary items, mostly military hardware.

A crucial factor which brought about the end of the war was the political and military co-operation that developed, over a long period, between EPLF and the coalition of Ethiopian opposition forces led by the Tigrayan People's Liberation Front (TPLF). The military collaboration between

EPLF and TPLF against a common enemy was never a secret. The cornerstone of the collaboration was their joint understanding of the right of the Eritrean people to self-determination.

NEGATIVE IMPACTS OF THE CONFLICT

The Eritrean case of uncompleted decolonization and resultant conflict is one of the sad accidents of history. During the protracted liberation struggle, Eritrea suffered a human tragedy of immense proportion, with EPLF admitting that about 70,000 combatants were killed. Many Eritreans were conscripted by the Ethiopian army to fight against their compatriots. Some estimate these civilian casualties to be as high 250,000. Moreover, about one-third of the population left Eritrea, seeking refuge in neighbouring countries, the Arab Gulf states, Europe and North America.

The majority of Eritreans lived either behind enemy lines or in contested areas and were therefore unable to benefit from the innovative approaches of EPLF. Their life was a day-to-day struggle as the economic and physical infrastructure of the country slowly degenerated. Relative to other countries in sub-Saharan Africa, pre-conflict Eritrea was economically and socially advanced, but decades of war and inappropriate policies by successive Ethiopian regimes destroyed these foundations. Society disintegrated – and its coping mechanisms were heavily damaged.

The large-scale disruption of social services, in areas such as education and health, contributed to the erosion of human capital. According to the Ministry of Education, the adult illiteracy rate in 1995 was as high as 80 per cent, and life expectancy at birth among the lowest in Africa, reflecting the neglect and damage suffered by the social service sector during the war. In some of the more educationally deprived areas of Eritrea, primary school enrolment was as low as five per cent in 1993–1994. Healthcare facilities were virtually absent in large parts of Eritrea under Ethiopian occupation, and were limited to a few hospitals in the garrison towns.

A social problem which has become prevalent is the large number of vulnerable groups, such as orphans, widows of combatants, aged combatants, disabled and destitute people, and households with broken family ties. Each of these groups requires specialized assistance, and the young nation has been struggling to cope with the situation with little external help.

The duration and brutality of the war profoundly damaged the national economy. As the Secretary of the Economy, Ato Haile Woldensae, stated in late 1991, "the economy is so devastated and the infrastructure so destroyed, that our present effort is to reach from the negative to zero". Every economic sector was affected – industry, infrastructure, and institutions. Eritrea had been one of the most industrialized African countries before the advent of Ethiopian colonialism. Many of its manufacturing industries, once employing a large portion of the working population in major towns, were destroyed and the remaining few were nationalized.

The first measurable impact of the lengthy war was the slow but steady decay of the physical infrastructure of the economy. Most roads became impassable and many bridges were destroyed. The railroad that connected the port town of Massawa to the capital, Asmara, and went westward to the towns of Keren and Agordet – a distance of 352 kilometres – was uprooted by the Ethiopians, who used the rails to reinforce military embankments. The communications infrastructure likewise fell into disrepair, until eventually the major towns were disconnected from each other. The same can be said about the provision of electric power. At the time of Independence, the electric power supply in the country was 22 megawatts for the entire interconnected system – barely enough to effectively run a sea-going ship. All in all, the infrastructure was in a state of ruin in 1991.

Conditions in Eritrean urban centres were similarly poor. Most of the sewage system was in a state of disrepair, the water supply system had deteriorated, the supply of electricity was insufficient and intermittent, and the roads were riddled with potholes. Homes became dilapidated as a result of the nationalization of urban dwellings. Telephone service in most towns was discontinued and, where it did exist, it was unreliable and of poor quality. Other urban institutions such as municipal services, banking, public transport, and so on had deteriorated, and some were halted altogether. However, Asmara was fortunate to emerge from the war with much of its physical infrastructure intact.

A negative aspect in the history of the Eritrean struggle is the civil war that took place in the early 1970s between ELF, the original liberation organization, and EPLF. An unknown number of Eritreans died in faction rivalry. Although short-lived, the conflict contributed to dividing the pro-Independence camp. However, by the end of the 1970s EPLF had established its superiority, and factions of ELF joined EPLF. The latter became the sole liberation movement and eventually brought about the liberation of the country in 1991. Remnants of ELF still exist outside Eritrea and have not been reconciled to the authority of the current government.

THE CHALLENGES AHEAD

EPLF has been renamed the People's Front for Democracy and Justice (PFDJ) and is now in government. The achievements of the past are a hard act to follow. Are the lessons learned being applied usefully in peacetime Eritrea? Wartime and peacetime administration differs enormously. Have the necessary steps been taken to cope with this change? Can the government effectively lead development and progress and still encourage grassroots initiatives and participation at every level? Will steps be taken to open up political space in preparation for peacetime policy dialogue? These are pertinent questions, and the government should take note of their significance.

The challenges faced by post-conflict Eritrea are varied and vie for priority. Perhaps the biggest hurdle the government faces is how to meet the expectations of the diverse groups in society: returning refugees, demobilized fighters, pastoralists, agriculturists, women, urbanites, vulnerable groups, and so on. Since liberation, these sectors of society have been struggling to mend their broken lives and it is important that they not be confronted with unnecessary obstacles, a case in point being the unresolved problem of land. Another challenge is the realization of the aspirations of female ex-combatants and civilian nationalists.

A formidable challenge for Eritrea today is learning how to deal with an outside world which does not necessarily share or even understand the values and behaviour associated with the liberation struggle, values and behaviour which persist in the post-Independence era. While many external actors recognize and appreciate the commitment of the government to build a self-reliant Eritrea, they feel that the Eritrean authorities lack understanding of the constraints under which they are working.

Thus, in confronting the transition from decades of war to a time of peace, Eritrea will make the change from a closed economic order inspired by a socialist premise, to an open economy that competes in the world market. This process will affect economic structures and priorities at every level, and requires time. The achievements of EPLF in the liberated zones – in terms of healthcare, education and women's rights – have yet to be made universal throughout the country. Democratic practices introduced during the war are now being institutionalized.

EXPERIENCES OF RECONSTRUCTION
Political rebuilding

With victory, Eritrean Independence transformed from an ideal into reality, sustained by political organization and armed movement. As previously noted, legacies from the liberation war would contribute to nation-building and peacetime political organization. The liberation army largely consisted of mobilized civilians, who were in turn assisted by non-military EPLF organizations. Because of the duration of the conflict, EPLF acquired experience in the administration of civilian society and attended to often contradictory civilian interests and military needs. During the war, EPLF developed parallel administrative hierarchies in the liberated zones and strengthened district and village level *baitos* (assemblies), making them more representative. Fighters adhered to well defined rules of accountability, as well as to military discipline. After 30 years of war, the Eritrean leadership now in power has extensive experience in mobilization and organization, which is being adapted to national reconstruction.

The political organization and trust developed between leadership and large parts of the population – as a result of war and clandestine civilian collaboration – became the basis of the peacetime government. Liberation fighters are now civilian leaders. EPLF is a *de facto* political party, the governing PFDJ. Parallel local administrative structures remain in place to organize reconstruction projects and voice local requests.

The political transition from war to peace has been generally smooth, but political and judicial institutions remain weak. The government in power, officially known as the State of Eritrea, remained provisional until May 1997. Even so, it enjoyed the support of the 105-member *Hagerawi Baito* (national council). The government consists of a president, 17 cabinet ministers and four specialized commissions and authorities. The country is divided into six administrative zones, or provinces, that are further divided into 55 sub-zones.

The government recognized the need to create political structures to accommodate Eritrea's ethnic diversity of citizens, who had high expectations that the achievement of Independence would bring a better life. The Constitutional Commission of Eritrea, composed of Eritreans representing different sectors of society, was established in March 1994 to draft a new constitution. The issues dealt with included: the form of government to be adopted (presidential, parliamentary, or mixed); civil and political rights, including political movements, rights of women and children, and human rights and duties; social, economic and cultural rights; legal and administrative structures; harmonizing the country's various legal systems; the electoral system; language policies; and military and security institutions. The objective was to design a constitution which would provide appropriate structures for nation-building and "national unity in diversity". The final draft of the constitution was based on extensive consultations with the public, as members of the commission travelled throughout Eritrea and held consultations with exiles outside the country.

[*Editors' note:* The new constitution was promulgated on 24 May 1997, the sixth anniversary of Independence, after final approval by the Constituent Assembly. An interim National Assembly was simultaneously established, charged with passing the necessary laws to bring the constitution into effect.]

Political expression

The EPLF government consolidated and centralized its power, while preserving forms of local governance developed in liberated zones during the war. There are no opposing political parties at present, but the constitution affirms the right to establish political movements. However, Eritrea does not permit political movements based on ethnicity or religion, as a preventive stance against the bloodshed caused by these groups elsewhere. Regional administrative divisions are designed so as to not separate such interests. A new press law is in preparation to establish the framework for conveying more diversified opinions in the Eritrean media.

In the present situation, without organized political entities, and with weak or *ad hoc* sector representation, it might prove difficult to maintain adequate consultation between the government and the people. The government has made and will continue to make major decisions affecting the fundamental well-being of large population groups, their land, basic rights and political activities. Popular participation, consultation and debate on these decisions are essential if the fragile national unity is to be preserved.

There is a challenge to incorporate the positive roles that could be played by non-governmental and civil institutions into the realm of political governance and social interaction. The role of civil society and local institutions in supplementing and consolidating civil governance is not to be underestimated. Eritrea ought to create a nurturing environment in which civil society is encouraged to consolidate national unity and democratic governance.

Security and national unity

Muslim and Christian Eritreans were partners in the liberation struggle and are now committed to Eritrean statehood. Compared to other countries, religious relations in Eritrea are not disruptive. Nevertheless, the government fears destabilizing influences from fundamentalist Islamic groups. There have been armed attacks, mainly originating in Sudan and allegedly involving Eritreans living there. The majority of these refugees are Muslim, and some still identify with ELF, the rival Eritrean political organization. Exile groups have published accounts critical of the current Eritrean government. The productive incorporation of these people into Eritrean society, should they return, will be a challenge.

Demographically generated tensions

Refugees and former combatants originally from highland areas are settling in fertile lowland areas when returning to Eritrea. They have become more numerous in these places than the autochthonous population and political, economic and social tensions can be anticipated. The central government needs to be sensitive to this when allocating resources and power.

Conflicting priorities

Even in the best circumstances, various government ministries sometimes have competing agendas. Food relief programmes and agricultural development policies, for example, must be continuously co-ordinated and monitored to ensure that the effects of one do not negatively affect the results of the other. For example, food-for-work (FFW) and cash-for-work (CFW) programmes run by ERRA and the Ministry of Agriculture generate income, increase food supplies and improve crop production. However, if these programmes attract so many workers as to cause a labour shortage in commercial agriculture, harvests will become smaller, thus weakening the private sector. When so much needs to be done, and so many urgent issues involve several ministries at the same time, co-operation and co-ordination are essential. Fortunately, the Eritrean leaders have worked together in the past and consult with each other formally as well as informally. However, the nature of consultation will necessarily change as governance becomes more complex when new sectors are brought into the process and demands placed on the system require increasingly specialized expertise. Even now ministries have to compete for scarce resources.

Centralization versus decentralization

Centralized decision-making was a military necessity during the war, but now Eritrea must adapt its governing arrangements to incorporate the nine ethnic groups in the country. Each group has its own language and the aim is to give equal opportunity to all nine languages. At present, Tigrigna is the dominant language, while English and Arabic are the *de facto* working languages.

The civil service will be reformed in line with the requirements of peacetime administration, such that the diverse social groups may effectively participate in civil society. Following the 1995 recommendations of a specially constituted task force, steps were taken to dramatically reduce – by 10,000 people – the size of the civil service and to reduce overly bureaucratic procedures.

At the local level, *baitos* have long played a strong role in local administration and conflict resolution. However, in some regions local organization was badly distorted by the *kebeles* (political structures) put in place by Ethiopia to maintain control. The *baitos*, which formerly excluded the participation of landless people, women and young, unmarried citizens, are now more inclusive, but their relationship to decision-making bodies at the national level needs further definition. Moreover, their role depends on whether the community is homogeneous or is divided along ethnic or other lines. There are elected government bodies at regional and subregional levels.

A decentralized, "grassroots" approach to local and regional development has distinct advantages, and the government supports this approach. To be successful, the approach must take into account the divergent interests of various ethnic and social groups, especially in certain potentially conflictual regions, and the inevitable conflict between urgent local needs and interests and broader, long-term national objectives and economic goals.

Women and social change

With social and political progress, various social groups seek a voice in shaping their future and, by implication, the national future. Eritrean leaders are becoming increasingly aware that traditional pre-war roles and expectations regarding women are unacceptable to many, especially to women who contributed to national liberation or who recently returned from exile. EPLF founded the National Union of Eritrean Women (NUEW) to promote the rights and defence of women, and give them economic and social assistance. The United Nations Children's Fund (UNICEF) has supported a number of projects aimed at encouraging education for girls in rural areas. These and other initiatives must be significantly augmented in order to expand the political and social space available to women.

Issues of Rehabilitation and Social Reconstruction

Social reconstruction builds on and derives from relief structures established during the war. ERRA was the key government agency for food aid and overseeing relations with donors engaged in relief activity. Since Independence, ERRA has become a quasi-state agency that now manages humanitarian assistance and oversees development initiatives. The operations of national and international NGOs are regulated by ERRA, which channels funding, projects and personnel to the appropriate ministries. However, ERRA – a vast bureaucracy striving to move away from decades of managing relief activity – is in a difficult period of transition, retooling and restructuring for a role in rehabilitation and development in the future. This is the same trajectory foreseen for the beneficiaries of current reintegration programmes. In other words, the intention of national and international agencies now providing assistance is to phase out relief as soon as possible and achieve self-sufficiency.

The National Service is a major programme operating under ERRA. The entire social reintegration programme vitally depends on the National Service, in which male and female Eritreans between the ages of 18 and 40 contribute 18 months of unpaid labour to their country. The National Service has not only provided the much needed human resources for a wide range of activities, but has also introduced young urbanites to the reality of conditions in the countryside and broadened the horizons of rural Eritreans. It is hoped that such interaction will stimulate a stronger sense of national identity and consciousness among those involved, particularly the young.

The Reintegration of War-Affected Populations

The repatriation and resettlement of returning refugees and former fighters can be a threat to peace and stability if post-war realities fail to meet their expectations. The process of reintegration is changing the demography and ethnic balance in some parts of the country. Likewise, the reintegration of refugees and ex-combatants has suffered setbacks because of scarce funding for specific integration projects and reconstructing the damaged infrastructure, while the national technical capacity to restore the productive system and provide health and educational services is limited.

Moreover, these various programmes and projects potentially give returning groups an advantage over others who suffered during the war but remained in their homes.

Demobilization is taking place gradually, with the first phases successfully accomplished. Reintegration is the challenge faced today. The army included about 95,000 people (3 per cent of the population) and 30 per cent of its ranks were female. These women were often the sole providers for their families, but when demobilized found themselves returning to a society much more inimical to their interests than the relatively egalitarian environment of the liberation movement. Among demobilized former combatants there are about 18,000 disabled people and many who are probably too old to fully re-enter a productive life. The government also provides support to the families of those who died in the struggle. So far, more than 300 million birr (US$ 47 million) have been spent on these vulnerable sectors of Eritrean society, a major commitment for a poor government.

Veterans generally do not have high levels of education or skill. Some sacrificed education in order to fight, and those who served for long periods often lost touch with their place of origin. On returning they find themselves distanced from civilian life and the job market. They expect government help, and their reintegration is a high priority for the government. They receive monthly cash allotments and there are special programmes on their behalf. The majority are in the rural sector, where agricultural settlements have been established to absorb their labour. They receive financial credit, vocational training, housing and social services. Many veterans with skills have found jobs in the civil service.

Most Eritreans would agree that the country owes a debt to the veterans who fought long and hard for Independence. However, Eritreans who were not combatants feel that they too made sacrifices. Resources for reintegration remain scarce and frustrations may increase as veterans continue needing assistance over the long term. Tensions may arise in places where the population currently welcomes the former combatants.

Mitias has been responsible for the reintegration of demobilized combatants since 1993. The term "Mitias" is derived from the obligation of a community to help a newly married couple establish their home. Mitias is a semi-autonomous body under ERRA, charged to implement a range of programmes and agricultural projects intended to benefit veterans. Despite wide acclaim for the dedication of the Mitias staff, and recognition of the need to achieve the desired integration, external donor response has been limited. Of the US$ 48 million requested, US$ 10 million was pledged, and of that only US$ 8 million was actually received. Donors typically have been reluctant to become involved in demobilization and reintegration programmes, but this attitude is changing and fairly generous support has gone to other countries in the region. Given the credible image that Mitias has achieved, it is hard to find concrete reasons for the low donor response.

The Eritrean diaspora was widespread, but most refugees fled to neighbouring countries, especially Sudan. The majority were in camps, where they were cared for by the Office of the United Nations High Commissioner for Refugees (UNHCR). Approximately 150,000 refugees returned, all but 25,000 spontaneously. There are still 3-400,000 Eritreans in Sudan. The Eritrean government has affirmed the right of all refugees to return to the country and to settle in the area of their choice, with full rights and guarantees of safety, regardless of their political position. To effectuate repatriation, the government established the Commission for Eritrean Refugee Affairs (CERA) in 1987. In 1993, PROFERI was established under CERA to implement projects, working with the various ministries. On the international level, UNDP, UNHCR, UNICEF, UNV, WFP and a few international NGOs have been involved in repatriation or reintegration projects.

In 1993 the government presented donors with the ambitious PROFERI for some US$ 262 million, aiming to bring refugees back and establish housing, social services, and small development projects for them, in three phases. PROFERI did not formally provide for the host communities, but the assumption was that rebuilding infrastructure and establishing health, education and other services would upgrade the quality of life for all. Disappointing donor response caused the government to scale down and begin with a pilot programme instead, at an estimated cost of US$ 16 million. This plan was carried out for some 25,000 returnees, with the government providing most of the funding. The PROFERI plan envisaged nine settlement sites – mainly in the fertile lowlands where returnees were expected to go – where the government and international assistance would be available. The number of settlements was increased to 12 as the influx exceeded expectations, particularly in the Gash-Setit and Barka areas, where 75 per cent of the returnees went. The remaining 125,000 spontaneous returnees not participating in the PROFERI project, and whose destination is outside the designated project sites, receive only three months' food assistance and no other help.

Most of the returnees, spontaneous or organized, have settled in lowland areas, especially Gash-Setit, although many of them came from other places and are not members of lowland ethnic groups. This is a cause for concern because of strains placed on local resources in communities where people are desperately poor. The paucity of resources is widespread and the fact that returnees are privileged exacerbates discontent. The situation should be studied, evaluating the absorptive capacity of specific regions.

Implementation of the pilot project followed negotiations and compromise between the government and the international agencies that would assist in repatriation and reintegration: UNDP, UNHCR, UNICEF and WFP. The design of the project reflected the government's determination to assume full responsibility for the administration and management of the projects under PROFERI. The United Nations agencies and the government agreed to the model of government execution, national monitoring and reporting back to agencies and donors. Reporting has improved over time. Planning is now under way for the repatriation of some 100,000 refugees in Sudan, but again international donor response has not been enthusiastic. Donors are not confident that the government of Eritrea has the technical capacity to manage and execute such a large programme.

A good deal is at stake. UNHCR cannot justify caring indefinitely for the 3-400,000 Eritreans still in Sudan. Their claim of refugee status is difficult to maintain, yet they are reluctant to return. Many have visited Eritrea, inspected their potential new homes and returned to Sudan. Eritrea cannot provide them with the food, education, healthcare and relative well-being they have in Sudan.

More donor support for PROFERI projects would help but would not solve the problem. At issue are the priorities of the Eritrean government and where returnees fit into these priorities. For example, UNHCR made US$ 2 million available for small-scale, community-based activities, called "quick impact projects" (QIPs), designed to alleviate some of the immediate pressures on returnees and improve the quality of life for local people. However, the QIPs proved more difficult to initiate in Eritrea than elsewhere because all projects established with foreign funding must be centrally initiated and approved, and the central government has not moved to develop QIPs or to consult with the communities about what projects they might want to set up. There is no official disagreement about the actual projects and their need is recognized. For example, a project for Arabic teachers has been initiated and another to provide living quarters for women working in fisheries may soon be under way. The question for the government is how these small-scale projects fit into larger plans. Even though funds are available, should these projects take precedence over others that are equally worthwhile? What will happen to the projects or the beneficiaries when there is no more money for QIPs? Can schools and health posts be permanently staffed? These are serious concerns for the government.

Similarly, conflicting priorities impede the reconstruction of roads destroyed in the war. Along with provisions for schools and healthcare, PROFERI requested funding for a system of roads. This received little response. International humanitarian agencies and CERA are interested in the construction of simple unpaved roads that would grant repatriate communities much-needed access to markets and make it easier to supply them with seed, fertilizer, and so on. The Ministry of Transport is more interested in building major asphalt roads that will connect the country and in the long run open up these same communities. The World Bank is funding the larger road system, but feeder road construction is not progressing.

Returnee reintegration projects, such as for former combatants, stretch the current national capacity. In time, national capacity can be improved through training and experience, as is the government's intention. Many current UNDP, NGO and government projects are aimed in this direction, although they are by no means exclusively targeted to programmes for returnees and former fighters. UNICEF projects have focused on training at the local level, so that people in and around returnee areas will be able to perform basic tasks in healthcare, sanitation and education.

A worst case scenario would be the shutdown of the refugee camps in Sudan, sending hundreds of thousands of people back to Eritrea. While Eritrea fears such massive, unplanned repatriation, even the planned repatriation of hundreds of thousands of refugees would create an emergency situation, threatening to upset the precarious balance of local populations, as well as natural resources. An additional concern relates to the identity of the Sudan-based refugees, as it is believed that some have been strongly influenced by Islamic fundamentalism and are hostile to the present Eritrean government. Thus, the resource question is compounded by security concerns. In this situation, the internal and external actors involved in repatriation and reintegration must consider and reach agreement on mutually agreeable options.

In regions absorbing returning refugees there is a growing demographic imbalance caused by the emigration of young men to work in the Arab Gulf states. Consequently, agricultural production at home has been declining because women do not traditionally participate in these activities. Large numbers of Eritreans survive on remittances, but these can be expected to diminish. Pastoralists who lost most of their livestock during the war are prominent among the emigrants, while others have been obliged to adopt a more sedentary way of life. Male migration is adding to the work load of pastoral women left behind, putting them in a vulnerable position.

Food Aid

Most of the humanitarian assistance to Eritrea was in the form of food aid. In recent decades, food insecurity has been endemic in Eritrea. Even after good harvests, food production satisfied only three-quarters of demand. Food insecurity was particularly severe among pastoral communities, caused by livestock depletion through war and drought. However, both pastoral and non-pastoral rural communities increased their production to the extent that, generally speaking, the food deficit decreased from one-half at the time of liberation to about one-quarters in 1995. The main reason for the improvement was the peace dividend, which allowed communities to improve their coping strategies. In addition, poverty alleviation schemes undertaken by the government – distribution of oxen and seed, financial credit, FFW programmes, and tractor services – were instrumental.

It is estimated that 30-90 per cent of the Eritrean population depended at some time on food aid. While the food deficit has decreased in recent years, food aid and food production programmes still necessarily constitute the major targets of foreign assistance. Food aid and other forms of relief are co-ordinated by ERRA, working closely with the Ministry of Agriculture and Fisheries, the Ministry of Transportation and CERA, as well as with food-related international agencies. The major recipients are vulnerable groups: people reintegrating into Eritrean society, drought and famine victims, and National Service participants. Nearly all pastoralists, both nomadic and agro-pastoral, receive food aid because they lost more than three-quarters of their livestock to war and drought.

The government's goals are mutually reinforcing, seeking to:
- reach a reasonable level of food security
- use foreign assistance only to the extent that it is absolutely necessary
- use food and other forms of assistance to promote development, rather than as direct relief.

With regard to the first goal, food security will not necessarily be achieved only through self-sufficiency, but also by increasing the purchasing power of the population. As documented in a 1991 University of Leeds study, in an average year local food production falls short, leaving a deficit of almost 50 per cent, which is dramatically increased by Eritrea's recurrent droughts. Therefore, increasing local food production requires a flexible approach that seeks to improve cultivation practices by applying appropriate technology while diversifying the economy, particularly in rural areas.

With regard to the second goal, foreign assistance plays an important role in achieving food security in the manner just described. Projects range from locust control to fisheries development to food monetization (raising money by selling donated food). Projects have often involved several donors along with two or three government ministries, ERRA and regional and subregional officials. Each may have different ideas about how to best prioritize and accomplish the tasks at hand. The projects require skilled and unskilled personnel who, by accepted norm, must be Eritrean nationals, and each project requires monitoring and sometimes extensive reporting documentation. The government is particularly interested in projects that include training and local capacity-building but, with only limited funding available, many projects have had to be scaled down.

The food monetization, training, and production enhancement programmes all aim to stimulate development. The government and international agencies share this goal and as a result agencies working in Eritrea tend to support projects that combine relief and development. Among the participating United Nations agencies are those specializing in relief (UNHCR, WFP) and those with a development mandate (FAO, UNDP, UNICEF). In Eritrea, UNDP and UNICEF have participated in humanitarian assistance and development projects, while WFP has expanded its capacity to channel food aid to more developmental purposes. The same applies to bilateral donors and NGOs.

Much emphasis is put on reducing food aid *per se,* in favour of FFW and CFW arrangements, which generate income and reduce dependency. The various techniques of using food and relief in ways conducive to development are complex and the risk of unintended, negative results is high. For example, food monetization could endanger rather than enhance food security if it is not properly managed and co-ordinated with other programmes. To be successful, monetization must be supervised by an institution capable of planning, implementing and constantly monitoring the process so as to not undermine evolving markets and to keep track of local and regional production levels. While ERRA is responsible for co-ordinating the food monetization projects, implementation engages a large number of national and international actors. Effective monetization depends on the ability of all concerned to communicate continually, to share information and to respond flexibly to changing situations.

Economic Rebuilding

The dire living conditions of Eritreans during the war did not end with EPLF victory. As other countries moved ahead economically, Eritrea was thrown into reverse, emerging from three decades of war as one of the poorest countries in the world. Its gross domestic product (GDP) per capita income is US$ 130-150, less than half of the per capita income in sub-Saharan African countries. The countryside outside Asmara was devastated by war, and rebuilding is now commencing from the ground up. The illiteracy rate is estimated at 80 per cent. Many of Eritrea's most educated and experienced professionals left the country and have yet to return.

After decades of war, Eritrea's economy is weak. Between 70 and 80 per cent of the population lives in rural areas and is engaged mainly in subsistence farming. A large portion of the urban population relies on informal sector economic activity because employment opportunities in the formal, public sector are limited. The informal sector is playing a constructive role in the rebuilding process.

Despite dismal post-war economic conditions, the self-help initiatives of Eritreans in villages throughout the country are encouraging and significant. In many places, communities have built schools and health centres, or dug wells and restored land entirely on their own or with very limited assistance from local or national government or NGOs. Economists believe that if this diverse activity could be counted in monetary terms, the GDP of the country would be significantly higher than the World Bank estimates. More importantly, perhaps, such self-help activity illustrates the will of the Eritrean people to overcome obstacles on their own, and their determination to build a better life. However, self-help initiatives add to the government's burden – for every health clinic and school constructed a health worker and teacher must be found.

The Eritrean economy is relatively diversified in comparison to other sub-Saharan African countries. According to a 1994 World Bank estimate, the share of agricultural output in GDP averages between 22 and 26 per cent. The share of industry, including manufacturing, mining and construction, is relatively large at between 26 an 31 per cent of GDP. Distribution services, including trade, transport and communication account for between 13 and 16 per cent of GDP. Other services, including the financial sector and administration, account for between 19 and 26 per cent of GDP. Currently, both investment and consumption in Eritrea depend to a high degree on development assistance. It has been estimated that the ratio of aid to GDP could be about 30 per cent. In 1994, Eritrea received US$ 210 million in development assistance from bilateral, multilateral and international NGOs (World Bank, 1994).

In its current economic policies, the government must balance the most immediate and pressing requirements of recovery with long-term economic goals. In the first category are the emergency needs of vulnerable groups and the reconstruction of critical infrastructure, housing, transport, and service sectors of the economy. In the latter category are the establishment of an export-based open market economy, promotion of regionally balanced economic growth, development and rehabilitation of agriculture and fisheries, revitalization of the private sector, and encouragement of domestic investment and foreign joint ventures.

The long- and short-term dynamics are obviously linked. A prerequisite for promoting exports and achieving regionally balanced growth is the immediate reconstruction of infrastructure and the restoration of agriculture and fisheries. The rebuilding of transportation, energy and communication facilities is also a prerequisite for attracting foreign investment and joint ventures. For the economy to prosper, food security must be achieved. As already noted, this will not be achieved solely by improved domestic food production, but will also depend on the long-term development of food and non-food exports. Of course, a diversified economy needs a more literate, healthy population, which necessitates the establishment of effective programmes for education and healthcare.

There is tension between the government's interest in strengthening the private sector and encouraging private investment, and its equally strong objective to revitalize national enterprises and productivity. Foreign and domestic investment have been limited, making it difficult to sell government-owned enterprises. Meanwhile, through PFDJ, the government has openly encouraged the state sector to set up new companies of its own, sometimes in joint ventures with national enterprises. Privatization has proceeded slowly, and the government's direct role in the economy remains strong. However, the role of PFDJ as an investor or entrepreneur may raise economic questions.

The private sector and the quality of the labour force would benefit if the large number of skilled and educated people who found refuge in Europe, North America and other African countries would return to Eritrea. The obstacles to returning are primarily economic, presenting difficulties in the areas of housing, income, education and amenities. The German government is offering attractive incentives to Eritreans in Germany who wish to return, and the Eritrean government is encouraging its people to come home. However, at this time it is difficult for Eritrea to meet the needs of those in the diaspora.

One of the first issues needing attention following Independence was land ownership and use. Land was unevenly and sometimes unjustly divided, with some villages much better endowed than others and, importantly, governed by diverse land tenure arrangements. Land has historically been managed by tradition, norms and laws at the village level, where *baitos* collectively determined not only who had access to land, but also how it would be used for pasture, cultivation or other purposes. The process ensured the local social and ecological management of a precious resource, but during the war local supervision did not produce positive results in terms of productivity or ecological management. The government's solution was the Land Proclamation of 1994, sweeping legislation declaring that all land belonged to the state. It is said that the government is seeking a once-and-for-all solution to the problems associated with land use, but the attachment of Eritrean peasantry to land is legendary and it may be not be possible to find an all-encompassing solution.

While the legislation has been declared, it has not been implemented, leaving questions of land use and inheritance unanswered. This situation effectively forestalls the utilization of land and discourages occupants from investing in its improvement. The legislation opens the way to resolving some conflicts, establishes greater equality in citizens' access to land, and provides for greater flexibility in agricultural planning. However, the legislation bypasses or reverses long-established traditions, norms and institutions, thereby diminishing the capacity of local institutions to resolve conflicts. Finally, the *baitos*, which have been identified as key institutions for channelling local participation in the political process, have now lost what was their primary function.

The urban situation entails a different kind of problem in which the government has to deal with property nationalized by the Ethiopians, and a number of associated technical difficulties. Very little urban land has thus far been released for private development, even for individual households, although doing so would have positive effects. For example, it would reduce the housing burden and thus the cost of living in Asmara.

Local-Level Initiatives

The protracted conflict had dire consequences for the coping strategies of rural Eritreans. To start with, mobility was restricted and people were not able to engage in off-farm income-generating activities. However, since liberation the entrepreneurial spirit of the Eritrean people has been rekindled and local initiatives have sprung up all over the country. In rural areas, sustenance from rain-fed agriculture alone was never a viable undertaking because of the dry climate. Therefore, most coping strategies of the rural population are based on diversification. For example, highland farming communities combine rain-fed cultivation in the highlands with pastoralism or irrigated agriculture in the lowlands. Similarly, communities of the eastern lowlands former Semhar province combine flood or spate irrigation with livestock production. Their main grazing area is in the Hazemo plain of the highland Akeleguzai province. In urban centres, the informal sector of micro enterprises initiated by individuals provides the livelihood of many people in spite of government efforts to regulate it. In rural areas, many community groups are involved in self-help efforts to improve their social and economic conditions.

The important role played by local-level initiatives in national reconstruction must be appreciated. Countless local initiatives are being undertaken throughout the country, involving a great number of people in various sectors of the economy. It is essential that these initiatives are encouraged and stimulated to lay the foundation for development from the bottom up.

For the rural population of highland Eritrea, a major means of supplementary income since Independence has been employment in urban centres, particularly in the construction industry. Many people also survive on a daily subsistence income, performing casual labour in urban centres. Both men and women are engaged in these activities. The involvement of women in the construction industry is a recent development, as this used to be considered a male activity. Employers in the construction industry now prefer female employees in some specialized areas. Other female-specific employment opportunities are found in domestic work.

The rapid development of urban centres and increased demand for food products has encouraged many people to engage in business. Raising livestock for milk production has become a major income-generating activity for people in satellite villages of the urban centres. Poultry production is another activity many people are involved in and raising chickens near the home is mainly the task of women.

Another entrepreneurial activity that has boomed in post-conflict Eritrea and benefits many rural people is the development of irrigated fruit and vegetable crops. It is worth going into some detail about this initiative as it illustrates the opportunity for grassroots efforts that contribute significantly to national well-being. The horticultural activities are concentrated along the banks of dry river beds and involve drawing water from hand-dug wells. Since liberation, this activity has been further enhanced by the construction of a number of micro dams, particularly in highland areas. The direct beneficiaries are the people who own land immediately below the micro dams. Individuals or families who have suitable land but lack the knowledge or labour necessary for development usually enter into a crop-sharing agreement with others. The horticulture sector benefits many people during the harvest, creating jobs picking and packing the crops.

In the Aala district of the Akeleguzai province, horticulturists have organized the Horticulture Producers Co-operative (HPC). The HPC is the first organization of its kind in Eritrea, and as such faces many obstacles to functioning as a co-operative entity. To start with, there are no regulations governing the activities of co-operatives in Eritrea and the group has been operating without knowing its legal status, instead drawing up internal regulations for governing members. Initially, the HPC was run by volunteers elected from its membership but, with the expansion of activities, it now employs a professional manager, secretary and accountant, who work together to manage the co-operative.

The main aims of the co-operative are to safeguard the interests of its members, secure reasonable prices for their products, advise them on what to produce and when, and make farming implements available. The HPC recently bought a truck to enable its members to transport their products to market at a reasonable price. The truck was purchased with funds from three sources: about 50 per cent came from a local NGO, the Catholic Relief Service, about 30 per cent came in the form of a loan from a local Catholic mission station, and the balance came from HPC savings.

Members of the co-operative speak of the great potential to develop the horticulture sector in Eritrea. However, they point out that this will depend on input from the government in the form of technical advice and assistance to enable the producers to compete in international markets. Direct government assistance in these areas has been minimal.

In Eritrean villages, economic and social organizations that have evolved are geared toward reducing vulnerability. In a situation where the formal social welfare system is largely unknown – excluding food aid – the traditional social system has mechanisms to reduce risk. For example, many individuals owe their livelihoods to support they receive from relatives and extended family members. During the war, this traditional help system played a crucial role, and the livelihoods of many people depended on it. In the post-conflict era, the traditional social organizations have been involved in more development-oriented self-help activities, such as the construction of feeder roads, schools and clinics. In some instances, communities are assisted by private donations that cover part of the cost of a school or clinic, and in a few exceptional cases this has even amounted to the donation of the entire building. The self-help spirit of the Eritrean people since liberation has been exemplary.

A major source of income for many Eritrean families, particularly those in lowland coastal communities, is remittance from one or more family members working abroad, especially in oil-rich Arab countries. More importantly, entire communities benefit from the investments of migrants in their respective areas of origin. In the Zula plain of the former Semhar province, contributions for the establishment of a transport company came mostly from migrants. The transport company was founded by local communities of the Zula plain who raised funds by selling shares. In this way the community managed to buy two buses and solved the transport needs of the population between the towns of Foro and Massawa. Again, this is a typical self-help activity and one which resolved a major constraint of the Zula plain communities.

A common solution to food shortage among sedentary farmers and pastoral communities alike in the post-conflict period has been seasonal labour migration. Among pastoral peoples, labour migration is a recent phenomenon occasioned by the loss of livestock and is common only among male household members. Seasonal farm employment is available during the dry season in the Gash-Setit flood plains or the neighbouring regions of Ethiopia and Sudan. Seasonal workers are usually paid in kind, receiving a portion of the crops they harvest. This can be enough to fill a large part of their families' food requirement.

Having lost most of their cattle, many pastoral communities are now left with small ruminants (grazing animals), usually tended by women and children near the home. For example, in the Denkalia province many former pastoralists in Afar are now dependent on various income-generating activities: seasonal employment in Assab, micro enterprises (trading) and sea-related activities. There is a division of labour between the sexes when it comes to sea activities. The collection of precious items such as snail shells is women's work, while men are mainly engaged in fishing. The sea items collected by women are sold in the markets of Yemen and Saudi Arabia and usually generate a good income. Fishing is an equally productive activity with most of the catch being exported to the same markets and the remainder sold locally. Shortages of transportation and preservation facilities are limiting factors for the local markets.

In addition to looking after the ruminants and performing household chores, pastoral women produce handmade crafts, mainly mats and embroidery. These activities have become a major source of income for many families. A go-between buys products from the individual producers and transports them to urban markets. For pastoral women, the most arduous job at home is food preparation. The staple food is ground by hand, a time-consuming and difficult task. In some pastoral areas grinding mills have been introduced by the government in collaboration with SOS FAIME of Belgium, an international NGO. The grinding mills save a great deal of labour and have transformed women's lives, allowing them to devote more time to craft work.

Community-based development will continue to be the most effective way of improving the quality of life for the rural population. Strategies to consolidate their structures and traditional coping mechanisms must now be devised and strengthened. Off-farm income-generating opportunities for individuals and co-operative groups should be expanded, and encouragement given to their initiatives. As mentioned, many rural communities are involved in development activities such as providing educational and health facilities and repairing feeder roads. The challenge now is to move beyond these initiatives and involve the communities in managing improved services, nutrition programmes, literacy and skills training programmes, maternal and child care, home economics and family planning, of which are all essential to poverty reduction.

The challenge is equally daunting in urban areas, where the priority may be to increase employment opportunities and encourage micro-enterprise activities. However, for these strategies to be successful the poor should be spared excessive government regulation and contact with authorities kept to the necessary minimum. The importance of the informal sector must be recognized, as most local-level initiatives are a means of poverty alleviation. If encouraged, these activities can be the basis for future development in Eritrea.

The Role of External Actors in Eritrean Rebuilding

The struggle to recover from the destruction of war, help people survive, and increase national productive capacity requires outside assistance. Some international actors have considered it a privilege to help rebuild Eritrea in collaboration with its committed government. The cardinal principles of Eritrean policy are to maintain national control over relief and development and to avoid, even at great cost, a dependency relationship with foreign donors. International co-operation is called upon to help achieve food security, rebuild infrastructure, and reintegrate returning refugees and former combatants. Eritrea still lacks trained human resources to carry out the economic transformation of the country and to provide basic services. The government's objective is to develop Eritrea's human resource capacity and it does not encourage the presence of non-essential foreign nationals working in the country. On the economic side, the government encourages direct foreign investment. The challenge is to promote and preserve national self-reliance, which requires reducing foreign involvement to an absolute minimum, while meeting the urgent needs of the Eritrean people and preparing them to be agents of national self-reliance and development.

Eritreans are bitter about the lack of international response during the years of famine and war. Although international presence was small during the war for independence, some funding did reach Eritrea through diverse channels, mainly NGOs. Considerable funding for the war effort and civilian survival came from Eritreans abroad. During the war, international relief was funnelled directly to ERRA, which organized humanitarian assistance for 20 years as a branch of EPLF. The general consensus is that ERRA was effective and deserves credit for the survival of much of the civilian population. International NGOs channelling outside support to Eritrea neither expected nor obliged ERRA to comply with strict bureaucratic procedures for project approval, monitoring, reporting and evaluation. Nor was the funding from Eritreans in exile conditional. The Eritrean people emerged from the war accustomed to relying on their own efforts and decision-making capacity to direct resources where most needed.

Following Independence, the government sought to continue the arrangements for receiving funding and to decide through its own mechanisms how best to use the funds. Donors would not and could not comply and the end of the war marked a major turning point. An increasing number of bilateral donors and international agencies offered assistance to Eritrea, at the same time insisting that Eritrea comply with procedures used for other aid recipients. Eritrea became one of a large pool of poor nations. International officials familiar with Eritrea credit its leadership for being effective, hard-working, honest and committed – qualities lacking in many other cases. Yet continued assistance to Eritrea must be justified in Brussels, Rome, Stockholm or Washington on the basis of demonstrated capacity to produce results. The projects are designed to take into account the interests and norms of the donors in addition to government priorities, and judgements about implementation are based on evaluations and reports sent to donors. Positive results are defined as efficient use of funds for previously established purposes. The Eritrean government is expected to fully co-operate in this process.

Bilateral aid has been targeted mainly to development in the agricultural and food supply sectors. Two programmes that have benefited most from bilateral aid are the Recovery and Rehabilitation Programme of Eritrea (RRPE) and PROFERI. Italian Co-operation and the German aid agency GTZ have been the most prominent donors to RRPE, while CIDA, EU, NORAD, SIDA and USAID have been major contributors to PROFERI. All have supported food aid, various aspects of development, technical assistance and early warning systems. Multilateral United Nations agencies (including FAO, UNDP, UNFPA, UNHCR, UNICEF and WHO) and the World Bank are present and contribute according to their specific areas of competence.

The government works bilaterally with United Nations and other agencies. Each has a particular ministry or department as its focus, and additionally works with the appropriate government body: the Ministry of Health, CERA (later called the Commission for Relief and Refugee Affairs – CORRA), or ERRA. Although the government relates to each of the agencies separately, the latter have had to work together, or at least to complement each other's efforts. Inter-agency participation between RRPE and PROFERI involves a range of activities, including transportation, education, health care, food assistance and production and income generation, covering relief and rehabilitation. In one instance, through CERA and with funding from the German NGO Orbis, the government established co-operation among agencies. The result was a vocational training programme for former fighters and refugee returnees.

Co-operation and co-ordination among participating agencies have improved and can be further enhanced.

Some international NGOs, such as Christian Aid, German Agro Action, Grass Roots International, Norwegian Church Aid and Save the Children UK have a long history of support for Eritrea. There have been 16 registered NGOs in the country. For the most part their role was limited to providing financial support for government projects and then monitoring them. Each agency could engage a maximum of two expatriate workers, although there was more flexibility for training projects. The government has evaluated the role of international NGOs in other countries and observed that their personnel frequently perform tasks that could be performed by nationals, there is little or no transfer of skills to nationals (and the few who are trained then find national salaries too low), and international presence creates a legacy of dependency.

There are a few national NGOs whose work is partially supported by international NGOs, but there are numerous restrictions on amounts and uses of funding. Despite the fact that some national NGOs pre-date the war and contributed to the war effort, the government is concerned that they might become conduits for international funding and, as in other countries, bypass official channels to compete with nationally determined priorities.

[*Editors' note:* On the basis of these assessments, in 1997 the Eritrean government decided to phase out the role of international NGOs working in Eritrea.]

Having concluded that it is not in Eritrea's interest to have international humanitarian agency personnel play a significant role in reconstruction, Eritrea seeks to meet these needs with its own human resources which, it is commonly agreed, are inadequate. There are not enough soil engineers, accountants, health officials, judges, computer technicians, and so on. One international donor recounted the development of a small agricultural project that was to have been staffed with three Eritrean nationals. It took two-and-a-half years to find staff, and then the project proceeded successfully. Such a delay is costly to both donor and recipient. The Eritrean government has decided that it is better to reach goals through a sustainable approach – maintaining overall control and training its own people to manage the tasks. Inevitably, these choices have meant slow progress on some fronts.

Slow progress can be attributed to cumbersome bureaucratic procedures in agencies and donor countries. In Eritrea, as in most aid recipient countries, pledged assistance is rarely delivered in a timely manner. Thus, tractors needed for the harvest arrived when it was over, funding for education projects came far too late in the school year, and trucks for the repatriation of refugees arrived four months after they were ordered. Eritreans estimate that promised "emergency" assistance may take 18 months to appear. In the meantime, the government has to pick up the tab and execute the task.

Members of the government and the international community have acknowledged that relations between government and donors must be improved. The current difficulties are rooted in differences in approach and over the kind of information that should flow from recipient to donor. What donors term "technical advice" is often considered by recipients to represent interference in the policy-making role of the government. Eritreans cite instances of donors seeking to establish large-scale projects with foreign technical expertise, whereas the government intended locally staffed small-scale operations. Donor agencies are perceived as designating beneficiaries quite differently from the government's proposals. International agencies and donors insist that they must be able to account for the use of their funds, should be involved in policy decisions affecting programmes they support, and cannot channel resources for government use without adequate provision for accountability. However, the Eritrean government is convinced that trying to satisfy donor demands will leave the country without its own policy direction, and that doing without assistance would be preferable to accepting unwanted conditions.

Since Independence, all parties have sought to establish mutually acceptable working relations. The international agencies admire and respect the Eritrean commitment to achieve self-reliance and now generally accept the principle of national rather than foreign implementation. The Eritrean leadership accepts that, if funding is to be maintained, donors must know how their funds are being spent. Joint planning of projects, monitoring and reporting seem to be functioning in mutually satisfying ways in most areas, although the resource base remains small.

Nevertheless, there is still a lack of understanding in the international community of what constitutes actions or expressions that infringe on national sovereignty. An incident that caused consternation both inside and outside Eritrea was the expulsion of two members of the international community for having expressed what were considered to be negative attitudes. The people expelled were involved in food aid, but a wider circle of international organizations and bilateral agencies felt threatened, and it was suggested that reduced levels of international assistance and participation in government programmes might result. It is not the intention to take a position here on what happened. The incident is noted to pose the question as to whether and how this unfortunate situation might be avoided in the future, in the interest of serving the needs of the people of Eritrea.

Many Eritreans are convinced that steps should be taken now to reduce foreign presence and assistance. Others are equally convinced that both must be maintained and accommodated until conditions have improved and immediate goals have been met. If there is a will for relations to improve, there must be a willingness on all sides to discuss, share information, and compromise.

REFERENCES

University of Leeds, *Food Needs Assessment Study*, University of Leeds, 1991.

World Bank, "Eritrea: Options and Strategies for Growth", *World Bank Report No. 12930-ER*, Vol. 1., Washington, D.C., 1994.

3

THE CHALLENGE OF REINTEGRATING RETURNEES AND EX-COMBATANTS

Teclemichael W/Giorgis (Rosso)

Social reintegration is a complex process that brings together people who have developed various attitudes and behaviour in diverse cir cumstances. They can act or react in ways that may help or hinder the action being taken to resolve the problems created by their differences. Social reintegration is not necessarily a conflict resolution process: the issue might be to assist particular groups to readjust or reassert their place in society, so they can live normal lives once again.

Reintegration involves economic and social aspects. Economic concerns include the distribution of resources, services, employment and other opportunities that promote people's material well-being. Social concerns include issues affecting people's values, traditions, capacities, aspirations and prestige, all shaped by political, ethnic, religious and psychological backgrounds and people's social positions. The issues to be addressed depend on the particular circumstances that led to the development of distinct societal groups. Although broad categories are normally used to classify people into groups, the groups are rarely homogeneous. In dealing with reintegration, care should be taken to identify crucial and urgent problems, and priority should be given to the most vulnerable sectors.

This chapter describes the problems of social reintegration that Eritrea has had to tackle in the post-conflict period. It outlines official policy concerning the two major groups – returnees from Sudan and ex-combatants – requiring reintegration, and examines critically the reintegration programmes. The chapter further presents case studies carried out in four settlement sites to determine the extent of social reintegration and the aspirations and achievements of returnees and ex-combatants, and looks at important cross-cutting issues such as the environment, gender and the provision of social services.

PROBLEMS OF POST-CONFLICT SOCIAL REINTEGRATION

Reintegrating returnees and demobilized combatants constitute two groups for which the government of Eritrea is continuing to develop specific policies and programmes. The two categories share the experience of having been physically uprooted from their former environments for varying periods of time, which distinguishes them from the rest of the population. They have had to move from place to place, undergoing tremendous hardship, their very survival often at stake. They have lost their assets and belongings, their jobs and even their homes. Survival has depended on support provided by charity organizations or the liberation front.

The challenges facing Eritrea after 30 years of war and recurrent droughts are enormous.

> The consequences of the war were not restricted to the many thousands of deaths in combat, the killing, imprisonment and torture of civilians, the general repression or the flight of refugees or internal displacement, but extended to the basic fabric of the economy and of everyday life (Cliffe, 1996:21).

Systematic destruction by occupation forces devastated the agrarian and industrial sectors. After 1960, successive Ethiopian governments deliberately dismantled Eritrea's economy by transferring industries and infrastructure to Ethiopia, forcing labour to migrate to either Addis Ababa or the Arab countries. Prior to Ethiopian colonization, Eritrean industrial development had advanced by African standards. In 1939 there were more than 846 registered transport companies, and in 1952 there were 728 light industries (Firebrace and Holland, 1984). But at Independence, Eritrea inherited an industrial sector comprising only 40 state-run enterprises and 600 privately owned small-scale businesses, most of which were not producing or only at low-level capacity (Cliffe, 1996:21).

The agricultural sector was also crippled by the labour exodus and the depletion of assets caused by the conflict and drought, especially since 1983. The population was subjected to starvation and became dependent on massive quantities of emergency relief supplies, both during and after the conflict. According to Cliffe (1996:30), crop production between 1986 and 1991 met only 14-25 per cent of national consumption needs (except in 1988, when it reached 46 per cent). The ERRA Food Needs Assessment Study calculated that between 80 and 90 per cent of the population was dependent on food aid for survival in 1991/1992.

Social dislocation was dramatic. Almost 700,000 Eritreans were forced to flee the country and seek refuge abroad, and the war's death toll is estimated at more than 200,000, of whom 65,000 were combatants. In addition, 70,000 civilians and fighters suffer from various disabilities caused by the fighting and land mines, while 90,000 children were orphaned. Moreover, large numbers of Eritrean youths were conscripted into the Ethiopian army during the conflict. And by 1991, when the conflict came to an end, the numbers of fighters in EPLF had reached 95,000 (more than one-quarter of whom were women). Among the civilians, many women were left to head households, as a result of conscription, flight, marriage break-ups and death.

Such massive social disruption had serious implications for efforts to rebuild the nation, and not only because of the large numbers involved. The dislocation especially affected the most active and capable sections of the population. The Food Needs Assessment Study conducted in 1991 by the University of Leeds revealed that labour shortage was one of the main reasons for low levels of food production and consequent malnutrition among rural households. Those who stayed home were primarily elderly people, women and children who were unable to join the fighting or to flee.

However, despite the destruction and disruption, the war helped to forge a strong sense of unity and national identity among the various ethnic groups. Across the country they rallied around the common cause of national liberation and defended their very survival, threatened by an immeasurably superior adversary in terms of human and material resources. Eritreans in the diaspora and those who remained in the country were organized in overt and covert mass associations respectively (unions of students, peasants, workers and women), and these systematic arrangements helped them maintain ties until Independence was achieved. Although the refugees were physically and economically cut off from their normal lives, their relationships with compatriots at home were not completely severed, nor were they necessarily estranged from what was going on in the wider community into which they are now being reintegrated. Indeed, their traditional loyalties were often reinforced by broader and stronger political ties. Despite their economically disadvantaged position, the combatants were in close social and political contact with the communities around them, fighting with them side by side.

Several other factors helped to form the social cement of the Eritrean nation. Liberation forces were recruited from all ethnic and social strata. This, together with the egalitarian distribution of social services and the democratic administrative structures that encouraged participation in the struggle, had a far-reaching effect in breaking down the various barriers that had traditionally divided the society. Indeed, the EPLF made great efforts to eliminate the traditional social divisions based on religion, ethnicity, regionalism, gender and class. Towards the end of the war, the absence of antagonistic political factions helped create a sense of unity and common purpose among combatants and the civilian population. To a certain degree, the EPLF was also successful in emancipating women and children from subjugation by men. It abolished feudal landholding rights, introduced legislation ensuring equal access to resources for women and other deprived groups, and attempted to do away with harmful traditional norms and practices.

Thus, it would seem that the reintegration of returnees and ex-combatants into Eritrean life had more to do with solving economic problems than with resolving socio-cultural and psychological differences. Little in-depth research has been done on impediments to the reintegration process arising from differing cultural values and, while it is difficult to differentiate between economic and social factors, it seems justifiable to say that social cleavages are not a major source of friction.

All in all, Eritrea suffered far less from the social divisiveness characteristic of other post-conflict countries. This was partly due to the fact that the adversary came from another country, to which it returned. Furthermore, Eritrea emerged from the war with a non-factional and disciplined army, dedicated to defending national unity and helping bring about social progress, justice and economic prosperity.

SOCIAL INTEGRATION POLICY

It was always recognized that peace and stability could not be sustained unless the legitimate demands of the sectors most adversely affected by the war were met. From the start, the nascent government allocated a large amount of its meagre resources for this purpose. Immediately after the war, the entire army was deployed to assist the population in returning to normal life. EPLF members agreed to continue their service without pay for two more years. This tradition is being carried on by the National Service Programme (NSP), started in July 1994, in which tens of thousands of young men and women help to construct roads, small dams, schools and health stations. Many of these activities aim to assist deprived communities in improving their socio-economic situation.

The refugees

All Eritreans have the right to return to their country. The return of refugees will have a complex impact on the population that remained at home. The refugees' exposure to different economic and educational opportunities, and to various political and cultural systems, have both positive and negative implications for the society as a whole. The gains in wealth and skills should contribute to national reconstruction, but the impact of their newly acquired values and lifestyles is difficult to assess.

Eritrean refugees in Australia, Europe and North America have had access to better educational and economic opportunities than refugees elsewhere. Most have acquired skills and professions which have enabled them not only to live independently, but also to assist families back home. These refugees have undergone tremendous cultural changes, learned new languages, and attained higher living standards. In the Middle East, while educational opportunities have been limited, most Eritrean refugees have worked in jobs and accumulated savings to enable them to survive when they return to Eritrea. A few have become successful in business and could make a significant contribution to the national economy by investing their wealth in Eritrea. It is estimated that remittances from abroad constitute the largest share of the country's external revenue.

The situation for the refugees in Sudan is very different. Most of the 500,000 refugees there are from the lowlands of Eritrea. They have experienced great hardship and have had to depend mainly on charity, seasonal agricultural labour and domestic work. They have had severely limited access to educational opportunities and rarely attended school beyond primary levels, which did not help them to improve their economic situation. This is due partly to the low economic levels prevailing in Sudan and partly to the Sudanese government's policy to confine refugees in rural settlement camps, restricting their participation in economic and social life. Health and educational services in the camps are woefully inadequate and the distribution of relief irregular and insufficient.

During the war, many of the refugees in Sudan were able to keep up with what was going on in Eritrea because of the relatively short distance that separated them from their home country. Despite their lack of resources, they contributed what they could to the liberation struggle. It is therefore likely that their values, culture and lifestyles have remained largely unchanged. However, this needs to be verified by in-depth studies to determine to what extent they have been influenced by various Eritrean factions, co-habitation with other religious and ethnic groups in the camps, and prolonged dependence on relief aid. The impact of the political-religious movement launched in recent years by the Sudanese government is also an unknown factor.

Whatever these changes may entail, the suffering of these refugees, often physically mistreated, renders their return a moral imperative for the Eritrean government. The government has made sustained efforts over the last five years to draw up programmes for their repatriation and reintegration. However, there has been a notable lack of financial contribution on the part of the donor community for such programmes. Except for a pilot project undertaken in 1995, PROFERI has become stranded, not only by lack of donor support but also by the reluctance of the Sudanese government to co-operate, as a result of constrained diplomatic relations with Eritrea.

The ex-combatants

In 1993, the government of Eritrea decided that a sizeable proportion of the liberation army should be demobilized and returned to normal civilian life. It was felt that the country was at peace with its neighbours, including Ethiopia, and that there was no threat requiring the readiness of such a large army. There were also economic reasons. It was recognized that maintaining a large army would consume a large portion of the government budget and would deprive the country of the most active members of the labour force needed for reconstruction.

Mitias conducted a study in 1993 to identify the main characteristics of the combatants, in order to understand how to best carry out the process of demobilizing and reintegrating them into civil society. The study showed that 80.9 per cent of the fighters were of rural origin, 6.1 per cent were from a semi-urban background and 13 per cent from an urban milieu. Forty-one per cent declared a preference to resettle in urban areas, 9.7 per cent preferred a semi-urban setting, and 13.7 opted for rural areas. The remaining 35.6 per cent were prepared to live anywhere, provided they received what they needed to establish a new life.

In looking at educational levels, it was found that 78.2 per cent had either never been to school or had attended only primary school up to grade five, 6.6 per cent had gone as far as junior secondary school, and 15.2 per cent had reached senior secondary school. The number of combatants who had been to university was statistically insignificant.

Regarding the marital status of the fighters, 48.8 per cent were single, 44.9 per cent had families, and 6.3 per cent were separated, divorced or widowed; 24.2 per cent had children under four years of age. The study showed that 85.2 per cent of the fighters were under 32 years old, of which 37.6 per cent were 18-22 years old. Of the respondents, 77.6 per cent were men and 22.6 per cent were women. Their ethnic origins correlated to a large degree with the proportions of the various nationalities that constitute Eritrea's population.

As far as health was concerned, 63.8 per cent considered themselves healthy, 22.7 per cent had some kind of disability and 13.5 per cent suffered from various illnesses. Half of the war injuries were severe, and half were relatively minor.

Thus, the needs and expectations of the ex-combatants were diverse. The challenge to develop suitable policy was compounded by the poor state of the economy and the need to maintain an army and public services. The government decided to carry out the demobilization process in several phases, which involved devising criteria for screening the combatants, as well as preparing the means to help them to reintegrate into society.

About 54,000 ex-combatants (out of 95,000) were demobilized between 1993 and 1995, in three phases. According to the July 1993 proposal for the demobilization and reintegration of ex-fighters, 26,000 combatants, including 4,500 women, were to be demobilized in the first phase. All of them had joined the fighting in 1990 or 1991, so it was felt that, as they were mostly very young and had been absent from their normal social environment for a relatively short time, they could be expected to be easily reabsorbed by their families and pursue their education or take up other activities.

In the second phase 22,000 fighters were demobilized, including 8,000 women. Considerations taken into account included age and physical fitness, and social and family situations which might affect their continuing service in the army. Individuals providing sole support to families or parents who had lost other family members were given priority for voluntary release. Women whose age and physical fitness qualified them for continued service in the army were allowed to choose freely whether or not to stay, depending on their particular childcare and family responsibilities.

The third phase involved the release of about 6,000 ex-fighters from the civil service when the ministries underwent a major overhaul and streamlining, in 1995. Some 1,000 of these ex-fighters were women. The main criterion for demobilization was the absence or low level of the skills and qualifications needed in the posts they occupied. This phase effectively completed the demobilization process, involving roughly 57 per cent of Eritrea's fighters.

The policy framework

No policy document has been drawn up specifically for the reintegration of refugees and ex-combatants. However, it is possible to extract certain social, political and economic goals from the government's Macro-Policy Document (Government of the State of Eritrea, 1994). The government aims to create a unified state in which citizens live in harmony, sharing equal rights and access to national resources and services. Self-reliance is a goal as well as a guiding principle in the social and economic transformation envisioned. It is emphasized that this principle should apply at all levels of society – national, community and personal. As much as possible, groups and individuals are encouraged to initiate efforts to improve their situation, drawing on their own resources and abilities.

Reintegration policies and programmes are no exception to this general rule. Interventions are designed to relieve groups from dependence on either the government or external bodies. Ideally, there should be no need for foreign assistance but, given the devastated condition of the economy inherited at the time of Independence, external assistance clearly has a role to play, at least for the time being. However, the long-term objective is to help the country and its people extricate themselves from chronic dependence. In this context the government has insisted on the national execution of all internationally funded programmes, with international organizations being asked to provide technical and financial support rather than substituting or undermining local capacities. Indeed, the government proposes nothing less than a reorientation of the usual donor/recipient pattern of development aid, in favour of co-operation based on partnership and mutual responsibility. Such an approach means that the recipient country is to be fully responsible for identifying its needs and for developing and owning its programmes according to its objectives and strategies for development. Co-operating partners were asked to assist in areas lacking expertise in clearly identified fields, and to monitor whether resources are used in accordance with stated purposes.

In February 1998 the government took action to abandon all humanitarian and grant assistance, stressing that international economic co-operation should be based on loans, investments and the promotion of trade relationships. Most of the international NGOs with offices in Eritrea were asked to wind down their programmes and are now closed.

The institutional arrangements

Since 1975 the ERA had been responsible for channelling all charity assistance to areas accessible to EPLF, including assistance to refugees in Sudan. In 1987 the need was felt for a body specifically responsible for refugee welfare; CERA was founded to meet that need. CERA was to provide counselling to refugees facing legal and human rights difficulties, to develop long-term solutions to these problems, and to help ensure that Eritrean's rights as refugees were protected and respected. In 1992, ERA was transformed into ERRA, with an expanded mandate including rehabilitation and the co-ordination of NGO activities. In 1994, Mitias, a semi-autonomous body, was established within ERRA to deal specifically with the reintegration of demobilized fighters.

As time went on, however, it was recognized that relief and rehabilitation programmes and the reintegration of refugees and demobilized fighters were, in essence, variants of the same goal of recovery. Therefore, in 1996 it was resolved to merge ERRA (including Mitias) and CERA to form the Eritrean Relief and Refugee Commission (ERREC), while maintaining the unique features of each programme. Thus it was hoped to minimize duplication of effort and fragmentation of resources, and to assure an integrated approach to programmes that were similar in nature.

It should be noted that the ministries are responsible for the execution of reintegration programmes as an integral part of their respective sectoral national programmes, while giving attention to the particular needs of the groups being reintegrated. In certain areas returnees are the sole direct beneficiaries, while in other areas they are not. Social services such as education, health, water and infrastructure are part of the regional planning process, which serves returnees, ex-combatants and local inhabitants alike. Shelter, food and agricultural inputs are types of assistance that are selectively provided to individual returnee or ex-combatant households. Even so, there are still parallel relief and rehabilitation programmes benefiting local communities, disproving the commonly held view that projects induce discrimination.

REINTEGRATION IN PRACTICE
The refugees

Assistance to refugees and other deprived groups was given not only after Independence, but was firmly rooted in EPLF beliefs and practices throughout the years of conflict. The present programmes cannot be fully understood without taking this experience into account.

By the mid-1980s, when EPLF had consolidated large liberated areas, it had already undertaken a number of programmes to curtail the outflow of refugees from Eritrea. During the large-scale famine of 1985/1986, EPLF was able to settle some 200,000 people who had been bound for exile in Sudan. However, its activities were hampered by lack of funds. Educational programmes and some limited health services were established in the settlement sites and some Eritrean refugee centres in Sudan. There were also plans to start economic development programmes for refugees in Sudan, including their settlement in more viable agricultural areas along the borders. Unfortunately, the latter plan was thwarted by war developments.

The commitment to put an end to the suffering of refugees in Sudan is reflected by PROFERI's current concentration on helping them. The PROFERI programme was negotiated by the Eritrean government and the collective external actors, represented by the Department of Humanitarian Affairs of the United Nations. PROFERI took into consideration the state of the national economy, infrastructure, housing, services and employment, as well as ecological and social situations in various areas of the country. CERA's role was to co-ordinate the various implementing bodies (ministries, local administrations and the returnees), and to liaise with UNHCR and other donor agencies.

PROFERI's objectives were twofold. The first was to facilitate repatriation of the refugees in an organized manner by providing them with logistical support. The second was to help them become socially and economically integrated in Eritrea. In its dealings with the international donor agencies, including UNHCR, the government strongly contended that the two objectives should be inseparably linked: repatriation alone would be a useless exercise, merely transplanting refugees to dependent returnee camps inside Eritrea. In the final negotiations, it was accepted that repatriation should be accompanied by further forms of assistance, enabling the returnees to re-establish themselves.

Implementation of the PROFERI programmme was to be divided into two parts. Responsibility for the operational and funding side of repatriation was vested in UNHCR, while reintegration responsibilities were taken by the government and its institutions. It was assumed that the other external actors would provide the necessary funding support to both components.

According to the original document, the repatriation and reintegration of the estimated 450,000 refugees were to be carried out in three phases, each lasting one year. Thus completion of the programme was envisaged in three successive years, starting in 1994. However, as adequate funds were not forthcoming, PROFERI started instead with a pilot project aimed at repatriating 25,000 refugees and settling them in nine pre-selected sites in the lowlands of Eritrea. This operation was completed during 1995. However, none of the major phases initially planned have got off the ground. As will be shown later, the entire programme has remained blocked, while spontaneous and unassisted returns have continued, induced by the great hardship faced by the refugees.

The assistance planned for the pilot project (which was a miniature replica of PROFERI), consisted of nine packages: relief, logistics, shelter, water, health, education, roads, agriculture and institutional development. Some of these addressed immediate basic survival, while others were long-term oriented. When the programme was conceived, the provision of food and household utensils was seen as an essential emergency measure, as all the refugees were assumed to be extremely poor. At the same time, the supply of food, in the form of FFW, was intended to encourage the participation of beneficiaries in various communal activities. In the pilot project, food in kind was given freely and in FFW programmes. However, in 1996 the government introduced a new approach to the utilization of food aid. The new monetization policy stated that all food aid would be sold to the people at reasonable prices and that the money generated would be used to finance rural development programmes. Vulnerable groups (elderly or disabled people) needing aid would be given cash amounts equivalent to the relief rations, while the rest would earn it by participation in CFW activities.

Repatriation requires efficient logistics and transportation. The organization of this part of the programme was the responsibility of UNHCR, which was already in charge of refugees in Sudan. Thus it was logical for them to assume responsibility for identifying and registering would-be returnees and for organizing their repatriation. In compliance with the principles governing the treatment of refugees, repatriation was voluntary. According to the programme, the repatriation component was to include the transport of returnees' small possessions that could not be profitably disposed of in Sudan. Economically, it made no sense to sell belongings at a loss before departure and then have to replace them at high cost on return to Eritrea.

On their arrival in Eritrea, the returnees were to be settled in selected sites in the countryside. A major criterion for selecting resettlement sites was suitability for agricultural activities. Any returnee resettling in one of the designated sites was automatically entitled to the complete reintegration assistance package. On the other hand, while there were no legal restrictions prohibiting settlement elsewhere, returnees who chose not to settle in the designated areas might lose their entitlement to benefits, which were allotted on an organized community basis.

The underlying assumption was that the refugees in Sudan had agricultural origins and therefore their reintegration into agricultural schemes offered the easiest solution. This orientation was also dictated by serious housing and unemployment problems in urban areas.

The new resettlement sites are in remote, sparsely inhabited areas of the lowlands, and are not easily accessible by road. Refugees had to be transported to these sites and the sites had to be connected to markets, health services and other communities. New roads were urgently needed and PROFERI was responsible for feeder roads linking settlement sites to the main roads. Stepping up the construction and repair of feeder roads contributed significantly to the reintegration of returnees as well as local inhabitants into the broader economic and social network of the country.

As for shelter, it was clear from the outset that the programme had to tackle the problem of housing as, unlike situations in which people return to their original villages where their homes may still be intact, in Eritrea entire villages had been razed. If the returnees were to survive the likely extremes of heat and rain, shelter had to be provided. Health facilities were also essential because of the high incidence of malaria in some areas. Given the prevailing conditions of poverty, malnutrition, poor sanitation and generally harsh environment, communities were prone to disease. Concerning education, there were numerous refugee children who attended schools in Sudan, but many more who were denied educational opportunities. Schools and health facilities established in the new sites were integrated into the local and regional system.

Safe and adequate water supplies for humans and domesticated stock animals were a must in settlement areas, particularly in the more crowded ones without surface water. Drilled and hand-dug water points provided clean drinking water. The programme also envisaged the provision of sanitary and water management training to enable the communities to organize and maintain their water supply.

According to CERA's 1995 evaluation, the agricultural component of the PROFERI pilot project aimed to help returnees meet their food needs through agricultural and pastoral activities. The project was modest, consisting of simple inputs – farm implements, seed, animals and tractor services – to the returnee households. It was assumed that a peasant would need a set of plough animals, and goats and sheep to complement crop production. Because of budget constraints, the package was calculated at the level of a poor peasant. Each returnee household received the same package, given in kind to prevent the possible misuse of cash disbursements.

The pilot project was already under way when it was decided that environmental protection and disaster mitigation activities should also be included in the programme. Although the eco-system's fragility had been recognized when the programme was prepared, environmental concerns did not constitute a separate component but were integrated into the programme as a whole. Each ministry was expected to ensure that in its area of concern certain standards would be observed to avoid possible negative environmental consequences.

Apart from the components briefly described above, all activities should be seen in light of the various rehabilitation programmes that were already operational in the region and that were addressed to all local inhabitants. The Agricultural Rehabilitation Programme, for instance, aimed to supply peasants with agricultural inputs, while the Rural Water Supply Programme attempted to solve acute water shortages in many places. Extensive relief programmes also provided assistance to the most needy. Except for the shelter component, the PROFERI package appeared to fit in with these overall recovery and development programmes.

The ex-combatants

Unlike PROFERI, the Mitias programme for reintegrating 54,000 demobilized fighters does not consist of a uniform package. It is an open-ended programme, couched in general rather than specific project terms. Mitias aims to give individual or groups of ex-combatants opportunities to identify areas in which they can best realize their potential. There are no restrictions confining assistance to a particular type of activity or location.

Agricultural settlement was initially expected to absorb a significant number of the former fighters, considering that most of them were of rural origin. Efforts are being made to diversify opportunities for the former fighters and to integrate them with other communities as much as possible. In fact, experience acquired during the struggle gives many ex-combatants greater flexibility compared to returnees and advantages that help them adapt to diverse situations.

As outlined in the Mitias programme document, the strategy is to promote both spontaneous and assisted reintegration (ERRA, 1994:4). Some of the demobilized fighters automatically reinsert themselves into normal civilian life and find jobs without government assistance. In the case of assisted reintegration, the nature of support varies according to the economic activity chosen by the ex-combatant and the facilities and resources available.

Assistance is provided in four basic areas: settlement in agriculture, self-employment in rural or urban small-scale businesses, waged employment in the modern sector (public or private), and training. In addition, special provisions exist for women ex-fighters and disabled combatants. Facilities such as training, counselling and guidance, credit, issuance of licences and land allocations are available for individuals and groups.

Agricultural schemes for the ex-combatants are based on relatively modern farming system components, compared to those of the basically peasant model adopted by PROFERI. Former fighters are not provided with inputs such as seed and tools, as their demobilization grants provide them with start-up capital and credit facilities are guaranteed by the compensation money they receive for military service. It is felt that ex-combatants, due to their experience, are better equipped than returnees to adopt modern farming methods. Because former fighters are believed to be a dynamic force that can help modify traditional attitudes, and because it is hoped that they will share their skills, efforts are being made to settle returnees and fighters at the same agricultural sites in several locations.

Those who choose to engage in agricultural activities are provided with basic training in agronomy, tractor operation and financial management. During the first year, temporary shelter, water, health services, transport and immediate food provisions are provided for those settling in organized new sites. Tractor ploughing is provided free in the first year, but from the second year settlers are expected to pay for their inputs, farm machinery rental and living expenses. If resources permit, they will be helped to construct permanent houses, with the cost repayable in instalments. Money collected in this manner is to be used as a revolving fund, so that the facilities can be extended to others. As with PROFERI, beneficiaries are first given two hectares of land, but if able to expand they may do so.

Ex-combatant agricultural settlement differs from returnee settlement in one important respect. The latter are resettled in designated sites, while the former may also settle in a location of their choice. However, individuals settling outside the project areas receive only credit facilities, technical advice and counselling. Mitias registered 4,334 ex-fighters (including 1,500 women) as volunteer candidates for agricultural settlement; 3,019 of these were provided with assistance according to the settlement scheme. This number is significantly short of the 10,000 former fighters expected to settle in agriculture, although it should be taken into account that the registered figure does not include spontaneously settled ex-combatants (Gaerke et al., 1995). The distribution of ex-combatants in agricultural settlement sites is shown in Table 3.1.

Table 3.1 Distribution of ex-combatants in agricultural settlements	
Settlement	**People settled**
Ali-Ghider	2,551
Sabunait	300
Jimeil	220
Gifate	300
Karmelo	27
Gahtelai	25
Haikota	25
Agordat	35
Total	**3,483**

Source: Mitias records.

Although Mitias considered the possibility that some ex-combatants might engage in fishery, this sector had been neglected for so many years that it would be some time before investment costs could be recuperated. Moreover, very few former fighters are familiar with the sea, and it is not surprising that, in spite of its potential, fewer than 100 ex-combatants decided to engage in fishing-related activity.

The Mitias programme does not emphasize grant assistance for reintegration, but credit is expected to play an important role. Access to financial institutions usually requires guarantees, collateral and detailed feasibility studies, but credit for ex-combatants has been made readily accessible and can be given under two conditions. Their anticipated compensation money may be used as collateral against credit, the amount depending on length of service during the war. The second criterion is the feasibility of their project. They may propose a project, individually or as a group, which is assessed by the Mitias credit office. If the project is considered sustainable, it is eligible for credit. If not, the office assists them to develop an alternative.

The credit mechanism operates on two levels. On the local level, credit officers can extend loans up to 30,000 birr. Larger amounts are referred to a higher committee composed of the Mitias office, the Commercial Bank and the Ministry of Local Government. Access to credit is simpler for groups who form a co-operative or a company and can collectively put up more collateral.

Few ex-combatants had a high level of formal education or professional experience, as previously noted. Various training programmes have been arranged by government institutions and by the private sector, and funding is sought from donors. Until now, most training has been related to the construction sector, including plumbing, masonry, carpentry, metalwork, and brick and tile making. Other fields include automechanics, leatherwork, dressmaking, embroidery and secretarial work. These courses last up to six months and participants receive a living allowance during their training.

In liaison with the Labour Office, Mitias also tries to find jobs in the private sector, United Nations bodies and government institutions that match ex-combatants' skills. So far, some 4,000 ex-combatants have been place in temporary and long-term employment. In addition, Mitias facilitates the issuance of licences for ex-combatants ready to open their own business. The government has also made available some small-scale enterprises and assets for individuals and groups of ex-combatants ready to acquire them on the basis of long-term payment. One of these enterprises is the state-run mini-bus service operating in Asmara. Likewise, taxis imported by the municipality have been sold to individual demobilized fighters. Another example is the distribution of the 5,000 hectare state-owned cotton plantation at Ali-Ghider, allocated to more than 2,000 ex-combatants and 500 returnees to be run on a private basis.

Except for a few small projects funded by external donors, most ex-combatant reintegration programmes have been financed by the Eritrean government. All in all, the demobilization money given to individual fighters amounted to 384 million birr, while the amount given to support martyrs' families was 296 million birr. Furthermore, some 4 million birr was spent on cash credits.

The problems confronting female ex-combatants, disabled veterans and orphans made specific demands on reintegration programmes. The government fully recognized the particular problems faced by women ex-fighters returning to civilian life. Partly because of the disadvantages they experienced before joining the liberation army, and partly because many of them have recently had childcare responsibilities, it is more difficult for them than their male counterparts to benefit from programmes designed to help them. Mitias studies show that about one-quarter of the women fighters demobilized in the first phase had children. In the second phase, 68 per cent had children. Moreover, many of them are *de facto* single parents, either because their husbands were killed in the fighting or because they are divorced or their husbands are at a different duty station.

Although special efforts have been made by Mitias to reintegrate as many women as possible, the women are hampered because childcare facilities are seldom available. Also, traditional attitudes confining women to domestic chores persist, making it difficult for women to take on the jobs most commonly available – mainly in the construction sector. The NUEW has also been trying to assist these women, but its aid has not been significant.

More needs to be done to meet the requirements of demobilized women. In recognition of this, Mitias established a Gender Unit to study problems and assess prospects. In addition, the unit provides counselling, guidance and training services for women.

More than 10,000 ex-combatants have sustained various disabilities and traumas, including some mental disorders. Women constitute 15 per cent of the disabled. Some 5,000 of the fighters with severe impairments are the direct responsibility of the government, which takes care of their basic survival needs. The government sponsored the formation of the

Eritrean War Disabled Fighters Association (EWDFA), which aims to foster socio-economic reintegration of the disabled.

Besides catering for their everyday needs, EWDFA is expected to identify areas for reintegration of the disabled, provide physical rehabilitation, and co-ordinate training and job creation opportunities. A vocational training centre for the disabled has been opened at Mai-Habar, while those with higher educational levels are trained for office work. Recently, EWDFA has made progress in organizing groups of disabled fighters, helping them establish businesses in bakery, milling, recreational centres, poultry and other trading activities in many urban and semi-urban centres. One of the most important plans is the creation of a trust to support economic ventures, financed by government funds. Although the total amount is not yet known, some assets have already been committed for the purpose. The Lilo Transport Company, comprising a fleet of more than 40 trucks, is one such venture.

Before the restructuring of the civil service, about 60 per cent of the disabled fighters organized through EWDFA were employed in various government institutions. A large number of them have now lost their jobs, once again posing the challenge of reintegrating them. Considering their disability and low education and skill levels, they are likely to encounter employment problems unless they can engage in self-run formal or informal sector business activities. The cases of people with severe mobility and mental problems will remain a formidable task for some time to come.

The war for Independence created an estimated 90,000 orphans, 10,000 of whom are children of martyrs. The government has entrusted the Ministry of Labour and Human Welfare with the rehabilitation and reintegration of these orphans. Children at orphanages run by the ministry receive full board and lodging, but centralized institutions are not considered ideal. The aim now is to promote decentralized community-based assistance, giving orphans more opportunities to develop individual potential in a normal social setting. Foster parent programmes have been initiated to send orphans to sponsoring relatives. Such families are given economic assistance, and the Ministry of Labour and Human Welfare monitors them to make sure that the orphans are well integrated and receive educational opportunities in their new environment.

ISSUES

The reintegration of returnees and former combatants is important not only because of the direct benefits to the groups involved. It is also crucial for the social and economic progress of the country as a whole. The overriding constraint is the lack of resources to carry out the reintegration process properly, to even temporarily mitigate personal hardship for returnees and ex-fighters, and to ensure that they are well integrated into the nation's social and economic life with the least possible delay. That said, there are a number of other issues which should be briefly examined.

Food aid

As we have seen, the war reduced agricultural production to the point that food aid became the main source of subsistence for the majority of the population. The government was concerned that massive and prolonged dependence on food aid would inhibit people from relying on their own efforts. In 1995, a policy was introduced which monetized all food aid.

The present policy provides food and other relief assistance to the most needy and vulnerable groups, while encouraging active, able-bodied people to earn their living, rather than await handouts. In principle and in practice, assistance to the needy is not withdrawn, but merely changes form. Funds generated by monetization are used primarily to finance rural development activities and provide relief cash assistance to groups unable to participate in such programmes. However, the donor community is unwilling to contribute badly needed food aid. While donors do not appear to disagree with the new policy, and even acknowledge the value of the strategy, when it comes to real action most donors try to impose conditions the government will not accept. Ignoring the main strategic issues, donors have been making counter-arguments about subsidies, prices, market liberalization, their role in planning and implementing programmes, and their own constitutional limitations in relation to monetization.

The hunger which became apparent in many returnee settlement sites when the research presented in this chapter was carried out in 1996, was a direct consequence of the reluctance of donors to provide food aid under the new policy. Donors attributed the problems to the ineffectiveness of the policy. The issue of food security is dealt with in greater depth in Chapter 5, but it is mentioned here as it directly affects reintegration programmes. As described above, food aid was an essential ingredient of reintegration assistance, to be provided for at least one year until the reintegrating groups had developed coping mechanisms in their new homes.

Strict targeting of assistance to the most needy, as now envisaged, will eliminate the privileges enjoyed by returnees receiving full rations irrespective of their means. If effectively implemented, the new measure will save scarce resources from being simply dumped, instead investing them with a view to long-term development.

However, one problem is that the new policy can deprive vulnerable groups, such as the elderly and female-headed families, of the communal labour support that was available through FFW programmes. Data on the settlement camps indicates that about 30 per cent of returnee households are headed by women. They do not have cash to pay for the labour needed to clear land, construct homes and farm their plots, so they face great economic difficulties unless special measures are taken. During field interviews for this research, settlers reported that, because people who can offer labour are being forced to work outside the settlements for wages, activities previously designed to be communally conducted have been curtailed.

Agriculture

PROFERI assumed that Eritrean refugees in Sudan originating from rural backgrounds had not changed their lifestyles, so their future in Eritrea was expected to be in agriculture, where they would readily become engaged. However, this assumption was not wholly correct. While most of them came from rural areas, many had long been exposed to and become involved in other activities such as driving, vehicle repair, small-scale trade, catering and domestic services, and wage labour. If the spontaneous urban refugees are also taken into account, the assumption is even less valid. The standard agricultural package also disregarded the fact that many women and elderly people could not be productive in such programmes.

While PROFERI is concerned with people settling in agricultural schemes, no one is forced to do so. Individuals must judge the situation and determine whether they need assistance and can fit into this programme, or whether they prefer to look for other opportunities. As already noted, there was some justification for concentrating on rural resettlement schemes. However, as no detailed refugee study was made before the programme started, the need for diversification was underestimated even within the framework of rural settlements. While some returnees might be inclined to engage in crop production, others might be more inclined toward pastoral activities. Still others may lack the skills necessary to engage in agriculture and may be more interested in small-scale trading in food, beverages and other consumable goods, or in working as semi-skilled wage labourers.

During field research, some recipients of packages in kind said that it would have been more appropriate if they had been given the chance to buy their own inputs on the market, as they would better know how to select the animals and tools adapted to their needs. Examples were given of animals that died as soon as they had been distributed to the households. Farm implements (pickaxes, shovels, sickles) imported by UNHCR were considered inappropriate to settlers' needs and thousands of them are sitting unused in ERREC stores. Settlers also reported that information about the planned large-scale purchase of livestock induced suppliers to raise prices. They claimed they could have bought animals individually at much lower prices. A member of the *baito* in Alebu also mentioned that some households had no children to tend the goats, which therefore wandered off and could not be retrieved.

Such problems may appear to be technical, but they had a bearing on the overall strategic thinking that took place about the reintegration programme. They revealed weaknesses which could be partly explained by the short implementation period. More importantly, there was no room for flexibility once the programme was drawn up and approved by the government and the donor community. Once the programme specifications and procedures were decided, there was no choice but to comply with them, and any alterations would have been interpreted as violations of the agreement. PROFERI negotiations lasted more than two years, after which time only a pilot project was feasible. There was little prospect for the introduction of adjustments. As with monetization, there was a bias that underestimated the capacity of beneficiaries to utilize funds properly, if received in cash.

It can also be said that insufficient rainfall aggravated the problems facing new agricultural settlers before they could produce enough for subsistence. Despite input packages given to them in the first year, the returnees found their position no better in the second year. As compensation for first-year failures, most settlement sites received tractor ploughing services for the second year. But the vagaries of nature continued to hamper progress in the agricultural sector. As infrastructure construction and commercial farming activities picked up in the Gash-Barka region, waged labour played a vital role in supplementing agricultural income.

Land

The question of land is a critical one. According to PROFERI, there was enough land to settle most of the returnees; the amount of land available was a determining factor in how many sites would be established and how many people should be settled in a particular site. A plot of two hectares was calculated to be sufficient to support a household, assuming that a peasant would use animal ploughing and family labour. The estimates were based on rain-fed cultivation.

According to the 1994 Land Proclamation, in principle all land in Eritrea belongs to the state and any citizen is legally entitled to use it. Given the small population of the country, land is therefore legally and physically available. However, the availability of suitable agricultural areas is dependent on the amount and rainfall distribution. The two hectare allocation envisaged by the programme can be met, as only 10 per cent of arable land is currently being cultivated. But are all the locations where land is available suitable for habitation? Does the settlement of new inhabitants provoke resentment among the existing communities? These are legitimate questions, especially in light of the fact that most identified sites are in the Gash-Barka region.

Some sites – Alebu, Tebeldia and Gergef – already have 4,500 settlers, far exceeding the original plan. Can the land, environment and services such as water and sanitation sustain such large communities? Obviously, the economic base of agricultural and pastoral activities cannot be similar to that of urban populations. It is true that the people have opted to live in these highly populated communities, prompting the question of limiting the size of settlements in relation to available resources. While sites such as Alebu, by virtue of being located on the main road, are developing into urban areas, remote settlements might not have such prospects.

Questions have been raised about the land entitlements of ex-combatants at the former state farm of Ali-Ghider. It is clear that they will remain entitled as long as they do not neglect their responsibilities in utilizing their land productively. Individuals not prepared to make the best use of the land can be evicted and the title transferred to others who need it.

In general, the allotment of land to ex-combatants and returnees does not seem to have given rise to hostility of any significance, as some scholars predicted. It is acknowledged, however, that in some places allocations were delayed because claimants contested land allocation, saying that they had used it long ago or that they had obtained recent concessions for commercial purposes. The effects of settlement on transhumant pastoral activities are difficult to identify while the programme is still in the pilot phase.

Shelter

The shelter component of PROFERI has been a major problem since the programme's inception. Questions have arisen concerning the type of housing to be provided, the appropriateness of providing returnees with houses while ignoring local inhabitants in many respects no better off than the refugees, and whether returnees ought to be encouraged to build their own homes. Some advocate that returnees use local materials to build their houses, as in the communities around them, for reasons of cultural suitability and concern about discrimination by the local population.

Others argue that the environment has been so degraded that traditional house construction methods, which involve cutting down trees, will jeopardize their future livelihood. Indeed, the scarce vegetation cover that remains (less than 5 per cent of the country is covered by vegetation) is found near the resettlement sites. If traditional building methods are adopted, the countryside will be doomed to desertification.

Thus, despite the attraction of being economical, traditional house construction has been ruled out. The debate now revolves around finding cost-effective alternatives. Some dome-shaped houses being constructed in the pilot project are made entirely of mud bricks, with some made of mud brick walls roofed with imported corrugated iron or cement tile roofing. Other houses are constructed of hollow cement blocks or have walls and roofs made of corrugated iron sheets.

Another issue related to shelter is the design of settlement villages. Are the shelters intended to suit only immediate needs, or should they serve for the long term? To what extent should the programme invest in testing models with an uncertain future? Is there a danger that resources will be wasted as people develop solutions that meet their own needs and desires? How durable are the proposed models with regard to natural forces such as rainfall, termites and heat?

As in so many cases, lack of resources is the major constraint. The programme has difficulty in even partially meeting the needs of returnees, let alone extending the provision of shelter to local inhabitants. This raises the question whether all returnees should be asked to participate in the construction of their houses or whether, after an assessment of their capabilities, a distinction should be made between those who can and cannot afford to do so. It is all too evident that shelter is lagging behind the other components of the programme.

CONSTRAINTS

The entire returnee reintegration programme budget was calculated at about US$ 262 million. Actual donations and pledges came to only US$ 32 million, including US$ 17 million in the form of food relief aid. Commitments were often tied to specific components or sub-components of the programmes, depending on the donor's interest in a specific sector. Therefore, certain sectors received funding while others did not get adequate financial support. To launch the PROFERI pilot project in 1995, the government had to finance two-thirds of the cost.

The reintegration of all Eritrean refugees in Sudan was originally planned to take place by 1997. Ambitious though this might seem, it would not have been impossible had funds been forthcoming. However, due to the lack of funds not even the first phase has been implemented. Some refugees have come back on their own, having lost confidence in the official plan for repatriation. Most had to leave their few precious possessions behind.

The government considered the role of the donor community to be one of filling the gaps in the reconstruction and development process. Donor contributions were welcome insofar as they did not interfere with the country's independent planning and procedures. Donors found this stance to differ from the usual aid practice, which assumes the absence of local planning capacity. The incompatibility of these perspectives might account for the limited response of international aid agencies to Eritrea's returnee reintegration programme.

Another important constraint is Sudan's persistent refusal to co-operate with UNHCR in organizing the repatriation of the remaining refugees. It is unclear whether this stalemate will be resolved.

As for funding the reintegration of ex-combatants, donor interest was also weak, and almost all financial support has been provided by the Eritrean government, thus diverting precious resources from productive investment.

PROFERI: AN INTERIM BALANCE

With the benefit of hindsight, PROFERI can be seen to have suffered from several handicaps. First, there was no information on the number of refugees, their socio-economic status and ethnic identity, where they were living and what they were doing in Sudan. UNHCR officially recognized some refugees while others had no status, so that official records were inconsistent. There is still no reliable information regarding the number of refugees remaining in Sudan, registered or not. Furthermore, certain ethnic groups are found on both sides of the Eritrea/Sudan border, and it is sometimes difficult to distinguish the Eritrean refugees from the local Sudanese people. The figures are distorted by the fact that people crossed the border to present themselves either as refugees or local inhabitants, depending on the assistance programmes taking place.

PROFERI does not distinguish between official and unofficial refugees. To do that, accurate information would have been necessary on the ethnic and geographical origins of the refugees, as well as on relationships between the different groups. Although organized resettlement of the returnees might seem the simplest administrative and logistical approach, it is debatable whether such a conglomeration of ethnically heterogeneous returnee communities can live together without a number of problems. For example, different ethnic groups have voluntarily settled together at sites such as Gergef. While the majority of people at Gergef are Tigre, there are minority Tigrigna and Saho groups. Schools have been established with classes taught in the Arabic language for children who spoke Arabic after attending such schools in Sudan. This arrangement will influence child development in minority groups.

When the settlement sites were identified, a detailed study of the regularity of rainfall, the dangers of flooding and the incidence of malaria should have been carried out. Some sites, such as Gergef, had to be relocated at higher altitudes due to floods, while Jimeil was abandoned after a year because the amount of rainfall was not sufficient to support agriculture. In some cases, such as the Gahtelai agricultural settlement using drip irrigation, the investment cost is excessive in relation to the number of people being assisted. Moreover, some of the beneficiaries lacked appropriate skills.

PROFERI aimed to facilitate the reintegration of all Eritrean refugees in Sudan, but in fact was able to help only the 25,000 refugees who returned in the pilot phase. More than 180,000 refugees have resorted to returning spontaneously. Paradoxically, they do not qualify for any of the PROFERI packages, because of the strict distinction between organized repatriation and organized reintegration. Most of these returnees have been left to manage on their own and appear to have devised successful coping strategies. Further study of their progress might give rise to doubts as to whether aid is indispensable in mitigating the social disruption caused by conflict.

The government's commitment to self-reliance notwithstanding, several years of food aid and relief handouts have led to a dependency syndrome that contradicts this strategy. It is particularly evident in housing construction and the clearing of farm land. Despite the principle of community participation and mutual assistance, settlers expect to be paid through FFW arrangements or to receive finished houses. Changing these dependent attitudes may take some time, but may occur if beneficiaries are given more responsibility. In the past, government institutions and NGOs have done things on behalf of the returnees. For example, the Ministry of Agriculture cleared and ploughed land, purchased tools, seed and animals for settlers, and CERA and NGOs constructed shelters. The role of governmental and non-governmental bodies is now being reconsidered, and beneficiaries are expected to assume greater responsibility for managing their own affairs.

Finally, there is the fact that the demobilized fighters, even if they come from rural backgrounds, have been exposed for years to a different lifestyle and values. They regard themselves as emancipated from the peasant way of life. Unless agriculture is organized in a more modern way, it will not be attractive to them. On the other hand, their wartime experience has equipped them with a work ethic and opened up opportunities. The challenge is to link this long-term potential with their immediate needs. As the economy picks up, ex-fighters may become absorbed by different sectors, but they need training in various skills. The dearth of training institutions is a serious bottleneck. For disabled and female ex-combatants the situation is even more critical.

CASE STUDIES IN FOUR SETTLEMENT SITES

Case studies were carried out in Alebu, Ali-Ghider, Fanko and Gahtelai, four returnee and ex-combatant settlement sites selected to evaluate the impact of the programmes. All sites are agricultural schemes. Ethnic composition and the nature of the programmes were taken into account when selecting the sites. Consideration was also given to the implications of the programmes for the relationships of spontaneous and organized returnees, and where possible to their implications for local inhabitants.

Alebu was selected because it was a site for returnees only. Situated some 30 kilometres east of Tessenei, on the main road to Barentu, it evolved as a settlement site during the PROFERI pilot project in 1995. It now hosts a returnee community of some 1,200 families (4,500 people).

Ali-Ghider was a private cotton plantation until nationalized by the Ethiopian government in the 1970s. During the 1970s and 1980s it changed hands several times between the liberation fronts and the military regime.

Starting in 1988, the plantation was run as a state farm, growing sorghum instead of cotton. In 1994 this 6,000 hectare estate was designated for the settlement of demobilized fighters and returnees. At the time this study was conducted, 2,551 ex-combatants and 436 returnees were settled there. Given the mechanization and irrigation services required to run the plantation, the former management structure had to be maintained. Settlers are responsible for labouring on their individual plots of two hectares. Technical and management services were provided free of charge during the first year, during which time the government also provided food rations, blankets, tents and kitchen utensils. The ex-combatants were thus able to use their demobilization money to hire additional labour and for other investments. From the second year onward, the beneficiaries were to bear the full cost of technical and management services.

Fanko, also known as Adi-Bidho, is located 37 kilometres south-west of Tessenei, a few kilometres off the road to Goluj. The settled population is 3,831, including 340 spontaneous returnees and 200 local inhabitants. The rest returned under the pilot project, coming from Shagareb and Semsem, two refugee camps in Sudan. They mostly belong to the Nara and Saho ethnic groups, and appear to be able to live together as a community without any problems.

The clay soil in this area is suitable for agriculture and there is enough of it to accommodate the present population. Each family is allotted two hectares, and there is enough grazing land and water for their livestock. Farmland clearing was organized on a communal basis so as to assist vulnerable families as well. Some animals were brought back from Sudan and together with livestock distributed by the project cushioned the settlers against disasters caused by lack of rainfall. Some settlers have experience in trade and at the time of the study more than 60 shops selling consumer goods constituted another source of income. However, as the roads and other infrastructure had not been developed, the diversification of economic activities outside farming and pastoralism was very limited.

Gahtelai lies at the foot of the eastern escarpment halfway between Asmara and Massawa. Its location on the main road has helped it grow into a town. It is inhabited by returnees, ex-combatants, local indigenous people and others from different places. It is surrounded by a lot of flat land suitable for agriculture.

Most of the returnees are Saho. Although originally pastoralists, they practised agriculture during their stay in Semsem. The indigenous inhabitants are Tigre. Most of the returnees in Gahtelai first settled in

Ghinda from 1991 to 1993, as spontaneous returnees receiving emergency relief assistance. To avoid prolonged dependence on relief aid, CERA requested assistance from AUSCARE to help relocate 600 families in the Gahtelai area so that they could take part in agricultural activities. In all, 240 houses were constructed and the same number of households was resettled in 1995.

A settlement scheme for ex-combatants in Gahtelai was also initiated by Mitias. Because it was believed to be beneficial to mix the settlers, 25 ex-combatants were settled with 25 local people in a project that was added to the CERA scheme. This Mitias project started with a six-hectare demonstration and training farm in drip irrigation. However, apart from these six hectares no new land was cultivated by the returnees, although the large flat area around Gahtelai had been partially used by private commercial farmers and is presumably fertile. It is expected that both rain-fed and irrigated cultivation will be practised in the area. There appears to be enough land to support the 240 returnee families and 25 ex-combatants. Meanwhile, some private commercial farms have also started operations in the area.

Social reintegration

In Ali-Ghider, the settlements' heterogeneity notwithstanding, there appears to be a high degree of unity among the settlers. When returnees were asked how they perceived reintegration with ex-fighters, they stated that they welcome it and support each other in many activities. There was not a single incident of friction or dispute between them. It is striking that, despite the absence of any police or law enforcement body, there is no sense of insecurity and no criminal activities have been reported.

One explanation for the harmony among the various groups may be the fact that the Ali-Ghider plantation was first owned by a private company and later by the state. Hence, the settlers may all consider themselves guests, with no one intruding on the land of others. Their social behaviour and interaction are marked by tolerance and respect for each other's customs and values. Furthermore, Ali-Ghider, a labour-intensive plantation, has long been a meeting place for various permanent and seasonal labour migrants. The local community does not resent the settlement of the returnees and ex-combatants; it does not have a direct impact on their livelihood. The settlement has almost certainly had a positive economic impact on the surrounding areas. Small enterprises are sure to benefit by increased demand for services. Work opportunities, however seasonal, have increased for the local community in many areas, including agriculture and transport.

Reintegration policies should not assume a dichotomy between returnees and ex-combatants. The issue is more complex, as members of both categories may possess more than one identity that reinforces or negates their association with various groups. For instance, members can belong to a certain ethnic or language group, sharing religious, educational and geographical backgrounds. But cultural, political and economic values can also bind or divide individuals and groups. Thanks to the experience of the liberation struggle, many of the potentially divisive ethnic, religious, geographical and occupational stereotypes have lost force. Therefore, contrary to what several theoretical assumptions suggest, there is no evidence of a lack of social cohesion among the various groups being reintegrated.

At an individual level, settlers face numerous problems. For example, they do not have adequate houses and facilities, and almost all ex-combatants still live in camp settings, as they did during the war. These and other factors impede their reintegration into normal life – the camp-like environment encourages them to retain their fighter mentality and identity, rather than consider themselves as regular citizens. They are also unable to establish a family life with almost all of them living away from their families. The settlement sites are referred to as *cambos* (camps) and are identified by numbers instead of *adi* (village), indicating that civilian activities are not in themselves enough to ensure reintegration.

It should be added that this phenomenon is not particular to Ali-Ghider. Even in urban areas, ex-fighters now working in the civil service live in former army camps and barracks (Gaerke et al., 1995). The main reason for this is the housing shortage and lack of financial resources. Although returnees and former fighters in Ali-Ghider are engaged in the same economic activities, their lifestyles are different. The former dwell with their families in traditional huts, while the latter have difficulty adapting to their new conditions. Such diverging lifestyles may increase the separation between the two categories, even though it is envisaged that they be integrated, each category having its own camp or village administration and council. They have not yet been able to form a common community organization.

On the other hand, while such differences exist they do not seem to hinder the two communities from living and working in harmony as long as they have a common understanding and similar goals.

As for the returnees in Alebu, on the whole they have retained the high degree of social cohesion that characterized their refugee community in Sudan. This conclusion is reached in Christian Sorensen's 1996 unpublished study, "Alebu: Eritrean returnees restore their livelihoods". Sorensen disagrees with Gaim Kibreab et al., who claim that the Eritrean refugees in Sudan have undergone changes which have either weakened or replaced their traditional values as a result of market relationships. Their original social and economic fabric is assumed by Kibreab et al. to have disintegrated and therefore they are expected to go through a difficult relearning and readjustment process after being repatriated.

The case of Alebu does not bear out such assumptions. According to Sorensen, several factors have contributed to the notable cohesion found there. Most importantly, the Wadel-Hilowi and Shagareb camps hosting refugees were located close to Eritrea, thus direct ties could be maintained. The refugees furthermore had strong nationalist feelings. The socio-economic situation in Sudan also was a factor. Sorensen seems to believe that Eritrean authorities shared the opinions of scholars in planning repatriation and reintegration, although such references are not found in government policy papers or programmes. On the contrary, the government has consistently recognized that Eritreans in Sudan maintain their identity, unity, traditional values and strong links with home.

It has already been noted that PROFERI can be criticized for paying insufficient attention to the new skills acquired by the refugees, and their resulting reluctance to take up the expected economic activities. However, social relationships remained unaffected. Because the refugees were economically deprived and dependent on relief assistance in Sudan, it is understandable that they look to aid to solve their problems. But this situation is not particular to the refugees – the majority of people remaining in Eritrea were also reduced to such dependency.

The community in Alebu is composed of several ethnic groups. Roughly two-thirds are Nara and Tigre, and the remaining one-third consists of Kunama, Bilen, Hidareb and Tigrigna. All these groups lived in harmony in Sudan, and this continued on their return to Eritrea. Formal and informal associations in Alebu cut across the various nationalities, and self-help groups are not based on ethnicity. In community activities, such as land-clearing and shelter construction, Alebu illustrates that the reintegration of returnees from various ethnic groups is not, in itself, a problem. The reintegration process has been relatively fast. Alebu has become a vibrant town, with modest housing, water, health and educational facilities and diverse off-farm activities.

In Fanko, social behaviour was found not to differ from that in Alebu. Ethnic diversity notwithstanding, the settlers had normal communal relationships. The local community willingly participated in the preparation of temporary shelters for returnees, demonstrating their positive attitude toward the newcomers.

The elderly and households without male labour find it difficult to manage agricultural activities on their own. As stated earlier, female-headed households make up about 30 per cent of returnee families. While it is encouraging that such problems are dealt with by traditional co-operative arrangements, it is doubtful whether these will sustain an agriculturally-based lifestyle for all. Other activities may develop, including sharecropping, lessening the burden on active community members who have been shouldering the responsibility for others.

Settlers expressed concern that their two-hectare allotments were not within a reasonable distance from their dwellings. Due to the size of the population, some farm plots were as far as four to five kilometres away. On the other hand, the size of livestock herds brought in by Fanko settlers are larger than those of other returnees, indicating that they were practising agro-pastoralism while in Sudan. However, the exact number of animals is unknown because there are no official statistics on herd sizes.

Although Fanko was progressing toward becoming a stable community, the construction of permanent shelter had not started at the time this research was conducted. The delay in construction, compared to other sites such as Alebu, has been a source of complaints. Funds are apparently available and construction could start when decisions are made about the type of dwellings to build and the method of implementation.

In Gahtelai, interviews with the host community indicated that there were no social cleavages hampering reintegration. Returnees were originally from the vicinity, although before exile they had not established organized settlements. Local community elders stated that they welcomed the return of their people, believing they would join hands in developing the sparsely inhabited area for mutual benefit. However, although the settlers joined the community's social and administrative structures and are sharing water, education and health services, they were not allotted land. Their survival depended mainly on irregular relief aid which, as described earlier, has ceased. Thus, there is an urgent need to help them solve their economic problems.

The ex-combatants and local people who were combined in the

drip-irrigation project in Gahtelai were still undergoing training in the third year. Although they received a monthly training allowance, they apparently did not derive any income directly from farming. Selection of the candidates had not been based on their capacity to adapt to the technology and manage their own farms, so many had dropped out, unable to cope with the training.

Aspirations and achievements

Most Alebu respondents complained that much of the assistance promised had not been received. They said that, when in Sudan, they had been told that the Eritrean government would provide them with everything, starting with a ready-made house, land, a complete package of agricultural inputs, provisions for health and education, water and free food. Gaim Kibreab witnessed such an information campaign being conducted through loudspeakers. However, on arrival they found they had to build new dwellings for themselves from scratch. No land had been cleared, and no school or health services established. With such expectations disappointed, some said they led a better life in Sudan.

It is true that relocation and rehabilitation is arduous. However, the difficulties encountered by returnees during the short transition period cannot be compared to their long-term stay in Sudan. The comforts that they claimed to have enjoyed were certainly exaggerated. Nonetheless, such complaints indicate that unrealistic expectations were created by announcements of programme provisions without definition of returnees' responsibilities and the efforts they would have to make.

Did a dependency attitude develop among the refugees during their stay in Sudan and if so to what extent? Without a doubt, they were largely dependent on charity assistance, especially in the chain of reception, transit and settlement camps. Restrictions on their mobility within the country kept them in poverty. This was a critical factor when PROFERI was discussed. While donors were much less interested in assisting the reintegration programmes, except for emergency relief provisions, the government insisted that, given the returnees' destitute situation, the programme must include assistance to enable them to resume normal lives. However, such material assistance was never seen as a solution in itself and the success of reintegration would depend above all on individual and collective efforts.

It can be difficult to differentiate between poverty and dependency, because both are a function of the availability of employment and productive resources, a conducive socio-economic and political climate, and skills and physical fitness. When such opportunities are lacking and people fail to see alternative solutions, it is a natural reaction to vest hope in external support. This preference for aid becomes problematic if people give up taking initiatives when opportunities do in fact exist. A dependency attitude is not only the fault of beneficiaries, as is widely believed. Several external causes can be noted. To some extent, aid has induced and perpetuated the tendency. Unless assistance is handled in a way that encourages beneficiaries to realize their potential, it will indeed be detrimental in the long run. Adequate education and community organization is needed to harmonize people's aspirations with existing assistance programmes. Therefore, sound policies and appropriate monitoring mechanisms must be developed to guard against the growth of aid dependency.

A case in point is the shelter programme. While the housing provided in Alebu seemed to meet the expectations of refugees, this was not the case in other sites with similar backgrounds. The organization of shelter construction in Alebu – which involved training, constant supervision, income incentives and community participation, and the provision of inputs and machinery – provided advantages other sites lacked. It does seem possible to match aspirations and achievements through proper organization and orientation.

In other respects, too, Alebu seems to be ahead of other settlement sites. Despite excessive numbers of settlers and the resulting scarcity of agricultural land, the people of Alebu were able to diversify their economic base. Alebu is located on the main road to Tessenei, so it is hardly surprising that it has not developed as a purely agricultural settlement. With the employment opportunities provided by trade, farming and pastoral activities, and water, health and educational services, returnees in Alebu are progressing toward full reintegration.

Finally, although most of the inputs envisaged by the programme were provided or are under way in Alebu, the community needed more support in their development efforts. Low rainfall in 1995 necessitated providing tractor services and other agricultural inputs again in 1996. This indicates that it takes time to build a self-sustaining community, especially one based on agriculture, as natural phenomena such as rainfall are not predictable.

Groups in the Fanko settlement site expressed various expectations and concerns about how to revive their economic and social life. Some elderly men and women who headed families said that they were unable to cope with tending livestock. Others mentioned that carrying out this task would lower children's school attendance. Most people valued education highly and were anxious that their children should receive more than primary school education. Older children experienced difficulties in attending junior secondary school in Tessenei because of the expense.

The shelter provided did not meet settlers' expectations. Based on information they received in Sudan, they anticipated finished houses but found only temporary shelter, constructed of grass or tree branches. Even two years after their arrival, the construction of proper housing had not yet started. Despite the hardship, people confronted the realities of rehabilitation with dignity and pride (Nielsen, 1995).

The ending of food aid rations led to another complaint. Settlers were given full rations for the first year, but they pointed out that they had expected to receive food until they became self-sufficient. Unfortunately, due to erratic rainfall, the first harvest did not produce enough to meet their subsistence needs. This problem, which is common to almost all the agricultural sites, illustrates that it is difficult if not impossible to plan one-year recovery programmes based on rain-fed agriculture, especially in drought-prone regions.

The returnees in Gahtelai, most of whom came spontaneously before the PROFERI programme was developed, had no great expectations of assistance. They said that, when the war ended, they decided to return home and live in dignity rather than linger on as refugees. They believed that the government would help them restore their livelihoods, knowing that charity assistance was becoming unavailable. As they were living in deplorable conditions, CERA decided to relocate them from Ghinda to Gahtelai, where houses were already completed. Although they were grateful for these houses, the returnees believed they could do even better if land was allotted to them.

In Ali-Ghider, it was found that the ex-combatants' level of expectation was different from that of the returnees. The former fighters expected more from the government than the returnees did, no doubt because of the sacrifices they made during the struggle and because they saw the government as their guardian. They seemed disillusioned by the time it took to return to civilian life and by the difficulties of making ends meet. They listed numerous hardships that they had to endure in Ali-Ghider and expressed their dissatisfaction about the assistance received. The project manager and Mitias officers indicated that the assistance packages had been provided according to plan, apart from some components which were still being organized, but the miserable position of the former combatants was nonetheless evident. The ex-fighters did not seem to realize that the support provided was going to be less than what they demanded, for there were similar or greater needs among other ex-combatants and in society at large.

It should be noted that, in the planning stages of the Ali-Ghider project, a comprehensive reintegration of returnees and former fighters was not foreseen, and the assistance package was not extended equally to both categories. Because returnees had already settled in the area and benefited from the national relief programme, they were not eligible for the one-year food allowance given to ex-combatants. Likewise, returnees were not included in the shelter programme, which had been specifically developed as a Mitias project for demobilized fighters. The only common provisions were the allotment of two hectares of land, collective technical management, and health service.

Profits from the project have been relatively good, compared to that of the two-hectare cereal fields in other settlements. While the latter had poor harvests due to insufficient rainfall, the cotton plantation in Ali-Ghider was only slightly affected due to the combination of direct rain and flooding from other areas. One harvest could not be expected to help the settlers overcome their difficulties, but the project was rewarding for most settlers, at least by Eritrean farming standards. It is claimed that the most successful were able to earn 20,000-30,000 birr a year, depending on costs. The project further had a considerable impact on the national economy. By supplying cotton and seed, it saved precious foreign exchange and helped revitalize textile and edible oil factories.

From an economic point of view, the Ali-Ghider scheme has been generally successful, although a few settlers could not absorb the know-how, were not prepared to work hard, or remained unable to meet financial requirements. The difficulties of some physically disabled people and women with children were also commonly raised issues. Generally, it is expected that individuals will have varying abilities for dealing with the problems encountered until sufficient experience is acquired and the infrastructure improved.

Housing has been a major problem for the former fighters at Ali-Ghider, as mentioned earlier. There are now plans to construct houses using revolving funds. Although Mitias officers claim that work was planned to start at the end of the rainy season, when beneficiaries could participate in building their houses, the project has been delayed. Until their homes are established, it is likely that ex-combatants will disperse as soon as they have harvested their crops. Apart from a few who cannot afford to leave, most do not reside in Ali-Ghider during the dry season.

By contrast, returnees in Ali-Ghider have resorted to their traditional huts and *agnet* (makeshift tents). As they were indigenous to the locality, it has been easier for them to settle in, establishing homes and community organizations, although housing conditions are still far from satisfactory.

It is the inclination of people to aspire to more than they have, making it difficult to measure achievement in terms of feelings expressed. Results will inevitably be disappointing unless aspirations are realistic. It is more appropriate to gauge achievements in terms of a project's realizable objectives. This suggests the need for continuous guidance and counselling in order to narrow the gap between expectation and reality.

The environment

The environment has recently figured prominently in discussions of sustainable development. While this comprises a broad range of issues, for present purposes the environment is considered above all in terms of the natural resource base, namely the water, soil and vegetation that directly affect the settlements.

Alebu was traditionally an agro-pastoral area, like other settlement sites populated during the pilot project. It was inevitable that the settlement of people would have an impact on the ecosystem. Land has been cleared for cultivation and construction, natural vegetation is cut back, felled or trampled by grazing and herding, and underground and surface water is used by people and animals. Although the Ministry of Agriculture has prohibited the cutting-down of trees, it is questionable whether these protective measures can be enforced, given settlers' heavy reliance on wood for cooking, heating and other purposes.

When the settlers first arrived in 1995, firewood could be collected from dead trees within a few metres of the houses. Women now have to walk 5 to 7 kilometres to collect wood because of population growth. Furthermore, as mentioned earlier, the amount of land available for cultivation and grazing is insufficient for the expanding population. Thus Alebu is often considered an environmental problem, even though an environmental component was incorporated in various sectors of the programme. For example, housing construction in Alebu was designed in a way that would avoid tree-felling. However, other activities have grown beyond the reach of environmental measures and – even though human and economic imperatives demand foremost attention in relocation programmes – strategies must be drawn up to minimize negative environmental impacts.

The success of such strategies depends on environmental awareness in the community. It was obvious that the temporary shelters and additional rooms built by settlers would be constructed by cutting down trees. However, it did not seem feasible or desirable in terms of time, finance and participation to construct permanent houses before the returnees arrived.

Similar environmental problems exist in Fanko. Nothing was done to replace the natural vegetation lost in land-clearing and shelter construction. Although felling trees was illegal, people continued to cut down trees for various purposes. Soil and water conservation activities were also minimal. Unless extensive reforestation programmes are introduced in time, Fanko may turn into a dust bowl.

In itself, the settlement of returnees and ex-combatants in Gahtelai does not give rise to immediate environmental concern, but with the added presence of other migrants and commercial farms, the depletion of natural resources can be expected.

Ali-Ghider, where the land was cleared decades ago, is different from the new sites but the large number of settlers is likely to adversely affect the area. New villages are planned on the periphery of the plantation, entailing land-clearing and tree-cutting for various purposes. As the infrastructure improves, the cultivated area is expected to expand. Large commercial plantations are being established by clearing land along the banks of the nearby Gash river. Thus, many environmental changes are liable to occur soon.

The major problem in Gahtelai is lack of water. The dam that supported commercial farming in the area has silted up and a new earth dam constructed after Independence has washed away. Given scant rainfall in the area, rain-fed agriculture does not offer great prospects. Moreover, wells supplying drinking water are salty. Settlers say that they use the water only for sanitary purposes and fetch drinking water from a distant well. If Gahtelai is to develop into a large agricultural settlement, the long-term water situation needs to be thoroughly studied.

It is absolutely necessary that environmental precautions be taken now, to avoid further degradation of the land surrounding Gahtelai. The escarpment immediately above Gahtelai is one of the few places in Eritrea with relatively good vegetation cover. The Ministry of Agriculture has already taken measures against the felling of trees there, and these should be complemented with reforestation and soil and water conservation measures. An environmental management department has been instituted within the Ministry of Land, Water and Environment. It is inevitable that significant achievements will take time, as implementing environmental conservation is not only a question of raising public awareness but is, above all, a problem of human and material resources.

Gender issues and the question of vulnerability

As has been noted, a major problem in most settlement schemes is the large number of female-headed households – 30 per cent in Alebu and 28 per cent in Fanko. In Gahtelai the majority of returnees are elderly people or female-headed families. This poses a serious social and economic challenge.

It seems unlikely that such a high degree of family disruption has occurred among refugees, despite the recorded figure of 30 per cent. Perhaps this question should perhaps be further investigated. While a large number of female-headed families can be expected in any post-conflict situation, it is doubtful whether war casualties are the explanation for these cases, many of which have been removed from battle situations for a long time. Families sometimes present themselves as two separate entities upon registration, expecting to benefit from double assistance. Some husbands may remain in exile while sending their families back, expecting assistance programmes to take care of them. Another plausible cause for the high number of female-headed households registered could be polygamous marriage practices, in which case several wives of one husband might register as separate families.

Whatever the explanation, the presence of so many female household heads – with limited experience working outside the home – makes it difficult to reintegrate them as self-supporting community members. Community support in the form of collective land-clearing, shelter construction, and so on, may not be available much longer. It remains to be seen if the communities can deal with such a high proportion of vulnerable members. Mutual assistance activities are currently being carried out in conjunction with external assistance, but whether or not the community will have sufficient resources and energy to continue these collective efforts when outside support ceases is a serious question. The withdrawal of FFW programmes is already diverting the labour force away from the construction and agricultural needs of individual families.

It is significant that returnee families that settled in Gahtelai are headed mostly by women or elderly people. The vocational training they received did not equip them for employment in construction activities. Furthermore, these activities are customarily the domain of young male labourers. Some trainees started self-help groups in metal work, manufacturing and repairing various household items such as charcoal stoves, dishes and beds. However, because people prefer to buy these items in Ghinda, there was little need for their services and they were unable to continue. Lack of employment is one of women's main problems. A few have opened tea shops. In Sudan women had access to seasonal jobs such as cotton picking or domestic work, but there are no such opportunities in Gahtelai. Because the food aid they greatly depended on has ceased, ways and means must be found to help them become self-supporting.

Households headed by elderly people or women predominate in Gahtelai because these most vulnerable groups have been given priority. This criterion for selection may have seemed logical when the original intention was that the level of assistance would comprise only housing. However, because the subsequent plan was to enable the integration of returnees in agriculture, the choice of people who were not physically fit or strong may not have been the most economically sound one.

In Fanko, too, female household heads presented problems for agriculture. A number of them took up other activities such as selling *swa* (a local beverage) and food. In 1995, many female household heads acquired skills such as embroidery. However, the problem was to find markets for their products. Their situation was determined by the number of children they had, whether or not they had extended families, and age. As could be expected, relatively young women who had children had greater social security than elderly women without children.

In Ali-Ghider, there are more than 550 female ex-combatants. Their problems are somewhat different from those of the returnees. The ex-combatants had overcome the traditional norms which inhibited them from participating in extra-domestic activities. However, as single parents, their childcare responsibilities prevent them from giving sufficient time and energy to agricultural activities. They expressed the need for daycare centres, especially because they do not have family members in the vicinity. Mitias recognized this need and undertook a study on how to make such facilities available.

Although agriculture is no longer considered an exclusively male domain, the disabled members and some women in the settlement still depend on hired labour. To help them obtain additional hired labour, Mitias recently made interest-free loans of up to 5,000 birr available. However, considering the extensive technical and management facilities and services available in Ali-Ghider, it is questionable if this experience is replicable outside the plantation.

There is no overall programme specifically addressing gender issues. The provision of shelter is a tangible demonstration of the priority given to women as family heads, rather than as women *per se*. The only gender-related activities for women are adult education and gender awareness seminars given by the NUEW.

The provision of social services

Basic social services such as healthcare and education started to function in Fanko as soon as the returnees arrived, but the structures are rudimentary because of lack of time and resources. The clinic and school are temporary huts and must be improved if they are to adequately serve. School enrolment is very low and students must sit on stones because of the lack of desks and chairs. In 1995 the school had three teachers, with 60 pupils in grade one, 60 in grade two and 35 in grade three. This was a small proportion of the total school-age population in the community.

The clinic was opened when the returnees arrived. A nurse and two health assistants are posted there to provide first aid and maternity services and treat minor illnesses. However, the clinic is constructed of grass and it is reported that termites frequently cause damage that takes time and resources to repair. Because the clinic is not well equipped, the returnees are often referred to Tessenei. Although a doctor from Tessenei visits Fanko once a week, he cannot provide satisfactory services given the absence of refrigerators and electric power, the scanty stock of medicines and the lack of diagnostic equipment. There is no ambulance and the public transport system is poor. In cases of emergency, the only way to reach Tessenei is to hire a truck, and this is an expense that is beyond the resources of the settlers.

Interventions now aim to meet urgent necessities but the community needs to be gradually assisted in planning and constructing sanitation facilities. There are no latrines and people defecate on the grounds of the settlement. The water supply could become a problem, especially during the dry season. Domesticated animals are currently supplied with water pumped into concrete basins by motorized power. As there is no surface water available, any failure in the system could be very serious. A supplementary reservoir or small dam is essential.

In Ali-Ghider, Mitias established a clinic to serve the settlers and the management staff. An ambulance was provided. This is particularly necessary because of the high incidence of malaria and harsh climatic conditions in the area. Clinic services are provided free of charge for the time being but Mitias cannot shoulder this expense indefinitely and it is foreseen that patients will have to pay fees, eventually making the clinic self-sustaining.

CONCLUSIONS

When the young government of Eritrea inherited a country with an almost completely devastated economy and a severely dislocated population – whether as refugees, fighters, or internally displaced people – many questioned the viability of the emerging nation. Some felt that the country could not overcome the obstacles to national reconstruction and reintegration without massive external assistance. However, against all odds Eritrea has preserved its national unity and social stability, and is making progress toward economic recovery, notwithstanding negligible donor assistance.

The lack of external aid has slowed the pace of repatriation and reintegration. The external economic assistance that would have enabled implementation of the three-year PROFERI programme did not materialize. The lesson seems clear: the needs that arise from devastation caused by war are not sufficient to qualify for outside assistance. Aid is not given based on demonstrated necessity, or even the capacity of using it properly. It is usually guided by donor priorities, whatever they may be.

The approach of the government of Eritrea has been determined by independent national priorities and emphasizes upgrading domestic capacities. The reintegration of returnees and ex-combatants is an integral part of the strategy for national recovery and development. Although there are separate arrangements for co-ordinating the reintegration of returnees and ex-combatants, various ministries are responsible for their respective sectoral components of the programmes.

External actors were expected to fill the gaps created by the lack of national resources and capabilities during the short transitional period. Their role was seen as limited to providing funds and technical support in specific areas. However, if such assistance undermined or replaced domestic capacities and initiatives, it was considered undesirable. Thus, the role of external actors was not an unrestricted one and was seen by them to unduly inhibit their actions.

This experience has thrown new light on aid mechanisms and

relationships that prevailed elsewhere during the last three to four decades. Some regard the Eritrean approach as a source of inspiration and a model for other countries. Others consider it too rigid, and attribute the low level of external assistance to the restrictive attitude of the Eritrean government.

That said, a surprising amount of economic and social progress has taken place in the short period since formal achievement of Independence, with very little external financial support. Nonetheless, Eritrea still has one of the lowest per capita incomes in the world, and there is certainly no room for complacency. The country does not suffer from the social conflicts and unrest that often occur in societies with similar war experiences. Neither ethnic and religious diversity nor the reintegration of refugees and former combatants have become a threat to national cohesion and stability. There is no evidence of the social tension and resentment that might have been expected.

Post-conflict situations are often characterized by vandalism, armed robbery and other crimes. In Eritrea, however, the demobilization and disarming of ex-fighters and their return to civilian life was carried out without need for military supervision. When the decision was announced, ex-fighters laid down their arms as willingly as they had taken them up when voluntarily enlisting in the army. Their return to civilian society does not seem to have caused any problems in social relationships. A systematic study of the psychological and behavioural changes resulting from the process has not been carried out, but it appears that there have not been significant shocks or depressions. This must be the result of the intensive and continuous political education that strove to form a dedicated and disciplined army with a clear vision of the mission and objectives of the struggle.

Similarly, the reintegration of returnees, even though the larger part has yet to be implemented, has not provoked problems in social relationships. Christian and Muslim returnees have settled in harmony. Ethnic and religious identities were not considered important when they chose to live together in the settlements. The returnees have developed a shared identity and consider themselves a single community. They are united by nationalist feelings and by their efforts to restore their economic livelihood.

It would be desirable to create economic situations suited to different social groups, but at this time the urban sector does not offer many opportunities. Agriculture is still the sector that can absorb the largest number of people, especially those returning from Sudan. Some refugees have acquired new skills in Sudan, but they are not statistically important enough to merit specific programmes. However, such small groups can be accommodated with some technical adjustments in the implementation of assistance packages.

The principle of self-reliance lies at the heart of the Eritrean government's policies. Emphasis is put on developing the country's human and material resources, and on the efforts of domestic actors as the key to social and economic development. This does not mean that all external assistance is rejected during the transitional period. However, it must not contradict the government's strategies and policies. The reintegration programmes reflect these principles. Assistance is designed to provide leverage, in the initial stages, to enhance the efforts of the refugees and ex-combatants themselves. Utmost care is taken to prevent dependency on aid. The maximum length of reintegration project assistance is one year, during which time it is expected that thebeneficiaries will achieve self-sufficiency. As noted earlier, however, the time span has not proven reasonable, particularly in view of the vagaries of the climate and related crop failures. One year is also too short a time to complete the multitude of activities envisaged to be carried out through community participation.

In the absence of refugee data, and given the still limited economic opportunities in Eritrea, PROFERI appeared to be a plausible programme. However, the experience of the pilot project showed that returnee groups were far from homogeneous in social and economic make-up. They included large numbers of female household heads, whose physical and traditional constraints did not permit them to undertake heavy agricultural tasks. The elderly, chronically ill and disabled were in a similar position. The programme was clearly not flexible enough to take into account the diverse social and physical needs of the returnees.

A serious shortcoming of PROFERI was the assumption that repatriation would occur only in accordance with their organized plan. Because of this, the programme excluded spontaneous returnees from planned assistance. While 25,000 people benefited from PROFERI assistance, more than 136,000 spontaneous returnees received no such support. Although the severance of diplomatic relations with the Sudanese government could not have been predicted, donor attitudes were also partly responsible for this rigidity. One of the negative consequences of the narrow scope of organized repatriation was that equally poor or even poorer spontaneous returnees did not receive assistance.

Had assistance been given to all returnees, more people would have been encouraged to come back on their own. Fear of losing assistance if they returned spontaneously probably deterred many refugees from re-entering Eritrea. Some donors have become aware of the need to treat spontaneous returnees the same as those who are organized, but others have yet to be convinced of the need to change the modalities that govern their assistance.

Another important question is that of aspirations. The achievement of national independence was the central goal during the struggle, subordinating all other concerns. All sectors of society made a contribution to the victory, albeit to different degrees. While everyone realized that the new nation was very poor and for the time being could offer very little, the drawing-up of PROFERI and ensuing publicity created exaggerated hopes and expectations. No doubt some of the information disseminated was inaccurate, but the fact remains that returnees in the pilot project complained about unfulfilled promises. This underscores the need to ensure that advance publicity is clear as to what may be realistically expected by returnees.

Table 3.2
Ex-combatant settlements with returnees and local inhabitants

Settlement	Combatants		Returnees	Local	Total
	male	female			
Ali-Ghider	2,001	550	436	–	2,987
Sabunait	240	60	–	–	300
Jimeil	180	40	–	–	220
Gifate	232	68	–	–	300
Karmelo	13	14	–	–	27
Gahtelai	22	3	–	25	50
Haikota	25	–	–	–	25
Agordat	35	–	–	–	35
Total	2,748	735	436	25	3,944

Such illusions may also be caused by other factors influencing expectations, including educational background, health, age, gender, exposure to various socio-economic conditions, and the role taken on during the struggle. These variations testify to the need for greater diversification of assistance. While the idea of new agricultural sites cannot be realistically questioned, given the limited options for urban settlement, it is now clear that assistance should take more account of different potentials and needs, without upsetting the principle of equitable treatment. Instead of supplying the elderly, the disabled and female-headed households with agricultural tools, animals and seeds, for example, it may well be wiser to give them the equivalent in cash so that they can invest it in areas where they feel they have opportunities. Some would argue that if people are given cash they will not put it to good use. This underestimates the sense of responsibility and abilities of the poor to manage their affairs and make their own decisions as to what is best for them.

Table 3.3
Returnee settlements with local inhabitants

Settlement	Organized	Spontaneous	Local	Total
Goluj	2,778	3,491	–	6,269
Fanko	3,291	340	200	3,831
Alebu	4,417	76	–	4,493
Gergef	3,008	45	–	3,053
Tebeldia	4,049	–	–	4,049
Um-Hajer	405	2,468	–	2,873
Adi-Ibrhim	1,233	52	–	1,285
Tekreret	1,215	124	–	1,339
Hagaz	569	1,264	6,000	7,833
Total	**20,965**	**7,860**	**6,200**	**35,025**

REFERENCES

Centre for Development Studies, *Eritrea 1991: A Needs Assessment Study*, final report to the Emergency Relief Desk, University of Leeds, May 1992.

Cliffe, Lionel R., "The Indirect Effects of the War and the Disruption of the Overall Economy", in Resoum Kidane, Lionel Cliffe, June Rock and Philip White, *The Patterns and Socio-economic and Environmental Impacts of Conflict in Eritrea*, Occasional Paper No. 14 in the series Environment and Development in an Age of Transition, Centre for Development Studies, University of Leeds, 1996.

CERA, *Evaluation of the Agricultural Component of the Pilot Phase of PROFERI*, Asmara, 1995.

Department of Reintegration of Demobilized Fighters (Mitias), *Annual Report, 1995*, in Tigrigna, 1996.

Department of Reintegration of Demobilized Fighters (Mitias), *Survey of the Ex-Combatants*, 1993.

ERRA, *Food Needs Assessment Report*, Asmara, 1992.

Firebrace, James and Holland, Stuart, *Never Kneel Down: Drought, Development and Liberation in Eritrea*, Bertrand Russell House, Nottingham, 1984.

Gaerke, Inge et al., *Promoting the Reintegration of Former Female and Male Combatants in Eritrea: Possible Contributions of Development Co-operation to the Reintegration Programme*, draft report, German Development Institute, Berlin, May 1995.

GSE, *Macro-Policy Document*, Asmara, 1994.

Kibreab, Gaim, *Ready and Willing...but Still Waiting*, Life and Peace Institute, Uppsala, 1996.

Nielsen, Soren Walther, *Capacities and Vulnerabilities in Times of Disaster and Recovery: A Case Study of Eritrea*, Roskilde University Centre, Roskilde, 1995.

Sorensen, Christian, *Alebu: Eritrean returnees restore their livelihoods*, paper presented at the conference Reconstructing Livelihoods: Toward a New Model of Resettlement, Refugee Studies Programme, Oxford, 1996.

4
THE STATE OF ERITREA'S INFRASTRUCTURE

BERHANE WOLDEMICHAEL

The deficiencies of the infrastructure in post-conflict Eritrea have become a major constraint on the country's economic and social development. The limited road network is hampering the development of production and distribution systems, links between the various regions, and the sustainability of social reintegration and environmental protection programmes. For example, the decision to concentrate returnee settlements in the Gash-Barka region was partially determined by poor road conditions and other infrastructure elsewhere in the country. Power and telecommunication services have degenerated to the point of a serious loss in production: a World Bank estimate suggests a loss of between 30 and 50 per cent of GDP (World Bank, 1994a).

The investment required to bring the infrastructure to a semblance of normality is enormous compared to the available resources of a country emerging from 30 years of war. Because resources are very limited, such investment must be carefully planned and efficiently managed. Investment in a stretch of road brings benefits to its users which can be quantified and compared to cost. In other words, investment in infrastructure in a certain locality has to be justified in terms of the benefits that will be generated, be they economic, social or even political.

Since Independence the Eritrean government has understandably placed much emphasis on the rehabilitation and reconstruction of the country's infrastructure. For the most part the work has relied on locally available resources, especially labour. The government has long experience in labour-intensive works, gained during the drawn-out struggle for liberation, and has made use of it ever since. However, by its very nature the rehabilitation phase was a response to some of the most urgent and obvious problems and required little in the way of socio-economic justification. This will not be the case for the long-term projects, which will have to be justified and prioritized, and will require a more systematic approach to investment in infrastructure.

This chapter is concerned with Eritrea's physical economic infrastructure and specifically with five sub-sectors: roads, ports, railways, energy and telecommunications. It is beyond the scope of this chapter to discuss the technical aspects of infrastructure, including technological choices, important though they are. Furthermore, each sub-sector is a major issue in its own right and cannot be covered exhaustively here. Instead, the aim is to describe the general challenges that Eritrea has faced in rehabilitating and reconstructing these services and to critically analyse the impact of policies for economic development in general and for poverty reduction and environmental sustainability in particular. An important aspect of the research examined interaction between infrastructure and other research areas featured in this book. For example, the policy mixes between social reintegration and road construction, resettlement and rural electrification, and crop production and processing facilities.

THE HISTORICAL CONTEXT

Eritrea had a relatively well-developed infrastructure during the Italian colonial period, as their intention was to turn the country into a settler colony. According to the 1939 population census, 15 per cent of the people were of Italian origin, while the inhabitants of Asmara, the capital, included 53,000 Italians and 45,000 Eritreans. In order to exploit the resources of the country, the colonists invested heavily in the development of infrastructure, especially in the productive areas of the Gash-Barka region and the main roads connecting Eritrea to neighbouring countries. Investment was also made in the development of two ports, Massawa and Assab, to facilitate sea links with the outside world. The Italian colony thus became a commercial and industrial centre. According to the 1939 economic census, there were more than 2,000 industrial firms in the country, resulting from the huge inflow of Italian labour and capital. With a population only half that of Somalia, the other Italian colony in East Africa, Eritrea had nearly four times as many industrial firms, and by the 1940s it possessed one of the most developed infrastructures on the African continent.

At the end of the Second World War, there were more than 1,500 kilometres of asphalt roads and 2,500 kilometres of earthen roads linking the main economic regions and settlement centres. The Italians had also constructed a single-track railway that connected Massawa with the western lowlands, a distance of 310 kilometres. In addition, there was a rope-way from Massawa to Asmara, a direct distance of 70 kilometres, which facilitated the transportation of cargo. This rope-way was dismantled during the British occupation and, together with the iron jetty at Massawa, shipped to Pakistan where it was sold. During the Ethiopian occupation that followed, there was no investment in Eritrea's infrastructure and decades of total neglect resulted in much of what existed being damaged, mostly beyond repair.

INFRASTRUCTURE AND DEVELOPMENT

The World Bank's 1994 development report is dedicated to the role of infrastructure in development. It is emphatic on the pervasive impact of infrastructure on economic development and human welfare, two of its main messages being that:

- infrastructure can deliver major benefits in economic growth, poverty alleviation and environmental sustainability – but only when it provides services that respond to demand and does so efficiently;
- infrastructure should be managed as a business, not a bureaucracy (World Bank, 1994b:2).

For countries at the low end of the development scale, such as Eritrea, investment in basic infrastructure clearly plays a direct and vital role in improving the welfare of its people. The construction of a link road to an agricultural area with high potential for development – or the installation of a water well near a village – can have a dramatic effect on the lives of the local population. For example, in the former case it can lower production costs and, with the possibility of easily and cheaply bringing any excess product to the market, farmers will be encouraged to produce more.

The argument as to whether infrastructure is a result rather than a cause of economic growth is somewhat irrelevant when it comes to the so-called developing countries. Their economic base is so low that the question is not about the need for investment in infrastructure. Of course it is needed, but it is important to determine its appropriateness. However, an infrastructure project may be designed that is appropriate and answers a justifiable demand, but these considerations alone will not guarantee success if efficient management capacity is lacking, be it for roads or telecommunications.

POLICY AND INFRASTRUCTURE

The government's macro policy outlines the strategies it wishes to pursue for the maintenance of peace and stability, the processes toward social, economic and political development, the methods of co-operation with external partners, the roles of the private sector and women, and many other considerations which have the overall aim to transform the war-ravaged economy into a modern, self-sustaining one (GSE, 1994).

There is no illusion about the formidable problems and challenges that lie ahead. The government has thus adopted a two-phased approach:

- The recovery and rehabilitation programme: a multi-sector programme aiming to address the immediate problems covering the restoration of essential agricultural and industrial activities, repair and rehabilitate social and economic infrastructure, and build and strengthen institutional capacity.
- The long-term development programme: which looks beyond the horizon of immediate problems and aims to solve structural constraints on development, and, by enhancing Eritrea's comparative advantages, to devise appropriate policies to create sustained economic growth.

The government's vision of the new Eritrea is one of a modern and technologically advanced country with an internationally competitive economy within the next two decades. The national development effort will thus be directed toward achieving:

- improved agricultural production through the development of irrigated agriculture, and through enhanced productivity of peasants, pastoralists and agro-pastoralists
- developed capital and knowledge-intensive and export-oriented industries and services
- an upgraded and technologically improved informal sector
- a developed tourism sector and high-grade conference and convention facilities
- a competitive international financial centre
- a developed and systematic public healthcare system
- broad-based education involving the dissemination of skills and languages and extensive human capital formation
- an effective social welfare and safety net system
- an upgraded and safeguarded environment that is free from pollution
- a decentralized and democratic political system
- an internally peaceful and stable nation that is at peace and harmony

with its neighbours
* a free sovereign state in which human rights are respected.

The main means of achieving these objectives are the development of infrastructure and of human capital through training (education, health), export-oriented agriculture and industry, and promotion of the private sector. Emphasis is on the need to establish an efficient, outward-looking market economy, with the public sector intervening only in areas where the private sector cannot engage because of externalities. It is further emphasized that all strategic public investments will be subjected to rigorous project preparation, operated on a commercial basis and carried out within the limits of a prudent fiscal policy.

The government has not found it appropriate to use the conventional way of listing priority sectors for development. It believes there is an equally vital need for rehabilitation, reconstruction and development in all sectors and, as such, its strategy is to remove the critical bottlenecks in every sector.

The government's Macro-Policy Document presents a carefully considered development strategy offering guidelines upon which specific programmes and projects can be based, but the difficult challenge will be how to carry them out. Policies are not end results in themselves; they remain mere aspirations until translated into development actions that can be implemented.

ROADS AND ROAD TRANSPORT

When Eritrea achieved Independence, its road network could hardly be called such. Many of the former primary routes were either completely destroyed or had reverted to gravel roads, passable only during the dry season. The many feeder roads that once linked villages to urban or market centres had become impassable by motor vehicle, thus seriously affecting the production of both rural and urban economies.

Moreover, the main roads had been constructed in the 1930s and earlier and were unable to meet the demands of modern road transport. Motor vehicles now have weight, volume and speed that far exceed the models for which the existing roads were designed. Sharp curves, steep gradients and narrow carriageways are among the inherited technical deficiencies. Therefore, requirements of the post-conflict period have involved major remedial construction work rather than simple rehabilitation.

During the war years, as road conditions and passenger transport services deteriorated, the vast majority of the rural Eritrean population found its mobility on foot or on animals (camels, mules, donkeys). Horse-drawn and hand-pushed carts continue to be an important way of transporting goods and people in urban areas. Most haulage trucks and buses were so old that at any given time only half were actually operational.

There have certainly been some dramatic improvements in the transport sector over the last few years. Its growth has been facilitated by improvements to the existing road network and construction of numerous feeder roads since 1991. The Ministry of Construction has been one of the most visibly active ministries, having successfully taken on one of the most immediate and major challenges facing the country. What became the Ministry of Construction had been the EPLF's department of construction, which performed wonders during the liberation struggle. For example they constructed the Bidho and Shenkolet earthen road.

Although the roads have improved, serious problems remain that hinder efficient haulage and passenger transport service. The Ministries of Construction and Transport, responsible respectively for public construction works and transportation, are severely affected by shortages of adequately qualified personnel in management, and specialized experts. This has been a restricting factor in designing and implementing reconstruction projects as far as roads are concerned. For example, there is a lack of qualified national experts and contractors who can supervise and manage large-scale civil engineering projects. The Ministry of Transport is also struggling in its effort to make safer roads and more efficient transport service. The problems include the large number of old vehicles and track roads, shortage of spare parts, lack of qualified auto-mechanic services, lack of operation facilities and effective inspection and follow-up capability.

The government has identified the following priority areas:

- development of potential agricultural areas, particularly those with the possibility of a quick return on investment
- development of social and economic integration among the various administrative regions and between Eritrea and neighbouring countries
- development of areas planned for social resettlement programmes
- development of potential tourist areas

In addition, expansion of the road network is seen as enabling many other activities. For example, the transport sector must be able to rely on road conditions to meet its declared policy of providing efficient, dependable public service.

The road system in Eritrea is classified according to function:

1. *Main or primary roads:* trunk roads connecting Eritrea with neighbouring countries, as well as those joining the capital to major production and distribution centres
2. *Secondary roads:* important connector roads to areas where significant development activities are taking place
3. *Tertiary or local roads:* feeder roads that connect villages and rural production areas to the primary or secondary roads
4. *Minor roads:* track roads providing access to isolated communities

In 1995, excluding urban centres, the network consisted of 588 kilometres of paved roads, 500 kilometres of gravel roads and 1,400 kilometres of earthen and track roads. Even after all the hard work that has gone into improving the roads since liberation, the network is still far below the standard that prevailed during Italian colonial rule.

The five-year plans for road construction

Following the guidelines and the general development principles contained in the Macro-Policy Document, the Ministry of Construction drew up a strategic plan of action for the road sub-sector, consisting of short-, medium- and long-term plans, each of which was to last five years. The short-term plan of action was of an emergency nature, as it addressed the period immediately after the end of the war, and the task was to rehabilitate and reconstruct those roads that required priority attention. The medium-term plan of action is intended to build on the short-term plan by upgrading and providing regular maintenance service to the existing road network and constructing vital new links. The projects that fall under the long-term plan are those that demand large capital outlays. However, it is envisaged that feasibility studies for the long-term projects will be completed during the medium-term plan of action.

Each five-year plan of action contains details of the projects to be undertaken, including their objectives and construction costs. Attempts have also been made in the action plans to provide rationale and justification for the projects in each phase. As already stated, road construction is very costly and it is important to take the utmost precaution to avoid expensive mistakes in later stages. The design of road projects should involve specialists in different disciplines, such as economists, sociologists, geologists, geographers, civil engineers and quantity surveyors. Feasibility studies of the major road work the ministry is currently doing had to be carried out by external consultants as there is a lack of in-house capacity to conduct such studies critically. Another problem for the ministry is its lack of expertise in the art of negotiation on the external funding of projects.

The Macro-Policy Document considers agriculture – the most important provider of livelihood – a priority sector for development. The Gash-Barka region has long been recognized as having significant agricultural potential which, if fully developed, could contribute greatly to the country's food requirements.

The only primary link road to Gash-Barka (Asmara-Keren-Barentu-Tessenei-Sabdarat) was constructed during the Italian colonial period and was considered the top priority for rehabilitation and reconstruction under the short-term action plan of the Ministry of Construction. When originally constructed, the 90-kilometre section from Asmara to Keren was paved with tarmac, while the remaining 300 kilometres was gravel-covered. During the course of the war, the gravel section deteriorated and became more like an earthen road.

Over the last few years, the Asmara to Keren section has been rehabilitated and partially upgraded and is now considered good quality. In 1992 the remaining section of the route was graded, but the work did not include gravelling the surface, so it did not take long to revert to its previous condition. The current state of the road is such that it takes up to eight hours for a four-wheel drive vehicle to travel from Keren to Tessenei, a distance of 250 kilometres.

Under the medium-term plan of action, construction is under way to upgrade the aforementioned primary road, while a new secondary link road is being constructed between Mendefera and Barentu. These are necessary, indeed long overdue interventions considering the importance of this region.

There have been complaints from some investors about the condition of the road to the Gash-Barka region. They have started banana plantations and claim that they have incurred losses as a result of the road conditions. There is not an attractive market for bananas from this region at the moment because of the high transportation costs. Discouraged, some of these investors have decided to get rid of the banana plantations altogether.

A major constraint for investors in the Gash-Barka region is the unavailability of other essential services, notably telecommunications and energy, which makes it difficult for them to diversify their activities and invest, for example in food-processing plants (the Gash-Barka region is suitable for many kinds of horticultural production). As the infrastructure services are interdependent, it will be important to work out what investments should be made in which services and when.

Another common complaint of growers in the region is about the lack of farm workers at critical periods. Most workers come from Ethiopia, so an improved road service would increase the supply of labour.

The regional context

As a small nation, Eritrea will have to develop trade with its immediate neighbours, as well as with the rest of the world. One of the prerequisites for this will be an efficient infrastructure and other related services.

IGAD, consisting of the African countries of Djibouti, Eritrea, Ethiopia, Kenya, Somalia, Sudan and Uganda, was recently reconstituted with responsibilities for subregional development and for the mediation of conflicts that may arise among the member countries. The development of economic infrastructures is one of the priority areas of IGAD, and several projects have been drawn up, including link roads, ports, and telecommunication services.

One of the IGAD-sponsored road construction projects (Gondar-Humera-Gedarif) aims to link Eritrea, Ethiopia and Sudan, with Eritrea being connected to this line by a supplementary road between Humera and Barentu. As already mentioned, one of the benefits will be its impact on labour supply to Gash-Barka, but a detailed study should also be conducted to determine the impact of the planned road network on the economy of Gash-Barka and the country as a whole. Such a study should also establish what complementary services might be needed to make the most efficient use of the road network.

There is little doubt that the IGAD-sponsored projects will help improve co-operation among the member countries, as the movement of goods and people will certainly increase, but effective use of infrastructure services will depend heavily on whether or not there is the necessary institutional capacity to make them work. IGAD is best placed to bring about such a change because the obstacles are usually of a political nature. If there is a political will to co-operate among the member countries, then efficient management will become merely a technical issue.

Impact on poverty alleviation

The significance of roads to the general development of a country was expressed by a high-ranking official of the Ministry of Construction during an interview:

> The construction of roads has social and economic significance. It eases communication between places and economic regions. It increases food production and facilitates marketing and trade at all levels (national, regional and international). The construction of micro dams, the provision of social services, the drilling of water wells are all related to the availability of roads.

The impact that road construction projects can have on settlement patterns and on the living conditions of people has been closely studied by social scientists. In Ethiopia, it is said that many towns along the main roads were originally temporary road gang settlements. These attracted small-scale businesses – such as tea and beer selling – and then grew under their own momentum to become towns

The end of the conflict and lifting of restrictions on people's movements immediately after liberation resulted in a great increase in passenger transport, and an impressive number of rural roads has been opened in the last few years. The impact of these roads is not only reflected in the numbers of people using motorized transport but, perhaps more significantly, by transformations taking place in the living conditions of the rural population. The case of Adi-Bidel, some 21 kilometres from Asmara, is illustrative:

- A regular bus service was established, reducing travel time to the main market in Asmara.
- Possibilities of diversifying income-generation have increased. Women are raising chickens around their homesteads and selling the poultry to traders, who have started coming from Asmara since the road was opened to traffic. Many men are also involved in trading during the dry season when crops are harvested. This trading mostly involves buying animals and varieties of foodstuffs (honey, butter and sometimes crops) from surrounding villages and from a weekly marketplace at Meqerka. They bring these purchases to their village and monitor market prices in the capital, then transporting the goods to the Asmara market for sale at the most opportune time.
- Opportunities for employment have increased dramatically. Many well-to-do urban-based sons and daughters of Adi-Bidel are constructing houses in their own village as they can now easily transport the necessary materials, thanks to the new road. Road construction activities thus benefit not only the people of Adi-Bidel

but those of the surrounding villages as well.

- There is greater access to health and education services. People who become ill can now be easily transported to Asmara, which used to be a difficult task as they had to be carried on a stretcher all the way. The junior school is some distance away from Adi-Bidel, along the new road to Asmara, and many of the male students can now ride bicycles to school. (Only boys ride bicycles; girls not living near the school have no choice but to drop out altogether.)

- Women no longer have to go to a nearby village to grind cereal, as Adi-Bidel now has its own grinding mill.

- Two local traders have opened small shops that sell foodstuffs and a variety of household items.

- Improved access to the market has made it possible for people to buy and use kerosene instead of firewood for some cooking (kerosene stoves cannot cook *taita*, the Eritrean staple food). Before the construction of the road, and in the absence of electric or gas ovens in the villages, people had no alternative but to use firewood, so in spite of a nationwide ban on wood-cutting, they continued to cut, often under cover of darkness and knowing the environmental damage they were causing. People are now able to transport firewood from licensed wood-selling stores in Asmara. This means that tree cover on the rugged land around Adi-Bidel is improving.

The construction of the road to Adi-Bidel has had a dramatic impact on the lives of its inhabitants – men, women and children. The community is aware that regular maintenance must be undertaken to keep the road in good condition, and they are more than willing to do their part. There are many villages benefiting from the road and maintenance input must be organized by the Ministry of Local Government, the relevant body in position to make such arrangements.

Community participation in planning and implementing road construction projects

The road to Adi-Bidel was built on an old track road that had existed during the Italian period, but it was hardly recognizable as it had been out of use for decades. One reason the road construction was such a success is the important role that the beneficiary communities played in planning and implementing the project. The communities themselves did all the work by hand, with support from the Ministry of Local Government, which is responsible for the rehabilitation and reconstruction of rural roads, according to an agreement reached with the Ministry of Construction. However, all technical matters beyond the capability of the Ministry of Local Government remain the responsibility of the Ministry of Construction.

The Asmara to Adi-Bidel road was constructed under the Eritrean Community Rehabilitation Fund (ECRFU) programme, which was managed by the Ministry of Local Government. The ECRFU is believed to have had a high success rate because of its participatory approach, motivating people with the prospect of improving the quality of their lives. The fund specifically targeted the rehabilitation of social projects, such as health centres, primary schools, water supply, rural roads, micro dams, hillside terracing and tree planting. An important aspect of these projects was that the communities had to contribute 10 per cent of the total cost, but in whatever way best suited them: cash, kind or labour. In this way the communities were made to assume ownership of the project. The ECRFU was phased out by the end of 1995, but has been reconstituted as the Eritrean Community Development Fund (ECDFU).

The active role played by the Ministry of Local Government in fostering community participation in the construction of rural roads is exemplary, as no project can afford to ignore the importance of such participation if it is to be relevant and sustainable. But participation means a lot more than consultation. It means, as with the case of Adi-Bidel, that local communities play an active role in planning and implementing projects and programmes.

Not all communities regard the construction of a road as advantageous. In the Gash-Barka region, a pastoral community decided to vacate its settlement following the nearby construction of a road. The reason was that the settlers were unable to cope with the intrusion of curious visitors, some even asking for food and water. In the northern Red Sea region, a community was sceptical of the benefits that the planned new road would bring them. They were worried that it would expose them to "merciless" merchants who, they feared, would arrive in droves.

Resource mobilization

The Ministry of Construction faces many problems, mostly created by a shortage of funds and lack of skilled and professional workers in technical and managerial fields. There is no simple answer to these problems. The ministry's needs will continue to grow as its activities expand in line with the country's development. Obviously, any external input must be used in specific projects in such a way that the project will not demand unaffordable resources upon completion.

This does not mean, of course, that external resources have only a small role to play. Eritrea will not be able to meet its challenges without external resources, but the question is how to use them in the most effective way. For example, Eritrea must borrow money for projects that guarantee a good rate of return on investment.

Regarding the Ministry of Construction's long-term plan: how are the various road projects to be financed? If the economic potential of Gash-Barka can be effectively exploited, the construction of a road of international standard from Keren to Gash-Barka will be a worthwhile investment. On the other hand, it may be premature to invest in projects such as the road from Massawa to Karora, or from Massawa to Assab. Road construction is very expensive, and a stretch of new road would absorb scarce resources that might be put to more productive use.

Regarding the Ministry of Construction's need for human resources, it may not be necessary to employ the required professionals. It could be more cost-effective to engage consultants for specific tasks. It may also be true that the ministry and the country as a whole would benefit if the task of road construction were carried out by private contractors. There may not be many experienced contractors with the necessary capital at the moment, but they can be encouraged. The ministry could support contractors with the necessary equipment – not without payment, of course, but under some arrangement. This would be in line with the more supervisory role that the ministries are expected to play when the new regions assume responsibility for the implementation of projects and programmes.

The economic considerations notwithstanding, the technical problems cannot be overlooked. Once it has been decided to build a road, it is up to the engineers to come up with the best solution for each case. A whole range of considerations is involved in designing roads: traffic volume, vehicles type and axle loading, nature of the terrain, climate and so on. Only after careful consideration of all these and other factors will it be possible to determine the required strength of the road and its surface.

PORTS AND PORT MANAGEMENT

The port of Massawa handles most of the sea traffic for Eritrea and the northern regions of Ethiopia. Assab, which was developed into an international port during the Ethiopian occupation in the 1950s and 1960s, serves mainly Ethiopia, according to the terms of the bilateral agreement reached after the liberation of Eritrea.

Massawa and Assab have six and seven commercial berths respectively. In 1994, the port of Massawa handled 781,000 tons of cargo, including the bulk liquid cargo handled at the petroleum terminals. International cargo made up 97 per cent of the total, which shows how diminutive Eritrea's export market is. The capacity is much greater at Assab, which handled more than 1.25 million tons of dry cargo and more than 1.5 million tons of liquid bulk cargo in 1995. Almost all of this was transit cargo destined for Ethiopia.

Like the road network, the port facilities were seriously damaged during the war. In Massawa, only three of the six berths were functional at Independence. Two of the berths were blocked by sunken ships and the third was badly damaged by aerial bombardment. All the berths have been operating since 1994, but their capacities are limited so they are unable to handle large containers. The available storage area can accommodate only 120,000 tons of dry cargo. This has become a major drawback in introducing extensive containerization, which requires a lot of open space.

Assab is located some 600 kilometres south-east of Massawa. As the war of liberation intensified in the 1970s and 1980s, the port, which is closer to the Ethiopian capital, Addis Ababa, received a huge amount of investment and was modernized and expanded. However, on the eve of Independence, the fleeing Ethiopian army plundered the port and inflicted considerable damage on the equipment and other port facilities. Only 15 per cent of the equipment is in a reasonable state. The total area of the port is 784,171 square metres, so there is no shortage of space, but the poor condition of equipment hampers efficient service.

A recent proposal for restructuring the port industry gives the ports of Massawa and Assab a semi-independent management system, perhaps following World Bank recommendations. A task force has been set up and is assessing ways to implement the proposed structure, according to which each port authority will be responsible for operation and management of the port on a commercial basis. The ports will be supervised by a board of directors, with daily operations being carried out by a general manager. However, policy matters will be handled by the Marine Transport Department of the Ministry of Transport.

The proposed structures aim to improve operations at the ports, but they will maintain a monopoly position for all cargo handling and storage. In the absence of competition, delays in dealing with cargo, problems of timely clearance from port stores, and high tariff rates may continue to beset customers.

Short- and long-term plans for port rehabilitation

The port authorities have drawn up short- and long-term plans for rehabilitating the ports. Massawa's short-term plans are contained in the First Five-Year Port Development Programme (1994-1998), which includes the rehabilitation of existing berths, asphalt pavement, construction of warehouses, purchase of cargo handling equipment, and so on. The construction of a voluminous open shed has been completed, and several rehabilitation works that needed immediate attention have been carried out. Massawa suffered more from the war than Assab, and has been the object of most of the rehabilitation work to date.

According to the Project Management Unit – set up to oversee implementation of the Rehabilitation and Reconstruction Programme (1993-1995), the total planned cost for port rehabilitation work was US$ 10.21 million, including US$ 6.99 million for the purchase of equipment, and the remaining US$ 3.22 million for civil works. However, only US$ 5.95 million was secured from external sources, leaving a gap of US$ 4.26 million. The main contributors to the port rehabilitation programme have been the EU, Italy, the Netherlands and the Eritrean government.

The policies and objectives of the Eritrean Port Authority, as stated in a report entitled "Marine Transport Development 1992-1995", are to:
- construct modern ports that meet international standards
- promote quick and efficient systems for providing port services and facilities by constructing modern transit ports
- maximize profit
- ensure a high degree of safety in marine transport
- introduce a container system
- stimulate national economic growth by encouraging international trade
- obtain a nominal rate of return on capital invested in the ports.

The establishment of free transit ports, construction of bonded areas, and installation of modern port equipment and facilities are also priorities. Moreover, upgrading port labour skills, ensuring proper allocation and utilization of skilled manpower, and improving formal training and working conditions are included in the programme. Since 1995, a project supported by the German government has provided advisory services to the port authorities, particularly with regard to upgrading labour skills and port management systems.

Survey on the functioning of Massawa port

A survey was conducted to identify problems facing the port authority's ambitious programme. It was felt that the best way to do this was to interview the main users (customers) of the port services, especially those in the import and export business. The Massawa port authorities were also interviewed. Interviews were conducted with 10 major investors. Because the sample was small, the results were not expected to have statistical significance, but they do indicate some existing problems. All but two interviewees were based in Asmara. The survey concentrated on four main areas:

1.   a comparative analysis of infrastructure services
2.   the degree of efficiency at the port of Massawa
3.   identification of problems and suggestions for their solution
4.   effects on business expansion and potential investors.

Survey findings

The respondents were first asked to compare roads, ports, electricity and telecommunications infrastructures in terms of relative efficiency. (Railways were not included as they do not yet provide service.) Telecommunications were found to provide the best service, followed by electricity. The port of Massawa was unanimously perceived as providing the least efficient service. The respondents considered this to be the major bottleneck for Eritrea's development. Three respondents, while acknowledging inefficiency, were understanding of the problems of the port authority. Two of them were experienced in the import/export business in other African countries and were optimistic about Massawa's prospects. They felt that there had been a great deal of improvement in recent years. One of them asked: how could Eritrea have done any better, given the circumstances in which it gained Independence?

One respondent said that the port provided good service but lacked the necessary equipment. This person thought port authorities were doing their best and were co-operative, but that their hands were tied for lack of equipment.

Another question aimed to identify the problems hampering efficient port management. Respondents were asked simply to list the problems, not necessarily in order of priority. The following list resulted:

Import problems:
- delays in processing goods through the port, particularly in customs service
- breakage during cargo handling, with the port authority not accepting responsibility
- unqualified personnel
- bureaucracy (too much paperwork)
- monopoly of services, customers have no choice other than to accept the available service; the one shipping agent (ERSTAS) is also governmental
- lack of new equipment, most equipment is too old and breakdowns are frequent
- high tariffs that are not reflected in the quality of service
- loss of goods, with no-one accepting responsibility
- customers are not allowed to go to the port during inspection and are forced to employ agents to attend on their behalf.

Export problems:
- difficulties in communicating with customers about the arrival of ships and their positions, which makes it difficult to decide when to deliver consignments
- delays in preparing bills of lading, which result in delays in getting money from the bank.

The respondents were challenged to suggest solutions which would improve the situation. They came up with some interesting and far-sighted answers:
- port facilities and stevedoring should be privatized; they were efficient before being nationalized by the Derg
- the port authorities should use international loans to improve all the necessary facilities; Massawa should not lag too far behind the best port in the world
- a maintenance system should be developed to keep the available equipment fully operational
- the port authority should do its utmost to train its workforce and fill positions with appropriately skilled workers, while bureaucratic practices in customs offices should be minimized; management capacity should be upgraded to meet international standards and customer handling should be improved; there is corruption in the form of favouritism toward friends or relatives and it could become a

serious problem; it must be eradicated before it develops further
- ERSTAS should be privatized to increase efficiency of service
- customs should be moved out of the port, to reduce congestion
- Massawa should be declared a free processing port

Finally, the respondents were asked about the effect of these problems on investment. The unanimous answer was that, for someone unaware of the improvements made in recent years, the existing problems discourage investment. "We are living in hope. Our slogan in Eritrea is 'Never kneel down!' As we performed miracles in the struggle, we hope to do miracles in development, too", was the response of three interviewees. Six were more cautious, with one investor saying that "Eritrea must compare itself with the best in the world. It is useless to compare oneself with the worst. With that in mind, we have a long way to go".

The response of the port management

The port authorities readily accepted some shortcomings mentioned by the investors, but they pointed out what they felt to be unwarranted criticism:

- The issues raised by customers when importing and exporting were confusing, as they included the tasks of different government departments, particularly customs and ERSTAS. The services provided by these two organizations should not be lumped together and considered as belonging to the port authority. For example, the export problems cited had nothing to do with management of the port. The port's responsibility covers loading and unloading cargo and does not involve much paperwork.
- Liability for loss of goods normally lies with the ships, and not with ports. However, responsibility for breakage of goods during handling has been under consideration by the port authority and due compensation may be given in the near future.
- The port is not meant to serve as a storage centre, and the authority has declared that it cannot be held responsible for any loss or damage to cargo stored for more than one month.
- The privatization of some functions of the port would not be advisable without a proper control mechanism to supervise the operations of the privatized sector.
- The decision to allow clearing agents, rather than the owners of goods, to be present during inspection was intended to speed up clearance procedures, as the former were supposed to be experienced and

licensed agents. If the documentation accompanying the cargo is correct, this procedure works well. Problems usually arose because the documentation for imported goods was not in order.

Analysis of survey findings

Without an understanding of the structural changes that were introduced, including their short- and long-term objectives, one cannot make meaningful suggestions concerning organization and management. Nevertheless, the investors interviewed raised important points, which may be worth consideration by the port authorities.

Two interviewees mentioned how efficiently the ports functioned before being nationalized by the Derg. Are there lessons to be learned here? If so, how relevant are they to current needs and future developments? The planning of the ports must look to the long term, encompassing not only the growing sophistication of port management, but also the physical facilities and equipment.

The proposal by one of the interviewees to move the customs offices out of the port to relieve the current congestion may have merit. One interviewee suggested that Massawa should be a free processing port. If this has not already been investigated, it may be worth pursuing.

At this stage, consultation with port users – shippers, truckers, importers and exporters – would be invaluable. The consumers or buyers of the port's services could make a significant contribution to the planning of port improvements, particularly with regard to management.

It is important that the challenges faced by the port authority be resolved, so that its institutional capability is improved and it can provide efficient service. Improvements in physical facilities may prove useless unless the authority has greater ability to deal with the changes. The responses of investors provide plenty of food for thought for port authorities (including customs and ERSTAS). As one investor said, "The port authority may have its own reasons for the current state of affairs, but these are of no interest to the importers who want to deliver their goods to the waiting customers." Customer satisfaction is a measure of efficiency, and the port authority ought to heed the concerns expressed by investors, in order to serve the development needs of the country.

Implications of ports for economic development

Ports form an integral part of a country's transport and distribution and ideally the whole system should be complementary, as a malfunction in one section can affect all other sections. Similarly, improvement in one can also positively affect the functioning of other services. The expected economic impact of several road construction projects have already been discussed. What plans does Massawa port have that would enable it to handle the expected increase in cargo?

The question of Eritrea's natural economic ties with neighbouring countries has already been raised in the discussion of roads. The country's two ports are potential magnets for achieving such links with, for example, northern Ethiopia (Massawa) and southern and central Ethiopia (Assab). When the political situation in Sudan improves, economic links with the eastern part of that country will probably resume. As emphasized earlier, Eritrea's future will depend on its capacity to make the best of its strategic location. The only reason for Ethiopian importers and exporters to use Eritrean ports despite their current problems is that they offer a better deal to their customers than other ports. But this situation could change overnight and there is no room for complacency. Eritrean ports must be prepared to improve their service. IGAD supports a plan to upgrade the port of Assab. The objective is to construct two new deep-water berths, aprons, sheds and equipment for a modern container handling port. This will greatly enhance the position of Assab as the main port for Ethiopian cargo. According to the plan, the benefits to be derived from the project include:

- a 30 per cent increase in container traffic
- a substantial reduction in the cost of transporting containers to Addis Ababa
- decreased loss and pilfering in the port
- a reduction of waiting time for ships.

These interventions will make Assab attractive to customers. The challenge for the port authority at Assab will be how to upgrade its management capability to cope with the expected workload increase. It is worth repeating that potential benefits from improvements in specific areas of a port can be wiped out if there are other bottlenecks in the system. Improvements in the port of Assab will increase the demand for land transport, therefore it is essential that the link road between Assab and Addis Ababa is upgraded. Perhaps this could be included in the next phase of projects sponsored by IGAD.

While road transport and port services are interdependent, the services are not only for import and export markets. The importance of infrastructure services for the expansion of domestic markets and their impact on poverty reduction, by providing opportunities for non-farm employment, should not be overlooked. Infrastructure development will play a key role in the social and economic integration of Eritrea's regions, as well as in enhancing the country's capacity to deal with the complex task of reintegrating returning refugees and ex-combatants.

THE RAILWAY SYSTEM

Eritrea had a functioning railway system only two decades ago. The line connecting Massawa, Asmara, Keren and Agordat was part of Italy's grand plan - not only to open up the agricultural potential of the Gash-Barka region, but to incorporate parts of the Sudanese and Ethiopian economies into that of Eritrea (Tseggai, 1994).

The line from Massawa to Asmara, a distance of only 118 kilometres, begins at sea level and winds its way up to an altitude of over 2,300 metres at Asmara, reaching a gradient of 3.5 per cent. It passes through spectacular scenery and, with its 30 tunnels and 35 bridges, was hailed as a major feat of Italian engineering at the time of its construction.

After the British Military Administration (1941-1952), the Ethiopian government acquired the railway system. In its heyday, the railway system was the biggest employer in Eritrea. In the mid-1950s it had about 1,600 employees, nearly 500 of whom were graded staff, the rest being daily labourers. In the 1956-1957 fiscal year, the railway between Asmara and Massawa handled over 200,000 tons of cargo, including slightly over 100,000 tons for export. Some 70,000 tons were imported, and the remainder consisted of local goods. Until the early 1960s, the Massawa-Asmara line had four regular trains running daily in each direction. However, this is insignificant compared with its record at the height of its glory: between March and October 1935, the line accommodated 38 trains in each direction in one day, which shows the potential of even a single track railway if it is well managed (IEG, 1965:7). In 1965, the following equipment was reported as being in good working order: 12 steam locomotives, four diesel hydraulics, eight shunting locomotives (steam), 19 diesel engine locomotives, 19 passenger coaches, 425 freight wagons, six water tanks, six fuel tank wagons and six service wagons.

By the early 1970s, the equipment was getting old and the line needed major improvements but, with the decline in the economy, freight traffic stagnated, as did the number of passengers. The railway no longer seemed viable and, as it became clear that the limited freight could be handled by existing road facilities, nearly a century of history came to a sudden end with the total closure of the railway in early 1976. What remained of the railway system was totally destroyed under the Derg regime; the rails were uprooted and used for constructing trenches, workshops were converted to serve military purposes, and whatever was left fell into a state of decay.

A 1996 survey stated that the facilities of the old railway system were "in a state of total abandon and must be completely restored...the technological part of the railway, such as signals and telecommunications, are completely absent". Surprisingly, basic structures such as the railway track, bridges, culverts and tunnels are recoverable, although they are in poor condition due to natural decay.

In 1995, the Eritrean government decided to reconstruct the line between Massawa and Asmara. Reconstruction work has started in earnest and is already some 40 kilometres from Massawa. As one official put it, the construction of the railway will be a "re-enactment of history" – it will bring back to life what was once a major facilitator of the Eritrean economy.

A feasibility study for the railway was carried out by the Ministry of Construction. The Ministry of Transport is laying down the lines but, according to one official there, this does not require much technical expertise as it simply follows the old line. Government officials foresee that the railway will be a great attraction for tourists, who are expected to generate most of the income. However, they acknowledge that the railway may not be able to compete with other means of transport for goods.

The line has an unusual gauge of 0.95 metres, as it was constructed to take advantage of surplus material and rolling stock available in Italy at the time. Old rails have recently been gathered from various places and are now being used for reconstruction. However, the narrowness of the gauge (the current standard is 1.1 metres) will present many problems. First, new rolling stock will have to be specially ordered and this will be expensive. Second, the existing system will not be able to handle container transportation, which is too bulky for the existing bridges and tunnels. Third, the steep gradient will not allow for heavy loading. So the main purpose will have to be the transport of people, including tourists.

The old rolling stock that has been recovered needs to be extensively reconstructed. Former technicians of these engines, now in their 80s, have been recruited to do the maintenance and train young engineers.

Two perspectives
Before deciding to reconstruct the Massawa-Asmara railway line, the government was faced with two different and opposing views.

The first view regarded the railway as a national project that would reflect the ingenuity, resourcefulness and determination of the Eritrean people to do things their own way. It gave weight to the immense pride that its completion would give to the Eritrean people, updating the national slogan "Never kneel down!" This view did not rely on quantifiable evidence to make its point, and cost was not considered. The "priceless" value of the project was felt to be more important, and the "do nothing" and the "do it properly by investing heavily" options were disregarded. However, the project was not merely considered some sort of monument, the railway was believed to be viable because economic growth and the rapid development of Massawa were expected to provide opportunities for tourism.

The second view was based on purely economic arguments. It provided a detailed cost-benefit analysis of the railway, showing how expensive the running of railway systems is and how their use has been in decline in recent decades. It brought evidence to show that railways were only cost-effective if there was a need to transport large amounts of cargo over long distances, or if there was a need for commuter and passenger services in densely populated areas. In other words, benefits were derived from economies of scale, for the operation costs were much higher and more sophisticated than for those of road transport. The economic point of view also took into consideration the current human resources situation and problems of institutional capacity in Eritrea. Proponents of this view emphasized that railways cannot function without built-in technical and administrative efficiency, for they form a complex system of facilities, the operations of which are closely interdependent. Potential benefits such as tourism, were also considered, but it was argued that the tourist industry had become competitive and sophisticated, and that the country would not, at least for some time, be able to provide the luxury services that the "spending" type of tourists demand. A few railway enthusiasts may come, but they will not be economically significant.

It appears that the decision to go ahead with the reconstruction of the railway was influenced more by the first of these views. However, the pride that it will bring to the Eritrean people can only be enhanced when it starts providing a reliable service and at a competitive price. Thus, questions arise such as: What organizational structure and management systems are being planned? How is the problem of the necessary human resources going to be resolved? Are adequate maintenance services being established? How about the co-ordinated action that would be needed between the railway and the port of Massawa? The concerns of the economic point of view are also relevant.

Planning is about forecasting future trends or outcomes, and many unknown factors have to be taken into consideration. The predictions of the economic point of view may turn out to be wrong, and a dynamic economy may change the present situation. In that case, the demand for cargo transportation will increase and the railway will have an important role to play. With the expansion of Massawa, the demand for passenger transportation should also increase. By then the shortage of human resources may have been dealt with, and a healthy and competitive transport service should be available to users.

If the potential of Gash-Barka is realized, it will not be difficult to prove that the economic perspective was wrong, and that the construction of the railway line could become justifiable in purely economic terms. The Italians thought it was a worthwhile investment during the colonial period, and the agricultural potential and minerals that interested them at that time are still there and unexploited. But the extension of a railway line to Gash-Barka is a long-term prospect, and attention should not be diverted from the immediate, pressing needs of the country.

Italy's plan had been to create an economic corridor by extending the Eritrean railway system to Kassala in Sudan and to Gondar in Ethiopia. Although this would obviously be a long-term plan, it is not unfeasible. With economic growth and an enabling political climate in the three countries, such an idea could be entertained. Perhaps IGAD could assess its long-term feasibility.

In conclusion, railway systems are extremely complex, and admittedly the points raised here are somewhat sketchy. Nevertheless, some key questions have been raised. It would be worthwhile to evaluate the ongoing project regularly to ascertain whether it is justifiable to continue. Unexpected problems may arise. The State of Eritrea's 1996 survey also raised some pertinent questions about the railway. They should be considered carefully, particularly the cautionary note on the need for proper restoration work and the implications for functioning and safety.

Energy

Eritrea has serious energy problems that have been aggravated by the long war. It is estimated that more than 80 per cent of the total energy demand and more than 96 per cent of household energy demand in Eritrea is met by fuel wood and biomass. This clearly reflects the present situation in the country – a small industrial base, electricity supply limited to towns, a disastrous effect on the environment created by ever scarcer fuel wood, and so on.

The depletion of forests

Evidence has been gathered about the damage inflicted by the Ethiopian army on the limited forest cover, on the pretext that it was serving as a hideout for guerrilla activities. The residents of Adi-Bidel, whose wooded area was destroyed in this way, have another explanation – soldiers in the Ethiopian army organized the cutting down of wood for the purpose of making money. The wood was transported to the garrison towns under their occupation and sold at exorbitant prices. There was a high demand for fuel wood at the time and people had no alternatives. For obvious reasons, concern for environmental protection was not a priority for the EPLF either, particularly during the first half of the liberation struggle. Thus considerable destruction of wood occurred in the EPLF base area in the Sahel, mainly for the construction of underground houses and for fuel wood.

The general underdevelopment of the country has also been a cause of tree destruction. One coping strategy of many people in rural areas is still the sale of fuel wood. Methods of producing energy for cooking and the use of wood in house construction in rural areas are also inefficient. In the Zula plain, near the coast, a study found that the construction of a 4x4 metre house required cutting 61 mature trees and numerous branches. A household usually consists of two such houses and a kitchen and, because of wood insects, the lifespan of a house is only five years. Cooking is done on an open hearth, and it was estimated that the preparation of the midday meal alone takes about six kilograms of wood, which results in an annual fuel wood consumption of 5.5 metric tons per household in that area.

The cumulative effect for Eritrea has been severe soil erosion and degradation, expansion of desertification, and loss of biodiversity, with all that this implies for food production. Whether or not the loss of the vegetative cover is irreversible is debatable; what is certain is that the depletion of resources for energy generation affects the quality of life, especially that of women who are responsible for domestic food-processing needs. The main sources of fuel in many parts of the country are now animal waste and agricultural residue – materials traditionally used to improve soil fertility. Moreover, the inefficient use of firewood in the rural areas also causes eye diseases and respiratory disorders in women and children, due to smoke and other toxic fumes during cooking.

The electricity supply

Electricity in Eritrea is generated from oil products, which contribute only 1.2 per cent to the country's total energy requirement. In 1994, the annual per capita consumption of energy, including traditional biomass, was 260 kilograms of oil equivalent (kgoe), compared to an average of 710 kgoe in other low-income countries in the same year. A measure of the state of Eritrea's industry is the consumption of commercial energy (electricity and oil products), which in 1994 was 0.06 tons of oil equivalent (toe) per capita, which is among the lowest in the world. Petroleum products are estimated to provide 16.8 per cent, and biomass to provide 82 per cent of total energy consumption.

Like everything else, commercial energy production was greatly affected by the war. The Ethiopian regime made no investment of any significance, and most of the generating capacity was in a poor state at Independence. The inadequate supply of electricity has thus been hampering rehabilitation and reconstruction programmes – demand is now increasing at a faster rate than the expansion capacity of the Eritrean Electricity Authority (EEA).

Most of Eritrea's oil is produced at the Assab oil refinery plant and production of electricity is by oil-driven thermal general units. Under a bilateral agreement between Eritrea and Ethiopia, the Assab refinery serves both countries. However, the refinery cannot meet all their requirements, and refined oil has to be imported to fill the gap.

Asmara and Massawa, as well as the small towns that lie between them, are served by an interconnected system (ICS) of electricity generation. All the main regional towns, such as Mendefera, Decamhare, Keren, Agordat and Barentu are supplied by self-contained systems (SCS). As most of the industries in the country are located in Asmara and Massawa, industrial consumption from the ICS constitutes 54.5 per cent, with domestic consumption taking up 30 per cent. In the SCS towns, domestic consumption takes a higher proportion than industrial consumption: 51.3 per cent as against 22 per cent, a further illustration of the uneven distribution of industrial production in Eritrea.

As part of the five-year plan that started in 1993, an 84 megawatt thermal power station is under construction at Hergigo, south of Massawa. A 132 kilovolt transmission line from Hergigo to Asmara will be erected, benefiting substations along the way, while the major towns with self-contained systems (Keren, Mendefera and Decamhare) will also be connected through 66-kilovolt transmissions. The total cost of the plan is estimated at US$ 200 million, but the completion of this plant should meet some of the urgent needs for energy.

Renewable energy technologies

Renewable energy technologies (RETs) are increasingly meeting the energy requirements of the rural population in many less-industrialized nations. The Eritrean government, recognizing the importance of these technologies, has been encouraging their introduction. Since Independence, a number of solar powered units, with a total capacity of some 150 kilowatts, have been installed for various community uses, such as water pumping, refrigeration, lighting and power supply. These facilities have been set up in health centres, schools and offices of rural development projects, radio communications and lighthouses.

Institutional framework

The government's major energy objective is to ensure a reliable energy supply at the least expense to all sectors of the economy, taking into account environmental considerations. The Ministry of Energy, Mines and Water Resources is entrusted with the overall responsibility for the formulation of policies and strategies and for implementing appropriate action to improve energy supply. It is also responsible for the supervision and co-ordination of the various activities so that the policies and programmes of the different parts are complementary. According to the ministry, energy planning and implementation are geared toward the achievement of the nation's overall economic objectives.

The EEA and the Petroleum Corporation of Eritrea (PCE) were constituted as semi-independent bodies and incorporated under standard company law to enable them to operate within a commercial framework. The EEA is controlled by a board of directors and is a self-managing and self-financing utility, although matters of policy are handled by the ministry.

The Ministry of Energy, Mines and Water Resources sees the following possible solutions to current energy supply shortages:

- review of thermal power-generation and consequent rationalization
- development of possible fossil fuel deposits
- development of mini-hydroelectricity

- development of renewable energy
- the importation of electricity from Ethiopia
- human resource development
- various training programmes in Eritrea and abroad to upgrade employee skills
- the follow-up of recommended new energy technologies, energy efficient appliances and co-generation options, and taking adaptive measures.

According to preliminary studies, the coastal geographic structures of Eritrea appear to hold good prospects in terms of hydrocarbon deposits and geothermal energy. Investigations are under way to identify oil and gas deposits. Although a long-term prospect, the potential for geothermal energy is estimated to be on the order of 150 megawatts. Both oil and gas potential involve capital, intensive drilling and sophisticated technology, and it is clear that specialized foreign companies will have to carry out such programmes.

Rural electrification

In the first five-year plan the ministry states its intention to undertake a feasibility study to bring electricity gradually to Eritrea's villages. Rural electrification is a special case of transmission and distribution, as the settlements are usually scattered and also because rural consumers are typically very poor. Nevertheless, many kinds of benefit are claimed for such programmes (Bridger and Winpenny, 1983:78–79):

- environmental advantages: if electric power were available, there would be saving of traditional sources of heating and lighting, such as firewood, biomass and kerosene lamps
- improvement of food security through the development of rural industry
- improvement of social life in the evenings and benefits for literacy programmes and health services
- cheaper water supply: electric pumps would be a saving on expensive alternative methods.

The main problem is that rural electrification programmes are usually not cost-effective. However, the long-term social, economic and even political advantages may outweigh the lack of short-term economic viability, and in this case the government may decide to subsidize it to cover the losses or the EEA may be in a position to cross-subsidize rural electrification from elsewhere in the system, considering it a long-term investment.

Woodcutting and the environment

Because of the disastrous loss of vegetative cover in the past, the government has been trying to enforce the protection of trees by prohibiting woodcutting. However, it is doubtful whether these efforts will be successful before alternative solutions for firewood are found. As it is, the current governmental regulations about woodcutting prohibit only the felling of live trees, and in the absence of dry wood people have invented all sorts of methods to "age" the wood that they cut. Cutting and selling wood is a survival strategy for many people in the rural areas and, despite the regulations, they will keep doing it.

The same problem is found in many other African countries, where governments have been trying to introduce and enforce forest protection measures. The assumption underlying such measures is usually that the use of fuel wood is the principal cause of deforestation or that wood scarcity will increase prices and eventually provide a strong economic rationale for afforestation programmes (Leach and Mearns, 1988). It is recognized, however, that a narrow focus on woodcutting and the symptoms of scarcity alone cannot solve the problem. The fundamental social, economic, political and environmental aspects of the issue must be understood.

The WSP survey undertaken in Gash-Barka showed that the different sectors of Eritrean society attach different value to tree-cutting. Among the sedentary farmers, trees are cut indiscriminately when clearing land for farming or building a house. In other words, a culture has developed which has little regard for the environment. For example, at the Adi-Ghider estate in Gash-Barka there has been no effort to plant trees, even for shade, which is surprising given the extremely high temperatures during the dry season. The planting of hedges and trees along the borders of individual holdings could have transformed the somewhat desolate landscape.

Another example is the impact on the environment of the settlement programmes for returnees, ex-combatants and others. No initiative has been taken to replace the trees that are fast disappearing to fill the need for fuel wood. The case of the *arkobkobai* tree (doum palm) is illustrative. This is considered a priceless tree by the traditional communities of Gash-Barka: life is unimaginable without it. The *arkobkobai* tree provides good shade and edible fruit which is believed to have medicinal properties. Its trunk is used for many purposes in house construction, while the leaves are used for roof thatching and handicrafts (such as baskets, mats, ropes, sun hats), making it a source of income for many people. Unfortunately, however, this valuable tree is being cut down indiscriminately to make room for banana plantations and for other farming purposes. There is some concern that the tree could even become extinct if cutting continues at the present rate.

In contrast to such a careless culture, the pastoral culture was found to be caring. "We do not cut to kill trees", a group of pastoralists explained. Their communities have extraordinary knowledge of many varieties of tree and their uses. They know exactly which ones to prune and when in order to provide feed for their animals. Only the leftovers of the pruned branches and sticks are used for fuel wood and house construction.

Given this situation, one may well ask about the prospects for improving the tree resources of Eritrea. The solution is afforestation on a vast scale. A World Bank study that has done much to legitimize the so-called "fuel wood gap theory" estimates that tree planting in sub-Saharan Africa would have to increase 15-fold to close the gaps projected in the year 2000 (Anderson and Fishwick, 1984).

The Eritrean government's tree planting programme, which is carried out by students and teachers during their vacation in the rainy season, is not sufficient. Much more needs to be done. For example, communities should be encouraged to assume responsibility for tree planting on communal land. As far as the *arkobkobai* tree is concerned, it may be necessary to introduce closure regimes to save it from complete destruction. The species grows along the perennial river banks, some 50 to 100 metres on each side, so another way to protect the tree could be to restrict farming to outside these limits. Also, in any reforestation programme in Gash-Barka it would be unwise to overlook the rich knowledge of trees that exists among pastoral communities.

The long-term solution to the fuel wood problem is not only to plant trees but also to increase efficiency in the consumption of energy. In the highlands of Eritrea the insulated fuel wood-efficient hearth system is used, but this has not yet been introduced to many parts of lowland Eritrea. Perhaps the Renewable Energy Department of the Ministry of Energy should promote this, and should launch a general information campaign on efficient energy use. Furthermore, these kinds of issues and environmental protection training could be integrated into the national curriculum of schools, making education more relevant to Eritrean realities.

Women and energy

Women in Eritrea are not only responsible for food processing but also for the arduous and time-consuming tasks of collecting fuel wood, fetching water and grinding grain. The example of Adi-Bidel has shown how road construction has improved conditions for women; they do not have to travel long distances to the grinding mill or do daily shopping and firewood collecting. Several innovative and low-cost approaches could be introduced to improve the quality of life for women, and energy policies should be linked to their special needs, particularly with regard to renewable sources of energy. The necessary institutional and infrastructural bases should be developed to support women's involvement in energy programmes and projects, such as reforestation and renewable resource technologies. Another approach could be the training of trainers to demonstrate and disseminate energy-saving techniques. Appropriate and successful policies for rational energy development must address the issue of women as energy consumers and the role which they could play in sustainable development.

The power supply

The electricity supply has greatly increased since Independence. Capacity has increased by more than 50 per cent. However, this progress has not been matched by an increase in distribution, despite the efforts of the EEA, which has the difficult task of improving the old electricity transmission and distribution system and carrying out the low-voltage conversion from 127 volts.

The following information is based on interviews with six industrial firms of various sizes in Asmara on the subject of power supply. All interviewees agreed that the power sector was not supplying them with reliable service. The problems were mainly sudden or unannounced interruptions in electricity supply and the belief that tariffs were very high. Interruptions in the current have created havoc in industrial production. One respondent estimated that since 1992 nearly 100 production hours have been lost, costing the enterprise nearly 350,000 birr. Another enterprise, which mixes products that require maintaining a regular temperature for a certain period, experienced numerous power interruptions in the middle of this process, rendering the end products unusable. The whole process had to be repeated, causing higher labour costs and wasted raw materials.

The interruption of current also raises electricity bills. Production machines require a lot of energy to start up and the interruptions naturally increase consumption and hence the cost of production. But, as the Ministry of Energy points out, the major cause is rather that the industrial machinery is very old and needs a large amount of energy to operate. The government has introduced cheap tariff rates for businesses with monthly electricity consumption of 100,000 kilowatt hours, and for fuel consumption of more than 360,000 litres per year, but only a few can benefit from this because most are small-scale industries.

The other major complaint was about tariff levels, which are much higher than in many other African countries – five times higher than in Kenya and two-and-a-half times higher than in Ethiopia. There are reasons for this. Unfortunately for Eritrea, electricity has to be generated by burning expensive fuel or diesel oil, whereas neighbouring countries can generate it from hydro power or geothermal power. In addition, energy is not subsidized, and the EEA has to ensure that it generates sufficient revenue to finance its activities without placing a burden on the government.

The fact remains that Eritrean industrial products are not competitive, which means that enterprises will not grow and provide much-needed job opportunities. The electricity sector must expand in order to reduce costs and, in turn, prices. The 1994 World Bank report rightly recommended the commissioning of additional capacity to ensure a reliable electricity supply at reasonable cost (World Bank, 1994a:159). While the aforementioned increase in generation capacity at Hergigo will go a long way in solving existing problems, there are questions of human resource development and management that will also have to be tackled.

The private sector

Government energy policy recognizes that the private sector could play an increased role in the production and distribution of energy. The Ministry of Energy, Mines and Water Resources states:

> As private investment aimed at strengthening and developing the power sector may not have a fast return in cost recovery, especially in the transitional period, basic investment in energy-producing infrastructure is expected to come from the government; however, long-term investment by the private sector has to be encouraged.

This proposal should be welcomed. It may turn out that the private sector will want to participate even at this early stage. But the role of the private sector should not be relegated to production alone – it can also play a role in distribution. This could be carried out by private companies under a profit-sharing scheme or similar arrangement, which in turn may further encourage distributors to invest in electricity generation. In this way the burden on the EEA can be eased, leaving the EEA to focus on regulating and controlling the efficient delivery of power.

Power needs for the development of Gash-Barka

The development of Gash-Barka has been mentioned several times in this chapter. What role will the energy sector play in the development of Gash-Barka? What plans are there for the short, medium and long term? What are the implications of these plans for human resource development and financial requirements? Power is a prerequisite for development, and these and other questions are better asked sooner rather than later.

With reliable electric power, which must be strategically distributed, roads and other related services, investment in food processing and other industrial production in Gash-Barka would become attractive. Many opportunities would result; jobs would be created, which would help increase food security, the stress on the environment would be relieved, and so on. Therefore, economic development of the Gash-Barka region must be approached in an integrated way. A case could be made for establishing some kind of co-ordinating authority.

TELECOMMUNICATIONS

It has already been mentioned that investors are of the opinion that telecommunications ranks first among the service-providing components of infrastructure. Nevertheless the Telecommunication Services of Eritrea (TSE) thinks that the quality of its service is below an acceptable standard. In an internal evaluation document, the organization's performance was criticized for its poor response to customer needs. The report further noted that the demand for service exceeded supply – the connected lines met only 30 per cent of total registered demand in February 1996. However, the TSE has made impressive progress since Independence, particularly in view of the fact that it inherited outdated systems providing inadequate services to only a few towns.

The challenges faced by the TSE are considerable. The rate of penetration, measured by the number of lines per 100 people, is the lowest in sub-Saharan Africa at only 0.3. The current staff is small, slightly more than 45 per 1,000 telephone lines, which helps explain shortcomings of the service. Apart from this, the quality of the staff is perhaps even more problematic.

Given the enormous unmet demand, the TSE has been forced to prioritize the allocation of available lines to government offices, international organizations, medical institutions and other bodies considered important for the service they provide to the country. This may be acceptable as a temporary measure, but the TSE will have to find a way to reduce the gap while keeping up with future demands.

Institutionally, postal and telecommunications services come under one body; the Postal and Telecommunication Services Authority (PTSA). As with other public utilities, the government is restructuring the status of the TSE so that it becomes a semi-autonomous, self-managing organization, with duties regulated by the PTSA. Some of the proposed powers and duties of the PTSA and those that apply to the TSE are as follows:

- to engage in the business of postal and telecommunication services for profit
- to establish training institutions, set the standard of the curriculum and train personnel
- to authorize, at its discretion, other government or private organizations or individuals to import and own communication equipment or operate and/or construct or engage in maintenance activities or specified telecommunication facilities in accordance with the rules and procedures to be issued by the authority (with respect to telecommunications only)
- to issue licences for the establishment and operation of telecommunication facilities.

According to the proposed structure, the purpose of the authority is to render efficient domestic and international postal and telecommunication services and to regulate postal and telecommunication services. Clearly, the intention is to enable the two branches of the authority to operate in a commercial framework, to become self-managing and self-financing. This appears to be a step in the right direction.

Development plans

The macro-development objectives of the telecommunication infrastructure have been stated as follows:

- to support national economic development by providing required services to agriculture, industry, trade, tourism and other sectors
- to assist in the implementation of national social goals, particularly in health and education.

In order to attain these objectives, the TSE plans to grow at an annual rate of more than 10 per cent. It is evidently taking its enabling responsibilities seriously, and anticipates being a step ahead of the expected economic growth of the country. To achieve its aims, short-, medium- and long-term plans with clearly defined strategies have been drawn up. The TSE's proposed short-term, or phase one, programme is described as a "high priority self-contained investment programme which provides for a balanced and integrated development of local, long-distance national and international services, scheduled for execution between 1994 and 1998".

The goal is to upgrade the quality of public service and achieve a target of three telephone lines per 100 inhabitants in the next 15 years. In rural areas where telephone service does not exist, the TSE is planning to provide service to within a distance of 20 kilometres in the first five-year plan (1994-1998), and 5-10 kilometres by the end of the third five-year plan, in 2008. The policy is to improve services by adding circuits that will remove congestion, modernize equipment, and introduce new services as demand dictates.

The plans are impressive in that they represent an integrated approach to developing the TSE's capabilities, including managerial and human resource programmes and consultancy services. According to a TSE document entitled "Development of the Telecommunications Network in Eritrea (1994-2008)", human resource development is a priority for the organization:

> Major upgrading and streamlining of administration, improvements in work co-ordination and supervision, laying down norms for operations, and determining staff strength needed to achieve the required level of services, are some of the major items which need urgent attention to ensure good execution of the expanded investment programme.

Admitting a lack of in-house capacity, the same document proposes that external experts assist in a number of areas, such as: reviewing the current organization and management set-up of the TSE; identifying major weaknesses and defining necessary changes in organizational structure; strengthening co-ordination and supervision of project works; developing a labour plan; conducting a tariff study; and improving planning and policy functions.

In other words, the TSE has developed mechanisms for the critical self-assessment of its operations. This is an important initiative, because a built-in system of problem-identification and rectification is a managerial tool for development.

Prospects and challenges

Eritrea is a small country with a limited population, and development will largely depend on its service industry. Expansion of the tourist industry, banking and financial services and agricultural and industrial export markets will all depend on an efficient telecommunications system. Access to information technology is now considered so vital that there are those who consider it one of the pillars of development, on a par with land, capital and labour. Indeed, in the last two decades, information processing and transfer systems have become the main artery of global society.

Therefore, the challenge for Eritrea will be to create the right regulatory environment to achieve rapid growth in the information industry. Given the constraints on the local telecommunications industry to generate sufficient income for re-investment, the TSE will have to devise mechanisms to attract private investment.

While it is not difficult to see the advantages of a developed telecommunications system for Eritrea, the disadvantages of not having one need to be clearly understood. The Gash-Barka region can once again be taken as an example. At the moment, only three urban settlements (Agordat, Barentu and Tessenei) are connected to the system and service is inadequate. If the development potential of the region is realized, the lack of an efficient telecommunications system will create many problems. Agricultural producers would not be able to follow market conditions, so that taking products to market would mean increased financial risk, whereas information technology for both local and external markets can enable farmers to store their products until the market stabilizes to their satisfaction.

Another example concerns the ports. The problems that investors had in finding out about the arrival of ships in Massawa could be solved by an efficient telecommunications system; the business community would be able to monitor the movements of any ship and deliver their products to Massawa at the right time.

Some people are convinced that information technology is the one area that may help poor countries such as Eritrea leap over whole stages of development. Indeed, the advantage that developing countries are believed to possess – lower labour costs to produce manufactured goods – may need to be re-examined. The growth in the sophistication of automated production, particularly the development of microchips, has greatly reduced the wage component of production. This has implications in favour of electronic engineering being included in the educational systems of developing countries such as Eritrea, particularly at the tertiary level.

Like many developing countries, Eritrea is struggling to deliver adequate medical and education facilities to its people. Information infrastructure can help deliver electronic health and learning services to rural areas, where most of the population lives. With information technology, for example, health officers in rural areas could consult doctors in central locations or educational materials could be transmitted to schools through electronic devices. The benefits that can be generated through telecommunications infrastructure are enormous. Some even believe that setting it up in remote areas could reduce urbanization. However, the TSE must meet many immediate challenges, and the aim must be to solve existing problems before planning for major investment.

As already mentioned, a major dilemma for the TSE is how to devise an acceptable tariff system. At the moment, although Eritrea has one of the lowest per capita incomes in the world, telecommunications tariffs are amongst the highest in the world. Income from domestic user charges is reported to be negligible; most income is from the TSE's share of revenue from incoming international calls. The high tariffs help generate much-needed foreign currency for re-investment. But this cannot be a long-term solution, as most of the population would remain deprived of telecommunications services. In this context, the TSE could introduce different installation and user charges for business and residential clients. Ultimately, tariffs must recover costs for the TSE to remain viable, but there may be ways to reduce investment costs and make tariffs more affordable. For example, relatively low-cost radio and satellite technology for serving rural areas is now available that makes it possible to reach even the most remote places and to base priorities on need rather than proximity to terrestrial networks.

Telecommunications can hinder development if unrealistic technical standards requiring heavy investment are introduced, or if unrealistic tariffs are set, making it virtually impossible for potential customers to take advantage of information technology. A telecommunications service can remain small and viable, but its purpose should go far beyond an immediate concern with viability. There could be situations in which telecommunications facilities are required immediately, but the cost recovery would come only after a long period of "economic gestation". In such cases, potential users or investors should be made aware of the services available and how they could benefit from them. In the long term, such an undertaking may come to fruition and become financially sustainable.

It is essential that end users of any service are involved in the planning process, as has been pointed out in the case of electric power service. A clear understanding of their position must form the basis not only of technological choices to be made, but also of appropriate pricing. Failure to understand users' needs could hinder development of the economy, and this can affect the growth of service, creating a vicious circle of underdevelopment. Involving economists and sociologists in the planning process would help ensure that important economic and social dimensions are taken into account, integrating the views of end users in planning telecommunications infrastructure.

CONCLUSION

Throughout this chapter there has been a continuous refrain: efficient and reliable infrastructure is crucial because it creates an enabling environment that fosters economic and social development. Where efficient infrastructure services exist, products are likely to be competitive and profitable. With profit comes the opportunity for investment, followed by demand for increased labour and then growth of an economy. In contrast, an inefficient and unreliable infrastructure service creates a bottleneck in the economy and products become uncompetitive. This results in loss of markets for national industrial products and will inevitably be followed by reduction in the labour force or even the complete shutdown of an industry. Eventually this causes widespread unemployment and poverty,

Another issue that has cropped up repeatedly in this chapter is how various economic activities are interrelated and how one activity can affect another positively or negatively. Concrete examples (banana plantations, roads, ports) have demonstrated these interrelations, and the obstacles that must be tackled have been analysed. The need for a co-ordinated planning approach has been a dominant theme in this discussion.

It might be appropriate to organize a campaign explaining these basic economic principles to employees in the service industry. For example, every worker at the port of Massawa should understand the impact his or her work has on a host of other activities and see how he or she bears responsibility for them, too. If these principles were introduced through in-service training programmes, it would not be too difficult to identify personnel responsible for expensive delays, for which others are now suffering the consequences.

In sum, the government's development vision, outlined in the Macro-Policy Document, is to transform the war-ravaged economy into a modern one characterized by self-sustaining growth. To achieve this, "the Government adopted a broad-based growth strategy that has aspects of rehabilitation, reconstruction and development covering all sectors of the economy". However, visions, policies, acts and even constitutions are not end results, but must be translated into actions that can be implemented. The process of thinking things through is of course important, but the processes of doing things are equally important. How can government policies be translated into action? Who should do what and how are activities to be co-ordinated? Such co-ordination is essential to maintain harmony and avoid duplication and waste. There seems to be a need for the establishment of some kind of institution responsible for supervising the integration of planning and co-ordinating the implementation of national programmes and projects. With the regions expected to assume more responsibility in the future, such a proposal assumes even greater importance.

REFERENCES

Anderson, D. and Fishwick, R., *Fuelwood Consumption and Deforestation in African Countries*, World Bank, Washington D.C., 1984.

Bridger, G. A. and Winpenny, J. T., *Planning Development Projects: A Practical Guide to the Choices and Appraisal of Public Sector Investments*, HMSO, London, 1983.

GSE, *Macro-Policy Document*, Asmara, 1994.

GSE, *National Environmental Management Plan for Eritrea*, Asmara, 1995.

IEG, *Railway Administration in Eritrea: A Short Description of the System*, Asmara, November 1965.

Leach, Gerald and Mearns, Robin, *Beyond the Wood Fuel Crisis: People, Land and Trees*, Earthscan, London, 1988.

State of Eritrea, *ETSS: Transport Sector Study*, Transport Survey Report, Vol. 1, Ministry of Transport, 1996.

TSE, *Development of the Telecommunications Network in Eritrea (1994-2008)*.

Tseggai, Araia, *Eritrea's Railway and Rope-way System*, Eritrea Profile, May 1994.

World Bank, *Eritrea: Options and Strategies for Growth*, World Bank Report No. 12930-ER, Vol. 1, Eastern Africa Department, Africa Region, Washington D.C., 1994a.

World Bank, *World Development Report 1994: Infrastructure for Development*, Oxford University Press, New York, 1994b.

5

FOOD SECURITY: PROBLEMS, POLICIES AND PROGRAMMES

HAILE AWALOM

Food security as a concept presupposes that a nation's basic food policies should aim to avoid malnutrition or starvation among the population. Policy consistent with this objective aims to overcome long-term nutritional deprivation among vulnerable groups, as well as to avert short-term deprivation due to adverse natural events or sudden changes in people's capacity to acquire enough food.

Food security has been defined as:

> Access by all people at all times to enough food for an active, healthy life. Its essential elements are the availability of food and the ability to acquire it. Food insecurity, in turn, is the lack of access to enough food (World Bank, 1986:1).

According to the macro-policy framework of the Eritrean government, it is also defined as:

> The existence of a capacity and ability to make readily accessible food to all Eritreans which is of sufficient quantity and acceptable quality at an affordable price at any time and place within the country (GSE, 1994).

Both definitions emphasize access to food. This is in line with the concept of food entitlement focusing on whether or not people have sufficient command over food. Therefore, availability and access to food are both stressed.

A clear distinction should be made between transitory food insecurity (a temporary decline in a household's access to enough food) and chronic food insecurity (an inadequate diet caused by continuing inability to acquire enough food). Transitory food insecurity may be due to a transient shortfall in either production or real income, as typified by famine, which can be caused by seasonal crop failures due to droughts or locusts, or, for example, a sudden rise in prices. Chronic food insecurity reflects a long-term problem of inadequate food (energy) intake due to low productivity and income of a society at local, regional or national level. Chronic food insecurity has been the lot of most of Eritrea's rural population over the last decades, due to the ravages of the protracted war and recurrent droughts.

This chapter examines the problems of food security in Eritrea, relevant policies drawn up by the government, and programmes that have been or are being implemented to tackle them. Special attention is given to the Gash-Barka region in western Eritrea, which is seen to have the greatest potential for agricultural production, while important issues such as environmental protection and women's participation are discussed in terms of food security.

THE IMPACT OF THE WAR ON ERITREAN AGRICULTURE

There was a time when agriculture contributed 50-70 per cent of Eritrea's GDP. Records indicate that, in the years before the war, the country was a net exporter of agricultural products. Large-scale agricultural farms in the lowlands produced horticultural and oil crops. As an agro-industrial region and fishing centre, Eritrea accounted for 40 per cent of Ethiopia's industrial output. It is estimated that, at the turn of the century, forest cover was 30-40 per cent.

In 1991, when the country was liberated, the agricultural situation was tragically different. The whole sector was ruined, as land had been left idle or become permanently fallow. Some three-quarters of a million people had fled the country, and those who remained were often too poor or too old to cultivate. Much of the land was mined, which meant continual risk to life and limb for would-be cultivators. Villages and agricultural land suffered indiscriminate bombing, while livestock and trees were deliberately decimated. As a result, the country's forest cover was reduced to 0.4 per cent of the total land area, and soil erosion was a serious problem in many parts of the country.

The exodus of much of the country's skilled and unskilled labour affected agriculture as well as industrial production. The destruction and neglect of Eritrea's infrastructure – roads, communication networks, schools, hospitals – impacted the rural and the urban world, destroying many markets and contributing to downward spirals of agricultural production and standards of living in rural areas. Indeed, by the mid-1980s, large sectors of the population had become dependent on food aid handouts for their very survival.

During the liberation struggle, the EPLF gave the utmost importance to self-reliance in all fields. While this was not possible as far as food was concerned because of lack of access to enough fertile land, a number of food production and conservation projects were carried out, although they were often hampered by the ongoing war and scarcity of resources. It was always envisaged, however, that independent Eritrea would give top priority to food security, through the rehabilitation and conservation of its resource base and the promotion of agricultural production and fisheries.

FOOD PRODUCTION AND FOOD NEEDS SINCE INDEPENDENCE

Since peace was achieved, determined efforts have been made to build up the institutional capacities of both the agricultural and fishery sectors. Soil and water conservation activities have been carried out in various parts of the country. Market linkages have been established for both domestic consumption and exports.

Statistics show a considerable increase in agricultural output since 1991/1992. Despite the prevention of a constant increase in production by vagaries of the climate, according to a 1994 FAO/Ministry of Agriculture sector review, the economy grew by nearly seven per cent in 1991/1992. A major source of this growth was a 10 per cent increase in agriculture (as well as a 7 per cent increase in industry and more than 8 per cent in trade and transport services).

The World Bank estimates the share of agriculture in GDP to have been 28 per cent in those years. However, this may underestimate the important role of agriculture.

As Table 5.1 demonstrates, the latest available figures (1994) show a smaller contribution of agriculture to GDP, due in part to a steep rise in the contribution of services (to 62.2 per cent) and a steady improvement in the industrial sector (to 21.4 per cent). The growth rate of GDP as a whole is calculated as being 9.8 per cent in 1994.

Food production in Eritrea remains well below national requirements, however, creating a situation of chronic food insecurity. The causes are many: low and erratic rainfall, soil erosion and deforestation, land tenure patterns and traditional agricultural practices, lack of proper pest control, post-harvest losses, shortage of trained workers, lack of investment in agriculture, and poor infrastructure.

Table 5.1
Key economic indicators in Eritrea, 1992–1995

Economic activity	1992 est.	1993 est.	1994 est.	1995 proj.
Real GDP growth rate	—	-2.5	9.8	6
Share of agriculture (% of GDP at FC)	28.5	13.1	16.4	—
Share of industry	19.3	20.7	21.4	—
Share of services	52.2	66.2	62.2	—
Inflation Asmara CPI index annual change	8.8	9.6	6.4	8

Source: World Bank, 1996:188, 190.

This chronic food insecurity is reflected in the general health of the population, especially in rural areas and more particularly among the most vulnerable, namely children. At a workshop organized by UNICEF in Keren in 1996, it was reported that the mortality rate for infants was 135 per thousand and for children under five years of age, 203 per thousand – among the highest in the world. The number of babies underweight at birth is 13 per cent of the total, while the maternal mortality rate is 710 per 100,000 live births. A 1993 survey found malnutrition among children to be moderate to severe, while height for age was 66 per cent, weight deficiency was 41 per cent, and risk of wasting 10 per cent. Again, these figures rank among the highest in the world. Malaria, diarrhoea and acute respiratory infections are largely due to the high prevalence of malnutrition among Eritrean children.

The country's food production situation, compared with its needs, is summarized in Table 5.2. According to an ERREC report presented at the Keren workshop, it is estimated that each year the country needs 360,000-450,000 metric tons of food grain, 45,000-53,000 metric tons of pulses, and 18,000-22,000 metric tons of oil. Between 1992 and 1995 the annual shortfall in food grains varied widely, ranging from 242,000 to 312,000 metric tons and depending largely on climatic conditions. For example, in 1993, the total production of cereals and pulses was as low as

86,000 metric tons, while in 1994 it rose to 265,000 metric tons. In good years, production can meet up to two-thirds of national requirements, while in bad years only one-third of the country's need is produced.

Table 5.2
Eritrean food production compared with needs,
1993–1996 *(in tons)*

Description	1993–1994 preliminary estimate	1995 preliminary estimate	1996 projection
1. Consumption needs	468,000	495,000	526,000
2. Opening domestic foodgrain stocks	32,000	100,000	16,000
3. Gross domestic production **Less:** post-harvest loss (approx.) **Less:** seed, feed, non-food use	86,000 - 14,000 - 15,000	265,000 - 30,000 - 15,000	149,000 - 14,000 - 15,000
4. Net domestic production	57,000	220,000	120,000
5. Closing domestic foodgrain stocks **(2+4)**	89,000	320,000	136,000
6. Net foodgrain imports needed **(1-5)**	379,000	175,000	390,000
7. Monthly imports needed **(6/12)**	31,583	14,583	32,500

Source: ERREC, 1996. Notes: Population figures include returnees and were calculated as follows: 1993-1994=2.6 million; 1994-1995=2.75 million; 1995-1996=2.924 million. Consumption needs were calculated according to ERREC's food ration system for cereals only, for example 15 kilograms/person/month. Pulses and oilseed requirements were not taken into account.

Table 5.3 shows the projected shortfall in domestic production, given the predicted population increase over the next eight years. Just keeping pace with current levels of food need, which are considered inadequate by the government of Eritrea, food supply will have to increase by 2.9 per cent annually, through domestic agricultural production, aid or imports.

It should be pointed out that 1992 was a good year, with widespread rain and only minor losses due to pests. If a poorer year, such as 1993 or 1995, were taken as the base level, the shortfall in domestic production would be even greater. The table is based on current productivity levels and area under cultivation, and does not take into account gains from additional cultivated land (in the south-west) or improved yields. Nonetheless, the table indicates some of the implications of continued high population growth.

Table 5.3 Projected population and food requirements, 1997–2004					
Year	Population (in millions)	Projected requirements (in tons)			% of 1992 production	
		Cereals	Pulses	Food oil	Cereals	Pulses
1997	3.10	557,289	55,729	27,864	45	11
1998	3.19	573,451	57,345	28,673	44	10
1999	3.28	590,081	59,008	29,504	43	10
2000	3.37	607,193	60,719	30,360	41	10
2001	3.47	624,802	62,480	31,240	40	10
2002	3.57	642,921	64,292	32,146	39	9
2003	3.68	661,566	66,157	33,078	38	9
2004	3.78	680,751	68,075	34,038	37	9

Source: Derived from ERREC food requirements.

An alternative way to consider the impact of population growth on the demand for agricultural commodities is to examine the yields required to produce the necessary goods. Table 5.4 shows the increasing yield requirements considering two sizes of cultivated area. It is assumed in this table that there will be 375,000 hectares (the 1992 figure) under cultivation until 2000, then increasing to the maximum potential of 1,050,000 hectares. Only cereals are considered in this example, but there would be a similar pattern for oilseed and pulses. In 1992 the highest aggregate cereal yield was 0.78 tons per hectare. If productivity could be sustainably increased, then the population could be fed from the current cultivated area, and the extra land could be diversified into high-value export crops.

This would require achieving a target yield of 1.82 tons per hectare, which is indeed feasible with improved management and pest control.

However, it must be remembered that seasonal conditions in Eritrea, as in most of sub-Saharan Africa, are highly variable and unreliable, as evidenced by the poor 1993 yield (0.26 tons per hectare). In such situations, even if all potential agricultural land were developed, there would not be enough cereal for domestic requirements. Achieving food security for a rapidly-increasing population requires marked improvements in productivity and an increase in crop area.

Table 5.4
Cereal yields required to meet
increasing demand,1996–2004

Year	Cereal requirement	Yield needed to meet requirements *(tons per hectare)*	
		375,000ha cultivated	1,050,000ha cultivated
1996	541,583	1.44	n/a
1997	557,289	1.49	n/a
1998	573,451	1.53	n/a
1999	590,081	1.57	n/a
2000	607,193	1.62	0.58
2001	624,802	1.67	0.60
2002	642,921	1.71	0.61
2003	661,566	1.76	0.63
2004	680,751	1.82	0.65

Source: Derived from ERREC food requirements.

THE ROLE OF FOOD AID SINCE INDEPENDENCE

Between 1991 and 1995, the difference between requirements and domestic production was largely offset by food aid from external sources. Table 5.5 shows the amounts of food requested and actually received. As is shown, for various reasons there were considerable variations in the food aid given each year, and the amounts do not correspond with what was needed. For example, in 1993, which was a poor year, only 32 per cent of the food aid requested was received, while in 1992, a relatively good year, 90 per cent of the food aid requested was supplied.

Table 5.5 Food aid requested and received, 1991–1995 *(in thousands of tons)*			
Year	Food requested	Food received	% of request
1991	270	270	100
1992	250	225	90
1993	344	110	32
1994	350	280	80
1995	181	129	71
Total	1,395	1,014	73

Source: ERREC Report 1995/1996.

Food items received and distributed to the various regions of the country from 1993 to 1995 are shown in Table 5.6. Some 90 per cent of food aid was in the form of grain cereals. As shown, the largest amount in quantity (but not relative to the amount requested) was received in 1994. All food was distributed in kind as FFW or supplied free.

Table 5.6 Types of food aid supplied, 1993–1995 *(in tons)*								
Year	Cereal	Rice	Pulses	Food oil	Sugar	Milk	Other	Total
1993	117,036	–	7,390	2,756	1,048	1,181	–	129,411
1994	162,792	–	11,110	5,275	4,230	1,036	3,080	187,523
1995	114,472	242	5,306	5,875	938	1,111	683	128,627
Total	394,300	242	23,806	13,906	6,216	3,328	3,763	445,561

Source: ERREC, 1996.

Finally, Table 5.7 shows aggregate food stocks and food aid between 1992 and 1996 in relation to agricultural productivity (numbers 11 and 12), which is still abysmally low.

Table 5.7 Aggregate food stocks and food aid, 1992–1996 *(in thousands of tons)*				
Description	1992/93	1993/94	1994/95	1995/96
1. Opening stock (*forecast, beginning of year*)	110	50	178	30
2. Production	260	86	265	149
3. Total domestic availability	370	136	443	179
4. Food use	460	378	389	403
5. Other use	40	23	40	22
6. Closing stock (*end of year*)	60	55	65	45
7. Total domestic utilization	560	456	494	470
8. Import requirement	190	190	320	51
9. Commercial imports (forecast)	50	65	51	100

10. Food aid
  - FFW
  - Emergency
  - Monetization
	140
	n/a
	n/a
	n/a
		255
		30
		175
		50
			n/a
			n/a
			n/a
			n/a
				191
				n/a
				79
				112

11. Area cultivated (*hectares*)	317,000	374,900	355,300	298,400
12. Yield (*tons per hectare*)	0.82	0.30	0.75	0.50

Source: EW&FIS, 1996 and FAO, 1996a.

AGRICULTURAL, LIVESTOCK AND FISHERIES PRODUCTION IN RELATION TO FOOD SECURITY

Agriculture

Very nearly one-third of the land in Eritrea is unsuitable for agriculture, being barren or desert, as shown in Table 5.8. The table gives figures for land use in 1995 and estimates for potential rain-fed and irrigated agriculture. If these figures are achieved, it follows that the area available for livestock grazing will be considerably reduced.

Table 5.8 Land use by area		
Land use	**Approx. area (ha)**	**Per cent of total**
Current		
Cultivated (rain-fed)	417,000*	3.42
Irrigated	22,000	0.18
Disturbed forest	53,000	0.43
Plantation	10,000	0.08
Woodland and scrub	673,000	5.52
Browsing and grazing	6,967,000	57.16
Barren	4,047,000	33.21
Potential		
Total rain-fed	1,050,000	8.61
Total irrigated	600,000	4.92

Source: EW&FIS, 1996 and FAO, 1996a.

While overall agricultural production is considerably below national requirements, what is particularly worrying is that the country's agricultural productivity, as we have seen, is very low and has not risen since Independence. More details are shown in Table 5.9.

Table 5.9
Cultivated area and harvest estimates, 1992–1995

Year	Crop	Cultivated area (hectares)	Harvest estimate (tons)	Yield per hectare (tons)
1992	cereals	320,700	251,300	0.78
	pulses	11,800	6,000	0.51
	oilseed	12,700	5,100	0.40
1993	cereals	338,500	86,850	0.26
	pulses	15,000	1,530	0.10
	oilseed	42,100	9,670	0.23
1994	cereals	330,310	253,400	0.77
	pulses	7,950	4,370	0.55
	oilseed	24,700	8,800	0.36
1995	cereals	298,432	122,460	0.41
	pulses	21,935	6,122	0.28
	oilseed	29,073	11,696	0.40

Source: Ministry of Agriculture reports, 1992–1995.

In an average year, most of the production comes from three provinces: Barka, Gash-Setit and Seraye. In the best year, 1992, six of the nine provinces achieved maximum cereal yields, while pulse yields were best in 1992 and 1994, with the performance of oilseed varying from province to province and from year to year. Variations in rainfall, as well as pest infestations, account for most of the differences.

Rainfall data is not available before 1992, and even since then some provinces have been represented by only one or two recording stations. The year 1992 was reasonable (Akeleguzay) to very good (Barka), while there was a different pattern for 1993, ranging from very poor (Barka, Hamasien, Senhit) to fair (Gash-Setit). There were intense rains and scattered hail storms in Akeleguzay, Hamasien and Senhit, while hot dry winds in the flowering and grain-filling seasons also reduced yields in Akeleguzay. In 1994 rainfall was reasonable in most provinces and very good in Akeleguzay, although hail storms reduced yields in the Sahel, Senhit and part of Akeleguzay. The 1995 season was poor in Barka but good in most provinces.

It should be stressed that, while rainfall records may be good, crop performance may still be very poor. The actual frequency and distribution has to be shown if the effectiveness of rainfall is to be calculated accurately. Among the reasons for poor yields are excessive run-off due to intensive rains, untimely rain distribution, and poor land management and pest outbreaks.

As far as pests are concerned, locusts and army worm caused significant losses in most provinces in 1993 (especially Barka, Gash-Setit, Hamasien and Senhit) and in 1995 locust swarms were particularly severe (Barka, Sahel, Seraye, parts of Akeleguzay and Hamasien, with yields in Senhit greatly reduced). In 1994 the main damage was in Hamasien and Senhit provinces.

Lack of inputs (mostly seed, fertilizer and tools) restricted production in some provinces in 1995 and to a lesser extent in 1993. In the 1993 growing season, Barka was severely affected by a shortage of the aforementioned inputs and labour, resulting in lower yields.

As for food sufficiency at the provincial level, there is a tendency toward surpluses in the western lowland provinces, while the highland provinces usually produce less than they require. Table 5.10 shows the average percentage and range of cereal and pulse sufficiency by province. Most provinces produce considerably less than they require.

All in all, with regard to national food sufficiency, it should be pointed out that even 1992 produced only 52 per cent and 12 per cent of the country's cereal and legume requirements respectively. This is a reasonable performance, given the prevailing low investment level. It would appear that with more investment and good rains and irrigation schemes, the production of cereals and pulses could be as high as 75 per cent of national requirements.

Livestock

Livestock makes an important contribution to the Eritrean diet, particularly among the lowland agro-pastoral and pastoral communities. Most of the products consumed are milk and milk products, meat and eggs – all sources of high-quality protein. Livestock is also a form of security – if there is a bad season the animals are easily exchanged for cash or food items.

However, across the country animal production is hampered by a shortage of feed, low in both quantity and quality, while water shortages and disease also affect production at different levels, depending on the province and the climate.

Table 5.10
Range and average percentage of cereal and pulse sufficiency at provincial and national levels, 1992–1995

Province	Cereals		Pulses	
	Range (%)	Average (%)	Range (%)	Average (%)
Akeleguzay	11–42	28	1–31	18
Barka	0–107	47	0	0
Denkel	0–7	4	0	0
Gash-Setit	36–185	98	0	0
Hamasien	19–46	38	4–26	15
Sahel	5–19	15	0–19	0
Semhar	25–105	58	0	0
Senhit	10–53	27	0	0
Seraye	22–95	67	8–62	37
National	17–52	36	3–12	9

Source: *Ministry of Agriculture report, 1996.*

Estimates of the national livestock population are patchy and often appear inconsistent. Table 5.11 shows the estimates at intervals going back 70 years. The table shows that from 1928 to 1973 there was a steady increase in all livestock production, after which there was a deterioration that reached its lowest in 1991. After Independence the figures go up again, and by 1995 sheep and goats had surpassed the 1973 levels, although this is not yet the case for cattle.

Table 5.11
Estimates of livestock population, 1928–1994
(in thousands of head)

Year	Cattle	Goats/Sheep	Camels	Equines	Poultry
1928	749	1,897	79	59	–
1938	591	1,491	68	51	–
1946	1,200	2,200	105	83	–
1965	1,300	3,200	180	109	–
1973	2,500	5,000	–	–	–
1987	970	3,001	–	190	456
1992	1,258	4,950	185	168	2,500
1993	1,396	5,100	191	276	2,573
1994	1,335	5,308	196	284	2,653

Source: Ministry of Agriculture, 1991.

Table 5.12 shows the quantity of livestock by province and estimated contribution to the average diet in 1992. The lowland provinces are clearly the livestock reservoirs of the country. About 60 per cent of the country's cattle and 40 per cent of sheep and goats are found in Gash-Setit and Barka.

The Tropical Livestock Units (TLUs) of the three central highland provinces, Hamasien, Seraye and Akeleguzay, amount to only 23 per cent. The breed of cattle favoured in the western lowlands is the Barka, which produces up to six litres of milk per day, and is also a fair producer of meat. As for the highlands, the preferred breed is the Arado, which is a better meat producer and draught animal than the Barka but produces only three litres of milk a day.

Another difference between the lowlands and the highlands is that oxen constitute only 12 per cent of the cattle in the former and more than 50 per cent in the latter. There are relatively small numbers of oxen (11-13 per cent of cattle) in the country as a whole, but the expanding demand for draught oxen in the highlands, due to the increased area under cultivation, has reduced the size of milking stock among cattle, sheep and goats. As a consequence, there are now fewer dairy products in the diet of the highlands population than in the lowlands. By timing their breeding and lactation operations carefully, pastoralists can ensure that there will be some milk for their communities throughout the year.

The quantity of sheep and goats is highest in Sahel, Barka, Gash-Setit and Senhit, with goats being in the majority. In the lowland provinces, goats are often multi-purpose, with specialized ones being raised around spate irrigation schemes in the eastern lowlands. The proportion of goats is greater in the highlands, where they are raised primarily for meat but are also milked for home use.

Table 5.12 Livestock population by province and contribution to average diet, 1992				
Province	Cattle	Sheep/Goats	Poultry	Contribution to diet
Akeleguzay	77,600	368,000	442,000	Slight
Barka	342,500	1,020,000	25,000	Very large
Denkel	38,600	170,000	0	Large
Gash-Setit	199,800	670,000	250,000	Large
Hamasien	110,000	110,000	520,000	Slight
Sahel	27,600	1,482,000	5,000	Large
Semhar	27,800	300,000	8,000	Large
Senhit	13,500	580,000	450,000	Slight
Seraye	11,900	120,000	800,000	Some
National	849,300	4,821,680	2,500,000	—

Source: FAO, 1993.

Most chickens are in the highland provinces, but their production is hampered by disease, as well as poor feed and management. If these obstacles could be overcome, and improved breeds introduced, chickens could play a significant role in improving the nutrition of the more vulnerable groups, as women benefit from cash generated by backyard poultry, and eggs are often fed to young children. The figures in Table 5.13 are comparable to those of neighbouring countries. However, if meat consumption is to remain at the levels shown, production will have to rise in keeping with the increased population, while higher consumption will require even greater production.

Table 5.13
Livestock products and per capita consumption, 1992

Product	Production per year (in tons)	Per capita consumption per year (in kilograms)
Beef	13,000	5.8
Sheep/goat meat	10,000	4.4
Milk	36,000	16.0
Poultry meat	3,250	1.3
Fish	1,500	0.47

Source: FAO, 1994.

Extensive livestock production as practised in the lowlands requires range grazing and long growing seasons. After Independence, livestock production was highest in Barka and Gash in 1992 and 1994. The poorer years of 1993 and 1995 were to some extent mitigated by the agro-pastoral and pastoral nature of herding.

However, there is little doubt that production in those years was adversely affected by the reduced availability of water. As for animal production in the spate irrigation areas, it was poor in 1993 and fair to good in 1994 and 1995. In poor years there is little browse available, but this is supplemented by crop residue. If the crops and the spate system are both poor, as in 1993, animal production is inevitably much reduced.

In the highlands, livestock production depends on browsing and grazing after harvest. In the fair to poor years, such as 1993, crop yields and natural vegetation were reduced and in turn diminished animal production and rendered livestock more susceptible to disease.

Fisheries

It is generally recognized that fisheries could make an important contribution to food security in Eritrea. The potential is considerable, but fish does not play nearly as great a role as could be expected. There are several reasons for this.

The fishing industry, hard hit by the closure of the Suez Canal in the late 1960s, further declined during the 1970s and 1980s when Eritrea was engulfed by war. When liberation came, the sector was practically non-existent – there were no fishing vessels or on-shore facilities and little or no expertise was available. The government of Eritrea had to take steps to rehabilitate the sector virtually from scratch because – as was the case in all the other sectors of the economy – fisheries suffered from an acute shortage of the necessary capital and trained labour.

The Ministry of Marine Resources estimated Eritrean fisheries production to be around 5,000 tons in 1995 (with an undetermined amount being illegally exported), while it has been estimated that the maximum sustainable annual yield would be well over 50,000 tons, and possibly even 75,000 tons. Artisanal catches out of Massawa increased steadily from 1992 to 1995 and were expected to reach 602 metric tons in 1996, while industrial landings, also out of Massawa, rose from 2,277 metric tons in 1994 (when they first started) to 3,261 in 1995. This figure was expected to exceed 7,000 in 1996 (see Table 5.14).

It appears, however, that this very fast expansion of the industrial fisheries sector could impede the growth of artisanal fishing. In 1995, there were already complaints that the bigger trawling vessels were rejecting large numbers of smaller fish, initiating a process that has reached disastrous proportions in other parts of the world. Most if not all of the industrial catch is exported, thus contributing to foreign exchange earnings, although not to the domestic consumption of fish.

Total fish consumption in Eritrea is calculated to be around 1,500 tons per year, which makes a very low per capita intake of 470 grams. According to a report presented by the ministry at the January 1996 Keren workshop, while fish consumption is generally higher in coastal zones than inland, it is still lower than would be expected, mainly due to lack of refrigeration facilities, scarce knowledge of fish conservation techniques and the limited experience of Eritrean women in preparing fish for consumption. Greater efforts should also be made to educate the public, starting with school children, about the nutritional value of fish. This is one of the priorities of the Ministry of Marine Resources.

Table 5.14 Annual fishery landings and sales, 1994–1995			
Type of fishery and landing site	Landing (in tons)	Sales (in US$)	Sales (in birr)
1994			
Industrial - Massawa	2,277.00	2,023,496.00	–
Artisanal - Massawa	370.81	–	2,224,860.00
Artisanal - Assab	21.89	–	109,450.00
1995			
Industrial - Massawa	3,261.52	3,396,869.92	–
Artisanal - Massawa	472.76	–	3,309,369.00
Artisanal - Assab	48.00	–	264,000.00
Total	6,451.98	5,420,365.92	5,907,679.00

Source: Ministry of Marine Resources reports, 1991–1996.

Agro-Industrial Capacity

Eritrea's few agro-industries are concentrated around urban centres because they have historically provided markets, and because of the perennial problem of transportation, an obstacle in the development of this sector since the early Italian colonial period. The following information briefly examines existing agro-processing plants and their development potential, as well as constraints they face.

There are two milk processing plants. The Asmara Milk Processing Plant produces milk, cream and some cheese, and is supplied with raw milk by small dairy farmers in the areas around Asmara. The milk is delivered in aluminium cans and checked by qualified milk inspectors for disease and contamination. After processing, the plant distributes to the market mainly through shop networks for private consumption. It is illegal to sell untreated milk (FAO, 1994), a measure intended to prevent the spread of brucellosis and tuberculosis from cattle to human beings.

Table 5.15 shows the Asmara plant's production and prices from 1992 to June 1996. There is very high demand for milk in this city and production is increasing (rising from 265,112 to 2,144,007 litres in four years), but several price increases suggest that demand still exceeds supply. Similarly, cream production has increased to 450 per cent of what it was in 1993, but here there has been no reduction in price.

	Table 5.15 Production and prices, Asmara Milk Processing Plant, 1992–1996			
	Pasteurized milk		**Cream**	
Year	**Production** *(litres)*	**Price** *(birr per litre)*	**Production** *(kilograms)*	**Price** *(birr per kilogram)*
1992	265,112	1.90	n/a	18.00
1993	2,761,279	1.90	5,973	18.00
1994	2,518,925	2.38	32,489	18.00
1995	3,674,078	2.60	52,902	18.00
1996*	2,144,007	2.60	27,290	18.00
Total	11,363,401	–	118,654	–

Source: Ministry of Agriculture reports, 1996.   *until June 1996*

The price of milk is currently favourable to both producers and consumers (according to the milk processors). However it is expected that the price of milk will rise considerably in the future because animal feed is becoming increasingly expensive. In addition, the City of Asmara has indicated that dairy farmers will have to relocate outside the municipal limits due to health requirements. This is likely to increase the cost of transport. The plant is unable to operate at an optimum level as the supply of milk is insufficient. Until this is remedied it will be difficult for the plant to further diversify its production and increase revenue.

Another factory, the Asmara Milk and Meat Processing Plant, also produces milk, butter and cheese, as well as pork products, including mortadella and cooked ham. The Elabaret Agro-Industry Plant supplies the raw milk and some of the pork, with the remainder coming from the factory itself. The products are distributed throughout the country, and some are exported to Ethiopia. The amount and prices of the main items produced by this plant are indicated in Table 5.16.

			Table 5.16		
			Production and prices,		
		Asmara Milk and Meat Processing Plant, 1993–1996			
Year	Mortadella kg – birr/kg	Cooked ham kg – birr/kg	Asst. pig meats kg – birr/kg	Butter kg – birr/kg	Cheese kg – birr/kg
1993	34,880 – 25	4,059 – 26	5,432 – 7	6,142 – 26	16,410 – 25
1994	39,900 – 25	4,333 – 24	8,058 – 7	15,117 – 22	30,415 – 23
1995	50,678 – 25	3,995 – 24	15,220 – 7	50,047 – 20	33,405 – 23
1996*	37,259 – 27	882 – 27	12,309 – 18	29,865 – 25	31,033 – 26
Total kg	162,717	13,269	41,019	101,171	111,263

Source: *Ministry of Agriculture reports, 1996.*   *until June 1996*

The 1996 price for assorted pig meats is higher than in previous years, as the producer price per kilogram increased from 2.75 birr to eight birr, due to the fact that in this year the Elabaret Estate was separated from the plant. Nevertheless, high demand for this product enabled cost increases to be passed on to consumers. Cheese and butter production increased steadily, without lasting price reductions, again reflecting the strong demand for these products.

As with the other plant, the shortage of raw milk affects production levels, and an increase in the supply is necessary if demand is to be satisfied. The machinery of this plant is also very old and badly needs replacing.

The main products of the Elabaret Agro-Industry Plant are citrus and other fruits, fodder for livestock, by-products (dairy products), tomato paste and processed meats such as ham. The production and prices of these items from 1992 to June 1996 are given in Table 5.17, which shows the importance of the processing part of the plant as well as the volume of fruit production. Declining prices for fruit, especially citrus, are attributed to the increased area planted with these fruits, as well as competition from imports. Some form of locally appropriate fruit processing would help offset these price falls – and could be expanded to serve export markets. The demand for processed meat, in particular ham, continues to rise.

Table 5.17 Production and prices, Elabaret Agro-Industry Plant, 1992–1996						
Product	**Production**					**Total**
	1992	**1993**	**1994**	**1995**	**1996***	
Main products *(production amounts are shown in quintals and prices are shown in birr per quintal)*						
Citrus Price	4,579.3 150–200	5,404.1 225–320	4,784.3 225–276	3,930.7 200–230	1,348.2 200–230	20,046.6
Mango Price	335.3 250	377.4 250	464.1 250	333.2 200	447.6 200	1,957.6
Papaya Price	0.6 110	32.5 110	634.7 110	656.9 110	188.1 110	1,512.8
Grapefruit Price	836.2 60	755.0 50	530.3 50	370.4 50	75.7 50	2,567.4
Tomato Price	3,714.7 125	5,698.3 125	4,864.4 100	7,335.6 100	2,920.2 100	24,533.2
Fodder Price	17,290.7 5–7	22,997.7 5–7	32,293.5 5–7	31,973.6 5–7	15,727.8 5–7	120,283.3
Grapes Price	– –	1,194 450	8.4 450	22.4 200	13.5 –	1,238.3
By-products						
Milk (litre)	300,651	470,663	873,141	850,230	455,155	2,949,840
Cheese (kg)	111,185	35,942	31,543	–	–	178,670
Butter (kg)	4,183	10,416	8,552	–	–	23,151
Ricotta (kg)	3,680	10,786	4,675	–	–	19,141
Cream (kg)	6,606	17,266	14,430	–	–	38,302
Tomato paste (70g tin)	14,800	57,600	930,200	138,400	–	1,141,000
Tomato paste (850g tin)	102,144	100,548	4,704	123,648	54,194	385,238
Ham (kg)	7,300	22,570	33,045	32,319	18,039	113,273

Source: *Ministry of Agriculture reports, 1996.*   **until June 1996*

The estate supplies most of the raw materials for agro-processing. Tins for the tomato paste are imported from Italy or Greece. Products are distributed in Eritrea and are consumed in the country. The plant is unable to meet domestic demand because of its ageing machinery, which requires increasing maintenance. Also, the plant is closed for two months of the year, which negatively affects its employees. Altogether, there are 235 workers on the estate, most of whom are in the production area, with an additional 66 professionals and National Service workers. Morale is poor due to low wages and loss of income during the two-month closure period.

Table 5.18
Production and prices,
Barka Cannery Factory, 1992-1996

Product	Production					Total
	1992	1993	1994	1995	1996*	
Shiro (kg)[1]	10,069.24	–	–	4,819.18	1,464.36	16,352.78
Price (birr/tin)	1.00–1.50	–	–	1.65–1.97	1.65–3.25	
Meat/meat and vegetables (kg)[2]	901.56	–	587.47	6,122.81	3,477.40	11,089.24
Price (birr/tin)	1.60	–	2.33–2.90	2.40–4.87	2.60–4.87	
Vegetable soup (kg)[2]	–	–	1,593.17	4,435.44	3,909.35	9,937.96
Price (birr/tin)	1.40	–	1.60–1.72	1.90–2.85	1.90–2.85	
Foul medames (kg)[2]	3.34	25.24	157.36	404.65	561.87	1,152.46
Price (birr/tin)	1.00–1.50	1.00–1.50	1.60–2.35	2.48	2.48	
Tomato paste (kg)[3]	25.39	37.99	–	7.88	10.28	81.54
Price (birr/tin)	8.45–21.00	8.45–21.00	–	27.50	27.50	
Bone/meat meal (kg)	14.35	–	24.65	96.70	–	135.70
Price (birr/kg)	2.00	2.00	2.00	2.00	2.00	
Fats (kg)	0.70	–	2.20	8.24	–	11.15
Price (birr/kg)	1.15	1.15	1.15	1.15	–	

Source: Ministry of Industry and Trade reports, 1996   *six months only
[1] Tin sizes 240g, 410g and 450g (1992 only). [2] Tin sizes 240g and 410g [3] Tin size 3kg; also 1kg in 1992–1993. Prices indicated range across tin sizes.

The Barka Cannery Factory produces tinned foods (*shiro*, meat, meat and vegetables, vegetable soup, tomato paste and *foul medames*) as well as fats, bone and meat meal for sale inside Eritrea. Production and prices of the main products are shown in Table 5.18. There was a general increase in the price of all tinned products from 1992 to 1996, reflecting sustained demand and increased ability to meet this demand. The prices of oils, bone and meat meal were throughout. The factory obtains its vegetables, salt and edible oil from Eritrean producers; meat, pulses and red and black peppers are imported from Ethiopia; chemicals (flavourings and preservatives) are obtained from Italy; and tins come from Turkey. An increase in domestic production of meat and pulses would help reduce import requirements.

The National Edible Oil Factory produces edible oil, margarine and shortenings, while by-products include *benello* (paint brushes) and husks as well as lint cotton, which is exported to several countries, including Italy and Germany. Such exports could be increased if there were sufficient raw materials. This is all the more important because of the depressed internal market for the main products, which is caused by competition from imports – accounting for, for example, the stagnant prices for margarine and shortening. The production and prices of these items are shown in Table 5.19.

In 1993 and 1994 cotton seed was imported from Sudan, but since then the Ali-Ghider Agricultural Estate (see below) has been supplying cotton seed, although not enough to sustain the factory's production. For example, in 1995 the supply of cotton from Ali-Ghider was sufficient for only two months' factory processing. If these supplies could be increased it would go some way to satisfy the factory's need of raw materials.

The Ali-Ghider Agricultural Estate, inherited in poor condition by the Eritrean government, has been undergoing a massive renovation programme to improve its decrepit infrastructures so as to be able to meet the demand for cotton. As explained in the chapter on social reintegration, Ali-Ghider is a major site for resettling ex-combatants, each of whom is entitled to two hectares of land. Farmers are given inputs (machinery, seed, chemicals, transport facilities and ginning) in advance and are expected to repay after they harvest. These inputscost up to 5,688 birr per farmer in 1996. To cover these expenses and still make an income for themselves, farmers need to produce around 30 quintals of cotton a year or considerably more sorghum or other cheap products.

Table 5.19 Production and prices, National Edible Oil Factory, 1993-1996					
Product	**Production**				**Total**
	1993	1994	1995	1996*	
Main products (production amounts are shown in quintals; prices are birr/quintal					
Edible oil	2,784	1,212	2,620	1,754	8,370
Price	534.84	557.76	880.92	986.32	
Margarine	228	100	175	71	574
Price	96.49	90.00	114.29	112.68	
Shortening	33	95	226	42	396
Price	969.70	978.95	115.04	119.05	
By-products (production amounts are shown in tons; prices are birr/ton)					
Lint cotton	245	104	263	374	986
Price	1,004.08	2,432.69	2,372.62	1,826.20	
Benello	1,141	504	1,160	1,821	4,626
Price	800.18	980.16	775.86	922.57	
Husk	708	332	584	869	2,493
Price	357.34	355.42	386.99	479.86	

Source: Ministry of Agriculture reports, 1996.   *six months only*

The area under cultivation on the estate increased considerably after 1993, as shown in Table 5.20, although the rising cost-price squeeze may restrict this expansion in the future. Yield levels are acceptable. In 1995 yields of cotton and sorghum amounted to 17 and 15 quintals per hectare respectively. Cotton yields are expected to rise to 40 quintals a hectare in the future, although more extension and training will be needed among the estate's farming community. There are a number of management problems remaining to be resolved, particularly the fixed costs that have created difficulties for inexperienced farmers who have not been able to achieve sufficiently high yields from their plots.

Table 5.20 Production and area cultivated, Ali-Ghider Estate, 1993-1995			
Crop *(Production in quintals; Area in hectares)*	**1993**	**1994**	**1995**
Cotton Production Area	4,595 706	43,000 2,441	66,000 3,840
Sorghum Production Area	496 84	12,834 1,225	4,942 321
Sunflower Production Area	– –	78 25	29 13
Sesame Production Area	15 10	– –	– –

Source: *Ministry of Agriculture reports, 1996.*

In addition to the factories mentioned thus far, Eritrea has several other agro-industrial plants. These include the Red Sea Tannery which processes leather for the domestic market, with some export to Italy and England, and the Asmara Pickling Tannery. The latter pickles sheep and goatskin leather for export to Italy and England, with only one per cent of production distributed within Eritrea. The shortage of raw leather is the main problem of both tanning factories, as it forces prices up, making selling prices less competitive internationally. In addition, the export of so many live sheep and goats to the Middle East has reduced leather supplies.

POLICIES AND PROGRAMMES PROMOTING AGRICULTURE AND FOOD SECURITY

Policies

In its 1994 Macro-Policy Document, the government of Eritrea defined its national development objectives. A broad-based strategy was adopted to achieve these objectives. It included human resource development, promotion of export-oriented industry and agriculture, infrastructure development, environmental protection and promotion of the private sector. This policy framework was to promote social justice and assure an equitable share for all Eritreans in the country's future prosperity.

In the field of agriculture, the main aims were to improve production through irrigation and enhancing the productivity of peasants, pastoralists and agro-pastoralists. Policies were formulated to shift agricultural investment activities toward private production (both peasant and commercial), irrigated agriculture, and areas with high production potential.

With the assistance of the International Service for National Agricultural Research (ISNAR), a national agricultural research strategy was prepared in 1995, covering the period 1996-2002. In line with the overall agricultural policy, research was to emphasize the production of high-value crops and the development of irrigation water resources to support an export-oriented agricultural sector. However, improvements in the production levels of traditional food crops and livestock would receive enough attention to achieve a certain degree of food self-sufficiency.

Priorities were established at two levels – production systems, and commodities and themes. The former were identified and prioritized within agro-ecological zones. Research would concentrate on the most important commodities and their constraints in each system. Ways of improving natural resource conservation and management would also be part of the overall research effort. Station-based applied and adaptive research and on-farm trials and production system improvement would be carried out, using research extension teams and involving farmer participation and feedback to adjust research plans and operations. In short, farm systems research – with full participation by farmers in the mainstream agricultural research to maintain the right focus – would be used to work out appropriate production approaches and techniques.

The document also established the relative importance of various commodities at the national level and divided them into high, medium and low priority crops. Their importance varied from one agro-ecological zone to another.

These new policies reflected a change of emphasis in the principles guiding agricultural development in Eritrea since Independence, which had been mainly aimed at helping subsistence farmers through the provision of inputs and the use of food aid for soil and water conservation.

Government policy aims to exploit local resources to produce as much food as possible in order to avoid reliance on handouts, and to prevent the distortion of local markets by highly-subsidized food aid. It is now recognized that, in the past, food aid undermined the work ethic and spirit of self-reliance, which are fundamental principles for the nation. In formulating this national policy, due consideration has been given to the serious threat to national security inherent in the unreliability of food aid donations and an unhealthy dependency on external charity and interests.

A clear stand was taken by the government on the whole question of food aid. It strives to:

- secure an adequate level of food aid to supplement national resources to meet the food requirements of the nation in general and those of the needy in particular
- eliminate or at least minimize the negative impacts of food aid, particularly the associated elements of dependency and price distortions
- implement full monetization of food aid as a preferred norm except in emergency situations requiring immediate assistance in kind
- ensure consistency and harmony of the terms, conditions and modalities of food aid with the general principles of "partnership in development" which govern the State of Eritrea's relationship with all multi- and bilateral partners.

(Consultative Meeting on Food Aid, Asmara, 1996)

Care is being taken to ensure that the conditions and modalities relating to food aid do not compromise national sovereignty and national ownership of policies, programmes and projects.

The government believes that food monetization policies contribute to flexibility, market-led prices (payable on the basis of wages), and relieve much of the need for supervision and control. At the same time there will continue to be "complete accountability and transparency during the utilization and distribution of food aid resources and funds" (ERREC, 1996). It is proposed that counterpart finance be pooled in a central fund for development programmes and food security activities, with reports provided regularly to all partners on how funds are utilized and assessing the impact on activities.

These food aid policies fit within an overall policy framework that aims to create a technologically advanced and internationally competitive economic base. Exports are being promoted parallel to efforts to improve production for local consumption, which will be led by the private sector but subject to some governmental regulatory measures. Attention will also be given to conserving natural resources and ensuring that all activities are developmentally sustainable.

As for the environment, a series of principles has been drawn up to guide policies and programmes, and these were spelled out in the 1995 National Environmental Management Plan for Eritrea. It recognized that good management of renewable terrestrial, coastal and marine resources was of strategic importance for social and economic development, and that there was a need to maintain the vitality and diversity of environmental systems. Obviously, this would limit the legitimate use of resources generated by these systems. Broad-based management (national and regional environmental legislation) is to be balanced with targeted management (establishing protected areas and rehabilitating heavily degraded ecosystems), while the involvement of local populations in the planning process was considered to be crucial, "recognizing that local people are the actual day-to-day managers of natural resources".

Given the country's scarce water resources and the advanced degree of soil erosion in many areas, programmes for conserving water and combating soil degradation must be central to all agricultural and rural development strategies.

Programmes

The Agricultural Rehabilitation Programme (ARP) was born during the 1983-1985 famine in the areas under the control of the EPLF during the liberation struggle. Initially, it was conceived as a short-term programme to provide basic agricultural inputs to peasant farmers who lost their resources during the drought years. It focused on the four provinces of Sahel, Senhit, Semhar and Barka – hence the acronym SASEBA-ARP. In 1988 a similar project was launched in the remaining three highland provinces of Seraye, Akeleguzay and Hamasien, and called SAH-ARP. In post-liberation Eritrea, the SASEBA and SAH programmes continued to operate as integral parts of the nationwide ARP.

The main objective of the ARP, and the Animal Health Programme (AHP), was to rehabilitate the rural population by helping communities increase their agricultural production and improve the ecological base of their environment. Since its inception, the main form of assistance has been the free distribution of agricultural inputs (seed, tools, animals, water pumps) and technical advice. As of 1993 these inputs were available on a credit basis. Other activities after Independence included soil and water conservation and cash cropping (through the provision of vegetable seed and water pumps), while tractor mechanization was introduced on an increasingly large scale.

In concrete terms, recent achievements of ARP and AHP include 992 kilometres of cropland terracing and 5,400 kilometres of non-cropland terracing (in 1994), 6,742 oxen and camels distributed free and on credit (1993-1995), 10,500 sets of farm tools distributed (in 1993), 2,314 metric tons of cereal seed distributed (1993-1994) and 3,114 farmers trained in extension and plant protection (1993-1995).

Table 5.21
Soil and water conservation
activities in Eritrea, 1992–1995

Activity *(unit)*	1992	1993	1994	1995	Total
Nurseries established (each)	10	19	11	4	44
Seedlings produced (each)	18,918,622	18,966,312	10,021,137	13,577,096	61,483.167
Seedlings planted/ replanted (each)	17,644,893	17,166,642	7,790,116	11,870,528	54,472,179
Terraces constructed and maintained (kilometres)	55,891	25,276	11,678	12,010	104,855
Feeder roads constructed and maintained (kilometres)	316	245	160	109	830
Land enclosed (hectares)	49,942	22,589	4,503	34,966	112,000
Constructed and maintained (each): - earth dams - ponds - wells	51 19 33	24 54 34	11 18 22	30 17 13	116 108 102
Constructed and maintained (kilometres): - embankments - canals - check dams	171 – 1,183	119 7 606	103 3 174	105 2 347	498 12 2,310
Diversions constructed (kilometres)	–	1	3	4	8

Source: ERREC, 1996.

While the first years after Independence were a transitional period for agriculture when the main consideration was to meet the immediate needs of the population (also through food aid), by the mid-1990s it had become clear that key areas should be given priority. An example of this is the rehabilitation of agriculture in the highland Debub Zone, where the target group is some 50,000 rural households and the main activities envisaged are cropland and non-cropland terracing, oxen restocking, supplying water

Table 5.22

Expenditure on FFW, CFW and free-distribution projects for soil and water conservation, 1995*(in thousands of birr)*

Province	FFW	CFW	Free Distribution
Asmara	635	–	160
Hamasien	5,126	–	139
Seraye	7,525	–	2,364
Akeleguzay	8,900	–	1,225
Semhar	3,436	–	3,776
Senhit	4,653	–	1,552
Sahel	2,503	–	3,293
Denkel	–	–	7,739
Gash-Setit	2,185	–	1,152
Barka	420	–	2,079
Other (Mitias, ERRA)	–	–	21,995
Monetized	–	29,379	–
National Service	18,381	–	–
Total	53,764	29,379	45,474
Percentage	42	23	35

Source: ERREC, 1996.

pumps and training farmers. This programme is a regionalized extension of the national-level ARP.

Clearly, an important part of the ARP was dedicated to conserving natural resources. FFW and CFW projects was used to protect water, soil, vegetation and forest resources, to construct feeder roads, wells and small dams, and to improve local food production through techniques such as cropland terracing. Table 5.21 summarizes the soil and water conservation activities carried out in both cropland and non-cropland areas. Terracing activities are most common in the highland provinces, where soil erosion is greatest. However, there is some terracing in the lowland provinces to prevent soil loss in vulnerable areas.

The introduction of monetization activities in soil and water conservation programmes is shown in Table 5.22. Highland provinces receive the highest amounts distributed because of their larger population and greater need to supplement food. National expenditure on soil and water conservation activities shows that the largest amount, 42 per cent, has been spent on FFW. CFW took up some 23 per cent, while 35 per cent consisted of free distribution.

THE ROLE OF DEVELOPMENT PARTNERS IN FOOD AND AGRICULTURAL ACTIVITIES

A number of development agencies have participated in rehabilitating the country's agriculture and efforts to ensure food security for the population. They include international and local NGOs, multilateral and bilateral agencies. The range of activities they have supported is wide, but the emphasis is on providing agricultural inputs, including livestock and veterinary services, water conservation and irrigation, crop production and horticulture, as well as the construction of schools and clinics. The agencies are concerned with food distribution to vulnerable groups – as well as FFW (now CFW) to vulnerable and targeted groups – and for activities of a developmental nature.

Important programmes and projects in the final stages of negotiation in 1995 are listed in Table 5.23. Most of them are of a bilateral or multilateral nature. They include activities such as establishing brick-making and ginning plants, irrigation development, marketing and providing credit, training in agricultural sciences, cereal and tree seed development, milk and feed legislation, and soil and water conservation.

Table 5.23
Donor involvement in recent projects

Project/Programme (duration)	Category	Donor	Components
Ali-Ghider Expansion Project (1996)	Bilateral Multilateral	Danida UNDP	Briquetting plant; establishment of ginning plant, acid delinting and seed cond.
Central Highlands Production (–)	Multilateral (on soft loan)	African Development Bank (ADB)	Irrigation and agricultural development, marketing and credit development
Institutional Capacity Building (1995–1999)	Bilateral	NORAD	Training for BSc, MSc
Institutional Support to Soil and Water Conservation (1995–1999)	Bilateral	NORAD	Office equipment
Environmental Information Centre (1995–1999)	Bilateral	NORAD	Training and equipment
Integrated Watershed Development Project (1996–2000)	Bilateral	Danida	Soil and water conservation
Dairy Development (1996–2000)	Bilateral	Danida	Milk legislation research, education, training, feed legislation
National Seed Development (1996–2000)	Bilateral	Danida	Cereal seed development
National Tree Seed Development (1996–2000)	Bilateral	Danida	Tree seed development
Water Resources and Irrigation Potential Study (1997–1998)	Multilateral	European Commission	Study
Soil and Afforestation Project (1996)	Multilateral	European Commission	Construction of soil conservation structure

Source: Ministry of Agriculture, 1996.

Assessment of Agricultural Potential, Policies and Programmes

It is generally agreed that Eritrea's main asset is first and foremost its hardworking and resourceful population, but there are a number of other important assets, including existing and potential agriculture in the eastern and western lowlands, in the fertile Hazemo plains, and in the pulse-growing central highland areas, and the increasing number of livestock in the Barka and Bash plains. There is also the possibility of growing horticultural crops almost everywhere in the country and of expanding intensive dairy, poultry, pig and apicultural farms, as well as floriculture, all of which can be tailored to meet domestic demand and earn foreign exchange.

However, the deterioration of the agricultural infrastructure has been a major obstacle. For example, it has prevented the development of rural enterprises as sources of income that would increase people's purchasing power. It would not be wise to rely solely on agriculture. Rural diversification should be diversified to increase opportunities for off-farm employment. Small-scale manufacturing, agricultural input, and output marketing and processing are key elements in building a more dynamic and integrated rural economy. The labour market needs to prevent people from being trapped in low-productivity employment when there are better opportunities elsewhere.

Eritrea's semi-arid climate and unreliable rainfall could lead development planners to conclude that rain-fed agriculture is not economically viable. But this would be a short-sighted view, over-emphasizing difficulties due to drought. The focus should not be on water scarcity, the resulting stress on plants, salinization and thus land degradation, without considering the possibilities of large-scale irrigation schemes. There should be a thorough investigation of conditions, and proposals for alternative solutions should be formulated. The importance of well-focused and relevant research cannot be over-emphasized. Agricultural extension, especially of the participatory kind, will play a key role in helping to upgrade the skills of the rural population and to increase their agricultural productivity. These are areas where the government must devote the maximum resources possible.

In past years, the first priority of agricultural programmes was to help the population recover from the devastation of war and drought. Even before liberation, programmes and projects were negotiated with potential donors and often targeted toward particular regions. Donor organizations were responsible for implementation. By 1995, it had been decided that implementation should be the responsibility of the respective Eritrean technical institutions, while donors should participate in the financial follow-up and supervision to ensure that funds are spent according to plan, local people were to be identifying priorities and problems, with the relevant ministries or agencies. This policy aimed to prevent development interventions from becoming donor-led and aims to ensure that they correspond to the country's objectives and requirements.

In connection with PROFERI, discussed in Chapter 3 of this volume, a number of problems in the agricultural field emerged, which can be summed up as follows:

1. Land distribution: when land is allocated to one refugee, the original owner asks the local government to reclaim the land. A clear land policy is needed.
2. Land clearing: in cases where land is distributed to refugee farmers, they are expected to clear it jointly before they receive the two hectares per household. But 35-50 per cent of refugee households are headed by women or elderly people who cannot clear the land on their own. As a result, the land area cleared and distributed so far has been only 0.9 and 0.6 hectares per household in Barka and Gash-Setit, respectively.
3. The provision of livestock: animals given to returnees have travelled long distances and are often in poor shape when they arrive. Sometimes there is shortage of water and grazing land, and mortality rates are high. Animals are also sometimes distributed to families that are unable to tend them; therefore, targeting is important.

LOCAL PERCEPTIONS OF FOOD SECURITY ISSUES

In April and May 1996, investigations were carried out in the western lowlands using Participatory Rapid Appraisal (PRA) techniques. The observation sites were in two areas in the Gash-Barka region, near Tessenei and near Barentu, as well as in Gahtelai in the eastern lowlands and Adi Shuma in the central highlands.

Farmers, traders and labourers in the Tessenei area were asked to identify the main issues that needed solving if they were to improve production and living standards. By far the most important problem noted by farmers was land distribution (ranked as such by 40 per cent), followed by need for credit (23 per cent), and lack of materials for house construction (15 per cent), mainly due to deforestation. Other concerns were the need to improve the water supply (for agriculture and domestic consumption), electricity and health services, and extension and training, as well as the high cost of hiring tractors in the area.

For traders, the most important issues were house construction and credit (35 per cent each), followed by need for extension and training (15 per cent), and for improved electricity supply (10 per cent). Water supply and healthcare were also mentioned. As might be expected, the labourers, whose income is very low, ascribe the greatest importance by far to healthcare (50 per cent), followed by house construction (25 per cent), and water supply (20 per cent). They also mention credit, extension and training.

A similar investigation in the Barentu area among farmers, pastoralists and traders revealed a somewhat different set of problems. For the farmers, the biggest constraint was the shortage of oxen (35 per cent), which had resulted in camels or donkeys being used for ploughing, which is slower and less thorough. The lack of cash was next in order of priority (25 per cent), followed by the rainfall problem (20 per cent) and the lack of farm implements and housing (10 per cent). For the pastoralists, the primary problem was the low availability of grazing land (50 per cent), followed by lack of rainfall (30 per cent) and need for cash (20 per cent). Due to lack of cash, pastoralists are often forced to sell some of their herds at very low prices. As for the traders, the need for cash and the need for housing (construction materials) were considered of equal importance (45 per cent), followed by the question of market prices (10 per cent).

In the Gahtelai area, the shortage of water was considered to be the greatest problem by far (80 per cent). Other problems mentioned were lack of oxen (10 per cent), lack of grazing land (seven per cent) and erosion (three per cent).

In the village of Adi Shuma, farmers were also asked to rank the sources of their revenue and to compare the current situation with the past. According to their responses, agriculture provided only 30 per cent of their income, while it used to contribute 60 per cent. Herding, which once provided 30 per cent, now contributed only 10 per cent. The sale of fuel wood, which used to provide 10 per cent of their income, now represented 50 per cent. According to the farmers, the Ministries of Agriculture and Education and the Water Resources Department were active in the area. Nonetheless, the information shows that the deterioration of agricultural production during the war years had levied a heavy toll on the already scant forestry resources, creating serious environmental problems.

COMMERCIAL VERSUS SUBSISTENCE AGRICULTURE

Cash crops allow producers to invest in improved technology or in off-farm investments, broadening their resource base. More fundamentally, they are an important source of income to meet the increasing demands of the cash economy, for example in education, health, clothing and purchase of foodstuffs not grown on the farm. As the enlargement of the cash economy is likely to continue, the importance of cash crops is clearly vital. At the national level increased production of cash crops, some of which can be exported, strengthens the GDP and earns foreign exchange. They are also often used by agro-industries, which helps diversify the economy.

However, cash crops usually require more agricultural inputs (chemicals and labour) than the traditional food crops and therefore represent greater financial investment and risk if harvests are low. They are often less adapted to local conditions and more likely to suffer from drought, pests and disease. Farmers have little experience in growing them, and crop management is still at a very early stage.

By adopting cash cropping, farmers also put themselves at the mercy of markets at the international level (if crops are export-oriented) or at the national level (if crops are for domestic consumption or processing). Price variations are considerable. Prices tend to go down as more producers enter the market, which means that an increasingly large agricultural area is required to generate enough cash to meet basic requirements. Producers become increasingly dependent on the sales of their cash crops merely to survive, while the area for subsistence agriculture is reduced. Returns from cash crops may not cover the cost of inputs needed to produce them, in addition to food required by the family. Market fragmentation and poor transport facilities can lead to artificially depressed prices, further exacerbating the problems.

If the national economy depends too much on primary production through the export of raw materials, it becomes vulnerable to international price variations. Too strong a focus on cash crops at the national level will increase the amount of food that needs to be imported.

Before the introduction of cash crops, the use of locally selected and bred varieties of food crops allowed farmers to meet food security needs reasonably well. This was when there was little need for cash for services such as education, and the overall productivity of the local environment was high. However this situation has changed over time with population increases, resource degradation and an increasingly strong cash economy.

There are still advantages to traditional food crop production. Traditional plant varieties are adapted to local conditions and local dietary preferences. They perform well with low agricultural inputs and are often multipurpose, providing grain, fodder and sometimes housing materials. Improved food crops seek to combine these strengths with greater productivity.

Producing food for home consumption rather than crops for sale reduces the risks of price variations, which are considerable at both regional and even national levels. In addition, the harvest from food crops is more easily available to the women of the household preparing food for the family, giving them greater control over the household's nutrition and diet.

Nevertheless there are a number of disadvantages to traditional agriculture. The need for cash often forces farmers to sell some of their food crops shortly after harvest when prices are low, forcing them to buy food later on, when prices are high. Although traditional food crops are less at risk from environmental hazards, they are still affected. If risk hedging strategies such as successive planting and crop diversification do not succeed, farmers are forced to sell their labour or livestock. Subsistence agriculture does not earn foreign exchange and so does not help reduce the national capacity to augment domestic food production by commercial imports.

In conclusion, cash crop production will make the greatest contribution to improved food security when regional markets are fully integrated and there is sustained demand for a crop from a large section of the population. Proceeds from sales can also be used to improve productivity of both subsistence and commercial agriculture. At the national level, certain high value cash crops can generate foreign exchange earnings which can then be used to fund food imports.

In sum, the contribution of cash crops depends on business capacity and the associated markets and infrastructure. Subsistence production, on the other hand, makes the greatest contribution to food security when markets for cash crops are highly fragmented, thus reducing returns and incentives for production. In small villages, remote from markets and other infrastructure, transport costs will often make cash crop production uneconomic. Therefore traditional and cash crops are important components of any food security programme and their relative importance will above all vary according to locality.

A Note on FFW and CFW

Food aid is provided through both FFW and CFW programmes that benefit communities and individuals through the construction of development structures such as roads and conservation works. These schemes aim at addressing three central issues: food insecurity, high unemployment and poor infrastructure (FAO, 1996b). Besides helping to improve the self-sufficiency of the participating communities in the long term, they also provide a head start in dealing with local food shortages before they become uncontrollable. The schemes are appreciated by the communities because they provide extra income and allow households to stay together rather than being forced off their farms to seek other work. Intra-household income control, which varies between groups, affects the preference for FFW or CFW, with women frequently preferring the former.

Government policy favours CFW for several reasons. It promotes the market economy, fosters growth of a wage economy, reduces local market distortions, and is easier to control and more flexible than FFW. However, women who prefer FFW explain that its value is slightly higher, and there is less chance of the benefit being spent by husbands on non-essential items, such as beer (Immink, 1995). There is, nonetheless, a definite shift toward the CFW programmes, both nationally and regionally, so a solution must be sought for women by involving them more in the programmes so they can exercise control over the resources they earn. Setting the price in the food aid monetization process is fraught with difficulties as it has to consider local prices for food and labour and ensure reasonable equity throughout the nation. This monitoring is done through the Early Warning and Food Information System (EW&FIS), which also gives advance notice of local food shortages so that remedial action can be planned.

The importance of communal projects funded under CFW and FFW depends on the area. In places such as Barka, the lower population means a scarcity of true communal projects which could utilize these programmes. This is also true of other more sparsely populated regions such as Denkel and, to a lesser extent, Sahel and Semhar. In these areas, free food distribution may be justified. Areas with a reasonably high population density, in particular the highland provinces, are more able to generate communal projects, such as tree planting and resource conservation work. Most, if not all development schemes are based on labour-intensive projects. It is more difficult to recruit the minimum number of people required in areas where population densities are low. Here, alternative approaches should be considered – perhaps smaller, more locally conceived projects.

The availability of infrastructure such as roads also helps in the planning of development programmes by expediting the delivery of necessary wages, inputs and materials and allowing participants to have access to such programmes.

Table 5.24 shows the differing importance of cash and food in funding environmental restoration projects in Gash-Barka from 1992 to 1995. CFW programmes started in the region in 1993 and were most important in 1994 (Barka) and 1996 (Gash). The increasing importance of monetized food aid in the form of CFW can be seen in the variations that are responses to regional harvests. In 1995, when the harvest was poor, the number of FFW programmes increased and the amount of monetized food aid decreased, to avoid increasing prices of the scarce food supplies. The figures for the first half of 1996 reflect the poor harvest in Gash in 1995.

Table 5.24
Distribution of food and cash *(birr)* in payment for environmental programmes in Gash and Barka, 1992–1995

	1992	1993	1994	1995	1996*	Total
Barka						
- grains (q)	6,632	1,000	6,817	34,660	65	49,173
- oil (l)	21,457	88,700	23,594	3,709	923	138,383
- pulses (q)	146	187	0	784	3	1,120
- birr	0	316,178	886,435	467,266	251,979	1,921,858
Gash						
- grains (q)	12,656	0	0	4,234	68,496	85,386
- oil (l)	61,726	26,127	580	5,829	119	94,380
- pulses (q)	2	0	0	0	0	2
- birr	0	495,032	99,143	0	543,557	1,137,732

Source: Ministry of Agriculture reports, 1996. Includes IFSP activities
*six months only

Incorporating the lessons of these investigations in new rural development projects would have the advantage that the community recognizes the problem and would therefore probably be eager to participate. Obviously, some of the issues raised do not lend themselves to projects (for example the shortage of rain), but others do – for example the shortage of housing materials often mentioned in such appraisals reflects the impact of deforestation. Discussions with villagers could lead to the setting up of a wood lot, comprising trees and other vegetation. The villagers would need to understand that this would be their wood lot and that they would be responsible for its upkeep as well as owning the products. The local *baito* would need to put together some kind of management plan, specifying the participating beneficiaries and their responsibilities. CFW or wage-based projects should be used for activities that are the village's collective responsibility, not benefiting a few privileged individuals or only a small number of people in the society. If a project is successful and acts as a catalyst for community development, enabling participants to plan and organize work on other important needs, further FFW and CFW efforts may not be needed. The community would have to understand that the FFW and CFW was to be a one-time contribution and would not be available continuously, except in special circumstances.

For reasons of flexibility, pricing, control, supervision and logistics, CFW is preferable to FFW. However, other elements to be considered include the relative financial situation and agricultural activities in a given area. Differences in vulnerability to food deficits can be compared between regions, in terms of whether they rely on a single source of income. Table 5.25 shows the relative significance of farming and livestock and off-farm income in a highland area (Adi Tequila) and a lowland area (Gash-Barka).

The table highlights the vulnerable groups in the two areas, with female-headed households in the highlands being particularly at risk due to low cash income and ownership of fewer animals. In both areas, purely farming households on average generate less annual income than households that supplement farm earnings with waged labour. The greater profitability of farmers in the lowlands is clear when the annual average incomes in the two regions are compared, with greater opportunities in the highlands for off-farm work. Cattle, usually cows, are less important than sheep and goats in the lowlands, which is in marked contrast with highland areas. A large proportion of highland cattle are oxen for cultivation and their large numbers, relative to the lowlands, reflect greater dependence on traditional farming (as opposed to the use of modern tools such as tractors), and greater importance of agro-pastoralism. The number of pack animals is similar in both areas. Income from remittances was not mentioned in the lowland survey group and thus the two areas cannot be compared in this respect.

Table 5.25
Selected farmers' household enterprises, income and average number of animals owned in the Adi Teklai highlands and Gash-Barka lowlands

Area and respondents	Average annual income (nacfa) from cattle	Average number of animals owned*		
		Cattle	Sheep/ goats	Pack animals
Highlands				
9, pure farming	1,346	19 (4)	1 (8)	1 (7)
8, farming/labouring	7,802	15 (3)	1 (7)	2 (7)
2, remittances	3,520	4 (1)	1 (2)	2 (1)
3, female-led households	1,730	2 (2)	2 (2)	2 (2)
17, male-led households	4,384	17 (7)	1 (15)	2 (14)
Lowlands				
13, pure farming	2,413	5 (6)	13 (6)	1 (10)
7, farming/labouring	4,099	0 (0)	6 (5)	1 (5)
20, male-led households	3,003	5 (6)	10 (11)	1 (15)

Source: PRAs conducted in Adi Teklai and Gash-Barka, 1996.
*Brackets indicate number of respondents with animals.

AGRICULTURAL PRODUCTION IN GASH-BARKA

The Gash-Barka region corresponds fairly closely with the provinces of Barka and Gash-Setit, which together form the western lowlands of Eritrea.

The Barka sub-region is located in the far west of the country and consists of plains and rugged mountains, 700-900 metres above sea level. The major soil types are fluvisols (deep, good for crops) and lithosols (shallow, suited to grazing). The annual average temperature exceeds 25 degrees Celsius. The climate is generally hot and dry from October to May, while the wet season usually occurs between June and September. Total average rainfall is 400-500 millimetres, while potential evapo-transpiration is 1,500-2,000 millimetres. However, rainfall distribution is extremely erratic and too unreliable for large-scale, long-term rain-fed crop production. Woodland savannah, bushland and thicket are the major vegetation types in Gash. Barka is predominantly pastoral, although crop production has increased over the last two years. Agricultural land is scarce in the northern, central and south-eastern part of the sub-region, especially as compared with Gash.

The total population of Barka is 206,000. Most of these people belong to the Tigre (Beni-Amer) ethnic group, and are followers of Islam. Land is mostly inherited, with temporary borrowing from friends and relatives being the second most common means of acquisition. Most holdings range from one to three hectares per household, and the vast majority of farmers practise traditional dry land techniques.

The Gash-Setit sub-region lies in south-western Eritrea, bordering on Sudan and Ethiopia, and consists mostly of flat to undulating plains and gentle slopes. In the northern and central part of Gash, the main soil types are cambisols, fluvisols and lithosols. Vertisols (deep and fertile) and cambisols dominate the sides of the Gash river in south-eastern and eastern Gash, but there are also fluvisols in these areas. Gash has a steppe climate, with an annual average temperature of 25-27 degrees Celsius. Annual average rainfall is 300-400 millimetres. Rain is more plentiful and regular in south-western Gash than in Barka, making Gash more suitable for crop production. The chance of drought is from one to three years every ten years. The sub-region's vegetation includes trees, shrubs and grasses.

There is a population of approximately 228,000 in the sub-region, composed of three main ethnic groups: Kunama, Nara and Beni-Amer. These groups have different languages and religions and differ in the extent to which they depend on crops and livestock. Women's roles vary. Unlike in Barka, there is little problem in obtaining access to cultivable land, which is usually inherited. The major constraint on agricultural expansion is the shortage of labour and traction power.

A crucial factor for the whole region is the availability of water. Ground-water resources are as yet unmapped. As for surface water, it is concentrated in three major river basins: Tekese-Setit, Mereb-Gash and Barka-Anseba. Only Setit is relatively permanent (depending on rainfall). The others generate spate flows from July to September. These rivers are the main sources of surface water for irrigation. Their flow rates, seasonality, and high sediment loads must be considered in development plans.

Legacies of the war

Thirty years of warfare have left their mark on the Gash-Barka region. This is reflected not only in the sufferings of the local population but also in the damage done to infrastructure. For example the hospital at Agordat was severely damaged by frequent air raids, while hospitals at Tessenei and Barentu were ruined and need to be completely reconstructed. Gash province, in particular, was a battlefield for many years.

Agriculture was also seriously affected. Large-scale commercial farms that produced horticultural and oilseed crops were abandoned and much of the land left uncultivated due to the lack of draught animals and the presence of mines. The Ali-Ghider cotton estate near Tessenei was one of the most important holdings, but its productive capacity deteriorated considerably when the Ethiopian Derg came to power and it was nationalized.

Since Independence there have been concentrated efforts to rehabilitate the remaining estates and encourage expansion of concessions in appropriate areas, but rehabilitation will take time and require a lot of capital.

As for the pastoral communities, they have lost large numbers of stock due to warfare and recurring drought.

Land-use systems and agricultural production

As we have seen, agriculture is important in Gash, where conditions are conducive to continuous crop production. Agriculture as a system entirely separate from pastoralism is less common, although with the expansion of concessions and the associated horticultural enterprises this is set to change.

Horticulture is mostly practised by farmers in the river basins. Water is lifted from deep, hand-dug wells or even bore-holes using the shadoof or, increasingly, diesel pumps. The major crops are bananas, onions and tomatoes. Other produce includes beans, chick peas, watermelons, lettuce, red peppers, cabbage and okra. Vegetable planting normally takes place in June; they are weeded in July and August and usually harvested in September. There is considerable use of fertilizers by commercial farmers in the irrigated area, but crop production is limited by a shortage of early-maturing seed of good quality.

Table 5.26 shows the fruit and vegetable concessions in Gash-Barka between January 1992 and December 1995. The old concessions are all irrigated and they produce horticultural crops. There are 211 new concessions that are irrigated, and 38 rain-fed. Most of the former concentrate on horticulture, with livestock also being important, while the latter are exclusively produce crops. The number of new concessions has been greatest in central Barka and near Tessenei in Gash – areas considered most suitable for commercial agriculture. There has been a fairly consistent increase in the area under concession in the two sub-regions, although Gash has maintained its dominant position.

Table 5.26 Fruit and vegetable concessions in Gash-Barka, 1992–1995				
Province and sub-province	**New concessions**		**Old concessions**	
	Investors	**Area** *(ha)*	**Investors**	**Area** *(ha)*
Barka				
- Central Barka	56	1,824.71	26	595.92
- Upper Barka	14	218	4	37.27
- Western Barka	10	69	–	–
Total	80	2,111.17	30	633.19
Gash-Setit				
- Upper Gash	33	1,415.68	3	151.00
- Omhager	6	32.50	2	13.00
- Tessenei	130	1,558.65	25	543.61
Total	169	3,006.83	30	707.61
Regional Total	249	5,118.00	60	1,340.80

Source: Ministry of Agriculture reports, 1996.

These concessions tend to produce a too-limited variety of products, leading to a regional over-supply of produce such as tomatoes, onions and bananas. The trend is likely to increase as new concessions are started up and there is a clear need to encourage the diversification of production.

In national terms, the concessions (both old and new) constitute 43 per cent of the total land allocated to old concessions and 30 per cent of the total number of applicants. Irrigated agriculture is important in both Gash (14 per cent of national irrigated area) and Barka (18 per cent of national irrigated area), while rain-fed agricultural concessions are most prevalent in Barka (26 per cent of the national total).

Dairy production is uncommon in both Gash and Barka (3 per cent and 2 per cent respectively of national total), which reflects the small urban population and the resulting low demand for milk and milk products. This is a potentially valuable niche of the market in the areas around the growing urban centres in the region, but it will need careful planning. The pastoral livestock production system has to be studied, and demand-driven dairy development schemes established.

The improvement of infrastructure, especially road networks to local markets such as Tessenei and Barentu, will no doubt have a direct impact on the expansion of these production systems. In addition, the development of a good road system to join the areas of production in the western lowlands with major markets (Asmara, Keren, Massawa) and with agro-industry will be needed if the full benefits of the agricultural concessions are to be realized.

The agricultural potential of Gash-Barka has been recognized internationally – two-thirds of foreign investors have applied for concessions in this region. It also has a higher proportion of company concessions, which reflects the greater average area and capital required. The size of these concessions could help them break into the international markets if appropriate crops and techniques are used and the necessary infrastructure carried out.

As for the system of mixed farming, the emphasis is heavily on cropping with animals being important for traction, transport and haulage, dairy products for home consumption and sale, and cash from sales. Although there is no seasonal shifting of homesteads, dry herds are often forced to migrate to better pastures in southern and eastern Gash, as in the agro-pastoral system, and the cropping practices are also similar. Mixed farming tends to be practised by the Nara and Kunama people, together with some of the Tigrinya-speaking population who live in the lowlands.

Sedentary livestock production is practised around large towns of the region and consists of Zebu and some Barka milking cattle. They graze the cattle on their own pastures during the rainy season. Later this is supplemented with crop residues, green forage and oilseed cakes. The milk is then sold on the urban market, but demand invariably exceeds supply. Those practising mixed farming usually do not cultivate land, as they rely entirely on local pastures and purchased feeds.

Agro-pastoralism is a mobile system characterized by short-distance transhumance of the family homestead and long-distance movement of dry herds. The household usually moves between wet and dry season camps, which are estimated to be located 5-10 kilometres apart. The wet season camp is located away from the riverine areas because of biting insects such as mosquitoes that cause malaria. During this season people farm crops, waiting until they are ripe before moving. The dry season camp is closer to the river to allow easier access to water.

Most adult males go with their herds in search of pasture during the dry season, often to areas in Gash but sometimes as far as Sudan and Ethiopia. The sheep and goats tend to stay with the household. This is a highly efficient way of coping with the arid ecosystem. The relative importance of livestock and crops varies among groups and depends on the number of cattle possessed. The Beni-Amer people, particularly in northern and central Gash-Barka, aim to return to pastoralism and work more toward increasing herd size than cultivating farmland.

Pastoralism involves the long-distance migration of cattle. Only a minority are pure pastoralists and they are concentrated mainly in northern Barka. Their numbers have declined in recent years because of war and drought. Pastoralists are heavily dependent on animal products for food. A 1994 FAO report estimated that people in lowland agro-pastoral and pastoral communities consume an average of one litre of milk per day, mostly goat milk. For households that rely wholly on livestock, the minimum number of small ruminants is 40 (Nauheimer, 1995). Below this number, losses caused by disease, rate of production and consumption exceed gains from production. Due to their slower reproductive rate, cattle and camels take longer to recover from losses than small ruminant flocks. This is a major cause of the declining number of pastoralists. When there is not enough livestock to sustain a pastoral lifestyle, the population often shifts to agro-pastoral production.

THE FOOD SECURITY SITUATION IN GASH-BARKA

Field investigations were carried out in different parts of the Gash-Barka region during a six day period in 1996 to sound out the views of people in four areas chosen as representative of the region. These areas were around Agordat, Barentu, Tessenei and Shambuco.

Main constraints on food security

The problem-ranking method of PRA was used in all four areas to discover the main constraints on current food security. After the problems were identified, farmers from around Agordat (5), Barentu (4), Tessenei (7) and Shambuco (5) participated in the investigation. Each farmer used 10 pebbles to rank each problem according to its gravity, and the results are shown in Table 5.27. It indicates that each area suffers from different constraints in achieving food security. Rain and pests are the only problems receiving common mention in three of the four areas. Indeed they are generally recognized as being the major obstacles to increased crop production in the region. But a number of more localized issues were mentioned.

Table 5.27					
Ranking of current constraints on food security in Gash-Barka					

Problem	Around Agordat	Around Barentu	Around Tessenei	Around Shambuco
Shortage of rain	6%	–	40%	42%
Poverty	–	–	–	12%
Shortage of farm tools, oxen and camels	–	32%	–	26%
Markets	66%	–	–	–
Shortage of seed	–	–	4%	–
Shortage of work opportunities	–	22%	–	–
High taxes	14%	–	–	–
Pests	–	18%	32%	12%
Health	–	8%	–	–
Low-cost of labour	4%	–	–	–
No tractor service	–	–	44%	–
Grazing area	10%	–	–	8%

Source: PRA conducted in Gash-Barka, 1996.

As shown in Table 5.28, respondents depended mainly on farming and livestock breeding for their income before the war. However, they were forced to diversify into new off-farm activities to cope with drought and famine. As far as their livelihood was concerned, the four areas were quite different before Independence. Around Agordat most respondents were pastoralists, while the majority are now settled farmers. Around Barentu there were a significant number of pastoralists as well as farmers, but now there are no pastoralists, fewer farmers and more labourers. In contrast, around Tessenei agriculture was the main occupation before the war and remains so today. And in Shambuco most people were pastoralists before the conflict as well as afterward – in fact their numbers have increased since the war ended.

Table 5.28
Livelihoods before and after the conflict
in four areas of Gash-Barka

Livelihood	Agordat	Barentu	Tessenei	Shambuco	Average
Farming pre-conflict post-conflict	15 75	70 55	95 85	70 90	63 76
Trading pre-conflict post-conflict	7 5	– 5	– 10	– –	2 5
Livestock breeding pre-conflict post-conflict	75 –	30 –	55 –	30 10	48 3
Labouring pre-conflict post-conflict	3 15	– 40	– 5	– –	1 15

Source: PRA conducted in Gash-Barka, 1996.

The farmers around Agordat felt that the major problem was a lack of effective demand. Many of them produce bananas, onions and tomatoes under irrigation, but the local markets are underdeveloped while the purchasing power of the local merchants is low. The only good market is in Asmara and the travel over rough roads to get there affects the quality of the produce. Competition from products imported from Sudan also affects the local market because the cost of labour and fuel there is relatively low. The second serious problem is taxation, which is considered high, especially for those with banana, onion and other horticultural enterprises. Also, land available for grazing is decreasing as agricultural areas are developed. Rain shortage was mentioned too, but the farmers regarded this as an uncontrollable phenomenon.

In the Barentu area the chief constraint was a lack of oxen and camels. Some farmers were forced to leave their plots unploughed because of the shortage of draught animals. The second most important problem was a general lack of work opportunities so that they could diversify their income. Pests were considered a serious constraint on crop production and were ranked third. The lack of healthcare facilities and clinics in the area was mentioned as influencing production by not ensuring good health, but this was seen as less important than the other issues raised. Shortage of food was also noted among the farm households during research in July 1996.

The three main problems of farmers around Tessenei were lack of tractor services, rain shortage and pests. Tractors seem to be replacing draught animals in this area, as no mention was made of a shortage of oxen or camels. Some farmers do not have money to buy seed, but this is generally considered less important than the other issues.

In Shambuco, lack of rain was mentioned as the most serious constraint on food security, followed by shortage of draught animals and farming tools, and pest infestation. Poverty was mentioned by some participants as contributing to food insecurity, as well as the reduction of grazing land due to agricultural expansion.

Contribution of current programmes to food security

The respondents were then asked about current rehabilitation programmes or projects in terms of their contribution to food security.

In Agordat, the respondents were operating irrigated farms. They felt that training was important in upgrading farmer skills, but only a few had participated, which limited its impact on general food security. The government credit service was considered very important as it allowed them to buy tractors, motor pumps and other items, while machinery services, such as tractors, were not felt to be contributing much to food security in the area. The bulldozer hiring service was considered very expensive.

As for the farmers around Barentu, the impact of the soil and water conservation project had lasted only a few months, so it was not rated important by participants. Conversely, in their view, building a school would play a great role in improving future food security as education would allow their children to seek employment in new fields. The construction of administrative offices was highly ranked because participants thought it would provide a channel for their concerns to pass to regional and national bodies. Well construction was considered very important because of the drinking water problem. However, seed provision and animal vaccination contributed to food security for only one year and was then discontinued.

The government tractor services in the Tessenei area constitute the one project relevant to people involved only in farming. However, this was ranked third out of four because of its high cost: 110 birr per hour for a four-disc plough, and 149 birr per hour for a 24-28-disc harrow.

Some 120 households in Shambuco had received animals. The numbers provided were sufficient for households to start farming and livestock breeding and so had great significance for food security. Seed, by contrast, was given to only a few farmers and so was not ranked. The Ministry of Agriculture tractor services are available to most in principle but there are few tractors, so the overall impact of this service was low. Only the returnees in the region were provided with farm tools, so the contribution of this programme to food security was low, as was the provision of credit. There were only about 11 beneficiaries in the region. The FFW and CFW programmes were very highly ranked, as they supplemented the income and production of most farmers, especially in the previous year when low rainfall resulted in poor harvests.

FFW and CFW were not mentioned in the other regions as neither programme was operational at the time of the visit. It was the transition period when FFW was being transformed into CFW and there were complaints about delays.

Demand and supply, 1993–1996

A merchant from Agordat was interviewed during the survey on crop prices from 1993 to 1996. He said that crop prices varied from month to month and even week to week. The overall average prices (birr per kilogram) cited are indicated in Table 5.29.

In the year after liberation, considerable amounts of food aid, mostly in the form of wheat, were brought into the area and brought prices down. When food aid supplies decreased, the price of wheat in the market began to rise. Finally, when the supply of food aid almost halted in 1995/1996, the price of wheat rose even more sharply. The price of other crops also went up because demand was growing.

The main grain supply areas for merchants in the region are Humera, Gondar, Guluj, Tessenei and Tokombia. Food grain consumption is very high as most of the population depends on trade for their living. Every day, four to five trucks supply the merchants and 50-100 camel loads are bought by the people living around Agordat.

Table 5.29 Grain prices in Agordat, 1993-1996 *(in birr per kilogram)*			
Crop	Crop prices each year		
	1993–1994	1994–1995	1995–1996
Wheat	.75	1.25	3.00
Sorghum	.75	1.00	2.00
Millet	1.25	1.25	3.50

Source: PRA conducted in Gash-Barka, 1996.

The Eritrean Grain Board (EGB) later supplied crops to the people at the rate of about 2,000 quintals every three days. The EGB price was 140 birr per quintal, while in the market it was 200 birr per quintal. All the grain supplied by the EGB was naturally bought very quickly, within three days. The merchant interviewed complained that the EGB had destabilized the pricing systems, but this accusation proved to be false. On the contrary, it appeared that the board's activities in the area had stabilized prices and prevented people from being exploited by local merchants.

Table 5.30 shows the increase in crop prices over three years. In Agordat and Tessenei prices increased annually, while in Barentu prices rose only in 1995, perhaps due to greater market integration or better production in the first two years. The provision of wheat from food aid affected grain prices in all areas, particularly the price of sorghum and would have had considerable impact on the income of local farmers in these years. Sorghum is more widely sold by farmers, compared with millet, which would account for the generally lower prices fetched in the markets.

Table 5.30
Prices of crops in three areas of the region,
1993-1995 *(in birr per kilogram)*

Area		Wheat	Sorghum	Millet
Agordat	1993	0.75	0.75	1.25
	1994	1.25	1.00	1.25
	1995	3.00	2.00	3.50
Tessenei	1993	0.75	0.75	1.00
	1994	1.75	1.25	1.50
	1995	2.75	2.50	2.75
Barentu	1993	0.50	0.50	0.50
	1994	0.50	0.75	0.75
	1995	–	2.50	3.00

Source: PRA conducted in Gash-Barka, 1996.

The prices of some household commodities in three markets in the area are shown in Table 5.31. As shown, the prices of consumer goods are the same in most markets. It is difficult to account for this without knowing the exact sources of such commodities. For example, if coffee comes from Ethiopia, it is expected to have an incremental price of at least transport costs from Asmara to Tessenei, yet the price of coffee in all markets is the same. This question merits further study.

The items in Table 5.31 are purchased with revenue from crop and livestock sales. In poor seasons, when crop surpluses are low, farmers without harvests are forced to sell assets such as livestock to procure basic food stuffs and the items indicated in the above table. Household budgets are adjusted accordingly. Barter is decreasing as the cash economy becomes more important, which in turn increases the dependence of farmers on cash crop production, be it food crop surplus or just cash crops.

Table 5.31 Prices of various household commodities, 1996 *(in birr per kilogram)*			
Commodity	Agordat	Barentu	Tessenei
Coffee	24.00	24.00	24.00
Sugar	5.00	5.00	5.00
Soap (one bar)	1.25	1.25	1.25
Food oil (litre)	10.00	10.00	10.00
Kerosene	1.30	1.50	1.60
Salt	1.00	1.00	1.00
Red pepper	13.00	14.00	15.00

Source: PRA conducted in Gash-Barka, 1996.

Table 5.32 shows the range of prices for horticultural products in the three major markets. While it does not show price trends over time, it does indicate how low prices can get. Making a living when prices drop becomes very difficult. As agriculture and horticulture expand in the region, this problem will become more acute unless some way can be found to develop markets for increased production.

Table 5.32 Prices of horticultural products, 1996 *(in birr per kilogram)*			
Horticultural products	Agordat	Tessenei	Barentu
Tomato	0.50–5.00	1.00–6.00	1.00–7.00
Potato	2.50–3.00	2.00–3.00	2.00–3.00
Banana	0.40–1.50	1.50–2.50	1.00–2.00
Onion	1.00–2.50	1.50–2.50	1.00–5.00
Cabbage	1.00–2.00	1.50–2.00	–

Source: PRA conducted in Gash-Barka, 1996.

Origins of market supplies

In the Agordat market, millet is from Guluj, while sorghum is mainly from Guluj and Gondar (Ethiopia) through Humera. Potatoes are from Asmara, while tomatoes, bananas and onions come from the nearby plantations. Prices are low when these products are harvested. Onions are also smuggled in from Sudan, while wheat derives from the food aid supplied as FFW or CFW.

Sorghum and millet in the Barentu market come mostly from the surrounding areas, while wheat is supplied by food aid and FFW and CFW programmes. Onions and bananas originate from Tessenei and Kassala (Sudan), while potatoes, tomatoes and cabbages are from Asmara.

In Tessenei, sorghum comes mainly from Kassala in Sudan, Gonder, Guluj and surrounding areas in Ethiopia, while millet comes from local areas. Bananas are supplied only from Tessenei, onions from Kassala and surrounding areas, but tomatoes are mainly from Sudan.

Crops

Sorghum is by far the most important of the food crops grown for local consumption. It is grown in large areas in both Gash and Barka, which results in low prices at harvest time. However, it is reasonably productive and useful in the household. The highest yields (12 quintals per hectare) are obtained in the irrigated areas in south-eastern and eastern Gash.

Pearl millet is the second most important food crop. It has a lower yield than sorghum but a shorter growing season, so it is harvested earlier and provides food during the "hungry season", before the sorghum crop is ripe. It is considered more drought-resistant than sorghum and so acts as a kind of insurance against dry years. However, it is popular among birds and requires labour close to harvest-time to prevent substantial losses. The highest yields of pearl millet (seven quintals per hectare) are obtained in the flood flat areas in south-east and eastern Gash, and also in the bed of the Barka river.

Maize as a food crop is grown in some seasons in Gash and eaten while green, serving a similar purpose as pearl millet. It requires more water than either sorghum or pearl millet and is thus not grown in the drier areas of Barka. It is of very minor regional importance.

Cash crops were never very important in the area. Farmers used to plant traditional food crops on their larger fields and if they did any cash crop production it was carried out on the smaller fields. But now sesame is the major cash crop in the region. It is expanding, both in area cultivated and amount produced. Yields are greatest (six quintals per hectare) in the flat and fertile areas in south-eastern and eastern Gash. However, it is a crop that is relatively labour-intensive – mainly in weeding and harvesting – and this is often a constraining factor. Farmers report little local demand for groundnuts, therefore prices are poor and so are the yields, so that less land is now being put under this crop.

Table 5.33 shows the area, production and yield of the crops grown in the Gash-Barka region from 1992 to 1995. The national average yield is included for comparison. As can be seen, the yields of both sorghum and pearl millet are substantially higher in Gash than in Barka (and than the national average) and they are both greater than in the highland regions due to greater soil fertility (particularly in vertisols), less long-term soil erosion (though this is starting to become a serious problem in some vertisol plains) and greater integration of livestock and cropping – although there is still room for improvement here. There is more use of manure in the lowlands, usually by pasturing livestock on the fields, rather than active collection and spreading. Fuel shortages in the highlands force farmers to use animal dung for fuel instead of fertilizer, thus further impoverishing the soil.

Table 5.33

Area, production and yield of crops in Barka and Gash, 1992–1995

(production in tons; area in hectares; yield in tons per hectare)

Crop	Barka				Gash			
	1992	1993	1994	1995	1992	1993	1994	1995
Maize production	–	–	–	–	1,200	40	550	–
area	–	–	–	–	1,000	200	500	–
yield	–	–	–	–	1.20	0.20	1.10	–
National avg. yield	–	–	–	–	0.69	0.23	0.77	0.34
Pearl millet production	3,600	140	11,340	3,285.1	20,700	1,400	16,640	3,624.2
area	5,200	13,000	18,900	22,146	23,000	4,500	20,800	9.906
yield	0.69	0.01	0.60	0.15	0.90	0.31	0.80	0.37
National avg. yield	0.80	0.12	0.70	0.19	0.80	0.12	0.70	0.19
Sorghum production	11,700	160	28,880	12,365.8	64,800	15,700	32,040	32,739.8
area	9,800	16,300	36,100	35,942	48,000	37,400	26,700	43,166
yield	1.19	0.01	0.80	0.34	1.35	0.42	1.20	0.76
National avg. yield	1.06	0.32	0.90	0.47	1.06	0.32	0.90	0.47
Groundnuts production	100	0	300	–	–	–	–	–
area	200	200	500	–	–	–	–	–
yield	0.50	0	0.60	–	–	–	–	–
National avg. yield	0.50	0.67	0.63	0.29	–	–	–	–
Sesame production	400	0	780	101.6	3,600	5,900	4,930	10,719.1
area	800	3,100	2,600	2,402	8,000	29,500	14,100	23,264
yield	0.50	0	0.30	0.04	0.45	0.20	0.35	0.46
National avg. yield	0.45	0.18	0.34	0.42	0.45	0.18	0.34	0.42

Source: *derived from Ministry of Agriculture reports, 1996.*

It is also interesting to note the increasing importance of cash crops (oilseed) in Gash, but not in Barka. Sesame, for example took up 10 per cent of the total cropped area in 1992 and rose to 30 per cent by 1995. However the total area planted with oilseed in Barka was 6 per cent in 1992 and went down to 4 per cent in 1995.

The crop varieties grown in the Gash-Barka region are local selections bred by farmers over centuries. As such, they are well adapted to the harsh climatic conditions often found in the region and their production during poor years would exceed that of many improved varieties, bBut yields are still low and variable. They could be improved by better management (pest control, more fallowing and crop rotation, greater application of farmyard manure), the introduction of improved varieties, more modern inputs such as chemical fertilizer, and greater use of irrigation.

The most effective intervention would be better management, where only minor changes are needed and the farmers recognize their value. The introduction of new varieties is more uncertain and long-term – they would have to be similar in taste and utility to the existing ones, as well as have higher yield and be more drought and pest resistant. This improved performance would have to be sustained under the traditional low input system for some years before farmers would be prepared to commit themselves to risky investment in chemical fertilizers. In the Green Revolution, small farmers who invested in the new and improved varieties often found themselves worse off because they could not afford the agro-chemical and other packaged inputs that the crops needed to achieve their high yields. Very often these new varieties performed worse in low-input systems than the traditional ones and their purchase price raised total cost with no improvement in performance. An agricultural policy that leads to tenant eviction would result in increased food insecurity.

Table 5.34 illustrates the national contribution of Gash-Barka in terms of area under crop cultivation and production from 1992 to 1995. Clearly the region is the major area for sesame, producing 92-100 per cent of the national crop. Gash is also a very important source of pearl millet (32-66 per cent) and sorghum (27-54 per cent) in most years. Pests and rainfall have a greater impact on yields in Barka than in Gash, as can be seen from the much greater disparity between area sown and amount produced.

Table 5.34
Production and area in Gash and Barka, 1992–1995
(shown as percentage of national crop)

	Gash				Barka			
Crop	1992	1993	1994	1995	1992	1993	1994	1995
Maize								
production	7	1	3	0	0	0	0	0
area	4	1	2	0	0	0	0	0
Pearl millet								
production	66	32	41	39	12	3	28	35
area	59	13	36	20	13	37	33	45
Sorghum								
production	49	35	27	54	9	0	24	20
area	38	27	20	33	8	12	28	28
Groundnuts								
production	0	0	0	0	25	0	20	0
area	0	0	0	0	25	4	21	0
Sesame								
production	90	99	79	99	10	0	13	1
area	91	90	77	90	9	9	14	9

Source: derived from Ministry of Agriculture reports, 1996.

The region's production per head of rural population in 1992 is shown in Table 5.35, with national figures given for comparison. The 1992 season was a good year throughout the country and reflects the potential from the system but, as annual subsistence needs are estimated at 145 kilograms per person, national production does not meet demand even in a good year. The relatively low production from Barka underestimates food security as it does not take into account the large contribution made by animal products to the regional diet (mainly milk and dairy products).

Table 5.35 Total crop production, 1992 *(cereal, pulses and oilseed)*			
	Gash-Setit	**Barka**	**National**
Production *(tons)*	90,300	15,800	262,400
Area *(hectares)*	80,000	16,000	327,200
Rural population	189,526	140,702	1,560,176
Production per rural person *(kilograms)*	476	112	168

Source: *Ministry of Agriculture reports, 1995.*

Constraints on crop production

Although the average size of farms is considerably larger in the lowlands than in the highlands, there are many farmers with no more than one hectare, which is not enough to produce sufficient food for the family in an average or poor year. Very often, this small farm size is linked to a shortage of draught animals. In areas where there is no shortage of land, the issue could be solved through land distribution, but in other areas there is need to increase crop productivity or introduce alternative crops.

Rainfall is seen an important constraint, although ranked below the shortage of draught animals, possibly because it is more difficult to solve the former than the latter. While rainfall affects farmers and their crop production, it only affects livestock marginally, when agro-pastoralists are forced to move earlier and to different areas. However, because of the tremendous reduction in livestock, agro-pastoralists have become more dependent on crop production and therefore more vulnerable to the vagaries of the climate than they were traditionally.

Pests, as mentioned in relation to individual crops, are ranked as one of the chief constraints. Tree and desert locusts are the most destructive, while birds and army worms are a menace to certain crops. Lack of control measures resulted in some crops being entirely wiped out by locusts in 1993 (in both provinces) and 1995 (in Barka).

In terms of risk, farmers consider it better to concentrate on food staples, rather than producing low-yielding, market-price dependent oilseed. This would have to be taken into consideration in designing systems to increase cash crop production.

Mention has been made several times of the shortage of draught animals in the region, as it is one of the major causes of restricted agricultural production in the region. It is a particular problem in south-eastern and eastern Gash. The preference tends to be for camels, which are better suited to the arid environment and are also multipurpose, being used for transport and as pack animals. There is the possibility of promoting the use of donkeys – they are much less efficient than camels or oxen, but better than no draught animals at all.

LIVESTOCK

The lowlands have a high percentage of breeding stock compared to draught animals, with oxen constituting only 12 per cent of the region's cattle. Milk from the breeding herd makes a major contribution to agro-pastoral and pastoral diets. Cow milk is generally available only in the wet season, but goat and camel milk is used in other seasons. This concentration on breeding stock enables livestock populations to recover quickly from disease and drought. However, it also restricts the number of animals suitable for traction and so the area of land that can be prepared for crops.

Table 5.36 shows the number of different types of livestock in the region and at the national level in 1994. There is not a significant amount of poultry in the region – some ducks and chickens are kept in Gash but statistics are not available (Schwartz, 1994).

The table shows the region's dominance in national livestock population. It contains almost 60 per cent of cattle, 40 per cent of camels and over 70 per cent of sheep and goats (mostly goats). The average household livestock holding is around 12 TLUs in eastern Barka and five in eastern Gash, as compared with the national average, which was 4 TLUs per rural household in 1992 (FAO, 1994). These numbers indicate heavy reliance on livestock, especially when the proportion of agriculture in the region is considered (see Crops, above). However, there is an increasing amount of land under cultivation, which is reflected in the total area under crops and the number and area of concessions in the region.

Barka is the main breed of cattle favoured in the region. It has high milk production (five to six litres per day), is relatively resistant to disease and has a high feed conversion rate, with good meat production. The preferred breeds of sheep are Hamele (large with long tails), mostly exported to the Middle East, and Sawakin, which comes from Sudan andis used for meat. The main breeds of goat are Barka, with a milk yield of

1-1.5 litres per day, and Lange, found mostly in Gash-Setit and used mainly for milk.

Table 5.36			
Livestock population in the Gash-Barka regionand at the national level			
Livestock	Gash-Barka region	Percentage of national total	National total
Sheep/goats	1,689,888	71	2,395,926
Cattle	384,610	58	668,102
Camels	271,162	92	293,918
Donkeys	52,428	38	138,585

Source: Ministry of Agriculture report, 1995.

Constraints on livestock production

Water shortages are a big problem in Barka and are one reason why pastoralists migrate in the dry season. There is an over-concentration of stock around the few water points, leading to degradation and overgrazing.

Another major problem is the lack of feed; agro-pastoralism and pastoralism rely heavily, if not solely, on range grazing. Feed availability interacts with disease. As there is little to be done to improve feed in the more arid areas, the main focus is on disease prevention. In most of the region, there is a prolonged dry period (October to July) when feed is scarce. Even when available, quality is low and does not permit high production levels (Schwartz, 1994).

The expansion of agricultural land also creates difficulties for pastoralists and their animals. Horticultural concessions have to some extent curtailed the productivity of agro-pastoral livestock, as they are usually in riverine areas which have traditionally been used during the dry season. Traditional dry season camps in northern Ethiopia are also becoming less accessible because of threats from gangs of bandits. Herders are forced to seek alternative and less attractive solutions; they are becoming more vulnerable to seasonal changes.

As for disease, the main threats to animal health are internal andexternal parasites, especially the latter. Trypanosomiasis is rife in south-eastern and eastern Gash (FAO, 1995) and livestock is also exposed to diseases such as rinderpest (FAO, 1995) because it is not far from the borders of Ethiopia and Sudan, where such diseases are prevalent.

Vaccination campaigns seek to reduce disease levels, although they are hampered by shortage of resources. It is calculated that 80 per cent of an animal population must be vaccinated to ensure a level of control against disease and rinderpest. At a coverage of almost 70 per cent of the livestock population, there is still some way to go. The high mortality rates from pasteurellosis and *peste de petits ruminants* (PPR) also justify priority on the vaccination list. Table 5.37 indicates animal vaccination that has taken place in the Gash-Barka region from 1992 to 1995.

Table 5.37 Number of animal vaccinations in the Gash-Barka region, 1992–1995					
Vaccination	1992	1993	1994	1995	Total
Rinderpest	139,200	31,712	236,562	261,150	668,624
Anthrax	0	921	26,755	2,627	30,303
Blackleg	0	921	27,954	8,309	37,184
Pasteurellosis	0	23,858	71,559	70,630	166,047
Sheep pox	1,000	4,985	24,601	307	30,893
PPR	0	0	218,450	169,400	387,850
Newcastle disease	0	0	1,132	2,160	3,292

Source: Ministry of Agriculture reports, 1996.

The need for natural resource conservation

Resource degradation can result from both subsistence agriculture and commercial agriculture. In Gash-Barka, the rapid expansion of concessions in riverine areas is having a major environmental and social impact. Forest cover is reduced, traditional food resources are lost and pastoralists' access to these areas is restricted. All these developments have implications for food security.

The large livestock population in the region has been causing serious damage to semi-arid and arid pastures, leading to a reduction in total grazing capacity, especially in eastern Barka. Much of the flatlands in both Barka and Gash now have greatly reduced grass cover, so that grazing takes place mostly in the hills. Degradation is likely to continue unless some way is found to match stock numbers to carrying capacity.

It is reported that in clearing land for horticulture, doum palms are sometimes felled (Robertson et al., 1994), as well as other riverine vegetation. This is a breach of forest conservation regulations, but strict enforcement is difficult because of the size of the region and the shortage of staff. Deforestation will also cause the extinction of wildlife in the region.

While hazards of erosion are very great in the highlands, the danger is not so great in the lowlands, where slopes are more gentle, but there are still some areas where soil cover has been removed. Gully erosion is severe, especially in fields adjacent to streams, where the soil is generally more fertile. Sheet and water erosion are also common, as well as wind erosion on the sandier soils.

Another potential resource problem is salinity, both primary and secondary. Primary salinity occurs due to natural factors such as salt lakes, while secondary salinity occurs as a result of artificial changes to the natural ecosystem, usually a change in the balance between evapo-transpiration and precipitation. In all parts of the region, this combination of evaporation and transpiration exceeds precipitation, so the water table remains at its long-term level. However, if vegetation is removed or significantly reduced, the balance between evaporation and transpiration changes – the former becomes more important, causing a general rise in the water table. As the water table rises, water passes through sub-soil layers usually containing significant amounts of salt, which is then carried to the surface and deposited there. There is evidence of salinity in some areas of central and northern Gash, with salt concentration in wells, accompanied by poor germination, stunted leaves and reduced yields. This could become a major issue as irrigated agriculture increases and there will need to be careful planning of any future irrigation schemes.

Conservation activities carried out in the Gash-Barka region between 1992 and 1995 are indicated in Table 5.38. The two main approaches to deforestation are enclosure and seedling planting. The former costs less, but as the land is communally owned there is little incentive for individuals to give up short-term benefits from the use of land for long-term advantages. An alternative approach to reforestation is the planting of seedlings. Between 1992 and 1994, 50,000 seedlings were planted in Barka province, and a further 500,000 were planted in Gash province under the

FFW programme. Seedlings have also been planted by schoolchildren, but there has been little maintenance follow-up and success has been limited. Future plantings of carefully selected multipurpose trees could address food security and firewood needs, while improving soil cover.

Table 5.38 Conservation activities undertaken in the Gash-Barka region, 1992–1995					
Activity (unit)	1992	1993	1994	1995	Total
Nurseries established (each)	3	3	2	–	8
Seedlings produced (each)	79,182	413,461	287,824	130,499	910,966
Seedlings planted/ replanted (each)	55,066	167,104	210,324	91,817	524,311
Terraces constructed and maintained (kilometres)	2,319	1,701	1,889	884	6,794
Feeder roads constructed and maintained (kilometres)	0.39	0.50	15.05	13.72	29.66
Land enclosed (hectares)	–	63	190	8,884	9,098
Constructed and maintained (each):					
- earth dams	–	–	–	–	–
- ponds	11	19	3	4	37
- wells	–	–	3	–	3
Constructed and maintained (kilometres):					
- embankments	–	–	–	–	–
- canals	–	–	0.32	–	0.3
- check dams	1.91	1.54	11.21	2.66	18.3
Diversions constructed (kilometres)	–	–	1.33	1	2.3

Source: *Ministry of Agriculture reports, 1996.*

Another response to the deforestation problem is the production of gas stoves. The Eri-Sok factory in Asmara has recently started to produce and distribute gas ovens, stoves and containers on the local market. During its first three months, the factory produced 5,500 stoves and 12,000 ovens. This should contribute considerably to reducing the demand for fuel wood, particularly in towns.

As for soil and water conservation, the most important measures are the construction of soil bunds, stone bunds and check dams. Soil bunds are constructed by pushing up an earthen ridge; terracing cropland in this manner helps increase soil retention and control erosion. Stone bunds are used in non-cropland situations, often on steeper land. They are designed to protect cultivated areas from run-off water from natural vegetation or bare areas. Stone bunds are much more labour-intensive than soil bunds, so their use should be restricted. Closures can be an effective replacement for stone bunds if the local community agrees to them. Check dams are low barriers of loose rock constructed in gullies to slow erosion and run-off and to retain sediment. This gives the water more time to infiltrate, and improves soil moisture. It also results in improved vegetation cover to control erosion, thus completing the cycle.

Water and soil conservation are linked – if water is conserved, so is soil. Ponds and wells are constructed in appropriate locations to improve water supply for both livestock and people. Large numbers of small water points supply the country in a cost-effective manner.

Existing agricultural practices contribute to resource conservation in various ways, but sometimes they fail to contribute. For example, while farmers often use contour cultivation on arable land, accumulating manure to improve soil fertility is not general practice. While livestock is often held on the fields for a week before cultivation, and the animal droppings are incorporated during ploughing and planting, farmers fear that this will make the crops conducive to weeds and pests, raising the temperature of the soil and killing plants, especially in times of poor rainfall. Crop rotation is little practised, and this also leads to a reduction in soil fertility. Where possible, farmers try to let part of their land lie fallow on a regular basis, but in some areas land shortage prevents fallowing, and forces farmers to apply manure to restore soil fertility.

The region's available grazing area is continually diminishing through soil degradation and the expansion of agriculture. This problem needs to be addressed through clear land-use policy and management practices.

The involvement of women

The extent to which women are involved in conservation and agricultural activities depends on their cultural group. Among the Kunama people in the Gash region, women and men share agricultural activities, although ploughing is generally done by men in male-headed households. In female-headed households women carry out all activities themselves, including ploughing. This is in contrast to the Nara and Beni-Amer Muslim groups, where almost all agricultural activities are carried out by men. In female-headed households in these cultures, women participate in weeding and harvesting, but ploughing is done by male relatives or hired help. Among the Beni-Amer in eastern Barka, women do not participate in development projects due to the Islamic Sharia laws and their customs – to go against them would bring dishonour to the family. The Nara women in Gash are also restricted (through seclusion) from being involved in development projects. However, women from the Christian Kunama ethnic group are active participants in development activities, and women from poor households are the most active labourers in CFW and FFW programmes.

If greater involvement of Muslim women in these schemes is desired, then activities will have to be designed that are acceptable under Sharia law. This could involve some form of gender separation. An extension and training programme will have to be conducted for both sexes, but mainly to increase women's role in productive activities.

THE POTENTIAL TO INCREASE FOOD SECURITY

Large-scale improvement of existing rangeland in the western lowlands is not easy, as environmental conditions are too harsh. However, there is potential to increase pasture production in small pockets where conditions are more favourable and demand is high. Improved pasture species could be introduced, preferably near water-points or riverbanks, although some form of protection from grazing would be needed. Species would need to be carefully chosen to ensure suitability.

As for crop production, it is estimated that approximately one million hectares of fertile soil in the south-west lowlands could be used in the future for expanded cultivation. Most of this would have to be rain-fed, at least for the time being, as surface and ground-water resources in the region have not been comprehensively assessed. Estimates of the area that could be irrigated vary from 107,000 hectares to 567,000 hectares (FAO, 1994). It is estimated that surface water irrigation from the three major river basins serves 5,000-6,500 hectares in the Barka-Anseba system, 30,000-251,500 hectares in the Tekese-Setit system, and 32,000-67,560 hectares in the Mereb-Gash system. The areas identified by the Ministry of Agriculture in the Gash-Barka region include all topographically suitable areas, and should be taken as the maximum potential for irrigation, spate being more suited to sites near seasonal rivers, while horticultural production will be best suited to areas with reliable ground or surface water supplies.

As horticulture in the region is not so attractive to farmers, mainly because of marketing difficulties, processing horticultural and agricultural products would be one possible solution that would ease the storage and transport of these crops. Indeed, food processing is suggested by the FAO as one of the priority research areas, together with storage, preservation, transport and packaging.

Livestock production and fattening for regional and national markets could be undertaken on concessions with irrigated pastures (suggested in FAO, 1994) around Barentu and Tessenei. The integration of crops and livestock could be increased, through the production of forage crops and milk or meat production, with spate irrigation.

The increased production of oil crops, associated with local or regional oil presses would encourage the expansion of agro-industries in the area, as raw materials become more readily available. Another alternative could be to develop a sustainable use for some of the woodland natural resources, for example *Boswellia papyrifera* (frankincense) or *Acacia seyal* and *A. senegal* (gum arabic), which can be exported. There is also the possibility of developing handicrafts, such as mats made with fibres of the doum palm, for regional markets.

The achievement of food security in Gash-Barka, as elsewhere in Eritrea, depends on implementing appropriate macro-economic policies and development strategies, as well as using methods to increase both agricultural production and productivity. The organizational capacity of the institutions involved needs to be improved (FAO, 1996b). Food security policies and activities must take into account the most affected groups in the region and take an integrated approach.

FOOD SECURITY: CONCLUDING OBSERVATIONS AND RECOMMENDATIONS

Some would argue that Eritrea should not pin all its hopes and efforts on food self-sufficiency in order to assure food security for the population.

The pursuit of domestic self-sufficiency is often regarded these days as a potentially high-cost and socially inefficient method for achieving the supply side of food security. It is pointed out that self-sufficiency is neither a necessary condition for achieving food security (as imported supplies can be used to close the gap between domestic production and consumption), nor a sufficient condition – even with self-sufficiency there may be significant categories of the population experiencing chronic or transitory food insecurity.

Even if self-sufficiency can be justified in terms of comparative advantage (if it is cheaper to produce domestically than to import), the marginal costs of balancing supply and demand can be reduced considerably by making more use of the world market, rather than depending entirely on domestic stocks. This is because the size of stock required to balance the domestic market using only domestic supplies is many times larger than the size of stock needed if imports are utilized to help balance the market.

It cannot be denied that food aid has played a vital role in helping the Eritrean population to survive, both during the struggle and in the post-liberation years. It has provided sustenance in the form of handouts – FFW or CFW programmes – to people whose labour has accomplished many essential tasks for agricultural production and the conservation of natural resources.

Food aid has been particularly useful in helping with the reintegration of Eritrean returnees from Sudan until they are able to produce their own food and earn their own living, while it has also assisted the population in semi-arid areas who are not yet able to support themselves as their livestock herds have not yet reached viable size. Food aid has also been essential for the survival of other vulnerable groups.

Nevertheless, the Eritrean government has become increasingly concerned about the negative aspects of food aid. There are two main drawbacks, the first is psychological and the second is economic. The first is that food handouts encourage a dependency syndrome and undermine the work ethic and spirit of self-reliance which underpins the country's whole approach to development. The second is that the country's intake of large amounts of subsidized food inevitably has an adverse effect on domestic food production, prices and marketing. Both drawbacks have been a recurring theme in this chapter, and these are the arguments that have led the government to opt for a policy of food monetization. Concomitant with this new policy will be greater efforts to target the beneficiaries in future, to ensure that they are indeed in greatest need (the aged, those in poor health or suffering physical disabilities) and that any assistance will, as much as possible, help them to become self-supporting.

It is argued that the various programmes related to food security and preventing environmental degradation that have been carried out using FFW and CFW have been relatively limited and that, if food monetization becomes a reality, it will be possible to carry out such important activities on a greatly increased scale. If properly organized, involving categories such as young people, demobilized fighters and returnees, the contribution to long-term food security would be incalculable.

If the ultimate aim of food aid is, as so often declared, to contribute to food security at least in the immediate and medium term, recipients should be allowed to use this aid in a flexible way. One of the benefits deriving from food monetization is the possibility of liberalizing the market and getting food to local markets and consumers efficiently, as the government has no interest in maintaining food subsidies indefinitely. Other advantages include stabilized food prices, limited food losses, and marked reduction in the cost of delivering food aid.

The main objectives of the food monetization policy can be summarized as follows:
- the stabilization of food market supplies and prices
- the insurance of minimum buffer stock reserves
- the motivation of local producers through the intervention of the market
- the continued monitoring of market conditions and advice on intervention if necessary.

A key issue in food aid monetization is how to determine the price of food aid in kind locally, so that it does not interfere with development objectives. If it is set at a low level, consumers will be happy but producers will not, and it will be a disincentive to domestic agriculture. If it is set at a high level, it will not be attractive to consumers.

What is the right price for an agricultural commodity? Economists may give quick answers but those would work only if there is a perfect worldwide information system with competitive markets, which as we know is never the case. Because of the distortions in the world economy, there are many distortions in the prices of commodities. But any deviation of domestic price from the international border price of a commodity, whether an import or export item, creates efficiency losses in production and consumption.

In setting prices, at least three criteria have to be taken into consideration. The first is the cost of production. This would appear especially applicable in deciding the bottom price of staple food crops in areas or countries that are to some extent insulated from world prices by high transport costs or other barriers. The cost of production focuses on private rather than social returns to agriculture. Its merits are that it is grounded in the real economic conditions of the majority of peasants and that it provides a direct link between farm incomes and farm prices.

The second criterion is border price, which needs to be adjusted and brought into line with domestic prices such as retail, wholesale or farm-gate prices. In practice the border price principle provides a reference point for discussing appropriate price levels, rather than a definitive guide. Of course, if government controls are abandoned altogether (including taxes, subsidies, floor and fixed prices) then border prices become the arbiter of domestic price levels.

Terms of trade are the third criterion. They refer to the trend of farm output prices relative to the prices of inputs and consumer goods that farmers purchase from the industrial sector. Terms of trade refer to agricultural output as a whole, not to individual crops, and therefore this criterion concerns the general level of farm-gate prices, not relative price levels between outputs. The terms of trade are calculated by dividing an index of prices paid to farmers by an index of prices paid by farmers for inputs and consumer goods. The aim of this criterion is to monitor the comparative level of prices between agriculture and industry. As with border price, the intention is not necessarily to adhere closely to annual changes in these relative prices, but rather to ensure that a cumulative divergence does not develop between farm and non-farm price trends, as a result of price policy interventions.

Taking all these price determination factors into consideration, the challenge for the Eritrean government is to set the prices of food aid so that they are not at odds with those of local producers. For the time being, taking into account such factors as local availability of food, degree of dependency, purchasing capacity of the population, and local food production levels, food aid prices will be set at current local prices. This set price is also expected to include all costs, such as transport, port handling, storage and losses, and retailers' profit margins. However, the purchasing power of the population in the various areas must be given due consideration. It would work against food security objectives to penalize the people living in the more remote areas, who are usually among the most disadvantaged groups of society.

It will be the task of the EGB to ensure that the monetized food aid is available in the markets of the various localities at the pre-set prices, without causing adverse effects on the existing local market prices. The EGB was established in 1993 to protect farmers and consumers through price stabilization and to supply farmers with seed after bad harvests. It works in conjunction with the zonal administrations, with the latter identifying priority areas. Market centres in surplus and deficit areas have been set up to increase trade movement between provinces. The main shortages are in storage facilities (at present they are using ERREC stores), transport and skilled workers experienced in market assessment and analysis. Poor harvests also complicate EGB operations.

The EGB has a pivotal role to play in food aid monetization. It needs to ensure that prices set are realistically, so the private trading sector can develop fully. There are two approaches which can be followed when monetizing food aid.

Food aid can be sold by the government or appropriate government bodies in markets where there is a food deficit. This maximizes the funds generated and improves the local availability of food. It should also reduce price distortions associated with food aid. Further reductions could be achieved if foodstuffs were sold in the deficit season (before harvest), when local supplies are low and prices are highest. This system would involve the government very closely in the marketing system, possibly to the detriment of local private traders.

The government could also sell grain at import parity prices at a central location and provide detailed market information to traders. This would allow them to assume the major role in marketing, with the disadvantage of increased handling costs. As infrastructure improves and trade increases, growing competition will lead to normalization of regional prices.

If the second alternative is adopted – meaning greater involvement of the private sector and increased supply – price monitoring would still continue to ensure sufficient competition, leading to a reduction of food prices to more stable levels in the "hungry season".

Regular information on prices, demand and supplies of major commodities will be essential both for traders and for the EW&FIS.

Summing up the advantages of food aid monetization, the following points should be noted:
1. Cash will be provided strictly to people in need – those who cannot, for one reason or another, engage in productive activities to support themselves.

2. Funds will be available for rehabilitation and reconstruction schemes, the objectives of which will be concerned mainly with future food security.
3. Immediate opportunities will be provided for supplemental income-generating activities in non-food sectors such as trade. For example, it is expected that a number of grain retailers will emerge, while the creation of food markets will help develop other markets, such as animals, through which people will enter a market-based exchange of commodities.

Given the precariousness of agricultural production, it is vital that there be an emergency stock of food grain – a minimum level of food grains should be set aside for emergencies. These stocks can also have a stabilizing effect on prices when deficits or surpluses occur.

Such a food stock is all the more important as negotiations for imports or free food aid, and shipment and delivery to the final consumers, can last three to four months. It is calculated that a stock level of 65,000-100,000 tons would be necessary to guarantee food for a four- to five-month period in order to avoid famine. This level should be maintained. In no circumstances should it be allowed to fall below a level equivalent to consumption requirements for three to four months.

In sum, the objectives of such a strategic grain reserve would be:
*   to counteract food shortages caused by artificial or natural disasters
*   to protect against regional and national food shortfalls
*   to bridge the gap between emergencies and the arrival of imports
*   to supply deficit areas with food
*   to ensure better distribution of food throughout the nation.

In order to avoid locking up the country's scarce financial resources in maintaining large reserves of food grains and to keep them at the minimum level, it will be essential to monitor the food situation constantly, so as to plan and arrange uninterrupted supplies of food grains to consumers.

It is recognized that such a grain reserve mechanism can be a double-edged sword. It is crucial to keep the right amount of reserves. If they are too large, not only will there be problems of storage losses, but there may also be price distortions for domestic crops which would adversely affect domestic farmers. Crop harvest predictions and projections should be as accurate as possible and constantly revised in light of the latest developments.

Monitoring the stock regularly involves collecting, processing, analysing and summarizing information at a centrally designated agency, which should then be expeditiously made available to decision makers and operators. To be able to make systematic and reliable estimates, an effective early-warning and food information system is required to assess crop harvests, rainfall and the number of people who may be at risk.

It should be kept in mind that importing food or any other commodity constitutes a leakage from the country and, from the national accounting viewpoint, is not an injection into the economy. Conversely, exports are injections into the economy and have a positive impact. It is important that the food balance not be confused with the objective of agricultural development. Clearly, it makes no sense to import more than is needed, even if it is a free food distribution, unless it is well planned and targeted to ensure that the most vulnerable groups benefit, or unless it is judiciously used for development purposes. Imports come in at the expense of foreign exchange and they should be most carefully scrutinized and compared with other purchases and investments that will have to be foregone as a result.

To address food security effectively, the technical, social and institutional aspects have to be examined with a view to increasing domestic production and reducing short-term dependence on food aid for development purposes.

The conservation of natural resources, particularly soil and water, needs to be explored in greater depth. However, such activities must be carried out so that they make an immediate impact on the livelihoods of the local population and provide long-term benefits to the country as a whole. Appropriate conservation and water harvesting techniques have to be researched and applied to agricultural production purposes, as the total kilometres of terraces constructed or millions of cubic metres of earth moved may not bear directly on soil and water conservation.

Existing farming systems in relation to land use and tenure need to be studied, as do cropping systems in the different ecological zones, with a view to introducing high-yielding varieties and mitigating drought. Crop versus livestock production, agricultural/agro-pastoral versus pastoral production systems – these issues should each be thoroughly investigated.

The rationale of food aid, used wisely for development purposes (especially considering the numbers of refugees who are expected to return home), has to be examined, along with institutional support services and the need to develop domestic production capacities.

The role of agricultural research is paramount. Basic and applied research activities are essential and should be accompanied by appropriate training and extension activities to enhance crop and livestock production levels. The synergy of the agricultural sector policy framework and other institutional support services in developing the agricultural sector to meet basic food needs will have to be kept under continual review.

The role of agricultural marketing and pricing systems has to be thoroughly studied and related to present realities. The use of rural financial markets for mobilizing savings, and the need for price-stabilizing measures such as grain reserves and stocks, must be carefully analysed.

REFERENCES

EW&FIS, *Rainfall Records*, Asmara, 1996.

ERREC, *1995 Annual Report – PROFERI*, Asmara, 1996.

FAO, *Eritrea: Agricultural Sector Review and Project Identification*, Report No. TCP/ERI/2353, 3 Vols., Rome, 1994.

FAO, *Eritrea – National Livestock Development Project Preparation Report*, 2 Vols., Rome, 1995.

FAO, *Food Requirements and Population Growth*, WFS/96/TECH/10, Rome, 1996a.

FAO, *Food Security and Nutrition*, WFS/96/TECH/9, Rome, 1996b.

GSE, *Macro-Policy Document*, GSE, Asmara, 1994.

Immink, M., *Linkages between Integrated Food Security Programmes (IFSP) and National Food Security Policies: The Case of the IFSP/Gash-Setit, Eritrea*, unpublished report for IFSP, Asmara, 1995.

Nauheimer, M., *Animal Health and Livestock Production in Gash and Setit: Assessment of the Sector and Proposal for Improvement*, unpublished report for IFSP, Tessenei, Eritrea, 1995.

Robertson, V., Bristow, S., Oxby, C. and Abu Ahmed, J., *Assessment and Management of Riverine Forests, Western Lowlands, Eritrea*, unpublished report for SOS Sahel, Asmara, 1994.

Schwartz, H. J., *Appraisal of Livestock Production in Gash and Setit Provinces*, unpublished report for IFSP, Asmara, 1994.

State of Eritrea, Ministry of Agriculture, *Reports*, Asmara, 1996.

State of Eritrea, Ministry of Industry and Trade, *Reports*, Asmara, 1996.

State of Eritrea, Ministry of Marine Resources, *Reports*, Asmara, 1996.

World Bank, *Eritrea: Options and Strategies*, Asmara, 1994.

World Bank, *Poverty and Hunger: Issues and Options for Food Security in Developing Countries*, World Bank, Washington, D.C., 1986.

World Bank, *World Development Report 1996: From Plan to Market*, Oxford University Press, New York, 1996.

6

HUMAN RESOURCE DEVELOPMENT: PRIORITIES FOR POLICY

Araia Tseggai

This chapter presents the results of a research project conducted in late 1996. Its terms of reference were to study and propose recommendations for a human resource development (HRD) strategy for the immediate future that would be consonant with the overall, long-term HRD strategy of the Eritrean state. Thus, the objectives of the research were to provide the Eritrean government and other key participants with a critical assessment of existing policies and programmes in the area of HRD, and subsequently to make policy recommendations relevant to internal and external actors.

To tackle this task appropriately, it was first necessary to explore the general conceptual framework on the topic of HRD. What did it mean? What were the relevant general issues? Which theoretical approaches were currently relevant to Eritrea? Second, it was important to understand the background leading up to the current realities of human resources in Eritrea. Pre-Independence philosophies on improving human resources needed to be examined for continuity in policy and action. Finally, the appropriate general recommendations for the future were to be presented. Preliminary investigations into the existing state of affairs of human resources in Eritrea were deemed necessary to extract the relevant information on status, policy issues and possible recommendations.

The development of human resources in post-war Eritrea should be understood in the proper context. The prolonged war experienced by Eritrea destroyed the basic economic infrastructure and institutions of the country and had a dramatic effect on the health and education of its labour force. The skilled Eritrean workforce was scattered, decimated and unable to take on the task of rebuilding the economy. It was clear that all levels of this post-war society had tremendous needs in health and education that could be serviced only through a flourishing economy, and to achieve that the key human resources needed for national reconstruction had to be developed as quickly as possible. Thus, the research primarily focuses on the section of the population that is instrumental in the struggle for national rehabilitation and reconstruction, and emphasis is given to education and training programmes that produce specific labour skills relatively quickly. Much had already been done toward training and retraining Eritrea's human resources. Long- and short-term programmes initiated by the Eritrean and donor governments, international organizations, NGOs and local grassroots initiatives were under way – yet much remains to be done.

It is also necessary to look at the positive legacies of the liberation struggle and their potential for the future. The long struggle granted EPLF rich experience that helped to upgrade the basic education and training of fighters. This legacy cannot be ignored in the study of the human resource endowment of the country. However, before engaging in a detailed discussion of the Eritrean government's philosophy and stated strategy for long-term HRD – with special emphasis on its proclaimed macro policy – it would be fruitful to establish a frame of reference for assessing the effectiveness of the policies. Thus, this chapter first addresses the general conceptual framework for HRD and attempts to link those concepts to the strategy needed to enrich Eritrean human capital for purposes of economic recovery and development.

THE GENERAL CONCEPTUAL AND STRATEGIC FRAMEWORK
Definitions of HRD
Generally, HRD is an all-inclusive concept that refers to the process of increasing the knowledge, skills and capacities of all people in a society. More specifically, and to quote pioneering experts in the field:

> In economic terms, it could be described as the accumulation of human capital and its effective investment in the development of an economy. In political terms, human resource development prepares people for adult participation in political processes, particularly as citizens in a democracy. From the social and cultural points of view, the development of human resources helps people to lead fuller and richer lives, less bound by tradition. In short, the process of HRD unlocks the door to modernisation (Myers and Harbison, 1965:2).

Such a broad definition needs to be narrowed to a specific and operational level to be relevant to the main research task. Therefore, from the operational perspective HRD is defined as "organized *learning* experiences in a definite time period to increase the possibility of *improving* job performance growth" (Nader and Nader, 1990:3).

This definition concentrates on intentional – not incidental – learning processes (formal and informal) organized by specified programmes (school systems, training courses) and periods of time with the aim of increasing productivity or performance in the workplace. Such an operational approach to HRD leads to programmatic planning to develop human resources in several ways, including:

- formal education, from elementary to higher education
- on-the-job training programmes, such as in-service and adult education
- "self-development", including correspondence courses, reading and learning from others
- improvement in health and nutrition, prolonging working life and productivity.

This chapter is primarily concerned with the economic aspect of HRD in Eritrea and so addresses post-war effects on the economy and prospects for economic betterment of the society. Therefore, the operational definition of HRD is more suited to discussing Eritrea's current strategy and more appropriate for identifying the necessary operational programmes.

HRD strategies

Having identified what HRD means for Eritrea, these programmatic activities can be framed in a workable, achievable strategy of development. Strategic success depends on defining constraints and then planning and implementing programmes accordingly. It must be noted that the biggest constraint on the realization of a planned HRD programme in any country is limited resource availability. Thus, choices must be made in line with stated priorities, and in Eritrea the government's macro policy seems to have set the nation's priorities. In this scenario of set priorities and limited means, the decision-maker entrusted with the task of implementation must create intelligent and feasible alternatives for HRD programmes. This constitutes the framework or arena of operational alternatives. The short-term strategy for Eritrean HRD deals with two main challenges:

- creating programmes and activities that provide the skills and competencies needed to fill the shortage of high-level workers
- dealing with the problem of underutilization of human resources in the national economy.

In the first case, the strategy is to implement national education plans, programmes and activities to provide the skills and capabilities needed for society in general and the economy in particular. It must be understood that mere physical "capacity-building" in ministries and enterprises without the inclusion of human improvement will lead to problems. The experience of other countries demonstrates that increasing physical capital when strategic human capital (skilled professionals) is lacking, leads to ineffective capital utilization and programmatic inefficiency or even failure. Therefore, for example, while schools with the necessary amenities are being built throughout Eritrea, the all-important end product must be qualified graduates. Instilling motivation and discipline to succeed in students is a major component of HRD.

The building of *incentives* is crucial for both the accumulation and the investment of human capital. In fact, investment in education may be wasted unless men and women have the *will* to prepare for and engage in those activities which are needed for accelerated economic growth and social and political progress (Myers and Harbison, 1965:18).

Employment is the second challenge to HRD strategy in Eritrea, where the overabundance of underutilized labour is as much a problem as the shortage of skilled workers. Continued underutilization or underemployment has the potential of becoming a serious economic and socio-political problem in Eritrea. Therefore, efforts are needed to reduce this problem through practical education and training programmes, and to prevent poorly designed school systems from producing graduates who cannot be properly utilized by the economy.

This discussion of HRD strategy indicates that Eritrea needs a long-term plan for dealing with development issues and a short-term plan for confronting the economic challenges of recovery and rehabilitation. While the former is undeniably crucial to pursue, the current task of rebuilding the Eritrean economy gives prominence to short-term strategies for developing human resources. That is why this chapter emphasizes dealing with urgent programmes and activities that are simultaneously subsumed in the overall long-term strategy of development.

LONG-TERM PERSPECTIVES

The Eritrean government has always had a strong, clear conviction that the key to rapid and sustainable long-term economic development rests with the development of human resources. Its pre- and post-Independence agendas on this issue are of interest.

The pre-Independence HRD agenda

Before becoming the government of Eritrea and throughout its existence, EPLF has considered it essential to improve and enrich its workforce in all aspects. EPLF often reiterated that the human element of the struggle was the decisive factor for victory, a belief reflected in the group's early slogans: "Preserve Yourself" (in battle), "Self-Reliance is the Key to Victory", "Let the Educated Educate", and "Man is Decisive for Victory, not Arms". EPLF stimulated an all-encompassing effort to educate the population during the years of struggle, as an imperative for the economic well-being of society after Independence. To this end, it had a broad scope of pre-Independence activities:

> If there is one memorable thing that foreigners know about the nature of the EPLF organization it is its ardent belief in educating the masses on issues of politics, culture, social relations and technical know-how.... Its steadfast struggle against illiteracy, especially adult illiteracy, is well-documented. It has stretched itself greatly to create [an] appropriate educational curriculum for the nation-to-be; translating important works into local languages; organizing cultural troupes capable of performing in languages of all the nine Eritrean nationalities, developing traditional art and music to higher thresholds of achievement; constantly introducing new and appropriate technology in its daily work; training by the thousands skilled professionals like nurses, barefoot doctors, mechanics and technicians, agriculturists and rural teachers.

The link created between the need for educating the masses and the resultant improvement of human resources became the cornerstone for the post-Independence perspective of EPLF on how to best handle the issue of HRD for economic recovery and development. By the time of Independence in 1991, the entire fighting force was literate and there were 105 schools with tens of thousands of students throughout the previously liberated areas of Eritrea. After Independence, the effort was to stay the course and further refine the framework.

The post-Independence agenda

Immediately following Independence, the government of Eritrea emphasized the pivotal role of human resources in the development of the Eritrean economy by specifying its position in the Macro-Policy Document (GSE, 1994). The document details the objectives and relevant policies of the major HRD issues: education and training, health, social welfare, rehabilitation of war victims and other vulnerable and disadvantaged members of society, gender, youth, and population. The Macro-Policy Document contains the following elements:

I Education and training
   A Objectives
      1. To produce a population equipped with the necessary skills, knowledge and culture for a self-reliant and modern economy.
      2. To develop self-consciousness and self-motivation among the population to fight poverty, disease, and all the attendant causes of backwardness and ignorance.
      3. To make basic education available to all.
   B Policies
      1. Universal primary education up to seven years will gradually be made available to all.
      2. Skilled labour requirements of both the public and private sectors will be met by steadily increasing enrolments at secondary, technical and vocational schools.
      3. Continuing education through formal and informal channels will be promoted to achieve higher literacy rates and enhanced competence.
      4. Tertiary education will be selectively expanded to meet the envisaged labour requirements of the country. For diversified skill acquisition, this will be supplemented by utilizing training opportunities afforded by the international community.
      5. Technical vocational training emphasis will be placed on importing multi-craft dexterity and skills that enhance the job adaptability and retraining potential of students.
      6. The government, community and direct beneficiaries will be made to contribute varying amounts toward financing educational costs. The government may resort to levying surcharges to meet part of the cost of education.
      7. Official recognition and/or professional accreditation of skill and academic attainment will be awarded only after undergoing government-established certification procedures.
      8. There will be no restraint on the provision of education by the private sector.
      9. Public school standards will be maintained by curricula issued by the Ministry of Education. Private schools are expected to follow the curriculum, but they will not be limited by its coverage.

10. Non-secular schools will be given accreditation of professional competence (in non-religious matters) only after completion of established national certification procedures.

II Health

  A Objectives

    1. To reduce and eventually eliminate deaths from easily controllable diseases.

    2. To enhance awareness of good health practices in order to improve the productivity of the workforce.

  B Policies

    1. Basic health services will be made available to the urban and rural populations. Priority will be given to primary healthcare and immunization programmes.

    2. Major health hazards will be given special attention and health services will be promoted.

    3. The private sector will actively participate in the provision of health services following rules, regulations, and operational modalities provided by the Ministry of Health.

    4. Community and beneficiary contribution in financing health services will be promoted.

    5. National health insurance schemes will be introduced.

    6. Information dissemination on health practices will be actively promoted.

III Social welfare

  A Objective

    1. To introduce a stage-by-stage comprehensive national social security scheme in line with the pace of the country's economic development.

  B Policies

    1. Development strategies aimed at meeting the basic needs of the population will be designed and implemented.

    2. Traditional social security and community self-help schemes will be encouraged.

    3. Appropriate monetary policies will be put in place to enhance private savings.

    4. Employment safety nets will be introduced through labour-intensive public works programmed in areas and periods of major economic distress.

5. Access to productive resources (land, water, livestock, credit) will be provided to the unemployed and underemployed.
6. Pension schemes will be introduced for public sector employees.
7. Victims of war and vulnerable groups will be provided with proper care and attention.
8. Children, youths, the aged and women will be provided with legal protection from economic, sexual and other forms of exploitation.
9. National capacity for disaster preparedness and prevention will be gradually developed and strengthened.

IV Rehabilitation of war victims and other vulnerable and disadvantaged members of society
  A. Policies
    1. Sufficient and necessary empowerment will be accorded to victims of war, disadvantaged persons such as demobilized combatants, refugees and displaced persons, and other vulnerable groups, in order to enable them to become productive members of society.
    2. Continuous sensitization programmes will be conducted to enhance and promote the participation of society in the care of these groups.

V Gender issues
  A Policies
    1. All efforts will continue to sensitize and enhance society's awareness of the decisive role of women in the socio-economic, political, and cultural formation of the country.
    2. Women's equal rights will be upheld and all laws that subtract from this right will be changed.
    3. Women's participation in education, economic activities and employment will be expanded.
    4. Appropriate labour saving technologies will be introduced to reduce the drudgery of women in the household and other activities (water, fuel wood, childcare centres).
    5. Mother and childcare services will be improved and expanded.

VI Youth
  A Policies
    1. Every effort will be made to cultivate in youth: love and respect for country; dedication to work and self-reliance; excellence in the arts, sciences and sports; and awareness of the need for tolerance, justice and democracy in the context of national political pluralism and cultural diversity.
    2. Recognizing the existence of a large number of unemployed youth, every effort will be made to expand employment and retraining opportunities.

VII Population policy
  A Policies
    1. Acquisition of a comprehensive and reliable demographic profile of the population will be accorded due priority.
    2. A population growth rate that is conducive to the economic and social development of the country will be promoted.
    3. Efforts will be made to ensure that the population is healthy and productive.

The above provisions of the policy on HRD are self-explanatory. They are continuations of the pre-Independence policies and practice of the EPLF. What remained was to construct a suitable framework for implementation

Capacity-building and implementation
Following the declaration of the Macro-Policy Document on HRD, the government established, under the auspices of the Office of the President, a special Office of Human Resource Development to concretize and specify the government's stated policy. A policy document entitled *Eritrea: Strategy for Human Resources Development – A Project for Capacity Building,* was produced by this office in late 1996, outlining the implementation scheme of the government's national HRD policy.

The basic strategy of HRD as espoused in this document is the systematic and planned expansion of the school system in Eritrea. The philosophical context of this strategy is crystallized in the document as follows:

> The nation's level of creativity, its wealth and the levels of living standards of its people are determined by the breadth and depth of its intellectual assets. The reservoir of these assets relies on the

learning capability and creativity of its people. Education, therefore, plays the most vital role in developing the nation's intellectual and creative power (...) education is viewed as a strategic tool for development, therefore the content of the educational system is to be reviewed carefully (...) The education system must be geared not only at raising the general social and scientific knowledge of the individual but it must also equip the individual with skills that would enable one to lead a productive and sustainable life (GSE, 1996a).

To summarize the detailed provisions of HRD listed earlier, the government considers the following objectives as the cornerstone of its national HRD strategy:

- to ensure an intellectually vibrant and motivated young generation
- to develop the workforce necessary for a dynamic, rapidly growing national economy
- to equip every Eritrean with requisite skills that enable one to earn and/ or improve one's living standard
- to enhance technological transformation and modernization necessary for the encouragement of an export-oriented economy, to develop the nation's intellectual and creative power
- to instil in every child and adult alike sound moral values to be diligent, efficient, responsible and loyal citizens
- to bring out the best in every citizen through a combination of formal and informal training schemes.

To achieve these objectives, the implementation framework includes formal and informal training, regular academic schooling, technical education, teacher training and training at skills-development centres. In short, it aims to build the necessary infrastructure and institutions based on a firm commitment to spreading basic education to all people in the country.

THE CURRENT STATE OF HUMAN RESOURCES IN ERITREA

A major bottleneck in the economic reconstruction of Eritrea is the absence of the right kind of human resources to tackle the various reconstruction tasks. Most skilled labourers and technicians were either killed in the war, emigrated to neighbouring countries, or have been working outside their field. No significant number of skilled young Eritreans has been trained to replace those displaced or killed during the war. After liberation, skilled Ethiopians who had been working in Eritrea left the country, leaving a vacuum in the area of skilled professionals and technicians desperately needed for reconstruction. Furthermore, since liberation, high school graduates have been too poorly trained to be considered an effective part of the solution without undergoing retraining. It is now common to see Ethiopian skilled labourers being imported, especially for construction work, signalling the extent of the problem and the urgency of the task at hand. Even the government has actively recruited foreign nationals for some jobs.

Employment and labour

Subsistence agriculture (crop farming, animal husbandry, fishing) is the mainstay of the Eritrean economy. It has been estimated that 75-80 per cent of the Eritrean population are dependent on it. In 1993, 67 per cent of the total labour force in Eritrea was rural. Of the rural population, about two-thirds were agriculturists, while the remaining third were agro-pastoralists and nomadic pastoralists. However, owing to the long war and recurrent droughts of recent years, smallholder productivity is low and most peasant farmers are unable to produce enough food to meet their needs. The decline in agricultural production and emergence of rural unemployment and underemployment has resulted in an increase in rural non-farm activities.

In the main urban centres, the civil service and public enterprises are the major employers in the formal labour market. More significant is that the majority of public sector firms and organizations are located in Asmara, the capital city.

The informal sector provides important economic activity in Eritrea, playing a pivotal role in creating employment opportunities for young people in the major urban areas. It is estimated that nearly one-quarter of the urban labour force is engaged in the informal sector of the economy.

As will be discussed below, open unemployment is a serious problem, particularly in the main urban centres. The unemployed are usually young, first-time job seekers. However, the large numbers of returnees and demobilized fighters re-entering the labour market is probably aggravating the situation further. In 1993, the Ministry of Labour and Social Welfare's Department of Labour estimated that 14 per cent of the urban labour force was unemployed.

Data on employment in Eritrea since 1991 shows unusual fluctuations associated with programmatic changes affecting the labour market. Thus, it cannot give complete and useful data on employment in Eritrea. Some examples are worth citing here to make the point clear. Many job seekers were conscripted into the National Service Programme beginning in 1994, thereby reducing the number of "placeable" job seekers. The number of job seekers soared after 1995 (data not available for that year), when the government initiated a "downsizing programme" of its bureaucracy, and laid off more than 10,000 civil servants. A large number of job seekers has been added to the list with the demobilization of some 50,000 fighters in early 1993. There is also an inflow of repatriated refugees from neighbouring countries. The trend of such events continues.

Yet there are prospects for increased employment, as new investments are being realized in Eritrea. For example, the Housing and Commerce Bank of Eritrea's investment in housing projects alone has resulted in the employment of more than 8,000 construction workers since 1994, in Asmara and Massawa only. Other such employment generating projects are springing up in many parts of the country, enough to make the future a bit brighter for Eritreans looking for more and better jobs. This is especially true for people who have been gaining the skills demanded by the market and who are graduating from the school system.

Education and labour

One of the important components in assessing the value and productivity of labour in a given country is the educational level attained and its position in the employment arena. The school system and its organization are the prime training ground for Eritrea's labour in the long run, especially when it comes to skills and technical know-how required by the economy.

The following description of the educational arena in Eritrea is abstracted from a Ministry of Education February 1996 publication, and gives a brief but important overview (GSE, 1996b).

The educational policy of Eritrea is firmly based on incorporating the experiences gained in this field during the struggle for Independence. The right of every citizen to basic education is recognized as the cornerstone of HRD in Eritrea, and the overall policy strives to correct the ethnic and gender imbalances that still exist in society. To summarize, the basic long-term educational policies of the government of Eritrea are as follows:

- promotion of the current education system that suits each region's economic condition
- provision of a basic education curriculum that takes seven years to complete
- use of the mother tongue as a medium of instruction in primary education
- use of English as a medium of instruction in secondary education

- strive to secularize and modernize education
- securing the simultaneous existence of government and non-government schools at all levels
- encouragement of communities to play a growing role in the management of education by strengthening ties between school and community.

According to policy makers at the Ministry of Education, the long-term HRD strategy for education and training consists of promoting basic education throughout Eritrea as an effort to significantly reduce illiteracy (which is estimated at about 80 per cent) in the short-run. This policy will enable the government to affect the slow rise of formal education while reducing the illiterate population by creating certain "stepping stones" toward literacy and then formal education. It is the considered opinion of the ministry that more of its efforts and resources should be expended on long-term HRD strategy planned in terms of decades, rather than on short-term skills training programmes.

The ministry is faced with the challenge of implementing its policies when budgetary allocations for the school system in Eritrea are among the lowest in Africa. The cost of implementing policy rests squarely on the shoulders of the government. Whereas in 1992 it cost about 34.7 million birr to run the country's educational programmes, in 1995 the cost jumped to 90.3 million birr. Nonetheless, the achievements realized in the five years since liberation are impressive:

- construction of 140 primary schools and rehabilitation of 191 since 1991/1992, with emphasis on educationally deprived parts of the country; this contributed to the growth of the Gross Enrolment Rate (GER) from 36.3 per cent in 1991/1992 to 49.7 per cent in 1994/1995
- training of 4,518 primary school teachers through Inset Preset teacher training programmes
- construction and rehabilitation of 30 secondary schools since 1991/1992, which increased enrolment from a total of 27,927 in 1991/1992 to 34,995 in junior secondary schools and 36,728 in senior secondary schools in 1994/1995; in terms of GER this is an increase from 20.1 to 23.3 per cent for junior secondary schools, and 12.2 to 15 per cent for senior secondary schools
- revision and development of a new curriculum at all levels has been undertaken; primary school textbooks in the various ethnic group languages have been revised and published; new English language textbooks (for grades 2, 3, 6, 7, 8 and 9) have been written; senior

secondary school textbooks for science, math and geography have been published in adequate quantities

- consolidation of regional systems to expand supervisory capacity for assessing education quality
- introduction of a new system of examination and assessment whereby a new National Examination Centre is formed to prepare and administer national school exams and prepare guidelines for school-based assessment
- the development of a comprehensive technical and vocational sector for school-leavers and the unemployed youth; there are currently six skill development centres giving 6-12 month courses on plumbing, electricity, building construction, metal and woodworking, auto mechanics and driving; a new commercial school offering courses in computing, business and secretarial studies started in Asmara as a pilot programme; a new arts and crafts school offers short courses on handicrafts, ceramics, tailoring and embroidery; the only two technical schools are being rehabilitated; future plans call for at least one technical school in each administrative zone, two skill development centres in each zone, and significant diversification of their curricula
- capacity-building through professional training is being conducted inside and outside the country and a substantial number of the ministry's staff have already benefited from it

Despite many achievements, the ministry still faces serious problems in extending educational opportunities to all Eritreans. Although progress is reported in the conventional academic educational system, the same cannot be said of vocational education and skills training. There are only two technical schools providing pre-employment training. In addition to academic education, they offer three years of traditional technical training such as metal and woodworking, auto mechanics, electrical fitting, surveying and drafting. The maximum output of the two technical schools is not more than 200 graduates per year. A third centre, the Mai-Habar vocational training centre, was conceived and established primarily to cater to the special needs of disabled war veterans. However, because of lack of resources, the trades taught there also fall under the traditional occupation categories. The centre runs a six-month training programme for some 100 war-disabled trainees who have attained at least primary education.

Various training activities to upgrade skills are also provided by government ministries, notably those of Agriculture, Construction,

Education and Local Government, as well as by the University of Asmara and various international organizations. However, the quality of such programmes is often questionable.

Eritreans once prided themselves on having an abundance of technical skills compared to other nations in the region and they are fully conscious of the benefits to be derived from good technical training. It is essential that this tradition is maintained by increasing the opportunities of vocational education.

RESEARCH METHODOLOGY

The research framework

Having explored the state of the labour force in Eritrea and the government's perspective regarding its improvement and development, the response was sought of those who were considered to be the building blocks of HRD – employers, trainers, policy makers and relevant international communities employing many Eritrean professionals – to factors reflecting the actual labour situation in Eritrea. These included the quality of labour, place and condition of work, needs of employers, training programmes for employees, and similar issues. A questionnaire-based survey, direct interviews with relevant people and an in-depth case study of one training programme were carried out.

This aimed to collect feedback from employers, trainers, policy makers and the international community regarding the current labour situation in Eritrea. It was decided early in the research that a survey of key employers in and around Asmara and Massawa should be undertaken. The selection was done carefully so as to be representative enough to infer some general conclusions. Then selected interviews and/or discussions with three key policy actors in the area of HRD were conducted. Finally, a case study analysis of the Otto Benecke Stiftung-Commission for Eritrean Refugee Affairs (OBS-CERA) training programme was carried out.

The research questionnaire

Questionnaires were sent to 70 selected individuals, firms and organizations. Of the 43 respondents, most were employers, along with some trainers and policy makers, and their input is summarized below.

The employers

Most respondents in this category (65 per cent), rated their employees' skills as medium quality. Only respondents from the university and school directors considered the skills of their employees (teachers) as adequate or high. Of the respondents, 11.6 per cent considered their employees highly unskilled, to the point that some seriously questioned the wisdom of introducing new technology and sophisticated machines in their plants with such employees. Some of the reasons given for the presence of unskilled labour in their plants are interesting: loss of employee motivation to learn the job due to very low wages; better qualified workers leaving public enterprises to go to new privately owned plants or to work outside the country, mostly in Ethiopia. A programme to replace the exodus of skilled Ethiopians in 1991 has not been seriously looked into by the government.

More than 75 per cent of the respondents considered short-term skills training for their employees to be of high importance. Even high school directors who were seemingly happy with their teachers' skills indicated the need for refresher courses, because many instructors were teaching subjects they were not trained in. A few respondents (9.3 per cent) considered short-term training ineffective in workplaces where machinery and methods are obsolete.

It is evident that there is substantial effort to institute short-term skills training programmes, if our respondent group is to be taken as a representative sample. Among the most often mentioned training programmes for employees are computer literacy, office management skills, refresher and upgrading courses, regular on-the-job training programmes (sometimes including training for newly recruited apprentices), and encouraging employees to upgrade their qualifications.

Regarding employers' ability to freely access the labour market and its concomitant effect on productivity and efficiency, the majority (60.5 per cent) responded affirmatively, indicating a slow shift from pre-Independence conditions, when labourers were provided by the Labour Department. Negative response came from school directors who head public schools under the Ministry of Education. Interestingly, plant heads stressed the lack of discipline or work ethic among labourers freely hired and outdated qualifications as the main drawbacks. Asked to assess the effect of hiring undisciplined and unskilled workers, many stressed the inability of their organization to expand, delays in implementing planned programmes, loss of business due to unproductive labour, inability to introduce changes and new labour systems to improve quality and efficiency, and resulting high production costs making their products less competitive and the salaries they can offer lower than desired.

Asked to rate the existing educational system's appropriateness for the kind of skilled labour they need, 30 per cent of the employers who responded considered it irrelevant to the work employees were doing, while 49 per cent considered it a contribution of medium relevance. Employers seem to have a strong need for technically trained graduates as opposed to those with only a general high school education. A cursory investigation into the proportion of specialized technical schools and those of general academic education indicates the need for more technical training facilities in Eritrea. Therefore, matching employers' needs with the qualified employees can come only through additional on-the-job training programmes.

The gender and health issues produced most interesting responses. Because the health conditions of employees are directly related to productivity and quality improvement, about 32 per cent of responding employers considered the provision of health services to their employees to be of high importance. One interesting aspect concerning female employees is the apparent "problem" of pregnancy, which employers did not feel could be effectively solved by employing substitute workers. In a follow-up question regarding gender equality in the workplace, various responses were observed. Some stated unequivocally that they were committed to gender equality, sometimes even instituting a quota system to promote women's employment. Others strongly qualified this equality by ability to do the job and by women's successful fulfilment of certain requirements. There were also some who saw problems in implementing gender equality because they consider some jobs (heavy manufacturing, driving) suitable only for men. Some pointed to lower school attendance by girls as a reason not to seek out and hire women for certain jobs.

As to the question of hiring disabled workers, the questionnaire did not address it. Nevertheless, the researcher sees the need for active enrolment of the disabled in many workplaces. Extensive study of this issue is justified and needed in Eritrea.

All employers in the sample were asked if they have continuous job vacancies. Seventy per cent do. Unqualified applicants, and tendency of qualified applicants to stay in the capital city of Asmara, seem to be the main reasons for the vacancies. Some vacancies, to be sure, are also due to budgetary shortages and pending organizational restructuring. The presence of unfilled vacancies in a situation of high unemployment is usually due to the inappropriateness of the skills possessed by the labour available.

Employers were asked if they tried to recruit skilled employees among Eritreans in the diaspora. About 28 per cent had done so with some success; in most cases the employees were Eritreans residing in Ethiopia and eager to return home. Of course, the biggest challenge in this exercise is the absence of an organized contact mechanism between the two sides. This can only be established if the Eritrean embassies take the initiative to serve as go-betweens for such purposes.

The trainers

As to the responses by several selected training programme directors and trainers, a few points should be included here. The respondents included trainers from the University of Asmara, the Asmara Technical School, Asmara Commercial School and a few specialized skills training programmes run by the government and international NGOs.

In most of the programmes, the basis of the curriculum is to establish training geared to meet the shortage of skills in the productive sectors of the Eritrean economy. Whereas many of the programmes aim to upgrade staff skills and build organizational capacities, some are oriented toward a specific group (returning refugees, demobilized fighters, SAWA graduates) that needs to acquire certain types of technical know-how in a very short period of time. The OBS-CERA programmes are typical of the latter type. Yet few are designed to provide skills needed in a locality in order for the community to function in an orderly economic fashion. Trainers felt that they were more effective in programmes that were practical and "hands-on". The chances of graduates from such short-term practical programmes finding employment in the economy were high, according to trainers. Some even managed to be self-employed, setting up their own small shops and workplaces.

Selecting trainees for such programmes is an important component of the potential success of the programme: academic preparation, gender, social background, physical fitness in some jobs, age, prior work experience and acceptable references are some of the factors used most often in selecting candidates. For example, at the Asmara Technical School, 15 per cent of enrolment is reserved for female candidates to encourage women to become educated in technical areas. Some training programmes under the supervision of the National Confederation of Eritrean Workers (NCEW) are similarly run.

One issue that seemed to be lacking or poorly organized is job placement of training programme graduates. Even though the Labour

Office of the Ministry of Labour and Social Welfare is organized to perform this function, much more must be done by each training facility to secure jobs for its graduates.

Lastly, our survey indicated the areas of training considered important and urgent in today's economy. The top six training areas, ranked in order of importance are:
1. technical and vocational
2. management
3. agriculture
4. small business development
5. teachers and instructors (all levels)
6. mid-level personnel (all categories)

As can easily be inferred, these training needs are related to the task of helping a nascent national economy, which is trying to harness its natural resources – human resources prominent among them – for purposes of development.

The international community

The international community was similarly asked to respond to questions regarding HRD and their role in it in Eritrea. Questionnaires were distributed to 23 offices, and responses were received from 17.

Nearly all respondents play a role – direct or indirect – in the development of Eritrea's human resources in these formative years. Most are involved in funding projects or programmes that contribute to capacity- and institution-building in the country. Almost all give training to their staff members, including training abroad. At the time of the survey, many NGOs were involved in training seminars and workshops, and sponsoring humanitarian programmes. Many of the international actors in Eritrea are engaged in various human development projects, including rehabilitating schools, training trainers, improving skills in housing construction, improving skills in agriculture and fisheries, disseminating techniques of pest control by farmers, school meal programmes, conducting study tours and administering fellowships, and funding the training of community development facilitators.

Interviews with policy makers

Interviews with policy makers were deemed important in this research because many policy makers did not respond to the questionnaire. Thus, three individuals concerned with labour, education and training, and health

234 • POST-CONFLICT ERITREA: PROSPECTS FOR RECONSTRUCTION AND DEVELOPMENT

education and delivery were consulted.

The representative of the Ministry of Education was of the conviction that HRD is a long-term process that would require a long-term plan to educate the citizenry in various stages and at various levels. For any HRD scheme to work, it must take into account and start from existing concrete conditions in the country. Basic education to reduce illiteracy must precede widespread and rapid training programmes that can contribute to the nation's economic development. It is only after this stage that the acquisition of skills and even formal education leading to higher levels can be successful. In addition, right now there are crucial resource and labour constraints on the country; whatever exists will bear more fruit if basic education is invested in now.

The representative of the University of Asmara strongly recommended overhauling the educational system. In his viewpoint, relevant education "would focus on producing learned farmers, learned pastoralists and skilled graduates fit for the commercial, industrial sector, as well as for the civil service". He argued that a system producing a twelfth grade graduate who cannot be productively utilized by the economy is an expense Eritrea cannot afford. We have to find ways "to de-school those already schooled in irrelevant education", he said. His concern was the continuing system of middle and secondary education guided by an irrelevant curriculum.

On the issue of health services in Eritrea, he argued that the predominance of primary healthcare over the provision of curative services was a necessary component of HRD policy. Not only is such policy less costly, but it is also more effective in maintaining the health of the population. Thus, it directly contributes toward the faster economic development of the country, where the human capital is more productive and long-lasting as a factor of production.

The head of the Department of Labour of the Ministry of Labour and Social Welfare, stressed more the introduction of modern labour laws in Eritrea that should be instrumental in increasing productivity while protecting the interest of the worker. The most important HRD policy strategy as far as labour is concerned is to push for continual on-the-job training to update the skills of employees. Preferential treatment should be given to investors with training programmes as part of their package. The new labour laws were meant to help realize higher and more efficient production levels, which in turn will result in higher wages and better working conditions.

The three selected policy makers recognized that Eritrea's most important resource that can be qualitatively improved is human capital. Policy to improve and enrich it should be a top government priority. Their differences reflect the transitional stage of the nation; opinions are hard to prove with quantifiable statistics or prior experiences. Their responses were helpful in pinpointing the issues.

The OBS-CERA training project case study

The overall objective of the OBS-CERA training project was to train labour needed urgently in all sectors of the war-ravaged Eritrean economy. Furthermore, the programme aimed to assist trained returnees in finding employment or becoming established as self-employed nationals.

From its inception, the OBS-CERA training project offered training programmes throughout Eritrea in collaboration with other organizations and institutions. In addition to training at its own sites attached to the resettlement programme for returnees from Sudan, OBS-CERA trained at private enterprises, sites organized by the NUEW, secondary schools under the Ministry of Education, and government department and public enterprises. The geographical presence of its training sites in the lowlands and highlands makes the programme exemplary in this respect.

The profile of trainees since 1993 indicates diversity and balance in age group, geographical origin, educational background and gender composition. In 1993/1994, 596 (32 per cent) of the 1,923 trainees were female. This exceeds OBS-CERA's target of 30 per cent female participation in the programmes. More interesting for our research, though, is the training programmes these women were enrolled in. The percentage of women in technical and agricultural courses was less than 10 per cent, and that was compensated for only by courses specifically organized for women (353 participants) in co-operation with the NUEW in fields such as mat and basket making, embroidery, tailoring, typing and fishnet making in the provinces of Semhar, Senhit, Barka, Gash-Setit and Asmara. But in courses such as commercial training, hotel catering, journalism, and telecommunications, more than 50 per cent of enrolees were women.

Training women in traditional fields such as mat or basket making, tailoring, embroidery or typing, does not create sufficient income-generating potential. According to the evaluation of the programme, training women in traditional crafts should be phased out. Female participation in these areas has decreased since 1994.

The profile of professional fields also shows diversity and proportion considered appropriate by OBS-CERA to respond to urgent shortages in

1993–1994. The training programme for the year shows that 561 participants (20 per cent) underwent training in construction, 228 (12 per cent) in carpentry, 165 (9 per cent) in mechanics, 148 (8 per cent) in metalwork, 63 (3 per cent) in electricity, 357 (19 per cent – including 353 women) in tailoring and handicraft, 160 (8 per cent) in agriculture, 109 (6 per cent) in commerce. The remaining 132 (7 per cent) were trained in mass media, hotel catering, and other fields such as fishnet making, telephone operations, meteorological observation and forecasting, and aerodrome control. Some 1,165 participants (60 per cent) received training in construction and related trades (masonry, carpentry, metalwork, mechanics, electricity).

One of the successes of the OBS-CERA programme is its ability to place most of its graduates into meaningful employment related to their training. Of the 2,266 graduates (1993–1996), only 288 (12.7 per cent) were still unemployed in mid-1996. The programme has an Office of Employment Co-ordinator who helps graduates find jobs and monitors their progress.

The OBS-CERA training project, although phased out in 1997 by order of the government, did have a positive impact on training individuals in many fields related to reconstruction efforts in a relatively short time. As such, the case study contributed to enriching HRD policies and programmes in Eritrea.

Summary observations and issues for further study

The research presented in this section pinpoints many important issues that require serious attention. The points raised indicate questions that need to be studied further, many of which are beyond the scope of this chapter. Among the most important issues which call for further study are the following:

- What is the best way to design relevant curriculum for training programmes? Who should carry out the task? How is it related to the labour needs of the economy?
- What selection criteria should be established for choosing programme trainees?
- Should the placement of trained graduates into gainful employment be the task of each programme?
- What rights of female workers must be legislated?
- Should there be a programme of affirmative action for female trainees and the disabled to redress age-old biases and discrimination?

- Is there a need to seriously review the educational system in view of the serious shortages of skilled labour resources in Eritrea?
- What system of incentives should be provided to repatriate professional and skilled Eritreans in the diaspora?

These are some of the questions that policy makers and researchers should address, along with the issues already mentioned.

Recommendations for HRD Policies

When giving recommendations regarding HRD policies in Eritrea, caution must be taken to put them in context. The country is new and the government is young. Most institutions are still in the process of becoming established and the lack of professionals to run them properly is a serious drawback. Therefore, some obvious general recommendations that can be made on the issue are out of place and premature in Eritrea. Only recommendations that relate to reconstruction and revitalization of the economy in the near future can be presented here, and briefly at that.

The following key recommendations are not necessarily for the government only. Nor are these exhaustive by any means. These are the most-discussed issues, raised primarily in response to the survey questionnaire findings. The main ones are:

- There are many unanswered questions relating to education and training needs in Eritrea. The lack of detailed analysis is a real problem. There is a need to establish an independent or semi-independent advisory body with the capacity to carry out policy-relevant research. Some of the responsibilities of the proposed body could include providing advice on training needs of the total economy, advising on curricula with the aim of making education relevant to jobs (rural and urban), and advising on how to make training more efficient and cost effective.
- As Ministry of Education statistics show, few student enrolled in primary education will proceed to the secondary level. Of those who complete secondary education, a negligible number will be able to attend the nation's only university. It is therefore important to define the *purpose of education*. At the moment, the need for a more work-oriented education at these levels is an essential and necessary consideration, relevance being key.
- The development of relevant HRD policies must rely on a well-researched and studied needs-assessment of all sectors of the economy, otherwise programmed activities may not meet the intended target.

- It is feasible to bring in high-level technicians and professionals from abroad at this juncture, with a clear plan to train Eritreans to take over from the foreigners in a known timetable. To persist in "doing it ourselves" may prove harmful in some economic activities.
- A well-thought-out policy to attract Eritreans in the diaspora to return home is needed. Pay may not be the paramount factor, but improvements in local school systems (in curriculum and foreign language facilities), establishment of clear professional linkages while they are still in the diaspora, housing, and establishment of a central information and processing centre are some steps which must be taken.
- A re-entrenchment in the health field toward giving prominence to the primary healthcare system is the better and preferred policy. The Eritrean struggle is relatively rich in its experience in this field and should be promoted. In the curative health delivery system, it is recommended that continual research be conducted to ensure optimal healthcare delivery and optimal professional performance of health workers within a system that is efficient and cost-effective.
- With regard to relations between national and international actors in HRD, more co-ordination of activities is needed.
- Finally, more thought should be given to the retirement schedule in Eritrea. In most professional and skilled fields, people are at their sharpest at the age of 55. Many more years of productive service may follow that age.

References

GSE, *Basic Education Statistics and Essential Indicators: 1994–1995*, Ministry of Education, 1996b.

GSE, *Eritrea: Strategy for Human Resources Development – a Project for Capacity Building*, Office of Human Resource Development, 1996a.

GSE, *Macro-Policy Document*, Asmara, 1994.

Myers, C. and Harbison, F., *Education, Manpower and Economic Growth: Strategies of Human Resource Development*, McGraw-Hill, New York, 1965.

Nader, Leonard and Nader, Zeace, *The Handbook of Human Resources Development*, Wiley and Sons, New York, 1990.

7

ISSUES OF GOVERNANCE IN THE ERITREAN CONTEXT

Alemseged Tesfai

The concept of governance came to the fore of the development debate toward the end of the 1980s, when the World Bank identified the "crisis of governance" as "underlying the litany of Africa's development problems". The Bank's 1989 publication **Sub-Saharan Africa: From Crisis to Sustainable Growth**, went on to list defects of African leadership authority and legitimacy such as "the absence of balance of power, the lack of official accountability, the control of information and a failure to respect the rule of law". The Bank recommended "independence of the judiciary, scrupulous respect for the law and human rights at every level of government, transparent accountability of public monies, and independent public auditors responsible to a representative legislative, not to an executive".

The call for accountability, openness and adherence to the rule of law was not new. What was new was that the World Bank, and thus the donor community, was adding its voice to the debate and making its recommendations prerequisites for aid and loans to African states. However, many found fault with the Bank's suggestion that sustainability, equity and participation were required for economic growth and that they be tied to the "imperatives of accumulation and order" (Moore, 1995:16).

Equity, for example, is seen by the Bank as essential for long-term political stability, without which growth is impossible. However, equity is conceived by the Bank not as "state or socially regulated distribution", but rather as encouraged by "improving the access of the poor to productive assets and to releasing the energies of ordinary people by enabling them to take charge of their lives". This would be accomplished by "giving the poor access to assets promoting this productivity" (Moore, 1995:16).

But who improves and gives such access to the poor? If the state is considered incapable of such an act, will the cut and thrust world of the free market allow it? The implication is that the Bank, or international capital, "would control the local state's withdrawal from the economy. Resources must (then) be taken away from the state and placed in the 'market' where all citizens will supposedly have equal access to them" (Moore, 1995:9).

In this line of thinking, the state would be relieved of its traditional role as a "buffer protecting the national economy from disruptive external forces" and as the "focal point for the organization and maintenance of domestic employment and welfare". Instead, "its role will be that of tailoring discrete geographical and social spaces to the whims of the world economic tsars and fashioning a civil society, made up of those with interests congruent with the 'global market places'" (Moore, 1995:19).

Many will regard this as cynical and unfair to the Bank. But Moore insists that the type of "participation" advocated by the Bank excludes "social movements considering making alliances coalescing around and permeating the state – especially a state that just might not be strong enough (i.e. have the capacity) to absorb any hegemony challenges posed by such movements" (Moore, 1995:19). Thus, he concludes, "a new emphasis has been reached, combining good governance (better administrative management in the state) with participation in 'civil society'".

Our intention is not to discuss these opposing views here, but to introduce current thinking on the subject. Governance, or "good governance" as perceived by the World Bank and other advocates of the idea, seems to anticipate a less dominant, more supervisory government and an independent, almost government-resistant civil society. Because popular participation in government policy-making and implementation is generally regarded as one of the keys to sustainable growth and development, the link between governance and the assurance of civil society participation is worth considering.

A point of heated controversy among scholars in Africa is whether or not a viable civil society exists in the various nations. Goran Hyden defines governance as:

> The use of political authority to promote and enhance societal values – economic as well as non-economic – that are sought by individuals and groups.... In the absence of any marked cultural differentiation, social separation and political opposition between the ruling élite and the masses, reciprocity is the basis of political

integration.... Reciprocity, then, is at the core of governance in
Africa and will be for the foreseeable future (Hyden, 1990).

Robert Fatton Jr. opposes Hyden's assumption that "the essence of
African politics is a common discourse of togetherness and commitment to
a common good". To achieve political authority, Fatton says:

> A 'general will' capable of ushering in a common good that
> transcends the purposes of antagonistic groups requires an idealism
> run wild. How can human beings truly share a community of
> interests when they are divided into classes of perpetrators and
> victims of exploitation? Governance imparts to politics a supreme
> benignity that conjures away the manifest realities of economic
> injustice, brutal repression and social conflicts (Fatton, 1992:4).

Fatton recognizes the influence of altruism, reciprocity, and
compassion in African politics, but stresses that in the prevailing context of
severe scarcity and gross material disparities this realm is besieged and
shrinking. So what appears to be the common good is "at best a very fragile
pact of consensual domination", that may break into coercion once the
"ruling class" fails to convince "subaltern classes" that "reciprocity
represents a credible contract without which their already limited life-
chances would be limited even more" (Fatton, 1992:4).

Contrary to what Hyden's reciprocity theory suggests, it is argued that
civil society as a "private sphere of material, cultural, and political
activities resisting the incursions of the state" does exist (Fatton, 1992:5).
Fatton singles out the petty-bourgeoisie (comprising the professional and
commercial elements operating relatively autonomously from the reach of
the state) as having played and continuing to play a fundamental role in the
resurgence of civil society by, for example, establishing NGOs and
voluntary associations "through which they are stating their claims for
positions of influence and power" (Fatton, 1992:5). He sees the petty-
bourgeoisie as the leaders of the multi-party movement and as the
champions, vis-à-vis the state, of democratization and privatization.

In a similar vein, John Keane sees civil society as:

> An aggregate of institutions whose members are engaged in a
> complex of non-state activities – economic and cultural production,
> household life and voluntary associations – and who in this way
> preserve and transform their identity by exercising all sorts of
> pressures or controls upon state institutions (Keane, 1988:11).

And what would the role of the state be? Keane warns against the
dangers of "idealising" civil society and "demonizing" the state: "Without
the protective, redistributive and conflict-mediating functions of the state,
struggles to transform civil society will become ghettoized, divided and

stagnant, or will spawn their own, new forms of inequality and unfreedom" (Keane, 1988:14–15).

Therefore, it appears that governance is a concept or "development agenda" that is relatively new, not clearly defined, and controversial. The controversy becomes more pronounced when noting that the neutrality of the concept is somewhat compromised by the standards of "good governance" often attached to it. Aside from the measurements already referred to, elements such as decentralization, political pluralism and regular free elections are added to the list of requirements that African governments must meet in order to achieve the standards of "good governance".

Even here, there appear to be contradictions and inconsistencies. For example, David B. Moore points to the World Bank's tolerance of the state-led development strategies of the Asian tigers. Some writers note that some authoritarian (not socialist or communist) states have proved more effective in the equitable distribution of wealth among their citizens than their more liberal (democratic) counterparts.

Political pluralism, generally regarded today as the prime test of democratization, is perhaps the most contentious aspect of governance as it relates to Africa. Mahmoud Mamdani argues that, although African social protest against colonial masters took the form of genuine social movements transformed into national political parties, colonial reform saw to it that political association lost its social base or context. By requiring that popular associations be registered and accountable to bureaucracies rather than to the people, colonial reform, Mamdani says, depoliticized the movements and professionalized the leadership. The net effect of this was to:

> ...drive a wedge between political and social movements. The point was simultaneously to contain social movements and to sever their link with political movements. Once adrift, political movements were easily reshaped by their middle class membership into state parties whose objective was limited to organizing periodic electoral contests (Mamdani, 1992:20–21).

Mamdani does not stop here. The absence of a social base for political parties in Africa deprives single-party and multi-party regimes of the status of being opposing alternatives. Rather, he says:

> They appear as different points in a single continuum: the soil that nurtured the single-party regime was prepared by the multi-party reform. Both begin with a definition of pluralism that negates its social and ideological dimensions, and limits it to its political aspect. The common heritage that one upholds and the other

repudiates, but around which both revolve, is of pluralism so narrow that its safeguards are meaningful mainly to political professionals (Mamdani, 1992:23).

Although Mamdani does not say so, the implications are that civil society, as defined above, lost its importance, as has the base. Even the reciprocity that Hyden talks about seems to have no place in Mamdani's formulations, as governments formed by one or more political parties detached from their social base cannot be expected to encourage or tolerate, much less create, the rapport necessary for a reciprocal relationship.

This discussion of the literature is, admittedly, sketchy. However, it indicates that governance – the word and the concept – is still a matter for debate, and has yet to be fully understood. Many of the points raised should be kept in mind during this discussion of the Eritrean situation.

The focal point of this research is the new administrative structure legislated by the Eritrean government. It must be viewed in light of the experiences of others. Is Eritrea repeating mistakes made by others or is it breaking new ground? Are there defined standards of governance that African states should adhere to, or should there be? Can there be governance as a country and culture-specific paradigm that is flexible and malleable according to existing conditions? These are some of the questions to be considered.

THE ERITREAN CONTEXT

Traditional administration

Pre-Italian administration in what became Eritrea differed from area to area. Feudal relations prevailed in the highlands (more strongly, perhaps, in Hamassien, Seraye, and the Roras than in Akele Guzai), while traditional forms were found among the Kunama and Nara. Feudal relations were not of the landlord/tenant or serf variation, except in the Roras to some extent. Eritrean communities mostly owned their land but had to pay dues in cash, kind or limited labour to overlords. Thus, feudal relations were never deeply rooted.

Communities were left to administer their own affairs. In the highland provinces the village *baito* was led by elders (rarely chiefs) they elected and who ran the affairs of the village. Regional power would often shift between powerful families depending on where the centre of power was. Land, family and penal laws were either written or firmly committed to memory. The *baito* was an all-male assembly.

Similar traditional administrative systems existed in lowland, pastoral communities. The Kunama people, for example, had a *baito*-type village assembly called a *dama*, where elders and wise men called *sukunda* made decisions in a gathering of the entire village. The villagers gathered at the *dama* could give their opinions and suggestions, and the *sukunda* had the obligation to give these due consideration.

These two examples indicate that traditional Eritrea had a rich and diversified system of administration before the Italian introduction of modern government.

Italian government (1935-1941)

The Italians established two levels of administration. The first was a colonial government with all the makings, apparatus and offices of modern government. It catered to the needs of the colonizers and their settlers, and introduced not only a modern state system, but also modern industry, commerce, agriculture and social services. These were directed and protected by European laws and enforced by an efficient police and judicial system. Eritreans were recruited to fill very junior posts in the colonial administration. This Italian set-up was to serve as the base for subsequent governments.

The second level of Italian administration concerned the indigenous or native population. Except where their interests so demanded – for example, when they needed to confiscate land or recruit Eritreans for military service – the Italians generally left traditional Eritrean administration intact. They did break the power of some local leaders or chiefs who presented a threat to Italian power, and then replaced them with their own loyal followers. Thus, village and district leadership became appointed instead of elected or earned through battle. The Italians also greatly reduced the privileges of the Rora (Habab) and western lowland feudal regimes, but maintained the *shums*, *kentibas* and *diglels*, feudal lords of various districts.

Control over indigenous Eritrea was maintained through a hierarchy of responsibilities and a line of contact going straight from each village to the colonial governor. Thus, each village had an appointed head who was responsible to a native sub-district head (generally known as the *meslene*), who in turn was responsible to the *residente* or provincial governor. The residente was accountable directly to the *Commissario*, the Italian colonial officer representing the state in a province. The latter would be responsible to the Governor General. The *residente* was the highest Italian official

Eritreans could access.

Disputes involving Eritreans were referred to the village *baito* to be dealt with in accordance with traditional laws. For more complicated cases involving reference to modern laws, a special *Corte Nativa* was established, with branches in the provinces. Cases involving Eritreans and Italians were referred to the Italian courts.

Therefore, the vast majority of the people of Eritrea had little if any direct contact with colonial administration. Italian rule is still remembered for its apartheid-type segregation and more especially for its denial of more than elementary education to the Eritrean population. Eritreans were excluded from the political life of the colony. Except for harmless, religion-oriented gatherings, no forms of association, political or otherwise, were even thinkable.

British government (1941–1952)

For the British, Eritrea was of interest only as part of an East African region where they were vying for supremacy. Their strategic designs focused mainly on territorial gains in Somalia, Libya and Sudan. Eritrea was considered an artificial Italian creation with no future as a country unto itself and was to be a dismembered compromise (or prize) to its neighbours.

This perspective determined British "governance" in Eritrea from the outset. Their first administrative act was to retain Italian laws, the government apparatus and even key Italian officers and judges. The Italian separate administration for Eritreans was also kept intact initially. This changed in later years, as Eritrean resistance strengthened and eventually the British were obliged to train and set up an Eritrean civil service, in preparation for the establishment of an autonomous Eritrean government federated to Ethiopia.

The British are often credited with having introduced modern education and press freedom into Eritrea. In 1946, they also allowed Eritreans to express their desires for the future by forming political parties. Although these represented significant contributions to the political development of the Eritrean population, the British political intentions and agenda already referred to were to have an overall negative impact on Eritrean politics in subsequent years.

Regardless of how Eritreans saw themselves, the British stuck to their initial perception that highland (predominantly Christian) Eritrea belonged to Ethiopia, and lowland (predominantly Muslim) Eritrea should join

Sudan. Further, the British were convinced that Ethiopia deserved an outlet to the sea. In other words, the British saw Eritrea as clearly divided between Muslim and Christian parts, with even further ethnic and regional subdivisions in each perceived religious sector.

Perhaps to strengthen their hand, the British never instituted a method for Eritreans to express political wishes at the grassroots level. Except for the *Mahber Fikri Hager*, a loose association of politically divergent personalities advocating certain civil and human rights, there were no labour unions and few or no gatherings that could develop into genuine, mass-movement political parties. Therefore, when political associations were formed in 1946, they not only reflected the religious and ethnic divisions in the country, but also became spontaneous mass followings of political figures. Political programmes were not clearly stated or understood by the supposed followers. Until the time of federation, mass defections and switches between parties were very common, indicating the absence of principled attachment to causes.

Remarkably, the divisions and general lack of organization notwithstanding, Eritreans resisted and frustrated the British (and Ethiopian) plan to dismember the country. However, this underlying unity or common feeling of nationalism was consolidated in an organized manner only later during the armed struggle. Toward the end of British rule, it was still raw and vulnerable. Thus the federal solution, which declared Eritrea an autonomous unit federated to Ethiopia under the Ethiopian Crown, was an imposition, a United Nations compromise between Ethiopian demands, British plans and the aspirations of the Eritrean people. Even in the election of the constitutional assembly, set up to discuss the Eritrean constitution drafted by the United Nations representative, the British could ignore with impunity political parties and affiliations and divide Eritrea into electoral districts based purely on religious and regional divisions and affinity.

Therefore, the British legacy was a government dominated by Ethiopia, with an assembly that did not represent the wishes of the people. The political parties were literally left out of the political processes of the day. In other words, there was little or no public opinion, much less an organized "civil society" in Eritrea in the early 1950s.

The "federal" period (1952–1962)

The first two years of the federal period saw an attempt in Eritrea to develop a free press, a broad-based labour union and a separation of powers between the three branches of government. However, this was short-lived as the democratic principles on which the Eritrean government was based clashed head-on with the Ethiopian monarchy.

The federal government was meant to be modelled after the United States' system of government, with executive, legislative and judicial powers clearly delineated. However, because a federal government separate from the Ethiopian government was not instituted, the latter had, with British collusion and in the name of the federation, usurped most of Eritrea's major sources of income: ports, roads, telephones and telegraphs, and so on. The Eritrean government was rendered bankrupt and dependent on Ethiopian "subsidies" from the outset. The "federal" (Ethiopian) government wasted no time suppressing free press, disbanding the fledgling labour union, exiling Eritrean nationalist leaders and eroding the foundations and existence of Eritrean autonomy.

The 1950s represented a landmark in the development of Eritrean political consciousness and in the Eritrean people's recognition that organization was the only means of asserting their rights. Ethiopia and its Eritrean puppet regime felt the frustration of appeals, student demonstrations and workers' strikes for the preservation of the federation and this led to the establishment of clandestine organizations and movements in the late 1950s that culminated in the beginning of the armed struggle by ELF in 1961. In other words, organized public opinion in Eritrea had to go underground in the late 1950s. The Eritrean government, itself under direct Ethiopian control and constant duress, could operate only as a police state. The story of the federal period was the story of the dismantling of Eritrean autonomy – and the story of suppressed public opinion seeking outlets beyond the official political system.

Ethiopian rule and the liberation struggle

Immediately after it's forced annexation of Eritrea in 1962, Ethiopia attempted to retain and use the more efficient (relative to Ethiopian bureaucracy) government machinery left over from the federal period. To prove that complete union was indeed the solution to Eritrea's problems, the Ethiopian administration also tried to show signs of liberalization in the economic sphere.

However, the struggle for independence by ELF was on the upsurge and Ethiopian repression had to match it. By 1967, most of the western lowlands were under military emergency rule and as the decade advanced the whole nation could be controlled only through brute military force and a network of spies, even in areas considered safe by the Ethiopian regime.

ELF's style of popular organization and the politics behind it differed little from the British approach to ethnicity and religion. The ELF divided Eritreans into five administrative divisions based on major geographic/linguistic/religious distinctions. It was a move that would have bred serious rifts and ill-feeling among Eritreans had it been allowed to continue.

It did not continue because in 1970, following abortive attempts at internal reform, opposing forces within the ELF founded EPLF as an alternative. A year later, ELF's attempt to eliminate the infant EPLF resulted in three years of internecine war that rocked the country. It was only after spontaneous popular interventions that the fronts agreed to a cessation of hostilities and started competing organizational work in their respective areas of influence.

In the 1970s, especially from the establishment of the Derg in 1974 until EPLF's defeat of ELF in 1980/1981, EPLF increasingly gained popular support. This was due mainly to EPLF's political programme and more effective and participatory system of administration, which contrasted favourably to the repressive methods of the Derg and the ways of the internally divided ELF.

It has been shown that the Italian and British colonial governments in Eritrea were super-impositions, detached from the life of society. It has also been shown that the Ethiopian government had to repress all forms of association, except those of its own creation, in order to rule. The EPLF method of administration stood in sharp contrast to these previous practices. It is often said that the EPLF unity of purpose and its people were the main reasons for the its resounding success. Whereas these were definitely factors, EPLF's whole approach to and handling of popular participation should be kept in mind.

EPLF's ADMINISTRATIVE EXPERIENCE

The formative years

EPLF was, in essence, an organization whose main duty was to fight and win the war for independence. In the early stages of its existence, its mobile nature allowed only for the establishment of small support units that catered to its immediate needs. Thus, such essential units as its health, logistics, training and information sections may be regarded as having evolved together with EPLF. These sections were as mobile as the fighting forces, and their members often had to shift from their specially assigned tasks to military duties.

The early 1970s were crucial for EPLF, as it had to fight both ELF and the Ethiopians for its survival. In order to gain public backing, small groups of fighters were given the task of organizing popular support and attracting new recruits. However, contact with the people brought with it involvement in their everyday affairs – health problems, various disputes, and so on. Because one of the main reasons for EPLF's separation from ELF was the latter's mistreatment of the people, EPLF spared no effort to establish a correct approach toward public affairs. As a result, the nuclei were formed of the mass administration units (MAUs) that were to play increasingly pivotal roles in EPLF's administrative responsibilities.

From its inception, EPLF had declared its final objective as being the establishment of a democratic state. The particular form that this state would take evolved over the years. The underlying intention of EPLF has, however, been directed toward political empowerment of the people and their eventual takeover of the responsibilities of government and administration.

During the formative years, up to the mid-1970s, EPLF had to compete with ELF for popular support, especially in contested areas. This provided an opportunity to refine its methods of work and approach and, by avoiding the mistakes of its competitor, gain more ground. By 1976, EPLF had grown both in strength and popular support and was gaining the upper hand. Its contact with the general population had also expanded and gone beyond propaganda work to include administrative and judicial duties that required more formal methods and directives.

The Department of Public Administration (DPA)

In 1977, the DPA was formed at the First Congress of EPLF. Its tasks included mobilizing and organizing people to the cause of EPLF, while also attending to their basic needs, for example improving their economic conditions and enabling them to protect themselves from the enemy attacks they were frequently exposed to.

In 1977 and 1978, EPLF and ELF occupied most of the Eritrean countryside, confining the enemy to the capital, Asmara, and a few other towns. During that short period, the DPA set out to establish two levels of administration: the people's committees and the people's assemblies.

The committees, generally seen as transitional, were established either in areas newly occupied or controlled by the EPLF or in those close to or behind enemy lines. The committees were usually very small and elected in village general meetings; their duty was to liaise between the EPLF and the villages concerned. All directives and programmes were transmitted through them and they could perform administrative, judicial and other tasks on behalf of the Front.

A step ahead of the committees were the people's assemblies or *baitos*. These could be village or *wereda baitos*. The *baitos* were fairly widespread in rural and urban areas in 1977–1978. They were set up in areas that EPLF regarded as secure and, in line with the political outlook of EPLF of those days, their membership corresponded to class divisions in the community concerned. For example, villagers would be classified as rich, middle-income or poor, and represented accordingly, with the poor forming the majority in the *baitos*. The *baitos* differed from the people's committees, which were elected in general meetings.

The duties of the *baitos* were far greater than those of the committees. From the members of the *baito* an executive body consisting of a chairman, secretary and heads of various committees was elected. The committees, which included justice, social affairs, security and economic committees, were granted relatively broad powers and within the directives of the DPA and under supervision of the MAUs concerned, these powers were actually put to effect.

The most prominent duties of the *baitos,* especially in the late 1970s, were to effect land redistribution and establish and manage various forms of people's co-operatives, including agricultural projects, community shops, furnaces and other economic activities tied closely to the communities. These operated with differing degrees of success.

However, the committees and the *baitos* should be viewed in the general framework of the DPA itself. Led by a member of the Politburo of EPLF, who was at the top of the administrative ladder, the DPA divided Eritrea into zones or regions, where geographical structure was to differ with changing military situations. The zones were in turn divided and subdivided into district and sub-district administrative areas, where different levels of MAUs were placed under the leadership of an appointed member of the DPA. Therefore, in the beginning the empowerment of *baitos* was restricted to the affairs of the village or an administrative unit of similar status.

The strategic withdrawals and after

At the end of 1978, massive Soviet support of the Ethiopian Derg resulted in strategic withdrawals of EPLF from areas it had liberated to its base areas in Sahel. This was a testing period, especially for the members of EPLF *baitos*, committees and members of the people's militia – which had also been formed in some areas as they were suddenly exposed to enemy reprisals.

Despite the danger involved, the DPA maintained its administrative network by continuing the activities of its MAUs, which did not delay in reasserting their influence in large parts of the areas from which they had withdrawn. By 1979, the initial shock of the strategic withdrawals subsided, as EPLF proved its resilience not only by repelling five major enemy offensives, but by also counter-attacking on the Nacfa front and incapacitating the enemy.

These were crucial years for EPLF. Once its base areas were consolidated, EPLF went about in earnest the business of laying the groundwork for a future government. In the First Congress several departments had been set up along with the DPA, including economics (encompassing agriculture, commerce and trade, and industry), political awareness, education and culture, social affairs, information and propaganda, and the old health and logistics sections – the latter being included in the defence department.

These departments, many of whose activities had begun as early as 1975, started to take on definite structure in 1980/1981. The base area had numerous underground complexes that provided sheltered offices, offering the security of settled desk work and at least the beginnings of a state machinery.

The situation outside the base area was different. ELF was still strong and, in the lull in fighting between EPLF and the Derg following the former's counter-offensive, old conflicts flared up. It had become virtually impossible to set up *baitos* along the old lines. EPLF's fighting forces, the Eritrean People's Liberation Army (EPLA), were so busy protecting the base areas that there could be no further liberated zones. At best, the EPLA could only attack selected posts, convoys or even towns behind enemy lines and withdraw to the trenches. This left the MAUs, representatives of the various departments of EPLF, members of people's committees, and the militias open to attacks by both ELF and the Derg.

This situation necessitated the creation of a new type of administrative set-up, the *bdho* (literally "challenge") committee. In status, it came between the people's committee and the *baito*. Its members were popularly elected to administer villages and areas on behalf of EPLF, but they were also armed to defend themselves as necessary. In the crucial years before the Derg's Sixth Offensive (and biggest), or the Red Star Campaign of

1982 and beyond, the *bdho* committees, along with EPLF's militias and later-formed regional army (or "territorial army", a paramilitary force whose movements were limited to specific areas), were an important arm of EPLF's administrative and military strategy.

In 1980 and 1981, civil war erupted once more between EPLF and ELF. This was the last of its type. ELF was totally defeated and had to disband. In the meantime, the Derg was preparing for its declared, "once and for all" offensive, which came in 1982. When this failed, another massive offensive, its seventh, followed in 1983. This did not succeed either, but the whole of Eritrea, with the exception of the base area, had become a battleground, necessitating expansion of the open and clandestine armed *bdho* committees, the militia and the regional army to defend the interests of the Eritrean struggle.

This situation, or method of administration through people's and *bdho* committees under the supervision of MAUs, continued without major changes until the Derg's major defeat at the Nadew front and the capture of Afabet by EPLF in 1988.

Some important characteristics distinguish this period of the EPLF's administrative experience:

- The *baitos*, people's committees and *bdho* committees had the power to decide on local disputes of any nature and on social and economic issues that concerned their areas of jurisdiction or authority. The MAUs always reserved the right of intervention where it was felt that EPLF's principles would be compromised.
- Serious or sensitive matters that involved security, military movements, or other matters requiring reference to EPLF's directives, policies or principles were the domain of the MAUs.
- Participation in all forms of administration made no distinction between the sexes and barred all forms of social discrimination. However, until the late 1980s, class distinctions characterized committee elections.
- Although the MAUs were the real administrative power, *baito* and committee members (and in the 1980s even ordinary people) were allowed to attend meetings and give their assessment and criticism on the performance even of district and zonal administrators. Some of the latter have been known to be removed from their posts by popular demand.
- The MAUs – and the *baitos* and committees under them – combined the tasks of executive, judiciary and legislature under one command. There

was no separation of responsibilities, an element that was later to create problems of transition.

• Although the DPA generally played the role of co-ordinator in such important tasks as distributing food-aid, enlisting new recruits, mobilizing for war and development efforts, central EPLF departments also started to be directly represented in zonal administrations. This practice was also to create situations that called for serious reconsideration.

Some reflections and observations

At this point, as EPLF's comprehensive administrative approach and structure started to change, it is worth reflecting on Eritrean "governance", as it developed within EPLF. No analysis can adequately treat this topic without an appreciation of the following distinguishing traits of EPLF.

The first consideration is that in essence EPLF was an organization whose main duty was to fight and win the war for independence. Its military responsibilities often dominated and sometimes eclipsed its other activities. It had to maintain a centralized chain of command, ensure strict military discipline through a system of laws, rules and directives, protect its essential secrets from reaching the enemy, and protect the unity of its ranks and the people from divisive ideas and elements.

These elements of tightness, closeness and centralization, justifiable under any military situation anywhere in the world, were everyday necessities. The victory attained cannot be conceived of had they not been enforced. Thus EPLF's efforts to create a democratic and decentralized base were always made in the face of constraints imposed by these elements.

The second point to appreciate is that EPLF was a volunteer organization and was perceived as such by its members. The tradition was passed from one generation of fighters to the next and was a commitment to EPLF's principles, an unshaken faith in a final outcome of victory, and a voluntary submission to the hierarchy of authority and its laws, rules and principles. With allowance for some deviations, the typical attitude of an EPLF member was never to wait for orders and to be accountable to their own conscience and sense of duty. Fear of authority or a desire for individual recognition were generally frowned on. Protecting EPLF's secrets, regardless of their classification, was a distinguishing characteristic of an EPLF fighter. Finally, as volunteers to a common cause, EPLF members saw each other as partners in struggle. In spite of hierarchy, the sense of equality that cut across the sexes was the norm.

The third point is the high level of popular support and voluntary popular participation, especially in the 1980s. With the exception of a small percentage attached to the Derg, almost every Eritrean supported the cause of freedom, be it physically, financially or spiritually. The absence of ELF from Eritrea meant that EPLF was without competition. It had the attention of the people and its contacts with them were real and constant. The MAUs in particular were regarded as part and parcel of communities, sharing their joys and sorrows. The old colonial separation of "us" and "them" was almost non-existent. What was good for EPLF was generally seen as advancing the cause of freedom, and few if any doubts were voiced regarding the wisdom of decisions and directives. Was this because there were no bad decisions or poor administration? Not necessarily, for those aspects were evident too, but freedom was in the air and all concerned were committed to expanding it further.

These three points are generally the dominant and distinguishing traits of EPLF administration, while sometimes allowing for laxity or severity brought about by extreme fluctuations in the armed struggle. The importance lies in the administrative culture brought about by their combination. How does this culture look?

EPLF has been described as a hierarchical organization with a chain of command strictly enforced by rules and regulations. In everyday life and work, however, the comradeship forged in struggle and the sharing of a common life and common premises often obliterated hierarchy and the aura and distance normally associated with authority. Thus, whether in trenches or offices, there developed within EPLF an informal style of communication, where trust and not legal or administrative accountability was the order of the day.

Paperwork – models and vouchers, application forms, memoranda, notices, bids and tenders – the weaponry of every bureaucracy, was rarely if ever used in EPLF. Regular meetings, seminars, assessment and criticism sessions, where policy decisions were discussed, accomplishments and performances weighed, failures and mistakes criticized and corrected and differences cemented, were instead the primary means of communication – top-down and vice-versa. Except in cases where rules were broken or discipline deliberately trespassed – matters that required stricter handling – accountability rarely meant anything more than criticism in a meeting. This was generally an effective method of correction, as few people withstood the stigma. Demotions, removals and detentions were avoided as much as possible.

In an overall centralized system, this style of communication and accountability created a flexible administrative method that avoided the rigidity typical of most bureaucracies. Although EPLF's departments were being established as strong and durable institutions, they were more flexible and less institutionalized in their internal operations. This more than anything else was necessitated by the constantly changing nature of the struggle. Continuity was ascertained in the general direction of the struggle and in the maintenance of EPLF and its essential parts as a strong and cohesive body. However, the parts and more specifically the various departments' importance and existence as separate bodies, always depended on their usefulness at particular stages. They were continually subjected to mergers, streamlining and even phasing-out, with their functions implemented on an *ad hoc* basis, if necessary. Institutionalization was seen as emanating not from charts and formulae, no matter how well devised, but rather from practical work and experience and from tested problem-solving structures and methods of work.

Another major area to consider is transparency. Was EPLF open in its internal and external dealings? What does transparency or openness mean? If it means complete openness and unreserved exposure, EPLF was not and could not be transparent. In fact, EPLF – leadership, rank and file, even its mass organizations and *baitos* – must rank as one of the most successful organizations at keeping secrets. Again, there were rules and punitive measures protecting secrecy. It was also the nature of membership to be closed to outside penetration, to refrain from exposing EPLF's internal affairs.

Naturally, there was a hierarchy of secrets and information that could go down to the grassroots or remain at certain levels. Overall, every member of the organization had the right to information, to ask questions and receive answers, to demand explanations, and to take erring superiors to task.

As is probably true anywhere else, transparency in administrative matters depends on the character of the superiors involved and on their level of access to information. In this respect, EPLF was no exception. Policies were made at the Central Committee level and transmitted downward, with ample opportunity given to discuss them in seminars.

As explained above, the DPA introduced the practice of holding open and public sessions where people were given the chance to air their views on every matter ranging from EPLF policy to the performance of their administrators. Periodic seminars and open question and answer sessions between EPLF leadership and rank and file or ordinary people were commonplace. So again, within a centralized information system and taking into consideration the need for military secrecy, the elements of transparency were there and attempts to institutionalize them did exist.

The last point to consider is the status of the rule of law in EPLF. "Law" here does not mean EPLF's internal rules and regulations, which have already been dealt with.

One peculiar aspect of EPLF is that there was no separation of responsibility between the three branches of government. As previously mentioned, the *baitos* in EPLF administration combined the executive, legislative and judicial powers. This was the situation until the end of the 1980s.

Judicial committees were not bound by any specific laws. The customary laws and practices of communities were referred to, but they did not necessarily have a binding effect. Thus, judgements were given in accordance with the DPA's general directives on justice, fairness and equity and within EPLF's general principles and policies. As there were no regular courts, court procedures did not exist. There were no delays in court proceedings, making justice fast and effective.

The system worked, in spite of its informal and extra-legal nature. This may be attributed to various factors. There was the level of rapport and trust that existed between EPLF and the people. People were not inclined to oppose EPLF's decisions, nor were they in a position, financially or physically, to withstand prolonged litigation. Furthermore, torn between the Derg's arbitrariness and EPLF's standards of justice and fairness, they usually submitted to the latter. The absence of a set of laws to refer to and the tediousness and futility of appeals also helped make the system effective.

To sum up, EPLF's administrative culture developed a flexible albeit dynamic system of administration with its particular characteristics of accountability, institutionalization, transparency and approach to the rule of law. This is the administrative legacy of EPLF – the essence of what they brought to the post-Independent state of Eritrea.

To this particular administrative set-up and system of thinking should be added EPLF's fierce determination to preserve and protect its independence. Its slogan of "self-reliance", which remained the basis of its relationships with the outside world, was and still is its second nature. The fact that it relied mainly on its own resources to fight and win the war gave EPLF a sense of freedom and confidence rarely seen, even in equally successful liberation fronts. Because it had no obligation to anyone, no debts to settle, it never saw any need to compromise its principles and strategic objectives. This has remained the cornerstone of its dealings with foreign government, parties, donors and NGOs.

POST-INDEPENDENCE ADMINISTRATION
The preparatory stages

With the capture of the Sahel town of Afabet in 1988, the enemy was forced to retreat from the whole of the western lowlands – the provinces of Barka and Gash-Setit – and defend the highlands from Keren, 91 kilometres north of Asmara. This sudden expansion of the liberated zones and the challenges it brought about led to a reconsideration of the administrative set-up.

The zonal administrative structure and the power of administrators had been fragmented, as EPLF departments were directly accountable to the divisions that represented them in the different zones. This meant that regional or zonal administrators had the power of supervision at best, rather than direct control and management. Given the physical distance between the parts and the centre and the ensuing problems of contact, this was creating problems of communication.

Another problem lay in the old style of administration. Sahel, Barka and Gash-Setit were huge provinces – geographically, the greater part of the country. The old, informal, flexible and mobile method of administration could not work under conditions of stability. It had to at least be strengthened by a more formal administrative structure.

Above all, EPLF's political outlook had changed considerably during the 1980s. This was articulated in its Second Congress in 1987, where the old socialist-leaning and class-oriented political philosophy gave way to a broad-based national democratic programme that cut across classes. The move had a fundamental effect on the administrative style of the 1970s and early 1980s, as the approach to popular participation also underwent a basic change.

EPLF's class orientation previously tended to reduce the role of traditional power bases. The middle to late 1980s, however, saw a return to tradition or the re-activation of traditional civil society in the political and administrative field. Along with the prospect of freedom, this created a positive impression in the communities, greatly increasing EPLF's popularity and helping to raise mass participation to levels previously unachieved.

These factors, and even more the need to empower regional administrations, were seriously considered. This was taken a step further after the capture of the Red Sea port of Massawa in early 1990 when, in a meeting in Afabet chaired by Secretary General Isaias Afwerki, plans for establishing local governments and working toward decentralization took shape.

Awraja (provincial) administrations with some autonomy were set up and started to operate. For the first time, representatives of the departments were placed under the regional administration. It was a time of heavy battling to recapture Massawa and EPLF's preparations for a final push toward Asmara. Although there was little time to really define and solidly install the new administrative set-up, some moves toward the creation of local government were taken. The old *baito* system was re-installed, at least at the town, village and sub-district levels. Sahel was an exception, where a zonal *baito*, the highest level at the time, was established.

A new element added to the old structure was the beginning of the separation of the executive, judicial and legislative branches. Thus, during the 1990–1991 period, the Department of Justice, which had been established at the Second Congress in 1987, started to organize a court system in the liberated zones. In the preceding years it had pooled some of EPLF's lawyers and worked toward drafting a new set of Eritrean laws.

However, this experimental administrative structure did not last long, as the country of Eritrea was liberated on 24 May 1991 and an entirely new situation materialized.

The challenge of Independence

Independence was not an unexpected or sudden event. It was the result of 30 years of war, sacrifice and painstaking work. The fact that, after the bitter battles, especially in the preceding three or more years, EPLF's administrative structure easily resumed the role of leadership – create a government, maintain peace and order, and operate a tattered and destroyed economy – is a feat sometimes not properly assessed and appreciated. Or it is simply submerged in the practical administrative problems brought by Independence.

The rush toward Asmara and high expectations

Sahel was the seat of EPLF for more than 20 years. Everything was rooted there. However, within months of Independence almost all operations were transferred to Asmara. Much has been said on the subject of the unruly, unplanned and uncoordinated nature of the rushed move to Asmara.

This massive shift caused an overwhelming congestion of fighters in the capital. Every department had to deal with hundreds of essential and non-essential members, almost all of them still completely dependent on EPLF for food and lodging. It was time-consuming and difficult to sort out, a process that for several months disrupted an otherwise smooth instalment of the new government.

The euphoria of Independence was the immediate reason for the move. Beneath it, however, were high expectations the level and strength of which even EPLF did not foresee. For a large portion of the population, especially those who had participated in the struggle, Independence meant not only freedom from the enemy, but also a panacea for all their economic and social problems. Perhaps this was a normal reaction under the circumstances, but considering EPLF's and the country's limited resources it was so intensively demanding as to be unachievable and impractical.

But it was there. For thousands of Eritreans, Independence had a hidden, often unexpected face. Many fighters came to realize the poverty level to which parents and relations had fallen. An even worse fate had befallen most parents of 65,000 martyrs. Hundreds of thousands of refugees had hoped that Independence would free them from their squalid existence in Sudan and elsewhere. And then there were the disabled, the internally displaced, and committed members of various EPLF organizations all waiting for rewards, solutions and special attention.

For the first time in its existence, EPLF was faced with dealing with the new element of individual interest, even in its own ranks. It was an alien factor, an attitude long forgotten (or suspended?) in the distance and camaraderie of the armed struggle. The bitter truth was that proximity to EPLF had dire economic consequences for the committed. The greater the dedication, the more severe the economic losses and, naturally, the frustration.

These were trying times for EPLF. To many outside observers, it may have appeared that EPLF would finally lose its grip, have its popularity reduced. To the extent that it was the object of expectations and the target of demands, appreciation of EPLF changed. But, as will be discussed later, the crisis subsided with time, proper handling and full or partial solutions to some of the major problems.

However, the truth was that EPLF had become the government and like all governments it was subjected to public scrutiny and complaint. The loudness of complaints during the first two years of government were an awakening for EPLF and the Provisional Government of Eritrea (PGE).

The Derg's legacy

Nothing positive can be said about the Derg's tenure of Eritrea. The country declined in every way. Deprivations of every kind and a decline in cultural standards and morality changed the face of the nation, particularly in urban centres controlled by the regime. Poor education and poor health services replaced the relatively high standards of the 1950s and 1960s. A new crop of unprincipled business people were allowed control of the market. There was deliberate laxity in the handling of Eritrean youth, who lost the discipline and knack for achievement of preceding generations. And a culture of distrust, fraud, and betrayal was encouraged to spread in communities at an alarming rate.

The Italian and British administrative legacy, which the Haileselassie regime had partly preserved, was gone. What was left was a provincial administration that served only the Derg's war effort and control mechanisms. The *kebeles* (local administrative units) and women's, workers', and farmers' associations were arms of or infiltrated by the *dehninet*, infamous agents of the Derg's atrocities and system of spying.

The so-called civil service was filled with unqualified or uninterested staff, usually corrupt and sometimes there for security and political reasons. Quite often, positions were invented specifically for their employment. Furthermore, the Derg introduced lengthy, tedious and unnecessary chains of paperwork, ostensibly to control corruption. In actual fact, it bred corruption, misappropriation and fraud.

EPLF inherited from the Derg a bureaucracy that had developed negatively. The Eritrean court system, known for its efficiency, fairness and independence until the middle of the federal period in the 1950s, had almost totally disintegrated. Most judges were corrupt or of low education and calibre, the same holding true for prosecutors and a host of unprincipled and greedy advocates and attorneys.

ESTABLISHING A GOVERNMENT AND SYSTEM OF ADMINISTRATION

The Provisional Government of Eritrea (PGE)

The PGE was publicly presented on the morrow of Independence, 24 May 1991. Although its formal reinstatement by Proclamation 23/1992 was delayed for another year, its duties commenced immediately with Independence.

The first act of the PGE was to declare itself transitional until a referendum two years later, when the Eritrean people were to decide if they wanted Independence. It was a gesture on the part of the victorious EPLF that was to gain it international appreciation and support, but more importantly it put to rest any possible notions that the Eritrean struggle was not popularly based.

Proclamation 23/1992 described the duties of the PGE as including the preservation of national and territorial unity, the establishment of peace and order, economic reconstruction, the set-up of democratic institutions, and the creation of appropriate international relations.

The proclamation set up a government with legislative, executive and judicial branches. The EPLF Central Committee was to constitute the legislature and was invested with supreme powers. The executive branch consisted of the PGE State Council which, under the Secretary General of EPLF, included the heads of 13 secretariats, the administrators of all the provinces, and the commanders of the armed and naval forces. The judicial branch was also established as a body independent of the other two branches and given the responsibility of protecting the legal rights of the government, associations and individuals.

The three branches of government were thus set up in Eritrea. What did this actually mean? What was the condition of each of these branches? How did they compare in terms of organization and experience? Was there, or could there be, an immediate separation of powers and responsibilities between the branches, as in some western democracies?

EPLF had always had a strong and centralized leadership. The Central Committee and the Politburo, both under the Secretary General of EPLF, combined legislative and executive powers. The judicial, as already shown, was virtually non-existent, with any evidence of it on an *ad hoc*, embryonic basis in the *baitos*. This merger of the three functions into one throughout the period of armed struggle, gave EPLF leadership great powers it put to good use in the march toward freedom. It helped it grow and operate with cohesion, confidence and effectiveness rarely seen in movements of its magnitude and longevity. Helped by the strong commitment to the causes of the struggle both in its ranks and in the population at large, EPLF rarely expected and never really encountered serious opposition, especially after the demise of ELF. It was a leadership almost totally trusted by its followers and equally accustomed to their unreserved and, most often, voluntary submission to authority. Therefore, at the time of Independence all the elements of a strong executive branch were present.

Not so with the other two branches. Eritrea had practically no legislative experience. Its only parliamentary body, the Eritrean assembly of the federal period, was partially effective for only the first few years of federation, when it attempted to control or protest Ethiopian moves to destroy Eritrean autonomy. Repression, election, fraud and physical harassment decimated the number of nationalist members in the Second Assembly of 1956, which became a passive, rubber stamp of Haileselassie's policies and intentions. The experience of the First Assembly was too brief to pass on as a tradition to the Eritrean public.

The next substantive Eritrean experience in this field came only with EPLF's *baitos*, confined to village and district levels. At best they may be seen as having formed the rudimentary stages of a national legislature. Their usefulness in the armed struggle was remarkable, as was their contribution to expanding the culture of representation and the practice of elections. But legislative experience as a national phenomenon, as a branch of power that could stand on par with the strong executive branch simply was not there.

It has been seen that the courts in Eritrea fell to an absolutely low level. However, judicial experience in the country fares much better than legislative. The Italians and the British had established courts modelled on their own systems. Until late in the federal period they were relatively independent, efficient, fast and fair. To the people of Eritrea – who through written and unwritten customary laws had mostly been guided by standards of legality and developed their own traditional methods and institutions of conflict resolution – the courts were popular and accepted as arbiters of last resort. Ethiopian rule changed all that by subjecting Eritrean courts to the authority of its corrupt and inefficient system. The decline of the courts was steady and almost complete by Independence. The same may not apply wholly to customary conflict resolution methods, which though partially retained were weakened by the war, interference of the Derg regime, and introduction of new approaches by liberation movements.

So to reiterate, neither the background nor the experience existed for the separation of powers between the three, unevenly developed branches of government. The immense problems inherited by the PGE demanded a firm hand and immediate attention. The sustainability of peace and order and the resuscitation of the destroyed economy demanded continuity. Only a strong executive branch could provide that. The formation of a government under the circumstances of 1991/1992, could not be entrusted to an untested method that had not evolved with or from the struggle. The priority was not to experiment with principles and structures of democracy – that could wait. This was the thinking that dominated at the time of Independence.

One fact is also often overlooked. Eritrea may be a new independent nation and the Eritrean state a new entity; however, EPLF leadership was neither new nor inexperienced. Although it spent more than 20 years outside the international frame of states, it had clearly articulated its visions for the future and how they could be realized.

Proclamation 23/1992 retained the superior authority of the EPLF Central Committee by instituting it as the legislative body and assigning it the right to appoint membership to the PGE State Council. The Secretary General of EPLF was retained by the proclamation as chairman of the Central Committee and the PGE State Council. The appointment of the President and judges of the High Court, on which the Secretary of Justice could advise and comment, was also the right of the executive branch. In other words, true to EPLF tradition and in answer to the demands of post-war administration, the PGE formed a combined executive and legislative body, with the judicial legally declared independent of the two.

Re-forming local governments

Of all the EPLF departments, the DPA was the one that worked most directly inside, with and through the people. Its achievements were phenomenal, often reaching deep into enemy territory, where even the Derg's *kebele* members were clandestinely enlisted in the ranks to carry out directives. Duties and tasks of the DPA often required the full-time dedication of its members, agents and operatives.

With Independence, many DPA non-combatant administrators felt obliged to attend to their families' economic problems, a responsibility that had long been sacrificed for the struggle. It had also been the fate of good administrators, before Independence, to be primary targets of the enemy's elimination or imprisonment campaigns. Those who escaped this fate would usually join the ranks of regular EPLF fighters, creating a gap in administrative experience. This gap widened with Independence.

A second problem was caused by changes in the administrative structure. Legislative, executive and judicial duties at the village and district stages were previously combined under the authority of the *baitos*. As discussed earlier, with the level of trust and rapport that existed between the people and the MAUs, this structure and method worked well for the purposes of the armed struggle.

Independence brought with it the need to separate the branches, even at lower levels. The courts, or what remained of them, were re-activated. This process started during 1990/1991, the years before Independence when the Justice Department set out to establish village courts through special election of judges in all the liberated provinces. Although Independence came before these courts started functioning, the idea of establishing a separate court system had taken root.

However, the actual establishment of the system was to take some time. There were two main reasons for this. First, the laws drafted by the Department of Justice in the late 1980s were more attuned to rural than national, including urban, issues. A national system of laws had to be prepared. This took about four months of serious work by the department, and resulted in the adoption (with the amendment or cancellation of some provisions) of the Ethiopian codes of law as the transitional laws of Eritrea. It must be noted that the court system was suspended for the duration of these months, leading to serious pressures on especially lower level administrative bodies that were refraining from adjudicating cases in the old manner, pending the establishment of the courts.

Second, when the courts finally started operating, they were hampered by the lack of qualified personnel. Half of the judges who had served under the Derg were found unacceptable on the grounds of inefficiency, poor qualifications and corruption. Their replacement was not easy and inexperienced people were employed and required complete training. To add to the problem, most of the village-level judges elected in 1991 and 1992, were found incapable of the duties assigned to them because they were illiterate or untrained. So courts were not established at village levels, a situation that was to continue for eight more months.

Thus, the first year of Independence saw a serious problem in the administration of justice. The three levels of the judicial system – the *wereda*, *awraja* and high court (the highest, including a session of final appeal) – were swamped with unfinished cases from the Derg period, cases accumulated during the courts' inaction and new ones. More incapacitated were the district courts, dealing with even petty disputes from all the villages under their respective jurisdiction.

The whole affair stood in sharp contrast to the relative ease and speed with which disputes were settled during the armed struggle. Inevitably, it was the administration that had to face the ensuing complications and deal with a quagmire of complaints.

It was not an easy time for the administration. As already mentioned, for many formerly committed *baito* and *bdho* members and administrators, administrative work had become a burden without reward. People started to demand remuneration for services rendered; the days of voluntary and free service were over.

After long deliberation, along the line of what began in Afabet in 1990, the PGE issued Proclamation 26/1992, which announced the establishment of a system of local administration. Among other things, the declared aims of this system were: assurance of balanced development throughout the country, encouragement of popular participation, regional initiative, and the attainment of a rational balance between centralization and decentralization. The three branches of government announced by Proclamation 23/1992 were also to be reflected at local levels.

Eritrea was divided into 10 *awrajas*, Asmara being the tenth. Beneath the *awraja* were the sub-*awraja*, *wereda* and *kebabi* (a group of villages or settlements) administrations. Except for the sub-*awraja* level, the *kebabi*, *wereda* and *awraja* administrations were to have legislative, executive and judicial branches. There was no legislature at the sub-*awraja* level, unless an urban centre was included. Sub-*awraja* administration consisted of only the executive and judicial branches.

Proclamation 26/1992 was a detailed law that dealt even with election procedures in the *baitos*. The distribution of responsibilities between the branches was also clarified. The prime responsibilities of the local level, including *awraja baitos*, were to issue local laws consistent with national laws, ratify the administration's budget, investigate wrongs perpetrated on the people by government authorities, and study, examine and ratify reports and assessments of the executive branch at its level. Laws passed by *baitos* had to be ratified by the Ministry of Justice, whereas its recommendations on various issues and popular demands were submitted to the administrator or executive.

The *Awraja* Administrator, who was made a member of the PGE State Council, was responsible to that body. Proclamation 23/1992 had dropped the DPA from the list of departments of the PGE. What is significant about Proclamation 26/1992 is that the *baitos* and the administrators are placed at the same level. Just as the *baito* was given the authority to examine and ratify the administrator's reports, so the administrator had the right to sit in every *baito* session and present the administration's point of view. But *Awraja* Administrators were not *baito* members, as they were directly appointed by the Secretary General of the PGE.

The process was different at the lower, *wereda* and *kebabi* levels. There the *baitos*, which were elected by popular vote, were to in turn elect village and *wereda* administrators from their own membership. The idea was to introduce a parliamentary system of administration, but to start from below and work up, toward the *awraja* and national levels.

To attract capable people to administrative jobs, the PGE decided to pay monthly stipends of 60 birr to the chairperson and 50 birr to the secretary of *wereda* and village administrations. Former MAUs, regular EPLF combatants, were withdrawn from both levels of administration, giving the civilian population the chance to elect its own people.

Elections were held in all the highland provinces and *baitos*, including *awraja baitos*, were set up at all levels. Several factors impeded the experiment. Chief among these was the failure of the *baito* to understand the system of·parliamentary democracy. Because the executive branch was being elected from within it, *baito* members started to feel that the executive branch was there to obey them, even at a personal level. No amount of explanations, seminars or educational meetings could redirect this thinking.

The same problems arose in the judicial branch. By 1992, the Department of Justice had reinstated village judges who were empowered to hear and decide on petty offences and civil cases. These judges have semi-official status, their pronouncements are binding, and *wereda* courts are obliged to accept appeals from their decisions. But they do not constitute part of the proper court system and are not included in the judicial hierarchy. They were assigned as a temporary solution to a pressing problem

These village judges also came into conflict with the *baitos*, which consistent with old EPLF practice, considered the judges subject to their authority. Furthermore, *baito* members even started to represent opposing interests in villages and *weredas*, creating dangers of rifts in the *baitos*. Old parochial sentiments, greatly reduced during the struggle, started to crop up and create administrative problems that could worsen if left unchecked.

To a government bent on preserving national unity, these sentiments and emerging rifts, though still limited, were not acceptable. Proclamation 26/1992 may be regarded as an experiment in decentralization and democratization at the grassroots level. It was an attempt to hand over some power to local administrations, but, from the point of view of the PGE, the gesture and its results were not encouraging.

The PGE had major programmes, such as the National Service Programme and land reform, which required a high degree of popular participation and a solid commitment of implementation from administrators. The upcoming referendum also required a set-up that would assure its fair and speedy completion. Neither the experience nor the disposition of the lower level *baitos* was likely to be of help in these matters.

So, after a lapse of about eight months to a year from the establishment of the *baitos* in accordance with Proclamation 26/1992, a change was effected. It was decided not to hold lower level *baito* elections in those provinces where such elections had not yet been held. In provinces that had held *baito* elections, the district *baito* was eliminated, with the former members of the executive being retained as advisors to a district administrator appointed by the government.

The *awraja* and village *baitos* were, however, retained as envisaged by Proclamation 26/1992. This arrangement continued through the period of the referendum up to the new regional and administrative restructuring ratified by the National Assembly in 1996. One aspect of Proclamation 26/1992 that was to change in the 1996 restructuring was the power of central government bodies, which were allowed direct access to their representative bodies down at the local government level. It was felt that this was rendering local administrators unable to co-ordinate their programmes and complicating communications both vis-à-vis the centre and the regions and within the regional administrations.

The Government of the State of Eritrea

The two years immediately following Independence may be regarded as a preparatory period when problems were sorted out, new administrative structures tested and, in general, when what was possible and practical was separated from what was not. A case in point may be the experience gleaned from the empowerment of local government at lower levels.

The great post-Independence problems facing the PGE in this period have been briefly reviewed. It is beyond the scope of this chapter to discuss in detail how the PGE tackled every major problem it faced. The maintenance of peace and stability, the first steps toward rebuilding the economy and the ruined infrastructure, its great concerns on the bigger social issues – refugee rehabilitation, helping families of martyrs, finding a solution to the problems of the disabled and war-orphaned children – were remarkable.

They were remarkable, especially in light of the fact that the PGE was still awaiting international recognition, pending the referendum. Its access to international trade, foreign currency, international communications and various forms of technology and technical assistance were limited.

The complaints and disaffection bred of unmet high expectations, the reduction in the quality of administration and the absence or slackness of the judicial process, and so on, may have appeared to be more acute than they actually were. For example, the strike by a small segment of fighters on 20 June 1993 may have had the appearance of an armed uprising. However, the abruptness with which it subsided on the PGE Secretary General's open and face-to-face discussion with its perpetrators, showed it to have been an expression of grievances taken a little too far. The old trust and camaraderie between EPLF leadership and the rank and file helped in its peaceful resolution. Neither was it really meant to unbalance the organization's authority and existence. Note must be taken of the fact that every regular EPLF member was serving without a salary and without complaining about it, a situation that lasted until 1995.

This example illustrates the depth of feeling and support for EPLF at the grassroots level. It was like a life-giving reserve that EPLF could depend on. The problems were transitional, as were the complications and complaints they brought about. When faced by broader issues of national importance, they were bound to be relegated to a secondary position, as they were during the referendum.

The months leading up to and following the referendum will always stand out as exceptional in the history of the nation. It was a time when a single objective – the attainment of Independence – ruled practically every Eritrean mind. The months before were spent in anticipation and the months after in celebration. The smoothness of the process, its dependence almost entirely on local resources and finance, and the unanimity of the result were manifestations of the high level of organization and popular participation that went into it. For EPLF, it was the reward of struggle and the impetus to carry forward its principles of, among others, national unity and self-reliance, two factors that contributed to the resounding success of the referendum.

In the wake of the referendum, the PGE issued Proclamation 37/1993, establishing the Government of Eritrea, as a transitional government pending the institution of a constitutional government. While asserting EPLF's special leading role in the period of transition, the proclamation also recognized the need to broaden the basis for participation.

Although the EPLF's Central Committee was retained in the newly constituted National Assembly or *baito*, 60 members were added to it.

These included 30 *awraja* representatives, identified as the chairs and secretaries of all the *awraja baitos*, and 30 citizens selected by the committee, including 10 women.

The National Assembly was given, among other things, the power of electing from its membership a President, who would chair the *baito* and the PGE State Council. Members of the council would be elected by the *baito* based on the President's recommendations. Furthermore, the *baito* was invested with laying down government policy, ratifying the government's reports and major agreements, and protecting the unity and sovereignty of the state.

The proclamation also detailed the general duties and responsibilities of the PGE State Council, the President and the ministries, commissions and authorities. As with Proclamation 23/1992, Proclamation 37/1993 asserted the independence of the judicial branch.

With respect to local administration, Proclamation 26/1992 was left intact, although a subsequent Legal Notice recreated a central administrative body renamed the Ministry of Local Government (MLG), whose duty was to co-ordinate the *awraja* administrations. Central government bodies remained directly responsible for the activities of their regional division.

In 1993 and 1994 the government started to disentangle itself from the "immediate problems of resuscitating the economy and rehabilitating certain sectors through a programme of recovery and rehabilitation" (GSE, 1994c:9). During these two years and as a result of the work of the preceding two years, many of the problems of post-Independence were either solved or were on the verge of being resolved. Assistance to families of martyrs, various programmes to help orphans, demobilization and rehabilitation of a greater number of combatants, care or rehabilitation for the war-disabled – these staggering problems were tackled one by one. Some are still unresolved, such as the problem of refugees, but at least all of the problems were put in proper perspective, enabling the government to proceed in 1993 to the second stage of its policy, namely addressing "the fundamental development problems and prospects of the country and to chart the direction of its future growth" (GSE, 1994c:9).

During 1993 and 1994, a series of public debates were held between various government representatives and the general public, especially the business community, on the present and future situation of the economy. Subsequent brainstorming sessions were held on all aspects of government policy, chaired by the President and involving government and private experts of various disciplines. These were followed by serious and co-ordinated work on the policies the nation should adopt.

All this resulted in the government's announcement of its macro-policy framework in which it expounded strategies for integrated development. After detailing a long list of development objectives, the Macro-Policy Document states that the government's growth strategy includes rehabilitation, reconstruction and development covering all sectors. The main component of this strategy is described as:

> ...human capital formation, with education and health as key inputs; export-oriented development both in industry and agriculture; infra-structural development to remove critical bottlenecks; environmental restoration and protection; and the promotion of the private sector (GSE, 1994c:12).

The establishment of "an efficient, outward looking private sector-led market economy, with the government playing a pro-active role to stimulate private economic activities" is seen as the centrepiece of this strategy.

In singling out, for the moment, what the Macro-Policy Document specifies regarding local administration framework, the objective of the policy framework is to:

> ...correct recognized weaknesses of the existing administrative system of the country such that it can facilitate over-all socio-economic development of the country, and to protect and develop the short and long term strategic interests and recognized advantages of the country (GSE, 1994c:36).

Having said this, the document goes on to detail policy on local governments as being to:

a) facilitate mobility of economic resources
b) encourage better and effective utilization of the country's global (sea, land, air) resource potential
c) allow Eritrea to have a lean but efficient central and local administration system and a highly qualified civil service
d) allow the country to set up decentralized and more participatory democratic institutions
e) facilitate the proper protection and conservation of the nation's resources.

At the beginning of 1996, a new local administrative set-up based on the macro-policy framework was announced. In the next section its main tenets will be examined in light of the administrative experience both of EPLF and the post-Independence government in Eritrea.

EPLF becomes PFDJ

In its Second Congress of 1987, EPLF had gone through changes in its political outlook and broadened its political base. In its Third Congress held in February 1994, EPLF, renamed the People's Front for Democracy and Justice (PFDJ), approved the **National Charter for Eritrea** that comprehensively expounds its vision for the future. It is an important document, which profoundly influenced the policies of the government.

The Charter begins by enumerating six basic goals as constituting the PFDJ's vision for the future (PFDJ, 1994:10–11). These are:
1. national harmony
2. political democracy
3. economic and social development
4. social justice or economic and social democracy
5. cultural revival
6. regional and international co-operation.

How are these goals to be achieved? The Charter states that the guarantees of the country's future are best assured by the continuation of the basic principles and views which were instrumental for Eritrean victory. Therefore, drawing relevant lessons from the experience of the armed struggle is stressed.

First among these basic principles is national unity. Although the Charter starts from the premise of the strong national unity forged during the years of struggle and sacrifice, it does not take it for granted. It goes on to underline the importance of preserving and enhancing the existing unity and of protecting it from the eventuality of "certain tendencies and thoughts" that might weaken it. For this to materialize:

> ...it is primarily necessary to build a national government which ensures unity and equality of the people of Eritrea, rejects all divisive attitudes and activities, places national interest above everything else, and enables the participation of all sectors of Eritrean society (PFDJ, 1994:12–13).

It goes on to reject sectarian politics and all forms of discrimination, and to advocate a secular state in which religious equality is respected.

The second basic principle is the active participation of people, which, in its organized form the Charter asserts (PFDJ, 1994:13–14), was one of the keys to the success of the armed struggle. Popular participation means more than voting in occasional elections. It means that "the people should participate in all decisions that touch their lives and their country, from the inception to the implementation of ideas". However, since participation cannot be effective unless people are organized, they should not only have the right to establish organizations but should also be encouraged and assisted to do so.

Recognition of the decisive role of the human factor in the nation's development strategy is the third basic principle of the Charter. The war was won through the sheer commitment of Eritrean fighters and through the "strong will, diligence, efficiency, work ethic, discipline, ability and skills and inventiveness" of the people. Strategies of development should, therefore, "aim at meeting the material and spiritual needs of people", where in an atmosphere of equal educational, training, and health opportunities, citizens can develop their capacities "free from oppression, fear, poverty and ignorance" (PFDJ, 1994:14–15).

Linking national to social struggles, or the struggle for social justice, is the fourth basic principle elucidated by the Charter. Popular participation, it maintains, cannot be sustained without programmes that help people change their lives for the better. Enthusiastic participation in programmes can only come when "people actually see that the political movement or government works in their interest, only when they see that promises are kept" (PFDJ, 1994:15–16).

The experiences of the armed struggle are referred to in concretizing the viability of this principle. Popular participation then, the Charter further underlines, was encouraged by the modern educational and health services made available to them from locally available materials and their direct involvement. Their political participation through the various assemblies and associations, and social changes – for example, improvement in the conditions and social position of women – are listed as evidence of the correctness of the principle.

The underlying philosophy behind this principle, the philosophy of social justice, is seen as "the narrowing of the gap between the haves and the have-nots, ensuring that all people have their fair share of the national wealth and can participate in the political, social and cultural life of the country, to creating balanced development, respecting human rights and advancing democracy". Note should be taken that this philosophy doesn't preclude development of the private sector or the market economy. In its section dealing with building the economy, the Charter stresses that the idea of social justice is to ensure an equitable distribution of national wealth among all citizens, narrowing the development gap between the centre and the periphery and ensuring balanced and fair distribution of economic development in the whole country, and "creating conditions which enable people to reap the fruits of their labour, improve their living standards through work, and honest work". In other words, honest work and honest profits are encouraged under this outlook.

Self-reliance, the fifth basic principle, has always been one of the foundations on which the struggle thrived. The Charter explains:

> ...politically, it means to follow an independent line and give priority to internal conditions; economically, to rely on internal capabilities and develop internal capacities; and culturally, to have self-confidence and develop one's own cultural heritage. Self-confidence does not mean to isolate oneself from the international community. It only means being as independent and self-confident a player as possible in the international community (PFDJ, 1994:16–17).

This old EPLF tradition of seeking internal solutions to internal problems, of not "copying anybody else's political models" and never expecting outside "experts" and "advisors" to do one's own job, is being re-asserted here. The need for experts and outside expertise, though necessary and accepted, is seen in the context and priority of relying on and developing one's own capabilities and expertise.

Finally, the Charter asserts another EPLF quality: the strong relationship between the people and leadership as the sixth basic principle. Leadership, according to the Charter, is seen not as referring to "the higher executive body, but in a broader sense, to the organized broad political force that provides leadership" (PFDJ, 1994:17–18). In other words, it is that quality found during the armed struggle at practically every level of responsibility – both inside and outside the regular EPLF membership – the Charter is referring to.

This existed because of the close physical and psychological relationship between the EPLF and the people, and especially the rural population. The Charter calls on government and political leaders to maintain the tradition and to be involved throughout the country. Continuing the proud leadership traditions of the struggle and striving for freedom from corruption and abuse of power are stressed, and diligence in learning and updating skills is recommended.

On the topic of governance, every principle enumerated here amply clarifies the PFDJ's approach to the issue. The Charter calls for the drafting of a Constitution to be ratified by broad public participation that sets up a strong government whose three branches check and balance, and that guarantees human and political freedom to citizens, assures balanced development throughout the country, fights corruption, sectarianism and discrimination in all its forms, ensures popular participation at the grassroots level in accordance with the principles of political plurality, openness, tolerance and accountability, and establishes democratic institutions, including a strong judiciary, various associations, and so on (PFDJ, 1994:20–21).

In other words, a broad-based democratic government is called for. The Charter clearly expresses what it means by democracy. It distinguishes democracy from the notion that evaluates democracy "in terms of the number of political parties" in existence or "whether regular elections are held". Instead, democracy is seen as:

> ...the existence of a society governed by democratic principles and procedures, the existence of democratic institutions and culture, broad public participation in decision-making and a government that is accountable to the people (PFDJ, 1994:21).

Thus, content is more important than "external manifestations", such as the number of political parties or regular elections. So the right of political parties to organization and free expression is not questioned by the Charter; "democracy" merely as the numbers of such parties is not accepted. Genuine democracy exists when "equating institutions – political parties, various grassroots associations, mass media and decentralized governmental agencies" are people-based. In other words, the Charter states, "governmental and non-governmental institutions must exist to ensure public participation from the grassroots to the national level."

In short, to paraphrase the Charter, democracy is less talk and more action. Democracy is public participation through organized inclusion in the political process. The existence of political parties for their own sake is not an indication of the existence of democracy. Political parties that, as Mamdani has stated, have lost or do not have social bases are not only undemocratic but will end up strangling the democratic process. So will parties based on sectarian – religious, regional, or tribal – ideas or movements.

The last section of this chapter relates the government's policies and programmes and the resultant actions to its stated principles of democracy. For comparative purposes, the section also reiterates the existing ideas and principles of governance.

LOCAL ADMINISTRATION

At the beginning of 1996, a new local administrative law was ratified by the National *baito*. As the direct result of the experience of pre- and post-Independence administration, the new set-up reflects the government's philosophy of governance and is based both on the PFDJ basic principles and the policy framework outlined in the Macro-Policy Document. In relation to the administrative experience, principles and policies that have been discussed, the basic tenets of the new law will be analysed. This section will also view the topic in relation to the general principles of decentralization, popular participation, accountability, transparency, the rule of law, and the level of government-to-people communication as proposed in the new set-up.

Rationale for a new administrative set-up

The division of Eritrea into *awrajas* was a set-up from colonial Italian times that persisted to modern times. This consisted of the *awrajas* of Hamasien, Seraye, Akele Guzai, Semhar, Senhit, Denkalia, Sahel, and Barka (later divided to introduce the Gash-Setit). Regardless of what initially prompted the Italians to choose this particular form of division, the *awrajas* have long been the means of colonial policies of divide and rule, particularly as overtly practised by the British and the Ethiopians.

Although these policies never matured to the level of creating permanent rifts among the people, they nevertheless succeeded in breeding parochial sentiments that often either stand in the way of the national interest or fall victim to the politics of division. During the war, EPLF succeeded in avoiding *awraja* divisions by opting for zonal or regional administrative set-ups corresponding to military strategy. This worked, but with Independence the old *awraja* system was reinstalled, more for the sake of convenience and continuity than because the government was comfortable with the arrangement, which it never was.

Apart from this, the *awraja* set-up had not taken development factors into consideration. Thus, regions with the same or similar economic resources and activity were placed under different administrations, creating problems for co-ordinated programmes of development. Similarly, geographic cohesion, an important factor for easier communication in a region and the development of infrastructure, was not one of the strengths of the *awraja* set-up. For example, the people of Erafale on the Akele Guzai coast had to make a detour through Massawa-Asmara to Adi-Keyeh, a circular trip crossing two provinces, to reach their *awraja* capital. For both political and economic reasons, the government decided to change the administrative set-up to one that suited its overall policies.

One of the policies that was an additional impetus to the change was the

Land Proclamation of 1994. Customary Eritrean land tenure was based on family and village ownership in most of the highlands, and government ownership or *demaniale* (so proclaimed by the Italians) in the lowlands. As such, it had long become the source of endless litigation, and grazing and farming practices that led to far-reaching soil erosion, deforestation and an inability by the agricultural population to cope with persistent drought and other natural disasters. So a change was effected in the land tenure system that declared land government-owned, but allowed lifetime individual usufruct and gave various forms of lease rights to citizens and other land users.

The Land Proclamation involves the redistribution and redefinition of village boundaries, as previous village agricultural borders are being eliminated. This calls for the rearrangement not only of village but also district and higher levels of administration, a condition for land law implementation now satisfied by the new administrative arrangement.

In addition to the overriding principles of national unity, popular participation and the needs of economic development, the preamble to the new law lists the following administrative reasons for its proclamation:
- co-ordination and all-encompassing direction and distribution of responsibilities
- establishment of a hierarchical assignment of duties and responsibilities
- striking a national balance between the principles of centralization and decentralization, with gradual progress toward the latter
- establishing administrations in every region, with executive, legislative and judicial sections.

Basic tenets of the new structure
Preservation of national unity
National unity has been identified as an overriding principle that touches on practically every government policy. The new structure proposes to enhance this unity through a more rational rearrangement of the old *awraja* classification.

Thus the number of regions – previously ranging from eight to 10 – has been reduced to six: Southern Red Sea Region, Northern Red Sea Region, Anseba, Gash-Barka, Southern Region and Central Region

The *awrajas* have been rearranged into an entirely different set-up. Old provincial borders and confines have disappeared and been replaced by geographically, topographically and ecologically more proximate and similar units. The coastal area, too long (more than 1,000 kilometres) to be formed into one unit, now encompasses two regions, with the adjacent plains constituting the hinterland. These two regions are marked for the development of marine resources, salt and mineral potential and major expansion of the tourist industry. The hinterland of the Northern Red Sea Region, up to the Semenawi Bahri escarpments and the Nacfa mountains, are areas with known potential for irrigated agriculture.

The Anseba region (with a potential for market-oriented crop production) joins the agricultural sections of the old Senhit with the predominantly pastoral areas of Northern Barka and southern and north-western Sahel. The great plains of the Gash-Barka, criss-crossed by seasonal rivers and with diverse flora and fauna, now form the largest and potentially most populous and dynamic region. This is the region where new settlements and major investments of an agricultural and agro-industrial nature are likely to take place, and where livestock production, already considerable under traditional pastoral and agro-pastoral practices, is expected to increase in magnitude and importance.

Finally, the densely populated former highland *awrajas* now form two important regions: the Southern Region, important for agricultural, industrial and trade activities, and the Central Region, including Asmara, the hub of all administrative, financial and industrial activities of the nation.

The question is often asked whether it was wise to change an old system that people were accustomed and attached to. Would it not involve, say, a rearrangement of ethnic or linguistic groupings that would create resentment and harm the stated objective of preserving national unity?

Because arbitrary border delineation often resulted in splitting cohesive groups, the concern is well understood. However, care was taken to avoid this from the inception of the idea of effecting regional rearrangements. In fact, this was one cause of the task's delayed finalization. On the contrary, the new rearrangement took the opportunity to adjust some of the irrational divisions of the *awraja* system, such as the Erafale enclave, which was alienated from its old provincial centre.

Border readjustments are not new in Eritrea, as every past government has tampered with the *awraja* set-up in one way or another. The intention, however, was different in the past. The Dekemhare area in Akele Guzai, for example, was made part of Hamasien at some point in the late 1930s and 1940s. The Logo-Chiwa and Tselema divisions between Hamasien and Seraye provinces, respectively, were a point of contention for many decades. Old *awraja* and district sentiments, sometimes corresponding to different linguistic and religious compositions, were often sources of confrontation. The Tor'a dispute against the Tsendegle, Saho-Muslim and Tigrigna-Christian neighbouring districts lasted for 80 years before cessation in 1995.

It was in the interest of colonial powers to continuously use differing *awraja* sentiments and border readjustments between to create ill-will and distrust. This divisive strategy, first introduced by the British in the 1940s and continued by the Haileselassie regime, was taken to extreme heights when the Derg attempted to cut Eritrea into three autonomous regions based on religious, ethnic or linguistic divisions.

The present regional restructuring looks at the issue from an entirely different angle. Eritreans are not, it is argued, obliged to respect the essentially divisive arrangement. Just because it thrived under colonial nurture did not mean it was so ingrained in the Eritrean psyche that it could not be challenged and changed. ELF fell victim to its seeming strength and deep-rootedness in its earlier stages, dividing its membership into five departments corresponding to the colonial linguistic-origin *awraja* divisions. It was a terrible mistake that was to have dire consequences for the future of the Eritrean struggle, a move whose repercussions have not been completely erased even today.

Eliminating the *awraja* and its subdivisions is seen as removing an impediment to nation-building in the broadest sense. During the armed struggle, EPLF made great sacrifices to eradicate parochial sentiments and attitudes from the rank and file. This served as a base for the high level of unity through which it won final victory. Succumbing to colonial administrative divisions was a regression to colonial and even pre-colonial and feudal arrangements that would have compromised the gains of the armed struggle.

The new structure is not engaging in *awraja* politics, simply uprooting it. There is no question now of animosity being aroused if an area of land is ceded to another *awraja* or district. This across-the-board rearrangement affects every *awraja*, district and even village, equally. Any initial shock, which there naturally was in many quarters, was caused by the newness, magnitude and sheer courage of the move. As the advantages of the new structure were realized, indignance and resentment dissipated.

The Land Proclamation, preceding the new structure by about 15 months, also played a major role in laying the groundwork. By declaring all land government-owned, the land law effectively eliminated village and district land boundaries. Customary rights of individual citizens to access agricultural and residential land were retained, but community ownership of land – a feeding-ground for *awraja*/district/village/clan parochialism – lost its legal base.

The Land Commission was asked if this eroded Eritrean social cohesion. The answer is no, as land adjacent to a village is given to its residents as a priority and the village is retained as an administrative unit by the new regional structure. In addition, the land law recognizes each village's grazing, water and forest lands.

So although these two laws allow for a greater degree of human mobility through the mechanisms they have created, they do not destroy the basis of social cohesion. No village, clan, linguistic or ethnic grouping is, in any way, split up, separated, or pressured to move out of its traditional habitat.

What is new is that there is more room for interaction between regions. The removal of the old parochial constraints is expected to breed a better atmosphere for co-operation based on mutual respect and the promotion of mutual interests. Unity is inconceivable without co-operation and the even economic development of various regions and different parts of the same region. That is what the new regional structure aspires to achieve.

The question of popular participation

How does the new regional administrative structure propose to assure the continuity of the level of popular participation that existed during the struggle? The EPLF experience and the PFDJ stand on the issue, as pronounced in the National Charter, state that popular participation becomes effective if organized at the grassroots level. But what, in the Eritrean context, does "organized public participation" mean?

In post-Independence Eritrea, the referendum and public debates on the constitution-making process are outstanding examples of popular participation. The referendum has been discussed and now public participation in the constitutional process will be briefly considered.

There is no doubt that the referendum has inculcated in the mind of every Eritrean the idea of the vote – the magic, in fact, of the individual vote. It is not possible to estimate the exact value of the constitutional public debates that were such an intensive activity of 1995 and 1996, but that they will contribute to the political awareness of citizens cannot be doubted. Given the complications involved in constitutional issues even to the learned, the majority of Eritreans, still not free from illiteracy, may not have grasped the full import of the debates. There can be no argument, though, that people have retained basic notions of democracy, social and political rights and of participation and political representation.

To the extent that popular participation of this nature helps form and canvass public opinion on a wide and spontaneous basis, it should be encouraged. But is it really effective? Perhaps it is as a one-time exercise. So is the referendum vote. The feeling that an individual voice or vote is in the Constitution or in the outcome of Independence is gratifying. It is when this type of "popular participation" degenerates into endless public meetings, seminars, group meetings, workshops, where the same points are belaboured over and over again, that the problem arises.

It seems that the new local administrative law attempts to set right this deviation from the true meaning of popular participation. At least that is how advocates perceive its role. As discussed, villages and districts were previously put under administrators elected from the memberships of village and district *baitos*. This led to problems that eventually led to the elimination of the district-level *baito*.

The new set-up avoids this. The village *baito* has been replaced by the village or *kebabi* session, the *kebabi* being a group of small villages or settlements joining to form an administrative unit on a par with the village unit. The village session includes every village resident, regardless of sex, religion or origin, who resides in the village and has reached 18 years of age.

The village session is empowered to initiate programmes and projects that concern its confines or affairs. It can discuss and give opinions and recommendations on programmes and projects destined to it, as well as study, comment and oppose reports submitted by the village administrator. It has the right to pass such oppositions and reservations to the subregional administrator. It can also help the administrator select members for village committees, which the law has set up to deal with the affairs of the village-*kebabi*.

The village administrator is appointed by the Regional Administrator, in conjunction with the Minister of Local Government. He or she is a salaried government official, directly accountable to the regional administrator (the hierarchical set-up is discussed later).

The idea is to enable every citizen to participate in the national political arena and decision-making process. Because the *kebabi* is also the smallest unit in the town administrative structure, the right extends to town-dwellers as well. How this inclusion of the population into the formal political structure will work remains to be seen. However, it should be realized that the practice of the village session (*megab'aya*, in Tigrigna) handling its own affairs and resolving its differences is a traditional practice in many parts of the country. But the present arrangement is a more advanced form than the traditional one, as women are included on an equal basis with men, a possibility that did not exist in traditional village *baitos*.

A pertinent question here is whether the village session will be adequate for full and effective popular participation. What guarantees are there that it is not going to be dominated by the village administrator? Should there not be additional guarantees of popular participation, such as civil society institutions independent of formal government structure?

The domination of the village session by the administrator assumes a meek and passive Eritrean public – not characteristics Eritreans are known for, particularly rural Eritreans. On the contrary, it is likely that villagers will use the session as a forum to air their views and grievances whenever the opportunity arises. It should be noted that one of the major complaints of rural residents, according to a random survey carried out WSP, is that in the years after Independence they have experienced fewer open discussions and confrontations with administrators. This complaint was more pronounced in former EPLF areas than Derg-controlled areas. The session, according to the new law, is scheduled to meet every two to three months, with special meetings allowed at the request of a majority of eligible residents or the decision of the administrator.

But what about other forms of popular participation? The first section of this chapter refers to the existence in Eritrea of a traditional civil society. This may take the forms of religious, self-help associations – the *ekube* (purely social associations and gatherings). These usually play a highly important social role in the lives of their membership, as they are venues where friendships are made and opinions formed. Furthermore, because age and the experience that comes with it are respected in Eritrea, community elders are considered and accepted as an important social force. They are usually not organized, but they have always been regarded as an institution to confer with. The same has always applied to the clergy – churches and mosques – the spiritual and highly influential leaders of Eritrean communities.

Civil society in this traditional sense has been and will continue to be an important force to reckon with. "No major programme of work", says an official of the MLG, "can succeed unless community elders and the clergy support it. It is standard practice, from the time of the armed struggle, to consult and convince them before any project is launched." Since elders generally also lead religious and self-help associations, it can be assumed that these are represented in the influential and unofficial institution of elders. Note that the Italians and the British, and to some extent Haileselassie too, used this body, sometimes in a semi-official capacity.

The reference to "traditional" civil society is not meant to separate it from a "modern" variation. Eritrean civil society is one unit, although made up of diverse socio-cultural backgrounds and interests. However, in relation to forms of association or organization, and in light of the definition of civil society as an "aggregate of institutions whose members are engaged in a complex of non-state activities" (see above), the distinction is appropriate.

In the late 1940s, the 1950s and part of the 1960s, Eritrea had fairly advanced trade and professional unions. The labour union that staged the famous national strike of 1958, a precursor to the armed struggle, is sometimes referred to as having been one of the first and most powerful of its kind in colonial Africa. The Eritrean Chamber of Commerce, on the other hand, was an institution of regional and international stature, unlike its incapacitated successor.

The Ethiopian Derg crushed these and similar organizations, only to replace them with subservient shadows of their former selves. The once famous Teachers' Association, for example, which as part of the Ethiopian association of the same name helped bring down the Haileselassie regime, suffered the same fate. At present, it concentrates more on making donations to worthy causes and catering to some of the everyday needs of its members. Similar examples abound of the dialectical discontinuation, as a result of the Derg's repression, of a culture of association and unionization in the colonial context, that was taking root in Eritrean society.

Today, there are plenty of issues that the Teachers' Association, for example, would like to raise with the appropriate authorities. The association's non-participation in the decision-making processes of the ministry, the question of teacher salary increment, and the daily two-shift teaching obligation currently in force are some points raised by association members. Similar issues are mentioned by groups such as the Eritrean Nurses Association, where complaints about the lack of job description, low salary and undefined working hours are voiced – all in interviews with WSP.

The causes of these problems seem to be linked with the general problems of the transitional period, rather than with deliberate attempts on the part of government authorities to shun or suppress legitimate associations and demands. The five years since Independence have seen a continuous attempt by the government to streamline and reorganize its civil service and governmental set-up, a process that is still going on. Some of the issues, especially those dealing with civil associations and their relationship to government raise constitutional questions that only the constitution will clarify.

Thus, in a period when laws and policies are being formulated, it may be difficult to demand and get clarity in complex and new relationships from a new government and state. For the government, the period of sacrifice, the time when the national interest subordinates every other individual or group need, is not yet over. Let there first be enough employment opportunities, enough schools and hospitals, and do not let people starve. In short, the line of reasoning seems to be to allow the economic base and political maturity that go into building the desired effective civil society institutions.

However, these are forms of civil society associations that originated in colonial times. It should be kept in mind that the most dominant and powerful associations today are those that "grew up in rebellion", inside EPLF – the NUEW, NUEYS and Confederation of Eritrean Workers.

These are umbrella organizations that draw their membership from all sections of society, including members of associations of the types discussed above. Although they have no formal links to the government or PFDJ, the historical connections continue in a broad unity of ideas and the pursuit of common objectives. There is a sometimes noticeable tendency to view these associations as part of the government and not as indications of a genuine or viable civil society.

Members of Eritrean national associations dismiss this notion and answer it by posing their own counterpoints or questions. Why, in the Eritrean context, is proximity to the government in philosophy and strategy deemed not genuine? Is distance from government the only guarantee to exert control on state institutions?

To discuss this in a more concrete form, let us briefly look at two of the unions more closely: the NUEW and the NUEYS.

The National Union of Eritrean Women (NUEW)
Established in the late 1970s, this union played an extremely important role, not only in organizing women to support EPLF but also in raising their level of awareness and participation in matters of social and economic concern. Its contributions in the field of literacy and primary healthcare

were, given the constraints of the struggle, quite considerable.

In the changed circumstances of post-Independence, the NUEW's role is focused on the preservation and advancement of the gains of the revolution. The fact that women within EPLF attained heights of parity rarely if ever seen in another historical situation, cannot be contested. At the time it seemed that the new status women were achieving would transfer to the rest of society with fewer hurdles than are seen today.

Eritrean society is patriarchal and left to its traditional attitudes and practices would choose to see women's roles not change in any significant way. Today it is not surprising to see even former women combatants falling back to the status they fought to eliminate. In light of their general disadvantage in terms of education and skills, their susceptibility to this fate is quite high.

True to the guiding principles of the revolution, the Eritrean government has taken significant steps to assure the firm establishment of women's rights. To mention a few examples: the Land Proclamation of 1994 makes no distinction whatsoever between men and women in the right of access to land – a possibility that did not exist previously. The new local administrative law, on the other hand, reserves 30 per cent of the seats in the regional *baito* for women, who also have the right to compete for any or all of the remaining 70 per cent. Their equal participation in the village-*kebabi* is also guaranteed.

These are just two of various similar instances. Mention should also be made of provisions for women in the Constitution. Apart from the tribute paid to women in the preamble, Article 5 provides that, without consideration of "the gender wording of any provision in this Constitution, all of its articles shall apply equally to both genders." This is meant to prevent any possible misreading of the Constitution, as most Eritrean languages do not have the neutral gender and the masculine formulation is frequent in formal legal writing. Article 7(2), which talks about democratic principles, further states that "Any act that violates the human rights of women or limits or otherwise thwarts their role or participation is prohibited". In other words, any form of discrimination against women is a constitutional offence.

There can be no doubt that government-level policy aims to consolidate women's gains achieved during the struggle. The fact that the Eritrean National Assembly, whose chair is the President of the State, endorsed the Draft Constitution, is further evidence of the government's commitment to the cause.

Therefore the NUEW operates in an essentially favourable atmosphere. In spite of this it is, like other governmental and non-governmental bodies in the country, beset by problems in organization, institutional capacity and efficient and effective communications. Still, every one of its 200,000-strong membership expects miracles of it. In addition, as if the question of women's rights were not already a national issue requiring national attention, NUEW officials say there is an unfair tendency to burden the union with responsibilities it cannot shoulder.

Nevertheless, the need for the union to be more aggressive even in areas strongly advocated by the government and PFDJ, is a point emphatically raised in NUEW ranks. The "quota system" in regional assemblies and equal right of access to land, all legally sanctioned, is all well and good. But is "affirmative action" on the part of government in itself a guarantee of gender equality? Traditional taboos still abound that hinder women's full participation in the political affairs and elections of their region and country. Many women find it difficult to break with existing religious and customary rules even on issues where national law is unequivocal – the land issue, for example. This is particularly true of Muslim communities, where Sharia law is practised. In short, women's consciousness even of matters pertaining to their own and their children's health, the "safe motherhood" problem, HIV-awareness and prevention, and so on, is at such a low level that the task involved here is beyond the present capacity not only of the union but even of the government agencies directly concerned.

There is, nevertheless, an increasing conviction in the union and those affiliated with it, that the basis of the improvement of the livelihood and position of women will, in the final analysis, rest in their economic empowerment. Consequently, in recent years the NUEW has been giving its attention to projects (some still at the pilot level) aimed at encouraging and training women to find diversified alternatives to their limited possibilities. With this emphasis, projects in agricultural co-operatives, credit services, animal breeding, handicrafts, and so on, are getting off the ground.

The logistic and capacity problems already mentioned have not enabled the union to speak in terms of thousands as far as economic beneficiaries of its projects are concerned. But the possibilities are there. For example, an affiliated businesswomen's association is going through the first stages of formal organization. Its intention is to help women in small-scale business or in the so-called informal sector. Along with the NUEW, it feels that training such women in the basics of marketing, simple record keeping, arts and crafts, cottage industries, and maintenance and repairs is the first step toward their empowerment. Some members of the union have been increasingly aware of the poor results brought about by training in skills traditionally reserved for women, such as typing and sewing. Hundreds of certificate-holding women have been unable to find employment in an over-burdened market. A shift to more technical skills areas is much desired.

With its problems and limitations, the union is well-advised to decentralize its activities and responsibilities. Ultimately, it is self-reliance in a diversified economic base at the grassroots level that will improve the condition of women. Chances of greater success will be enhanced by focusing on the types of project activities just mentioned, but also by upgrading NUEW institutional capacity as a matter of priority to improve effectiveness.

The National Union of Eritrean Youth and Students (NUEYS)

As a result of the war for independence, Eritrea lost a whole generation of youth in the educational, technical and cultural sense. Most martyrs were young people, as are the disabled and the majority of refugees. The generation that grew up under the Derg was intentionally diverted from school, work and most societal values and discipline. Therefore, in terms of planning and projecting for the future, perhaps the problem with deep strategic implications for the government is the question of youth.

By moving fast to proclaim as law and seriously implement a national service programme for the nation's youth, the government has set out to right what was becoming an alarming development. The decision, initially controversial and unpopular among many youth and parents alike, is now proving of significant national value. Similar results are showing in the annual vacation, one-month work programmes organized by the Ministry of Education for young high school students.

The NUEYS is at the lead and centre of all activities involving its more than 100,000 members nationwide. In terms of activities of a public nature, this union undoubtedly stands at the top of the ladder. Its educational programmes include health campaigns, especially for the prevention of AIDS and other communicable diseases. Peer counsellors and educators disseminate such information. Local and national knowledge contests and quizzes organized or financed by the NUEYS are encouraging youth and children to improve their general knowledge. Other activities include campaigns of reforestation, organizing national clean-up days, and establishing agricultural youth co-operatives at differing levels of participation and with varying degrees of success. Every year, about 600 young people from all over the country are trained in youth leadership courses and 270 are employed in voluntary workshops to be trained in different trades.

Compared to the NUEW, many feel that the NUEYS is more active. But the NUEYS has the advantage of dealing with youth, most of them with practically no responsibilities and is not pressured for immediate material benefits and solutions to economic problems as its women's counterpart is.

Both of the unions have had substantial dealings with, and have received sizeable grants from various outside sources, mostly NGOs. Whereas this is greatly appreciated and put to effective use, sometimes differences of opinion arise with regard to setting priorities or choosing project areas.

For example, one of the most successful areas of NUEYS activity is mass sport, an activity in which thousands of children's and youth teams participate throughout the land. Of 13 foreign-funded projects, none is tuned to sports and, in an unusual turn for NUEYS, it has been unable to interest other possible funding organizations. Yet this is a matter of top priority for the union.

In some projects – vocational training, co-operative farming and AIDS prevention campaigns – priorities from both sides merge. But there are priorities insisted on by funding parties that the union would prefer to postpone. Conflict resolution, human rights and democratization, prevention of female genital mutilation, and so on, are issues that, though important, are simply not ones that a project can solve. They involve culture, politics, societal values – things that take time and basic societal transformations.

The NUEW similarly mentions a few examples. In order that their programmes can help women become economically self-sufficient, daycare centres are important. The union had to solicit the help of its Eritrean women members in the diaspora to get funding for one such centre. No organization, not even UNICEF, could help. However, the union got offers of funds for projects involving democratization, human rights, and dissemination of the Convention on the Rights of the Child, among others.

The main point is that popular participation in decision-making in Eritrea is still of a mass nature. The war has left so many people in similar social and economic conditions that most social demands, though varying by degrees, are quantifiable in a few categories. In other words Eritrean

288 • POST-CONFLICT ERITREA: PROSPECTS FOR RECONSTRUCTION AND DEVELOPMENT

society, still mostly rural, largely poor and unemployed in the urban areas, is not yet economically diversified enough to be organized along diversified lines of interest. Therefore in the foreseeable future its relationship with the government or the state is perhaps bound to remain of a "reciprocal" nature, to quote Goran Hyden.

Thus it may well be that, as far as inclusion in decision making is concerned, the village-*kebabi* session will remain a very important means through which people can express their views. Hopefully, this will also serve as a forum where tolerance of differences of opinion, so essential to the future development of a healthy and independent civil society, will flourish.

Local administration and communication

The local administration law institutes regional administration in accordance with the following hierarchy:

- at the regional level: an executive branch (the administrator and his or her staff), a legislature (the regional *baito*), and the judicial branch
- at the subregional level: an executive branch (the governor of the subregion and his or her staff) and the judicial branch
- at the village level: the village-*kebabi* administration, the village-*kebabi* session (*megab'aya*), and the judicial branch.

Note should be taken that there is no *baito* at the subregional level and that the district level of administration has been eliminated.

It has been shown how the idea of decentralization, particularly the empowerment of local administrations, was debated and even attempted implementation in the years and months before Independence. Also shown was how Proclamation 26/1992 attempted to tackle the issue. Although (according to that law) central government bodies could give directions to their regional divisions and representatives only with the "knowledge" of the *awraja* administrator, they still retained substantive powers.

Thus, placement and hiring of regional staff was the responsibility of central government bodies. The same bodies could transfer their *awraja* staff by informing the administrator and reciprocally the administrator could do the same. Finally, the *awraja* body had the duty to present its quarterly progress report to both the administrator and its parent central government body. This was over and above the direct government projects reserved for the body concerned.

In practice, this arrangement allowed central government bodies to bypass the administrator and deal directly with their *awraja* parts. It was to prove difficult for co-ordinated work at the *awraja* level, as the *awraja* divisions felt more attached and responsible to their parent bodies.

Another problem with the 1992 set-up relates to the failure of district *baitos*, already explained, and the similarly not-so-successful post-Independence experience with the village *baito* resulted in its replacement by the village-*kebabi* session.

The present law upgrades the strength of regional administration by confining the powers of central government bodies to policy making, providing technical expertise and training services, undertaking only central government regional programmes directly, organizing training, providing statistical services, and so on. All their communications, including matters dealing with the placement and transfer of personnel, are now communicated through the Minister of Local Government down to the regional administrator. The regional administrator is now directly responsible for making regional plans, implementing various government policies, and directly co-ordinating the activities of the various regional departments.

This is considered a major step toward decentralization of central government powers, as the authority of the administrator has been enhanced by the newly expanded responsibilities. This is true to the extent that central government bodies can no longer bypass the administrator and deal directly with their corresponding departments. It is a process still in the making and more concrete information about its progress and outcome, especially in terms of institutional and labour capacity at the regional level, will presumably be available when the structure is in full swing. As a process, this is not expected to mature until the end of the decade. In the meantime, the Institute of Management, which is run by Asmara University, is undertaking intensive courses in management, accounting and other pertinent subjects with the aim of filling some essential gaps.

The process of decentralization is more complicated than it appears and as the new law states in its preamble, the general aim is a balance between centralization and decentralization in administration. So, whereas in the aspect just explained the move is toward decentralization, there is another aspect that makes the system still considerably centralized.

Thus, the regional *baito* and executive branch, each invested with considerable regional administrative and legislative responsibilities and authority respectively, and a system of adequate checking and balancing between the two, are nevertheless responsible to the MLG for final approval of activities, plans, proposals, and so on. For example, regional development plans – budget proposals prepared by the administrator and approved by the *baito* – become operable only when the Minister ratifies and returns them to the administrator for implementation. *Baito* opposition or reservations on an administrator's performance or plans are openly deliberated on and transmitted for action to the Minister. Similarly, resolutions and decisions by the *baito* considered beyond its regional jurisdiction may be suspended by the administrator pending their final resolution by the MLG. The administrator's powers are also limited in the area of appointment, transfer and dismissal of regional officials, as this is the responsibility of the Minister at the regional and subregional levels and requires the Minister's approval at the levels of the village-*kebabi*.

The rationale behind this half-way pause toward more decentralization is, first, that both the institutional and personnel capacity of regional administration in not yet ready or developed enough for greater autonomy; second, for some time to come the regions will remain dependent on the central government for financial and technical assistance. True, the new law opens the way for them to secure their own regional financial resources, but this will have to wait until the means of these resources – local taxes, regional development projects – start to generate income. Thus, a ministry pleading the case of the regions at the central government level is essential. Finally, there is the need to co-ordinate and prioritize the competing labour, financial and technical assistance of the regions, until they develop their own avenues.

Is this not, in effect, taking authority away from the various government ministries and other agencies and concentrating it in the hands of the MLG? If so, how is the Ministry expected to cope with all the communication between itself and the regions, between the regions and the ministries, and so on?

If the only line of communication open to central government bodies is the MLG, will this not encumber the necessary flow of information from the regions to the former for policy formulation? Particularly in matters of high technicality, should not a direct line be open to regional and central expertise for a freer flow of information and exchange? If the new structure allows for this, it is not evident, but the issue is being raised at both levels.

Officials at the MLG maintain that the Ministry's power is actually less than it appears to be on paper. In practice, the Minister's intervention will occur only on those occasions when national laws and policies are trespassed or when there are competing and conflicting demands from regions requiring settlement. Otherwise, as long as regional administrations and *baitos* operate in a spirit of co-operation and in their legal confines and jurisdiction, the intention is for the MLG to facilitate rather than block regional matters. The same presumably holds true for communication between ministries and regional counterparts. In fact, based on the short experience, Ministry and regional officials are already feeling that there might be more decentralization than there appears to be on paper. The strength and personality of officials in the respective areas is also expected to contribute to the speed and measure of decentralization.

Practice will, of course, demand and affect its own readjustments. The tug-of-war between centralization and decentralization, which is bound to continue for some time, cannot be seen in isolation. There is, for example, the related progress toward institutionalization, in both central and regional spheres. As roles and functions crystallize and assume definite and identifiable forms, communication in the central government and with the regions will certainly change and at a faster rate than may now appear. It is important to keep in mind that improving telephone and fax systems and the appearance in Eritrea, albeit embryonic, of computer networking are bound to greatly affect present conceptions of communications, decentralization, institutionalization, and so on.

Meanwhile, the constraints that these important aspects of governance and Eritrea's negative experience with the *awraja* set-up impose today are influencing the solution. Eritrea has always known strictly centralized administrations. The *awrajas*, as has been shown, had been weak links in the hierarchy of administration that generally played a negative role. Their disappearance and the creation of the regions does not mean that old parochial and sectarian sentiments do not exist. In view of this, jumping from centralization to complete decentralization, if at all such a situation can exist, is fraught with unknown quantities and eventualities. So, the argument goes, caution and a step-by-step approach to the whole issue are essential.

Again, the whole issue of decentralization should be viewed from a broader perspective, for decentralization goes beyond administrative decentralization to the empowerment of communities. Peter Koehn and Goran Hyden list community mobilization and participation, needs assessment, project identification and selection, planning and budgeting, project implementation and monitoring and evaluation as process areas meriting attention for the further introduction of decentralization in the country (Koehn and Hyden, 1996). They explain that the new local administrative initiative in the country creates favourable conditions for the type of decentralization they suggest. Detailing a three-phase decentralization approach that deals with different levels of the process areas listed above, they estimate that the initial and intermediate phases of decentralization would take two to five and five to ten years, respectively. After that the advanced phase would be attained (Koehn and Hyden, 1996:27-30). Are such formulas and projections really applicable? But their suggestion goes to prove that, if the choice is to decentralize, then serious steps to that end are prerequisites.

Today, for example, the activities of the ECRFU – a community-based development fund involving the government, World Bank and community contributions – has used 70 million birr for 140 projects throughout the country. The success of the ECRFU has now prompted its elevation from a rehabilitation to a development fund (ECDFU) with a current fund of 350 million birr for further projects. The process normally followed for choosing project sites goes from local demands or initiatives, to approval by the local *baito*, to approval by the ECDFU and then the finished project returns to the community for implementation through popular participation.

Several similar projects involving community participation and government and NGO co-operation – such as the Zula Project that Koehn and Hyden take as an example in rural participation and the ACORD Savings and Credit Scheme in Seraye – are mentioned as beginnings of decentralized forms of development projects. However, because international NGO involvement in Eritrea is on the way out, this form of decentralization (effected through NGO-driven and financed local institutions) is unlikely to continue.

The question of the volume and diversity of communications directed toward the MLG creating problems has already been considered. It is felt by local administrative officials especially, that a second level in the new structure will create communication problems in the subregion.

The elimination of the *wereda* level that used to administer several village groupings within subregions, has now opened the subregional administration to direct contact with the administrative village-*kebabi*. It was initially intended that an administrative village would consist of a few small villages jointly administered, or of larger and more heavily populated individual villages administered as separate units. Although the principle is the same, some populous subregions are being compelled to increase the number of administrative villages to make them manageable. For example, at the time this study was undertaken 119 villages in the Adi Quala subregion had been organized into 27 administrative villages, and 82 villages in the Diba-Riwa area made 25 administrative villages. Such an arrangement was convenient for the administrative villages as each of the aforementioned averaged 4.4 and 3.3 villages per administrative village, respectively.

However, the burden of work and problem of communication for the subregional administration can easily be imagined. So a new rearrangement, aimed at enlarging village administrative jurisdiction, was under way. But, if stretched too far, some administrative villages might grow as big as the old districts. This is an area that presumably is being worked on.

On a different plane, in the WSP Working Group meeting on governance the feeling was expressed that the level of communication between the government and the people had declined considerably, especially compared to what it was during the armed struggle. That there is a decrease in communication and rapport cannot be seriously contested and the post-war causes of that reduction have been discussed in some detail. But the meaning attached to it is a contentious issue.

Has a distance really been created between the government and the people, or is the government being subjected to an unfair comparison with an "idealized" EPLF experience, whose own communication problems may have been forgotten, to quote Ato Yemane Gebreab (of the PFDJ)? In the absence of sophisticated public opinion polls that would show the government its level of popularity, determining its closeness or distance from the people with any degree of accuracy will remain a problem. It was probably the same with EPLF. If public opinion was gauged at the time when EPLF was undertaking its campaign of compulsory conscription, the results may possibly have been alarming even among its most ardent supporters.

This is a transitional period and people may be blaming their problems on the government for reasons beyond its control. Government steps that negatively affect certain segments of the population contribute to feelings of ill-will. The loudest complaints against the government have resulted from the dismissal of former Derg party members from government jobs, civil service streamlining that brought about thousands of government employee lay-offs, and strict controls on the massive and unrestricted profits demanded by businesses.

Other government measures regarding the national service, land, and local government laws created shock waves that subsided only with subsequent high-level public explanations. There may be other actions generating deep concern but these are the ones that had widely ranging consequences across the country. In the interest of brevity and for the purpose of this review, the Land Proclamation will be considered in relation to the issue of government-to-people communication.

In all public gatherings held in eight of the then 10 provinces, a question consistently asked was why the Land Commission had not consulted with the people before it came up with a finished document. Why, indeed, were public consultations not held on what the proclamation's contents should be?

This issue was often discussed between the commission and the committee tasked with the final draft of the Land Proclamation. The committee's studies and conclusions were based on EPLF experience on land matters – the result not only of in-depth research (unfortunately not yet published) by the DPA, but also of the EPLF's attempts at land reform, the outcome of which did not satisfy the committee.

In its long dealings with the people, the EPLF had actually come to the conclusion that the solution to the major problem of land lay not in the token reform (including its own) attempted since Italian times, but in major rethinking and complete transformation of the concept and system of land ownership. So the decision that land ownership be vested in government had been reached before, not after, Independence. Thus, the PGE State Council's directive establishing the Land Commission in late 1991 asserted the government's intention to transfer ownership rights.

State ownership of land was preferred for a variety of reasons. The old communal system was becoming the cause of major conflicts that often created instability in the maintenance of public order. Customary farming and grazing practices and land use were bogged down in old laws that neither allowed nor encouraged the introduction of new technology and major public or private investments. Beyond this, the old system discriminated against women and some minorities, was a breeding ground for parochial sentiment that slowed the rapid progress of national unity, and was inconsistent, because the same communal rights prevalent in the highlands were denied the lowlands, where land was state-owned.

Furthermore, fundamental and controversial issues such as according women equal rights of access to land was not likely to be accepted by most men if the topic were open to public discussion and decision. Such would have been the fate of transferring land ownership from the hands of communities to the state and the resulting elimination of village, clan and tribal land boundaries.

As far as communication is concerned, the real issue here is how much of its policies and intentions government is supposed to make public in order to pass the test of transparency. Should a government postpone programmes and policies it is convinced will enhance the process of democracy and development in order to gain the consensus of a people who may not clearly see the future value of the change proposed? The Tanzanian Presidential Commission on Land spent many months consulting with representatives from every corner of the country and submitted what it thought would satisfy popular sentiments and demands on land. The government of Tanzania rejected the proposals and issued its own law.

The key point here is that assessing government-to-people relationships on the frequency of contact made between the two or, to put it more plainly, on the love-hate scale of public feelings about government is simply misleading.

It would be difficult to argue that at the initial stage of each of the laws mentioned – national service, land and local administration – public reaction ranged from shock to frustration to resentment to support. It is possible that at the beginning the balance tipped toward the first three reactions. With time, National Service has become part of Eritrean life. The complaint now is not about the content but the delay in implementing the land proclamation. The local government law is being implemented without impediments. In fact, as a result of the favourable conditions created by the two other laws, land and community disputes originating in Italian times – such as the famous Tor'a-Tsendegle and Adi Quita-Birkito conflicts – have been resolved through use of customary conflict resolution machinery.

Government-to-people communication is more substantive than would appear in surveys or polls taken at specific times. Instead, it can be more accurately assessed over time and with the cumulative result and effects of various government policies and programmes. In the meantime, government should take care that people understand its long-term intentions.

Random interviews showed that residents of former EPLF-controlled areas were more prone to complain about poor administration and neglect than those from areas with relatively less EPLF presence. The reason clearly given was that contact with the former is not at the level it was during the armed struggle. The whole nation now demands an equal share of government attention and services, advantages that were concentrated in fewer areas before Independence. If people in Sahel, the EPLF base area, complain of neglect, it would be justifiable from their point of view, since the fringe benefits of the EPLF 's massive presence in the area are no longer there. The government needs to clearly state and make known to the public its problems and good intentions. A good practice of the past five years has been the public question and answer session that the President holds every September. The famous capitol seminars, where the highest-level government officials explain and are questioned on various government policies, have also played a major role in informing the public. Similarly, various television and radio programmes air interviews, panels and debates on public issues.

Considering the amount of public relations work that is needed to really explain and inculcate in people's minds the problems of transition, and considering the amount of hard work and patience needed to attain even minimum levels of development, what is being done is not enough. Transparency is not necessarily the problem. A recent interview given by the President to the PFDJ magazine, *Hidri*, is a document of openness rarely matched in similar interviews anywhere in the world.

Rather, the problem is to carry out organized and consistent public discussion processes that involve as large a part of the nation as possible. The Constitutional Commission encouraged participation but it was temporary. Government needs a permanent means to reach the public and hear its problems.

The village session may be one means of canvassing public opinion. As part of the government structure it may not be considered as effective as, for example, unions, associations and special interest groups, but until these expand or mature it can be of considerable importance and influence.

Thus, to the extent that the Eritrean government has so far been concentrating on uprooting the causes of poverty, illiteracy, rebuilding the infrastructure, and so on, and to the extent that it has been tackling post-Independence problems, its contact with the realities and needs of the people is intact. On a deep social, psychological and strategic basis, its communication with the people is blameless. On the narrower, day-to-day level of communicating ideas, decisions and actions, there is room for improvement and refinement.

A NOTE ON THE PRIVATE SECTOR
The background
It is generally agreed by people in government and the private sector that a "business community" did not exist at the time of Independence in 1991. Seventeen years of Derg "socialism" had decimated what was a

dynamic, though chiefly Italian-led private sector. The once vibrant Chamber of Commerce was weak and had long been silenced, and the market was ruled by a new breed of merchants who approached business in an entirely different way.

Alternately known as the "Children of the Seventies" or the *"Ayer Bayer"* (Amharic for "Air to Air"), the merchants were mostly individuals with little or no entrepreneurial skill, who entered the market as a result of spying links or other connections of material benefit with the Derg's authorities. The reference to *Ayer Bayer* is quite revealing. Typically, a Derg official would give a favoured person an exclusive right to import an essential commodity not in stock in Eritrea – and there were quite a few of these due to the war. This permission usually took the form of a letter properly signed by the authority concerned. The beneficiary, usually not licensed to trade, would then sell the permit to a licensed business that would actually import the commodity. Inevitably, the beneficiary and the official would share the ill-gotten gains. Hence, "air to air" meant letters, speculations, anticipation of commodities flown in chartered planes, and so on.

It was possible in those days to wake in the morning as a pauper and go to bed in the evening with one's first million, or part of it. Eritrean business suffered in the process. Corruption, bribery, the black market and the like replaced the old principles of market and business dealings. Money went into the hands of inexperienced and unprincipled people who did not know how to use it. The concept of profit lost its accepted meaning, with business's appetite and greed soaring to insatiable heights. No consideration was given to the consumer in the quality or price of commodities that filled the market.

In 1991, the Eritrean government set out to deal with this extremely confused and confusing situation. However, because it had its own limitations in terms of concrete knowledge of the sector and capacity to deal with it, the first two years and more failed to show substantive progress in the move toward rehabilitation of the business community. In fact, this was a period of loud complaint and ill-will on the part of the community.

According to some business people, the reason for the bad start in government-to-business relationships was attributable to an underlying mutual suspicion between the two. The government, or at least many of the officials concerned, many business people contend, saw the community as inherently bad, fraudulent, corrupt and corrupting. Whereas this preconception or pre-judgement had a sound basis in the experience of the preceding years, it failed to take into account, they further argue, that adherents of lawful and principled business practices were, although weakened, ready and willing to bring back the vitality and respectability of the private sector. This attitude of the government, it is stated, led to the formulation of policies that discouraged rehabilitation of the sector.

The most frequently cited of such policies relates to the stringent licensing rules that required the deposit of large sums of money in the bank to prove capacity and worthiness. The complaint was based on the fact that sureties of this nature failed to take into consideration an individual's capital goods, entrepreneurial skills, business experience and good-will; the requirement actually had effects contrary to what was desired. This was so because, first, it discouraged potential business skill and know-how without ready access to cash; second, it enabled the *Ayer Bayer* to use their hoard to obtain licenses; and third, it opened the way to trickery and fraud. For example, some people deposited borrowed money in the bank only to withdraw it as soon as the license was obtained.

By the admission of the present licensing office, apart from problems posed by the surety requirement, the process of acquiring a license involved three separate offices, each requiring weeks or months to finish its part. This meant that getting a license would take as long as eight months. A system inherited from the Derg, it became evident that it was cumbersome, frustrating, and to many applicants, very discouraging.

The practice and its negative effects on business were not hidden from the government. Neither were the community's complaints, opinions and suggestions, which were registered with the appropriate authorities in public meetings and open seminars.

However, the government was more interested in long-term business policies and strategies than in solutions for immediate problems such as the license issue. Despite claims to the contrary, and given the existence of a potentially productive section in the community, the government was still convinced that the private sector was too weak and ill-equipped – financially and technically – to raise the country's economy "from the ashes of war and destruction", as the Macro-Policy Document puts it. Thus, solutions to existing problems had to be seen in and related to the broader context of national development objectives.

The macro policy and after

The Macro-Policy Document gives a great deal of attention to the private (including the informal) sector as the "lead actor in the economic activities of Eritrea". It affirms that economic activities are open to participation with "no restriction and discrimination". The government, through its public sector, is limited to activities such as the provision of infrastructure, investment in human capital, securing financial and credit institutions, and the regulation and maintenance of a stable economic and political system in general. It is also responsible for taking "all necessary policy and other supportive measures to promote, encourage, and develop the private sector and protect its interests" (GSE, 1994c:14–16).

Within this broad statement of national development objectives, the document spells out its investment policies for all sectors of the economy, including its monetary, fiscal and trade policies. Every one of these policies lays the foundation for encouragement and free development of the private sector. The land and local administration framework policies already discussed were meant, among other things, to provide the above policies with the necessary basis for social mobility and easier access to the country's resources, factors vital to the expansion of the private sector.

The Macro-Policy Document is not just a statement of intentions. The government's genuine desire to abide by the principles of the document started to show even before it was published. Thus, the new Land Proclamation and the Investment Proclamation were made into law in August 1994, three months before the macro-policy paper.

The Investment Proclamation of 1994 eliminated requirements of the previous law such as enormous bank deposits in order to obtain a license for investment. Low income tax on capital goods, speedy licensing mechanisms, loans and foreign exchange allocation, business travel facilities, and allocation of land to investment projects are all leading principles of the proclamation.

Immediately after publication of the investment law, customs tariff regulation was revised to suit both national and foreign private business and investment in the country. Thus, capital goods, industrial spare parts and raw materials and intermediate goods pay a nominal import duty of two per cent plus a three per cent sales tax. Goods for export and re-export are exempted and sales tax paid on imported raw materials that are re-exported as finished products is refundable.

Similarly, a new income tax proclamation greatly reduced old rates inherited from the Derg. Thus, personal income tax, previously having reached 85 per cent, was limited to a progressive range of two per cent for earnings below 200 birr, to 38 per cent for income above 150,000 birr. Tax on corporate profit ranges from 25 to 35 per cent. In commercial agriculture it ranges from two to 20 per cent.

The new incentives showed a marked increase in the number of projects approved by the Investment Centre. Some 240 such projects, worth a total of approximately 1,900 million birr, have either been established or are in progress. Manufacturing takes the lead in with 92 projects worth 613 million birr; hotels and restaurants have 40 projects worth 785 million birr; agriculture has 28 projects worth 90.5 million birr, and fisheries have 27 projects worth 216 million birr. The complete or partial removal of many constraints of the initial years – inadequate owner supply, poor transportation and faulty communications systems and networks – have contributed to steady growth in investment.

Perhaps most decisive in the move toward the encouragement of the private sector is the ease, simplicity and speed with which business licenses of every kind are being issued by the appropriate office. Termed as "one-window shopping" by all concerned, it is a process that requires no appointments, starts at one end of a large hall on the ground floor of the Municipality of Asmara, and in half an hour finishes at the other end. If the sought-after license is for a bar, restaurant or hotel, the process might take longer because the premises have to be inspected. Otherwise, as long as the applicant is at least 18 years of age, not a government employee and not serving a prison term, then on payment of a fee he or she emerges with a license within the specified time. From January to June of 1996 alone, 4,163 licenses were issued and 9,513 renewed. This contrasts sharply with the 850 licenses issued in all of 1995 under the old system.

The licensing practice signals an attitude on the part of the government that is favourable to the expansion of a free market. The previous system involved government agencies in making decisions on who was eligible for all forms of business. Every application for a license had to be screened, the assumption being that the official responsible had the power and appropriate knowledge to decide who goes into what business. Today, the licensing office leaves decisions on business ventures to the entrepreneur or applicant.

Although this is a welcome development, some business people are sceptical about the easy availability of licenses as, in their words, "business is still being invaded by unprincipled people, who may give to it a bad reputation", and examples are cited. The License Office does not deny this possibility but gives it very little importance, maintaining that those who complain are established business people who would not mind exclusive control of the market. At a time when demobilized fighters, families of martyrs and returning refugees are looking for a livelihood, those who want to try their hand at business should be given the chance. The more licenses issued, the tougher the competition, which is all the better for private sector development. There are signs already, it is claimed, of the old *Ayer Bayer* weakening and giving way to genuine competition.

The constraints

One investor involved in both commerce and construction describes customs tariffs as very reasonable, personal income tax as most favourable and conducive to the employment of workers, commercial and corporate taxes as fair, and licensing as among the "simplest and fastest in our region". Nevertheless, there are still formidable obstacles to the sector's fast growth and development.

Many – including officials at the Ministry of Finance – see this evidence of the government's determination to push the sector forward as inadequate because it still needs to be backed up by administrative and revenue services, and financial institutions. It also requires ports and transportation and communication facilities to work efficiently. Some of these such as road, sea and air transport, although improving steadily are problems whose sheer enormity stands in the way of a quick resolution. They are thus likely to go on impeding the expansion of the sectors for some time to come. On the other hand, electricity supply and communications – telephone, telex and fax services – are improving at a much faster rate and are expected to reach reasonably high standards in a few years' time.

The factors requiring most immediate attention, though, are within the business sector itself. For the sake of brevity, only two of these will be reviewed: customs regulations and credit or financial services.

The process of clearing and forwarding imports and exports has not changed much from previous periods. Although some business people point to the relative efficiency of Eritrean customs posts, compared with the practices in some neighbouring countries, and to the non-existence of corruption, the room for improvement is still enormous. There is simply no correlation between the situation in airports and ports and what the government has declared in its laws and macro policy.

A recent study by the Ministry of Finance identified the problem as emanating from lack of clarity in rules and guidelines, especially as these are a carry-over from the Derg's highly inefficient system. As in the old licensing process, here, too, the customs office simply does not entrust customs declarations to transit officers or individual business people, whose honesty is often doubted. Until now, it was routine for the customs officer to fill in declarations and check prices, processes that often lead to frustrating delays.

A detailed description of the customs situation is unnecessary. Suffice it to say that the Ministry of Finance has identified the bottlenecks causing confusion not only in customs, but also in income tax processes. For example, customs officers, transitors and banking and port authorities must be given well-defined and complementary, rather than vague and conflicting responsibilities.

However, the problem is not confined to a deficiency in the government's method of tariff or tax collection. The low capacity and lack of basic knowledge on the part of transitors and business people is also a major factor. Transitors are often untrained and sometimes even incapable of filling out a declaration form. In the area of income tax, the great bulk of medium- and small-scale business people and traders simply never declare their respective annual income for the purposes of taxation. The task is thus left to the tax office to track down every culprit every year and estimate their income, a practice that inevitably triggers off some very loud protests. To assure a steady flow to the government treasury and avoid wasting time and resources, a system is being devised whereby such businesses are classified by type, size and likely levels of income and a presumptive tax fixed accordingly. In other words, there will be no more tracking down petty tax evaders.

The second major area of the business sector requiring immediate attention is credit or financial services, a situation vital to growth in the private sector. This requires some deeper knowledge of the banking system and for the purposes of this chapter a layperson's description is given.

The Commercial Bank of Eritrea began as a continuation or replacement of the Commercial Bank of Ethiopia's branch in Eritrea. Because the latter was only a regional bank and dealt mainly in short-term commercial loans, its activities were confined to retail business. Loans requiring long-term credit were handled by specialized banks, such as aid and investment banks and the housing bank. In the absence of such banks in Eritrea (the housing bank having started full operations only in 1994), the whole burden of handling the credit demands of the country fell to the Commercial Bank, and this arrangement continues.

On Independence, the government inherited an almost bankrupt institution. Eighty million birr, loaned in the name of the numerous nationalized enterprises and not even used by them, was and still is registered as the bank's debt to its clients, the Eritrean public. The reason the enterprises did not use the money was that the Derg had used it for other purposes. In addition, in its hasty escape from Eritrea, the Derg carried off close to 300 million birr of public savings. Retrieving this huge amount from the newly installed Ethiopian government was not to be an easy matter. With part of the money still under negotiation, the Eritrean Bank had to pass through a period of inaction before some of the money was returned and it could start normal activities. This situation played a part in slowing down revitalization of the Eritrean economy in general and the private sector in particular.

The Eritrean public either had no money to deposit or was not entrusting its savings to the Derg's banks. In June 1991, total deposits were a meagre 280 million birr, including the 80 million "loaned" to public enterprises and the large amounts shipped to Addis Ababa. However, as soon as the bank started its activities, deposits increased at a very high rate. In June 1995, 3.3 billion birr was on deposit in 200,000 accounts.

Money sitting unused in a bank is not good for the bank or the economy. Short-term loans were so low in volume in the pre-1995 period that the bank was losing an average of 90 million birr per year in interest on savings deposits. To off-set this and to fill the gap created by the absence of specialized aid and investment banks, the Commercial Bank was involved until 1996 in medium- and long-term loans to accommodate industrial, agricultural, tourism and other such demands. The result was a sharp increase in the amount of money loaned, from 804 million birr in June 1995 to 1.3 billion birr in June 1996, providing a temporary respite to the bank's predicament.

Despite these problems, the bank has done badly. The need to increase and upgrade staff capacity and to introduce a faster networking system is evident. Banking laws are yet to be issued or be made more comprehensive. However, the main problem still lies in the weakness of the private sector. Despite claims to the contrary, the amount of money in the hands of most Eritrean business people is not enough for the types of major investment projects they propose. Barring a few exceptions, Eritrean entrepreneurs prefer to go it alone in business. Joint ventures, partnerships and private limited companies with other business people are generally avoided unless the other parties are members of a family or a close relation. So the concept of pooling capital for a common investment project or enterprise has not yet been embraced by the Eritrean business mentality.

Therefore, the bank is involved in filling gaps in equity shares, for example granting loans to entrepreneurs whose funds fail to meet the amount required for a given project. Most of the 628 million birr loaned to members of the private sector falls into this category.

What are the main activities of the private sector? What types of business are Eritrean entrepreneurs or business aspirants involved in or entering? Two sets of figures from the Licensing Office give a rough picture.

As of 12 February 1996, a quantified report from the office records 23,711 different business activities. Almost 68 per cent of these are classified as follows: 6,769 individual activities or licenses in the import/export sector; 5,341 in retail trade of edibles and cleaning material; 1,465 in wholesale of non-edibles; and 909 in wholesale of edibles, including beverages. A total of 16,115 licenses are concentrated on these five activities. The sample does not take into account retail and wholesale activities similar to the above.

Our second example comes from a follow-up to this report for activities quantified between February and June 1996, this time examining licenses issued during these four months. Of a total of 3,122 new licenses, the following activities took the lion's share: 856 import/export; 699 wholesale of non-edibles; 490 wholesale of grain and cereals; and 246 taxi services. This means that 2,291 or about 73 per cent of new licenses are for these four activities. This contrasts sharply with manufacturing ventures of all forms for the same period, totalling only 90, mostly in wood and metal working businesses. The figures do not accurately reflect actual activity; obtaining a license does not necessarily mean activity begins.

An additional observation of note is the activities women are involved in. According to the License Office, well over 80 per cent of women now obtaining licenses are concentrating on extremely limited areas of activity. The most prominent of these are hairdressing and beauty salons, and restaurant and bar activities. Of 233 licenses in the former sector, 156 (68 per cent) have gone to women. Of 867 licenses in the latter sector, 521 (60 per cent) are held by women.

The above information tells the interesting, though partial story that the Eritrean private sector is dominated by small-scale trade, artisanship, manufacturing and services. As a recognition of the vital role of these activities in the economy of the country in general, and in people's livelihood in particular, the Macro-Policy Document provides for upgrading and technologically improving what it calls "the informal sector", clearly the largest source of employment next to small-scale peasant agricultural occupations. What exactly is being done to realize the macro policy's vision for the private sector?

THE FUTURE OF THE PRIVATE SECTOR
The baseline survey of the private sector

As a first step toward realizing the macro policy's stated aim of revitalizing the private sector in general and upgrading its small-scale and informal part in particular, an impressive baseline survey of the sector was issued in July 1996 that focuses on micro, small and medium enterprises (MSMEs), but also deals with large-scale enterprises and fisheries. Time constraints and the scope of this chapter do not allow an in-depth look at the contents of this study. It presents a detailed and comprehensive picture of the state of the private sector in Eritrea, based on area canvassing, including street-to-street and door-to-door surveys, and field work over a period of three months.

In its executive summary, the study indicates that an estimated 55,000 enterprises provide employment for roughly 130,000 people. Of these, 92,288 people are employed by 52,191 MSMEs; 26,603 people by 191 large-scale enterprises – 8,812 people in 2,358 modern agricultural enterprises and 2,500 people in 400 fishing activities.

By MSMEs the study means companies that employ 1-2 (micro), 3-9 (small) and 10-25 (medium) people – any company employing more than 25 people is considered large-scale. The study indicates that a majority of these MSMEs are located in urban areas and operating in the field of trade, with food and drinks and wood and forest-based material industries taking second and third places. Large-scale enterprises are also mostly situated in urban areas and are mainly involved in manufacturing, particularly in the fabric industry.

The executive summary of the study also points to the significant role of women in the private sector. They account for 43 per cent, 12 per cent and 6 per cent respectively of MSME ownership. The study indicates that female-owned enterprises account for almost two-thirds of those in the manufacturing sector, about two-fifths in the trade sector, and one-quarter in services. However, the study further points out that female dominance in the manufacturing sector is "due to smaller activities such as brewing of local drinks, basket and traditional broom-making, net-making and the production of certain juices". Thus, their importance and share in the sector is not commensurate with their numerical participation. As pointed out in relation to female share of licenses, women employed in service and trade are confined to hairdressing salons and braiding and in the hotel, restaurant and bar business respectively.

Another interesting revelation of the study relates to the activities of the private sector outside urban centres. Of the total of 52,191 enterprises, 20,746 (39.7 per cent) are in rural locales. The remaining 31,446 (60.3 per cent) are located in urban centres and rural towns. The employment figures are 63,811 (69.1 per cent) in urban and 28,477 (30.9 per cent) in rural locales respectively.

The main purpose of the study is not merely to provide statistical information, but to identify the problems and constraints facing the sector, with a view to helping the government come up with policies, plans and programmes for solving them. Thus, the survey provides the following ranking of problems for each MSME group:

Table 7.1
MSME problem rankings

Problem ranking	Size of enterprise and problem		
	Micro	Small	Medium
First	Market	Market	Raw materials
Second	Transportation	Raw materials	Market
Third	Space/site	Space/site	Skilled labour
Fourth	Equipment	Lack of training	Utilities

A further important revelation of the survey is the fact that small-scale trade far outranks manufacturing. To reverse this the manufacturing sector needs to be planned, following the careful identification of items or areas of priority. The formidable problem of finding adequate markets for finished products, along with facilities for their exposure and distribution, has also been made evident.

For a starter at the pilot level, studies have been conducted on the improvement and expansion of the old Medeber in Asmara. This is an amazing centre in the north-eastern part of the city, where artisans from all over use scrap metal and other discarded materials to manufacture anything from horseshoes to metal plates and spoons. Possibilities of expanding this activity and improving the products, services and safety measures are being looked into. The final aim is to encourage the establishment of similar centres in other towns, so that artisan products and services will be more easily available in all locales. However, the MSME experiment is still in the rudimentary stage.

The main topic of governance will now be returned to and concluded. The baseline survey has started a move toward a fundamental understanding of the state of the Eritrean economy that will play an extremely positive role in its growth and diversification. As the above ranking and the information leading up to it indicates, the government now has at least some of the essential elements for rational planning in the revitalization of the sector.

What kind of private sector?

Assuming that the adult population of Eritrea is about one million, approximately the number that voted in the Referendum in 1993, then the 130,000 people employed in the private sector make up 13 per cent of the general adult population. Considering that 70-80 per cent of adult Eritreans are employed in small-scale agricultural activities, the business community constitutes a formidable section of the rest of society. It is also important to note that, of the 130,000 people employed by the business sector, 92,288 (71 per cent) are in MSMEs.

Eritrea may not be a "nation of shopkeepers", as England was once called, but the role MSMEs are playing in maintaining the livelihood of their members and the members' families cannot be ignored. In addition, it should be noted that MSMEs are the highest source of employment for women. The principles of social justice and equitable distribution of national wealth adhered to by the government and PFDJ have been discussed at length. The baseline study is expected to play an important part in providing the government with the opportunity to take a rational and balanced approach toward developing each part of the private sector.

Social justice, by definition, demands that the private sector not be dominated by a few capitalists and financiers to the detriment or at the expense of the majority. As far as possible, extreme inequalities need to be avoided or reduced. The opening-up of the market to free competition, as evidenced by the easy accessibility of business licenses to practically all who apply, seems to be a move in the right direction. However, at present, not only is the competition highly unequal to begin with, but such constraints on the Eritrean economy as the absence of a large market for local products, lack of raw materials, still largely unresolved problem of transportation; and low level of skill and business know-how within the business community itself, stand in the way of making even preliminary progress toward the final objective.

Thus comes the stage at which the foundation or infrastructure for fair market competition must be laid down. Because the private sector is still weak and not cohesive – the once dynamic Eritrean Chamber of Commerce is yet to be fully reorganized – the burden of revitalizing the economy in general and the sector, in particular, has fallen to both the government and PFDJ. As PFDJ's intervention in the economy raises a few questions, it is worth a brief look.

A few years ago, a common complaint of practically every Eritrean business person was that the government was dominating the market through PFDJ's economic activities. Remnants of such arguments still abound, especially in areas of trade that people feel should be left to private business. The counter-argument is that PFDJ's enterprises are private and they pay taxes and dues like every other business, and so on. Great detail is not needed here as there is nothing in the records to prove otherwise. However, the reason for the activities and whether the front's massive intervention in the economy is always justified should be put in proper perspective.

PFDJ officials strongly argue that the front's major aim is more the revitalization of the Eritrean economy than the strengthening of its own economic base, although its determination to be economically self-reliant is also in place. To realize its former aim, the officials maintain, the front is investing in strategic areas that are outside the financial and physical capability of the Eritrean business community; it is providing partnership opportunities and deals to major foreign and international investors; it is helping local entrepreneurs and investors obtain the extra capital they need to stand on their own feet; and, lastly, it is protecting consumers and keeping prices down by entering market competition and setting profits close to accepted or legal levels.

This researcher was surprised to find a high degree of support among some potent business people for many of the aims and economic activities of the PFDJ. Strategic commodities such as cement or bricks imported or locally manufactured by the front's enterprises are seen as highly positive contributions to the growth of the private sector, as are massive imports of food items, especially in times of bad harvest. Although there is plenty of criticism of the Sembel Housing Project's designs, the front's attempt to solve the housing crisis is also supported.

Barring some reservations concerning the PFDJ's choice of local partners, the idea of helping local entrepreneurs help themselves is also generally appreciated, with some ventures cited as exemplary. If its stated objective of helping local export items find markets abroad is achieved, this will definitely be a major breakthrough for the private sector. Furthermore, PFDJ's intervention is also seen by many as the protection of the Eritrean economy from domination by foreign capital, as was the case with Italian business control before the Derg.

What is not accepted or properly understood is some of the PFDJ's activities, especially in the retail trade, which many feel it should withdraw from. According to PFDJ officials, some of these activities and the entities that engage in them are carry-overs from the days of the armed struggle. Since the PFDJ's economic activities started in 1994, it is only now starting to take full stock of its enterprises and getting in a position to separate the essential from the temporary and transitional. This is expected to be followed by the front's gradual identification and eventual retreat from some of its non-essential activities.

Another advantage of PFDJ's economic activities, as seen by members of the community, is that they also concentrate on providing goods and services to rural and remote areas normally beyond the reach of the rest of the private sector. Thus, schools, clinics and transport services are being extended to unprivileged sections of the country. It is also notable that these activities are creating employment opportunities for a workforce that remained idle for years. The Sembel Housing Project alone is employing and training 4,500 male and female workers. Total employment in PFDJ's economic activities is about 15,000.

Thus, as long as PFDJ lives up to its promises of eventual withdrawal from many of its current activities – opening them up for public shareholding or outright sale to the rest of the private sector seems to be the argument in the business community – its role will be regarded as positive and vital.

So, what kind of a private sector is likely to emerge under these conditions? Presumably, one that is based on and favourable to the role of MSMEs, as the overall commitment to social justice and equitable distribution of wealth will continue to be the guiding principle and policy. One would hope that the government will forge ahead with its plans not only of expanding and diversifying the economy, but also of finding a market for local products, so that MSMEs can survive competition from larger enterprises. Contrary to the current situation, in which MSME numerical dominance is not reflected in its share of the market or of profits, a proportionate or fair part of capital itself should fall under MSME control if any semblance of equity is to be achieved.

This is not to say that large-scale enterprises should be limited in their activities or be suppressed in favour of MSMEs. But despite the government's gradual sale of some of its public enterprises to private capital, this sector is likely to remain outside the scope and capacity of local capital. Major investments in areas such as mining, energy exploration, communications networking, large tourism ventures and heavy industry are linked more to foreign than to local partnerships. Usually the government or PFDJ is the Eritrean partner. The importance of large-scale enterprises being unquestioned, a balance should be struck with MSMEs for the development of a healthy private sector.

An additional reason to expand and diversify the MSMEs is gender. Despite the government's efforts to continue EPLF traditions concerning the equality of participation by women, post-Independence progress in this area has not been substantial. The private sector, especially MSMEs, is probably the area where women's successful participation and empowerment may best be assured. But, according to accounts of the License Office, they need advice, training and a lot of technical assistance.

This section may be closed with advice offered by several business people to the government and PFDJ. First, that the government be more communicative and informative and that government officials stop regarding the business community with suspicion and instead accept its members as partners. Second, that laws governing all aspects of business be clearly stated and consistently implemented. Third, that PFDJ concentrate on strategic as opposed to retail business. Finally, that the Chamber of Commerce be reinstated as an independent forum for the private sector and as a bridge and facilitator in communications between the government and the sector.

It is incumbent on members of the Eritrean business community to realize, on the other hand, that this government neither accepts nor tolerates fraud, dishonesty and corruption in business. Its adherence to equity and justice are non-negotiable and cannot be compromised. The greed and total disregard for the most elementary societal values – respect and consideration for the rights and interests of others – cannot be allowed to continue. Profit must be limited to legally and morally acceptable levels. Professionalism in business should be aimed at. Finally, the Eritrean business community should realize that its financial and technical capacity is limited and that its resurgence is partially dependent on its understanding of and co-operation with the government's plans and policies.

If the improvement in relations between the government and the business community seen over the last two years is an indication, the future looks promising for the private sector.

INTERNATIONAL ECONOMIC CO-OPERATION: THE ERITREAN VIEW
The legacy of independent thinking

One of the purposes of this research on governance was to investigate the present relationship between the government of Eritrea and the various United Nations agencies, NGOs and other such foreign-based entities present in the country. Together with the private sector discussed above, this issue could have been an Entry Point unto itself as it raises questions of fundamental philosophical, policy and practical significance.

Eritrea's approach to dealings with external or international actors in the areas of trade, aid and technical assistance, has become a focal point in serious discussions with radical implications for established views. Its origin is the armed struggle, in which EPLF jealously guarded its principles of self-reliance and independence while maintaining working relationships with chosen outside supporters and sympathizers. A sign of the times in this respect was that the EPLF was practically never forced or pressured by outside forces to adopt attitudes or courses of action contrary to its fundamental beliefs and strategic plans. Forgoing essential help (even food supplies for its ranks) in the interest of the preservation of its independence, was not a rare act.

The question now is, can the Eritrean government, as heir to EPLF's legacy, afford to continue the stubborn defence of its independence in the face of the economic realities of the world today? Will its economic problems and massive task of national reconstruction eventually force it to succumb to the politics of aid and all the compromises that condition it? In any case, will its attitude and determination, even if genuine and admirable, really be appreciated by those whose financial and technical help the government will need anyway?

It has been mentioned that "self-reliance" was not merely a slogan for EPLF and its membership. It is unfortunate that the human aspect of the struggle has not yet been properly documented and made known outside the EPLF itself. The war was won because adversity was faced and overcome by a combination of supreme individual efforts. It was also won because reliance on limited resources taught a determined people how to persevere and more importantly how to be inventive and resilient in the process.

So the question has a philosophical background. It is not really confined to the policies and principles of a government. It is rather concerned with the character of a liberation movement, its leadership and national supporters. The notion that the feat of the struggle will be repeated in the challenge of reconstruction is a national faith. On the other hand, it challenges current thinking on international co-operation, as existing relationships and philosophies are being put to task.

The concept of partnership in development

The main document on the government's strategy, the Macro-Policy Document, states that the objectives of its policy on international economic co-operation is to "serve the aims of the national macro and development strategies and policies" and to "enhance and promote regional and international economic co-operation" (GSE, 1994c:48). It further describes these policies as being intended to:

a) strengthen bilateral and multilateral economic and financial relations
b) promote export-oriented economic development
c) encourage foreign capital inflow through direct foreign investment
d) encourage Eritrean investment abroad
e) encourage trade, scientific, technical and cultural co-operation with all nations
f) create an atmosphere conducive to international emergency assistance and grants.

This list makes it obvious that the policy focuses more on bilateral and multilateral relations, direct and reciprocal investment, and so on, rather than on assistance and grants, the last item. Even here, the stress is on the creation of a "conducive atmosphere" for such assistance and grants. Presumably, this means that emergency assistance and grants should be seen in the context or as part of and supplementary to the other more substantive and long-term areas of economic co-operation.

The off-shoot of this broad policy is the principle of "partnership in development", whose tenets may not be clearly understood by all concerned. In discussions with members of the international community in Asmara, this researcher came across different interpretations of the concept. One dismissive reaction sees it as pure sloganeering, as "there can be no partnership in an atmosphere of inequality". According to this view, no matter what the Eritrean government calls the relationship, the fact that it is in a "donor-recipient" situation will not change.

A more tolerant, though amused, member of the international community admits, that in 20 years in the aid business, he had never questioned or in any way noticed or heard mentioned the negative connotations imputed to the "donor-recipient" set-up and terminology, as in this country. Though supportive of the principle, he fails to see how a government could enter into partnership relationships with individual organizations, since the more appropriate counterparts for such agreements are other governments.

From these sample views of important members of the community, it may not be wrong to conclude that the concept of partnership in development is not coming across as clearly as is desired. Is the government really saying that it stands on equal footing with the economic powers of the world? Is it claiming that it has as much to offer in partnership exchanges as the high and mighty? Or is it introducing a new way of rendering aid, grants, and technical assistance more effective and of mutual benefit to parties concerned? In other words, what exactly does partnership in development imply?

The most comprehensive statement on the concept is found in a leaflet prepared by the then Ministry of Finance and Development entitled "Partnership in Development" (Ministry of Finance, 1995). According to the leaflet, the principle is based on the premise that development is "principally a domestic challenge". It is seen as a question of giving priority to the creation and sustainability of an environment conducive to the involvement and participation of domestic forces and private capital.

The chief mechanisms the paper chooses for the resource transfers required to set off on this route to development are trade and investment, which it views as capable of creating relationships of mutual benefit, permanence and reliability. On the other hand, external assistance is perceived as having a "facilitating and not an initiating role, its main importance being bridging short-term and transitory resource gaps". The main effort, therefore, is directed at building up trading relationships with the world and encouraging investment.

The leaflet, however, admits that the current massive and complex problems of reconstruction and rehabilitation allow "no alternative to the additional flow of resources through external assistance". This is justified to the extent that it will not only "ease the current scarcity of resources", but also "provide much needed additional import capacity thus enabling the government to undertake investments in infrastructure and human resource development". This form of technical assistance is welcomed without regard to the source and as long as it "does not encroach on our sovereignty and independence of decision".

Thus, partnership in development is the old EPLF adage of self-reliance and resistance to outside domination and direction adapted to the challenges of statehood. It is neither a rejection of assistance and grants nor a self-deceiving claim to parity in manifestly unequal relationships. There is a philosophical aspect to the term "partnership". It would seem that the main concern is not with the proportions, percentages, or exchanges of shares between would-be partners. Such a formulation or interpretation of the concept undoubtedly does not favour small and disadvantaged Eritrea. In any case, they are subject to negotiation and agreement. The concern is more basic.

As a new entry into the international community of states, Eritrea has the advantage of reviewing the result of at least 30 years of aid and technical assistance in many of its fellow African and other Third World states. Although it was destroyed economically, the fact that this nation emerged from its war for independence much more united than ever before in its history, is an advantage that policy makers feel responsible to uphold and sustain. One person's mistake is another's lesson. The fact that most traditional "donor-recipient" relationships have had the opposite of their intended or stated aims has not escaped the government's perception.

The Ministry of Finance's paper categorically states that the "traditional relationship that polarizes partners into separate camps with one relegated to a passive role of performing according to the bidding of the other is no longer appropriate". It goes on to explain that such an arrangement:

> ...disregards the fact that the issues being addressed by external assistance are of greater concern to the country being assisted, and that their resolution would be enhanced if the assisted country plays a focal role in articulating and prioritizing the problems and in designing and implementing their solutions. This point cannot be over-emphasized because no responsible government can abdicate its responsibilities for the well-being of its people. This is not to foreclose the need for open dialogue on programmes, policies and priorities submitted for external financing.... However, if after such dialogue, it is evident that the two entities are committed to the same goals and as long as the interest and mandates of the one coincide with areas identified and prioritized by the other, then the two should work as partners for the same goal – development. This would require a fundamental reassessment and reformation of relationships between the parties (Ministry of Finance, 1995:5).

The essence of the concept is to be found in this lengthy quotation. One who views or assesses the formulation in terms of a one-to-one return in material or financial exchanges will probably fail to see the point. What is there in it for the donor except, perhaps, gratification?

The counter-argument here is that technical assistance is a temporary need on the road to the type of full partnership desired by both parties. Eritrea has a thousand kilometres of unexploited coastline, and as yet virtually untapped wealth in natural resources, and a potential for tourism. These are areas where partnerships in trade and investment can and are being made. The various mining concessions with major international investors, agreements to develop the islands as resort areas, private partnership deals by PFDJ and other members of the business community, may be mentioned as examples.

The core of the principle of partnership in development, therefore, is that the sooner international technical assistance is freed from the conditionalities that, at least in the Eritrean context, render it an imposition and arbitrary, the more effective it will be. Here, the ministry's paper points to specific aspects of traditional technical assistance as impeding the desired progress. These include the indiscriminate assignment of highly-paid expatriate personnel, who do not always assure appropriate expertise and effectiveness and thus often fail to provide the much-needed transfer of knowledge and skills. In addition, restrictions on where and how the assistance may be used are similarly underlined as highly prescriptive. The first, procurement tying, says the paper, "restricts purchases to the country that provides the assistance and, by so doing, interferes with the competitive...[and choice of]...free markets". The second, use restriction, "ties use of funds to a specific project usually earmarked and designed by the party that provides the assistance" – and that party is not always right about the appropriateness of that particular use.

In other words, the line of argument is to let procurement and choice of use area be the decision of the assisted. Worries about possible misplacement or misappropriation of funds, legitimate and acceptable, may be alleviated, according to the pamphlet, through a "transparency of the operation being financed and accountability of the government funds" made available to the assisting party.

Finally, the paper identifies five broad categories in which technical assistance in the context of "partnership in development" is solicited. These are:

a) support to physical infrastructure with particular emphasis on ports, electricity and telecommunications

b) productive enterprises with emphasis on cement and glass factories
c) human resource development with emphasis on primary healthcare delivery, basic education, and the development of technical skills
d) private sector development with emphasis on the provision of credit facilities and promotional services
e) balance-of-payments support to allow for substantial increase in imports and for a build-up of foreign exchange reserves to an appropriate level.

Some reactions to "Partnership in Development"

It can be concluded from discussions with members of the international community in Asmara that there is plenty of support and goodwill regarding the dedication, hard work, honesty and absence of corruption characteristic of the Eritrean government. Efforts are also generally made to understand and cope with the problems and deficiencies that the war situation has imposed on various aspects of the Eritrean administration and its institutions.

However, as mentioned earlier, the concept of partnership in development does not seem to be fully understood by many members of international agencies and NGOs. In the first place, there is a lack of knowledge of the magnitude of sacrifice both EPLF and the people of Eritrea made to get where they are. The fact that the Eritrean struggle was shunned by the international community and that it thus depended heavily on its own resources is not always kept in mind. For Eritreans, self-reliance is a cultural trait which achieved religious proportions during the bitter war for liberation. Information about the struggle is meagre and outsiders fail to link government actions and reactions of today to established norms of thinking and behaviour of only a few years ago. As one interviewee put it, the abruptness and fierce defence of Eritrean interests by some Eritrean authorities often puzzles and injures foreign counterparts because they fail to realize which "button of sensitivity they had unknowingly pressed".

Perhaps this exaggerates the reaction a little, but such problems of communication often divert attention from the real issues. The real issue is how to react to the new set of thinking, attitude and relationships that the concept of partnership introduces. To a community accustomed to think and act as a "donor" and a "giver", partnership creates a difficult situation. In many other countries, "donors set the conditionalities. Here, they are told what to do", an interviewee states.

Along the same lines many, including members of United Nations agencies, feel that to, operate comfortably with the principle, it should be accepted by their respective headquarters. Why? Because these are policy matters that introduce new methods of work and operations that established multilaterals find difficult to accommodate. It may be easier, it is contended, for bilateral relationships that do not have to deal with bundles of paperwork and rigid bureaucracies.

Such arguments may have some administrative basis. One cannot discount, on the other hand, resistance on the part of donors to see their traditional powers stripped. The introductory remarks of this chapter referred to tendencies, accepted as standard practice in many African nations, to regard donors as policy makers and also as implementors. Suggestions of a link between donors and civil society institutions that would relegate state authority to one of supervision are also seriously considered. The Eritrean context clearly rejects this and would reserve policy decisions and project implementation for the government, while allowing policy discussions and project implementation follow-up or monitoring to those who are assisting the government.

Considering the possibility of the "donor" world rejecting the partnership arrangement, the government's insistence is also seen as a bold move that should be given a chance. The saying "no country developed through foreign aid" is heard more and more often. Dependence breeds dependence. The negative effect of foreign aid, especially food aid, on the industriousness and work habits of populations of dependent states is well-known. It is no exaggeration to say that the weakening of the legendary hard work, inventiveness and accumulated skills of the Eritrean working force is partly attributable to food aid dependency. Hence, the government's decisive and controversial decision to monetize food aid, so every single grain is sweated for and deserved.

There is, however, a general consensus in both government and the counterpart international community on steps the government should take if the principle of partnership in development is to work. As a general statement of principle, ideals and general targets, the macro policy has to be put into practice and be visible to all concerned at the operational level. The rationale for decisions and the atmosphere and grounds on which they are to be implemented may not always be clear.

So, it is further argued, there is a scarcity of basic information on the government's set of priorities. There is also a general feeling on both sides that the problem is one of communication rather than of the lack of plans or priorities at the activity level. For example, anyone who felt that the government was ignoring small-scale enterprises will be surprised to see the baseline survey, a preparation to major projects for the awakening of that sector. It is doubtful if anyone outside the circle that prepared it knew that such a massive survey was being undertaken. But why so much secrecy, even in non-essential, not so sensitive areas?

There is the cultural aspect. Eritreans generally refrain from discussing their own affairs. The plans, projects and priorities of a family rarely if ever reach the ears of the next-door neighbour. The established tradition in EPLF never to discuss, much less brag about, individual feats has already been referred to. This was the nature of the front itself, its collective behaviour. It is gradually being recognized that it may be advantageous for the government to slowly disentangle itself from some of the unnecessary limitations imposed on communication. Nevertheless, government officials contend that maintenance of a low profile, in spite of some of its problems, will probably remain a strength and an asset. If the principle of partnership in development is to gain ground, it may be because things have been and will continue to be done without the outside world knowing about them. Few if any people knew about or thought possible the daring, all-Eritrean reconstruction of the railway, already substantially on its way to completion.

In the meantime, since dealings with all United Nations agencies, NGOs and other such non-Eritrean bodies engaged in the area of international economic co-operation, aid and technical assistance, are channelled through appropriate government bodies, the importance of continuing dialogue between the parties cannot be overemphasized. A regular flow of relevant information is appropriate and beneficial. The need to upgrade the operational capacity of government bodies and personnel dealing with international counterparts should also be given adequate attention. As the Ministry of Finance correctly pointed out, efficiency, transparency and accountability in mutual dealings are also keys to the success of the principle of partnership in development.

CONCLUDING REMARKS

This chapter began with a cursory review of current thinking on governance. It also suggested that the term and concept of "governance" appears to still be in the process of clarification, as different definitions and interpretations of the paradigm are being contended.

It seems generally agreed, however, that governance concerns the overall range of activities and relationships that links governments and people. If this is correct, then governance deals with the complex fabric of interaction through which the government and the governed work toward the attainment of a common goal. This kind of approach toward the concept would be objective and would give the student of governance the opportunity to study specific government-to-people relationships on their own terms. The problem arises when the paradigm is turned into a set of standards a government has necessarily to comply with to earn the title of a "good" government.

Such a problem is the World Bank's requirements for "good governance" that African states especially have to meet in order to qualify for aid. A 1995 IDS policy briefing paper lists a set of "ingredients" of good governance that most donors would like to find in recipient governments. These are:

- democracy (particularly multi-party democracy)
- respect for human rights and the rule of law
- efficiency, accountability and transparency in government and public administration.

Many donors, the paper continues, include the following additional ingredients of good government:

- popular participation
- equity and poverty concerns
- a commitment to market-oriented policies.

The merits of each of the above principles of good government are not in doubt. They are qualities that any government would like to have. The Eritrean macro policy is based precisely on these principles. The PFDJ Charter contains every word, concept and spirit of the above list.

These are pronouncements, visions and intentions. Some of them have been realized, others not. Many are being worked toward and may be attained quickly, others may lag behind. An enthusiastic donor with the above checklist is therefore bound to be disappointed, and Eritrea is fated to fail the test of democracy, as no other political party or organization exists except for PFDJ.

There is something arbitrary and unfair about the whole approach. It is based on assumptions that do not necessarily hold true to every African government. The assumptions seem to be the following. First, to quote the IDS report:

> ...'bad government' [is] undermining development. Corruption, poor control of public funds, lack of accountability, human rights abuses and excessive military expenditure, have all been holding back development – particularly in Africa (IDS, 1995).

Second, it is assumed that all African governments depend on foreign aid and donations, not just for development purposes but also for their own existence. Third, in light of the weakness and lack of dependability of African governments, it is incumbent on the donor community to step in with the weapon of aid and ensure the democratization of governments. As seen in the first section of this chapter, there is the added suggestion that bad government can be circumvented by linking foreign aid with civil society institutions and building democracy outside the sphere of government.

To a government such as Eritrea's, committed as it is to preserving its strong tradition of political and economic independence and self-reliance, both the checklist and the assumptions that go with it can only be offensive. In more ways than one, the psychological composition of the people in government has not changed, or it has changed very little from the days and ideals of the armed struggle. Serving without salaries for four years is simply not the trait of a corrupt bureaucracy. The fierce reaction of the government to any semblance of corruption and misappropriation of public funds is indicative of its serious intent to deal with the tendency harshly.

This is a government that insists not on foreign aid and donations, but on partnerships and ventures of mutual benefit with the advantaged of the world. It is also a government that has gone to the extent of eliminating food aid handouts to free its population from the devitalizing habit of dependency. Its laws limit the number and activities of international NGOs to those whose presence and usefulness it accepts.

It is, then, a government that has been known to forgo certain types of aid and donations that compromise principles it upholds as important and not negotiable. Given the embarrassing IDS report of African governments being bad, corrupt and abusing power and funds, the Eritrean government's attitudes and actions breathe new air to an area that, apparently, has been taken for granted for quite some time.

This chapter has shown the genuine efforts of a government and a people struggling to live by the ideals, principles, promises and hopes they paid for so dearly in the long war for liberation. A nation that has suffered alienation and extreme hardship from the cynicism of international power politics and superpower competition and alliances, its culture of self-reliance proved the most secure route and guarantee to its salvation. That the maintenance of this principle should be seen as the basis for national reconstruction should come as no surprise.

Furthermore, there are some unique aspects of the Eritrean experience that deserve appreciation. Eritrea emerged much more united and much less "war-torn" than other nations that went through the same process. Perhaps this gave it the strength and confidence to avoid the grudge and bitterness toward its internal and external antagonists that might otherwise have marred its post-Independence politics.

The war did, however, destroy the economy and greatly weaken the reasonably high cultural standards Eritreans had achieved, in terms of administrative efficiency, educational excellence, various types and levels of skill and expertise and, in general, in terms of a tradition of hard work and individual self-reliance. That the government inherited a void in most of these areas, will perhaps remain the chief problem in this period of reconstruction. If there are any obstacles to the realization of the government's plans, they will come not from a lack of vision or direction, but from the yet undeveloped means for such realization.

The Constitution now ratified by the National Assembly contains 58 articles providing for, by any standards, the supremacy of democratic principles and the establishment of a democratic system of government. Every element of "good governance" and more are included in its provisions. The Constitution will instigate changes and adjustments in practices, habits, relationships, constraints and even laws and structures carried over from the struggle or colonial heritage. But to expect the Constitution to provide a panacea for every perceived problem would be to repeat the same innocent expectations of the day of Independence.

In the final analysis, it will be the commitment and the practice more than declarations and the ideals behind them that matter. Eritrea has a strong government that delivers. It is also a government that is free from most of the weaknesses and malaise that characterize the "bad" governments of the world.

Of immediate importance is the evolution of responsible and accountable government. However, the legislative and judicial branches are yet to attain the stature and maturity of the executive branch. The making and enforcement law, the establishment of the rule of law and due process as supreme are yet to be mastered. Getting out of the habit of quick executive decision making and implementation and accepting the routines and drawn-out process of the courts and legislature will probably prove difficult. But it will have to be done if the new Constitution is to have any meaning.

Although Eritrea has an influential traditional civil society and workers, women and youth organizations with a great history of active

322 • POST-CONFLICT ERITREA: PROSPECTS FOR RECONSTRUCTION AND DEVELOPMENT

322 • POST-CONFLICT ERITREA: PROSPECTS FOR RECONSTRUCTION AND DEVELOPMENT

participation during the armed struggle, their post-Independence roles need to be better defined and tuned to meeting the challenges of peacetime.

Civil society organizations can only be genuine, dynamic and effective if they have a diversified socio-economic base. But building the economy without regard to the fair and equitable distribution of national wealth would be self-defeating or betray the general understanding or social pact that correlates independence with social justice. None of the values and principles of "good governance" – popular participation, accountability of government to the people, respect for human rights – can be achieved without the prevalence of social justice, as guaranteed by equity in wealth distribution. This refers equally to Eritrea's most glaring "deficiency" in that prescribed checklist of good government, namely multi-party democracy. Eritrea has emerged from the war with a remarkable degree of unity that has, rightfully, prompted resentment of its being termed "war-torn". As a unity forged in war and sacrifice, it has its strong side. But it is a unity in the context of a highly traditional society not yet free from parochial and sectarian attitudes and cultures of various shades.

For some time to come, at least until the economic resurgence that is starting to take shape begins to create new social bases and national relationships, the likelihood that multi-party politics would divide the country into regional and religious factions is a real possibility and danger. For what purposes would a nation sacrifice the unity and peace it enjoys to party politics it is not yet ready for and whose eventuality holds dubious benefits for its future? The argument here is not that multi-partyism is bad. On the contrary, and in spite of PFDJ's positive role in helping the government maintain peace and stability and launch economic reconstruction, the need for alternative politics cannot be waved aside. The timing, however, is important and political and social conditions themselves should demand the eventuality.

In the meantime, the economy is the issue, the key to everything else that will follow. The test of governance in the Eritrean context depends to a great extent on progress made in the various policy areas discussed in this volume. The nation has taken on the challenge that its particular perception of governance is the key to the objective of development. The road ahead may be rough and full of obstacles, but so was the armed struggle.

REFERENCES

Fatton Jr., Robert, *Predatory Rule: State and Civil Society in Africa*, Lynne Rienner, Boulder and London, 1992.

GSE, *Establishment of Local Government Proclamation 26/1992*, 1992a.

GSE, *Investment Proclamation 59/1994*, 1994a.

GSE, *Land Proclamation 58/1994*, 1994b.

GSE, *Macro-Policy Document*, Asmara, 1994c.

GSE, *Proclamation 37/1993 to Determine Structure and Duties of the Government of the State of Eritrea*, 1993.

GSE, *Proclamation 23/1992 to Determine Structure and Duties of the Provisional Government of Eritrea*, 1992b.

GSE, *Study of the Private Sector in Eritrea*, July 1996.

Hyden, Goran, Reciprocity and Governance in Africa, in James S. Wunsch and Dele Olowu (eds.) *The Failure of the Centralized State*, Westview, Boulder, 1990:245–269.

Keane, John, *Democracy and Civil Society*, Verso, London, 1988.

Koehn, Peter and Hyden, Goran, *Decentralization for Social Planning in Eritrea*, paper for MLG and UNICEF, January 1996.

Mamdani, Mahmoud, *Democratic Theory and Struggles*, in *Democratization Process in Africa: Problems and Prospects*, CODESRIA, 1992.

Ministry of Finance, *Partnership in Development*, January 1995.

Moore, David B., Development Discourse as Hegemony: Toward an Ideological History, 1945–1995, in David B. Moore and Gerald J. Schmitz (eds.) *Debating Development Discourse: Institutional and Popular Perspectives*, Macmillan and St. Martin, London and New York, 1995:1–53.

PFDJ, *National Charter for Eritrea*, Nacfa, 1994.

World Bank, *Sub-Saharan Africa: From Crisis to Sustainable Growth*, Washington D.C., 1989.

8

THE CHALLENGES OF POST-WAR DEVELOPMENT: A REVIEW OF WSP RESEARCH FINDINGS

ALEMSEGED TESFAI

In a leading explanatory paper entitled *Rebuilding War-torn Societies*, WSP stated the objective of its "action-research project" as being to assist the international donor community, international organizations, NGOs and local authorities and organizations to understand and better respond to the complex challenges of post-conflict periods (WSP, 1994:8). It further identified the main tasks of transformation of a fragile cease-fire into a lasting political settlement, provision of emergency relief to groups and regions unable to meet their own needs, and initiation of political, economic, social and psychological rebuilding to lay the basis for future sustainable development.

Although the WSP approach is generally broad-minded and advocates an integrated, participatory and objective appraisal of particular post-war situations, the tasks identified may not be relevant in all post-war situations and societies. In the Working Group and Project Group discussions in WSP-Eritrea, the response to the term "war-torn" ranged from outright rejection to reservation to discomfort.

In projects of this magnitude, where set values and practices are challenged, premises and generalizations must be free of preconceptions, rigidities or misinterpretations. In the Eritrean context, the achievement of WSP objectives can be assured only if Eritrean specificities are recognized. What does WSP mean by the term "war-torn"?

WSP identified peace, relief and development as overriding objectives which must be pursued simultaneously, while recognizing the intrinsic link between peace and development (WSP, 1994:8). There can be no argument about the latter. The rest of this review will deal with the form that relief and development are taking, and should be taking, in Eritrea. However, the liberty will be taken of separating the "peace" element from its companion objectives because the answer to the question of how war-torn Eritrean society is depends on how peace in Eritrea is perceived and acted on.

WSP's notion of peace in post-conflict societies seems to stress its fragility. WSP focuses on the difficulties of determining where war ends and peace begins, as well as the infeasibility of demobilizing combatants as long as no alternative sources of livelihood are available. Although post-conflict political reconstruction is correctly seen as the broad task of setting up a participatory, accountable, decentralized government and state machinery, the type of peace achieved is still perceived as the "result of military victory of one of the parties, or of mutual exhaustion of the combatants, or imposed by external forces and actors on an 'unfinished civil war'" (WSP, 1994). Similarly, in the broad context of social reconstruction, WSP refers to deep rifts of ethnic, political, religious and communal bitterness that must be bridged, and to the collective social trauma engendered by the horrors of war.

Thus the term "war-torn" presupposes a post-conflict society still politically and socially divided, or at least in danger of a return to civil strife. As WSP points out, for such war-torn societies the priority is obviously the attainment of peace and stability. Because there can be no relief or development without peace, time and vital resources have to be dedicated to securing it. National and international policies and programmes must recognize this precondition.

In this sense, Eritrea is not a war-torn society. As the previous chapters indicate, there are no historical grounds for social discord along ethnic, religious, regional or even political lines. Unlike many African countries (for example Angola and Mozambique, where independence brought bitter civil wars), the end of foreign rule in Eritrea ushered in an atmosphere of reconciliation. The EPLF, to its credit, set the tone by abstaining from undertaking any reprisals on either captured enemy troops or, more importantly, Eritrean nationals who worked, fought and even spied for the Derg. A few weeks into Independence, the only signs that a 30-year war had raged in the country were the destroyed infrastructure, ruined buildings and, on closer inspection, the ravages of poverty, physical disintegration and psychological scars on a long-suffering population.

The first two years after the war saw a jubilant population that literally danced its way to the referendum and full sovereignty on 24 May 1993. This volume's chapter on governance describes some of the problems of the period, when the disappointment of unmet expectations created some confusion and disillusionment. However, this feeling was expressed more through words than actions. It did not contain the elements of violence, organization, depth of feeling and sectarianism that normally cause widespread frustration and unrest, and it subsided with the realization that the expectations could not be met in the prevailing conditions.

These feelings of frustration were essentially the result of what was and still is the primary problem of post-war Eritrea: poverty (rather than peace or the lack of it). For Eritrea, war ended and peace began within a week of the Ethiopian army's eviction. The Eritrean war was a war of independence against foreign domination. The Ethiopians tried without success to create religious and regional animosity. The blessing for Eritrea was that its own sad period of civil war ended 10 years before Independence, in the middle of the war for liberation. EPLF, now PFDJ, was and still is the only political organization in the country, and enjoys an uncontested national following. What remains of ELF is divided and scattered outside Eritrea in small factions with practically no social base in the nation.

An indication of the peace prevalent in the country is the unbelievably rapid and orderly manner in which EPLF combatants marked for demobilization answered the call to disarm. About 54,000 combatants, including 16,000 women, did so without incident in a three-phase process ending in 1995. The fact that alternative employment opportunities were scarce did not stand in the way of this impressive procedure. It is possible that weapons remain illegally in private hands, but their unlawful use is unheard of.

Eritrea thus provides a special case, in which the political and social characteristics of war-torn societies do not exist. The implications of this are profound. Of the "triple objectives" of post-war societies identified by WSP, perhaps the most decisive, peace, is an asset in Eritrea. But it is peace in the context of poverty and a devastated economy. There is no doubt that its sustainability can only be assured if the war-torn economy is rebuilt. Furthermore, it is clear that the existing peace should not be taken for granted.

Toward an Integrated Approach

WSP presented the aim of its action research as "to clarify policy options and redefine relevant strategies" for both international and local actors (WSP, 1994:8). It also aimed to contribute to better integration of various forms of international assistance – humanitarian, economic, political and military – in a coherent policy framework, to encourage better alignment of external assistance with local efforts, and thus bring about a more efficient and effective use of limited and overstretched local and international resources.

To do this, WSP devised a conceptual framework of "mixes" as a tool of an integrated analysis and approach. The first is called the "policy mix", in which the task is to study the multiple positive and negative interactions among various policies, agendas and mandates that simultaneously address the same problem. The objective is to better understand how the different policies interact in order to minimize contradictions and improve synergy in a more integrated policy approach.

The second concept, the "level mix", refers to relations between local-level actors, initiatives and social dynamics and the plans and projects worked out by national government and international actors. In this case, the objective is to improve national and international actors' understanding of local-level initiatives and resources, in order to optimally build national and international projects and policy on local initiatives and resources.

Finally, the "actor mix" refers to the interaction of collective actors behind the policies. The focus is on the relation between internal and external actors. The objective is to achieve a healthy balance by making international aid complementary to national resources and initiatives so as to strengthen national capacities and reduce vulnerabilities, thus promoting national self-reliance. This implies that external and internal relations are to be seen not only in terms of aid, but also in terms of wider economic, political and social relations of co-operation, with the latter ultimately replacing the former (WSP, 1994).

The difficulty involved in making sense of the maze of interactions that such an approach demands must be appreciated. The identification of the main tenets of the Entry Points described below should help set the stage for the following discussion.

The "policy mix"

Unless the principles underlying Eritrean policy and practice are properly understood, it is difficult to appreciate the way things "mix" in the country. Policies are formulated to respond to present and future needs, but always in the context of fundamental principles. These principles include maintaining national unity, assuring the active participation of people, recognizing the decisive role of the human factor, working toward the prevalence of social justice, self-reliance and effective leadership, as pointed out in the chapter on governance.

A quick glance at the contents of the government's Macro-Policy Document will show these principles built into every policy and objective listed. The idea is that policies will become viable and sustainable as long as they do not contradict the aforementioned principles. In other words, policies may be amended or altogether changed, but principles are not up for negotiation.

This has significant implications, especially in the transitional period. The government's post-war policies are not the product of this particular post-war period, nor are they confined to its needs as they look forward. They were actually first formulated in the period following EPLF's Second Congress, held during the armed struggle in early 1987. This was the congress that decisively and formally announced the EPLF's ideological shift from socialist centralism and class orientation to the more pragmatic principles of social justice and participatory democracy. In the months that followed, high-level discussions and a task force – specifically established for the purpose in 1988 – provided the new approach with the clarity and base it required. The macro policy is an offshoot, indeed a post-Independence version, of the visions of those days with very little change in substance.

The chapters in this volume – reflecting WSP Entry Points – examine the government's policies on social reintegration, infrastructure, food security, HRD and governance. These represent only a part, though significant, of the policies included in the macro policy framework. Components such as the fiscal, monetary, trade, science and technology and, more importantly, environmental policies have either not been discussed or have received only passing mention. In addition, the sheer breadth of subject matter, especially in the Entry Points on infrastructure, governance and HRD, has hindered WSP researchers from treating their respective topics with the thoroughness deserved.

Policies of the rehabilitation period

Practically every WSP study has identified institutional and labour capacity shortages as a major problem. Administrative decentralization, for example, is slowed by weak zonal administration structures and shortages of trained personnel. The industrial and service sectors lack relevant and appropriate skills and expertise, and infrastructure has been described as facing the same problems. Policies' relevance and positions or negative interaction should to be seen in the context of these shortages. Policies that fail to take into account the means and grounds for their own implementation would be poorly formulated. If development depends on how policies complement each other and how their overlap and contradictions are resolved, then the reasons for their formulation and the grounds on which they are to be implemented should be clearly understood. Furthermore, the objective of development and the speed and manner of its progress must be carefully charted.

Thus the integrated approach to development, though slow and incremental, serves the principles of national unity, social justice and self-reliance. It equally serves the related principles of even distribution of resources, the decentralization process and the narrowing of the urban/rural gap, which are essential to the maintenance of peace and national unity.

Is such an integrated approach sustainable, in view of the scarcity of resources and limited institutional and labour capacity? How has the Eritrean government been resolving the competing needs of various sections of the population and sectors of the economy? Surely the need to prioritize conflicting demands must arise even in the context of a transition period?

A re-examination of the Entry Point studies may shed light on the questions above. This discussion will be made clearer by examining policies from long- and short-term perspectives. The challenges of the first few years of post-Independence – the period of rehabilitation – were different from those being posed by the period of development that followed. Although the two perspectives are closely linked and should not be regarded as mutually exclusive, the "policies" of the period of rehabilitation should be understood in the context of the special characteristics of transition.

WSP research established that the war adversely affected or destroyed practically every aspect of social life, the economy, the administrative machinery and services in the country. Because almost everything had to restart from scratch, it was, and still is, difficult to establish priorities. The main roads were heavily damaged and had to be repaired. Schools, hospitals and clinics – needing not only physical repair, but also curriculum, equipment and staff readjustments, purchases and changes – had to continue operating. The Derg's administrative set-up, already weak and inefficient, had to be replaced quickly to establish order and institute government. And then there was the question of catering to the needs of nearly 100,000 combatants, 10,000 disabled fighters, the families of 65,000 martyrs, and thousands of spontaneously returning refugees, almost all dependent on the EPLF.

Understanding how the period before the referendum of April 1993 came to survive the confusion of competitive demands would require a separate study. EPLF came equipped with its old ideals, which were immediately translated into action. Problems needed prompt and effective response, calling for pragmatism, flexibility and resilience, more than coolheaded policy formulation.

This meant that the policies could operate only on an *ad hoc* basis. Forged in the armed struggle, they could not be expected to address all the issues of post-Independence. What worked for a liberation front was not necessarily appropriate for a full-fledged government. The rules of the game, relationships, popular demands and expectations, were naturally different. Thus the front's policies had to be tested and fine-tuned, amended or entirely reformulated to suit new realities. Components such as monetary, fiscal and investment policies were almost novel and had to be newly devised. The foundation had to be laid for the revival of the private sector, long incapacitated by the Derg's socialization programme. Even time-tested EPLF policies such as education, health and local government could not adequately respond to the demands of peacetime, not so much for lack of principle or clarity as for lack of institutional and labour capacity.

Therefore, the transitional period up to the formulation of the government's macro policy framework in 1994 may be seen as preparation for identifying areas of priority for development strategy. This was also the time when policies were crystallized in the domain of practice.

Thus, for example, the basic weaknesses of the government's educational and health policies have been identified, or are in the final stages of being identified. The HRD chapter points out that the vacuum in the area of skilled professionals and technicians created by the war is not being filled because the educational system is not well-oriented to meet this demand. The problem is not just institutional, for it has to do with the way the whole system has been geared toward academic rather than technical and practical education. The suggestion that ways should be found to "de-school" those already schooled in irrelevant education may not be just a passing comment.

In the meantime a great deal has been accomplished, especially in building schools in remote areas and making education accessible to children in their mother-tongue. However, in terms of relevance, the system may be creating more problems than it is solving, since the job market is increasingly swamped with untrained and unskilled junior and high school graduates or drop-outs. Vocational schools and the university, in their present capacity, can accommodate only a small percentage of the school-aged population, even of those who qualify.

The same and more may be said of the health sector. Neither the EPLF's immense and proud accomplishments on this front, nor the health infrastructure that was added after Independence, can fulfil the country's demand. This sector is deemed among the most deteriorated, relative to pre-war and EPLF standards. The HRD chapter suggests that prominence be given to primary healthcare, while research to ensure optimal healthcare delivery and optimal professional performance of health workers in a system that is efficient and cost-effective is recommended. The experience so far, however, shows that conventional approaches to the solution of the health problem have not been successful. It is this realization that seems to have led to the rethinking of the whole labour development strategy prepared for nationwide implementation.

In terms of infrastructure, restoration of existing roads and telecommunication services was the dominant task during the initial post-war period. Restoration of the ports to reasonable operating standards and assurance of the basic energy supply are major accomplishments. The chapter on infrastructure identifies many of the problems in each sub-sector, but may not sufficiently stress the fact that rehabilitation work has so far been accomplished mostly through local resources. For example, a recent *aide-mémoire* by the World Bank on the progress of the RRPE shows that as of April 1996 total foreign expenditure on the infrastructure part of the project was only US$ 58.01 million. Of this, US$ 26 million went to road construction, with equipment taking the greatest share at US$ 18 million. The rest of the foreign infrastructure funds were allocated as follows (in US dollars): ports 9.43 million; water supply 6.97 million; power 12.52 million; and telecommunications 3 million. These figures do not include expenditures of the ECRFU.

These figures indicate the extent to which the burden of infrastructure, especially road rehabilitation, has fallen on government and local resources. The human and material resources spent on upgrading the Asmara-Massawa road alone – an almost non-stop endeavour over five years – greatly exceed the US$ 26 million of foreign funds spent on equipment, materials, civil works and technical assistance for road rehabilitation.

More than in any other sector, this illustrates the role that past principles and determination have played in the task of rehabilitation. Infrastructure rehabilitation and development demand high technology and expertise. Labour-intensive methods are time-consuming, and the results may not meet certain standards. Reconstruction of the old railway line is criticized for reasons ranging from cost to safety and project sustainability concerns. Similar criticisms are heard regarding the tendency of some already repaired roads to fall back into disrepair.

Many lessons have surely been learned from these experiences and some underlying problems are being tackled. However, it is important not to lose sight of the implications of depending mainly on self-resources for development. The building of a self-reliant economy demands that this approach be taken seriously. This should be seen as strengthening foreign grants and loans, the message being that every factor so acquired has been put to effective use and can be accounted for – an element allegedly missing in many other countries. As for mistakes and possible erroneously chosen priorities, tragedy will result if they are not identified and corrected. Making such mistakes should be part of the whole process. The old EPLF adage that only those who work make mistakes is very much alive.

Agricultural policy has also been undergoing improvement and change, as WSP food security research has shown. In spite of signs that the economy in general is growing, the chapter on food security points out that agricultural productivity in Eritrea is still low, caused by recurrent drought and the general use of traditional low-input, low-output agricultural systems to reduce risks. This difficulty is most profound in subsistence rain-fed agricultural areas, where problems are addressed by the government through various projects and extension activities. These problems require more than temporary solutions.

Agricultural production is low not only because of the farming and livestock-raising techniques used but, as this research established, also because of environmental degradation and vulnerability to drought and other natural disasters. In the first few years since Independence, the government and its Ministry of Agriculture worked out an agricultural development strategy, which it has started to implement. The strategy involves the establishment of national and international markets for agricultural products, changes in land tenure to improve land use, and increased emphasis on soil and water conservation.

Reintegrating returnees from Sudan was a task for the early period of rehabilitation as far as government policy saw it, but it dragged on. PROFERI has been discussed in the chapter on the challenges of reintegration. In the early 1990s, a misunderstanding arose between the Eritrean government and UNHCR on the terms for resettling refugees in Eritrea. The government saw it as an all-encompassing programme linked to its development strategy, involving the complete integration of returnees. UNHCR's mandate was more limited to the physical repatriation of refugees, followed by a relief programme lasting some months. Implements and tools to set them on a rehabilitation course were also seen as adequate measures. In other words, the United Nations agency's mandate did not allow it to be involved in developmental matters. The Eritrean government, on the other hand, could not see any point in creating refugee enclaves within its borders, albeit of its own citizens, that would be a great problem to administer and sustain. The Eritrean position would obviously involve a change of UNHCR policy or mandate in this particular case, but the government's logic seems to be that if UNHCR (or any other) assistance is to be relevant and effective, it should be geared toward solving the problem, not transferring or compounding it.

So PROFERI succeeded in repatriating only 25,000 returnees in a pilot project, 115,000 fewer than the number of spontaneous returnees. The remaining refugees, more than 350,000 of them, are still in Sudan with their return further complicated by Eritrean-Sudanese relations.

The pilot project, however, has provided some lessons for future handling of repatriation and reintegration activities. First, PROFERI's assumption that Eritreans returning from Sudan would choose to resettle in agricultural areas and take up agriculture-related activities because they originate from rural areas has not proved true. Many have adopted other, urban-related trades and will not accept rural resettlement. A second lesson is the need for proper data collection to help meet returnee requirements and preferences regarding labour. Third, the allocation of pre-determined parcels of land in all areas was found not to have taken other factors, such as rainfall, into account. In addition, settling returnees in areas already inhabited or used by pastoral communities almost invariably caused some friction, and there have been some land claims that have delayed land distribution and clearance. The issue of shelter, too, has taught important lessons. The types of housing preferred by various projects have not always been suited to the environment or cost-effective. The unforeseen problem of providing housing to returnees and leaving out the local inhabitants who in many cases are not better off, has raised serious debate.

In short, the chapter on reintegration points out that more in-depth studies should have been carried out in the areas where sites were planned in terms of the regularity of rainfall, availability of water, incidence of malaria and the presence, albeit sporadic, of pastoralists grazing their herds. This will no doubt help make the next phases of returnee reintegration more appropriate and sensitive to the points raised.

The chapter further makes the point that the reintegration of returnees and ex-combatants has been greatly constrained by lack of funds. As discussed earlier in this volume, the very limited donor response to PROFERI in 1993 forced the government to allocate funds that would normally have been invested in economic programmes. External assistance has been negligible compared to the 10,000 birr given to each of the 50,000 demobilized fighters, the costs of training and counselling them and, as in the case of the Ali Ghider plantation, the millions of birr committed to help clear land, build shelters, obtain seed and initial tractor and other services.

External grants are often tied to specific projects or components. This does not give the government and implementing agencies any leeway to adjust their interventions according to priorities that might change in the meantime. Funding instruments and budget lines of donors also specify the implementation period, after which funds may no longer be available.

In conclusion, a potentially exemplary programme of the rehabilitation period has failed. However, the process continues, albeit slowly, depending on local resources.

Policies of the development phase

It is now taken for granted that Eritrea has passed the rehabilitation stage and is entering the development phase. It is felt that many initial post-war problems are more or less in the past. To clarify, some of these are:

1. The process of demobilizing about 54,000 combatants is over. The task of fully reintegrating them has begun as a component of the development phase and strategy.
2. Initial help (in the amount of 10,000 birr per family) has been provided to the families of martyrs. Again, more permanent solutions to the most needy are being handled as a responsibility of the development phase.
3. The government has completed a three-phase programme to restructure its bodies and streamline its civil service to a more manageable and effective level.
4. The new land law, though yet to be implemented largely in rural areas, is being effected in urban and peri-urban sections of the country, creating opportunities for solving the urban housing problem and

encouraging industrial and services investment.

5. The infrastructure – roads, ports, telecommunications and energy – have attained at least minimum standards in the services required for initial development needs.

6. The new zonal administration set-up is in place and relations between the regions and central government bodies is expected to take a permanent form once regional elections are undertaken.

7. After a period of confusion and inactivity, the private sector is awakening, with licensing, taxation, banking, fiscal, monetary and other related laws and policies being developed.

8. The government's intention to privatize enterprises nationalized by the Ethiopian Derg regime have been announced and the organizational framework to complete the process has been set up.

9. The constitution-making process has been finalized and a new national Constitution enacted.

There may be problems in the rehabilitation phase, such as those of the Eritrean refugees in Sudan, that will need more attention and effort, but the general attitude is that solutions will occur in the process of development.

In discussing its particular Entry Point, each chapter has referred to the government's Macro-Policy Document as the starting point of the policies discussed. The document is, indeed, a set of principles, objectives and general policy that gives coherence to the government's development strategy. As a guideline, it sets the framework in which different government bodies formulate their respective policies and plans of action. The policies that this WSP research has been focusing on are offshoots of the macro policy framework that set the stage for launching the nation's development strategy.

It is indicated above that Eritrean policies are also statements of principle. One of the enduring legacies of EPLF is the continuing effort to establish a link between theory and practice. Ideas are accepted or rejected in terms of their concrete and practical value. "What, in concrete terms, is WSP research going to accomplish?" was a typical question posed by government and PFDJ members. This reflected a deeply ingrained approach that applies to policy and decision-making and that often determines relationships. The policies of the development phase are, therefore, characterized by pragmatism and a common theme or underlying principle.

HRD may be the best place to start, as it is the area now getting the most government attention. It may be premature to talk about priorities at a time when development strategy is being worked on and policies are being reformulated or readjusted, but HRD may be considered to be at the centre of the process. Throughout this analysis, the twin problems of post-war Eritrea have been identified as shortages and inadequacies in labour and institutional capacity. Development of the human factor as a precondition for growth and development has already been established as a right – or a human right – of a people who have paid dearly for liberty and social justice.

The principles on which HRD is being built – universal basic education in the mother-tongue, adult literacy up to the basic education level, relevance and response of basic and adult education to local needs, opening skills to the majority of the population, and relevant higher skills and expertise at the tertiary level – set the basis for achieving the human requirements for growth and development. The addition of health and civic education to the national curriculum is meant to produce results too obvious to require discussion here.

The fruition of this strategy will depend on a variety of factors. One of these is the infrastructure, both physical and social. The main test of HRD strategy will be if it reaches underprivileged areas and underprivileged citizens, especially women. Accessibility, in other words, is the key to success. The subjective factor in this respect – the government's commitment, harnessing popular participation, committing available resources and raising funds – cannot be a major problem as it has passed the test of time. Schools, clinics and especially roads may prove more difficult, for reasons ranging from expense incurred to physical remoteness and inaccessibility of some areas.

The reverse reason is also a problem. The construction business is short on expertise and skilled labour. It is a highly competitive field where other forms of the infrastructure, especially the ports and the impending boom in urban and rural residential and industrial housing construction, are vying for position. There is too much demand for the existing limited capacity. The type of relevant training proposed in the chapter on HRD may help in meeting some of the short-term demands in question. However, the capacity of training centres and the university being what they are, the short-term solution will only be able to cover part of the demand.

Therefore, short-term HRD problems will have to be confronted with more efforts to attract Eritrean expertise in the diaspora, a task that involves accommodating generally higher salaries, housing and special schools and health protection demands. It is usually assumed that the country's labour development needs will still not be adequate. Foreign expertise is already being hired and some building activity is being handled by foreign construction companies. The implication of this for overall HRD strategy in the country is no secret. The danger of local labour replacement and consequent dependence on outside expertise is a possibility. For this reason, HRD is seen as a process not confined to formal and adult education alone. Foreign expertise is hired both to solve immediate needs and to train local personnel who will take over.

The years of war have disrupted the smooth and normal transfer of basic skills to the younger generation. Pre-war Eritrea boasted a wealth of medium-level technical skills that enriched Ethiopia and could even be gainfully employed in the Middle East. The older generation has not yet died out and the collective memory of hard work and inventiveness is still within reach and can be salvaged. The private sector has a vital role to play here, and plans and projects to encourage micro and small enterprises should be conceived in the light of their importance for skill acquisition and transfer. Laxity and complacency among young people are now being tempered by the National Service, an 18-month exercise that combines military training with production activities. This is a component of HRD whose short- and long-term benefits are already showing. What follows National Service is naturally of great national concern, as adequate job opportunities are needed to accommodate thousands of eager youths. In other words, maintaining the momentum of the programme is a condition for its total success.

Closely linked to this is the supreme national effort to ban the "culture of dependency" from the minds and habits of the population. This is a malaise enforced by years of food aid handouts, whose cure is at the base of the HRD agenda. To say that massive endeavours such as infrastructure development that require popular participation are thinkable in the face of such malaise is not to understand the magnitude of the problem. The research on social reintegration found that some returnees expect to be paid for work designed to meet their individual needs. For example, instead of being enthusiastic to complete construction of their houses and improve their living conditions, they complain about not receiving finished houses. Dependency on food handouts in times of insurmountable problems and crises is one thing, but making charity an excuse for not working is quite another.

Thus HRD is not merely about education and healthcare, nor is it confined to the immediate and future training needs of the country. It is also about human behaviour and work habits that must be restored or learned anew. Every nation has its dependants, groups and even sections of the population vulnerable to natural disasters or the onslaught of market competition. Every society also has its vagrants and dependants by choice. Eritrea has had its share of such people and charity, alms-giving and nurturing poor relatives have always been national religious and cultural attributes. What is totally unacceptable to the government today is the level and extent of food-aid dependency. In times of crisis it may not be avoided, but its persistence in times of peace cannot be condoned.

The food security policy in Eritrea attacks this threat of hunger and dependency by working towards making food available and accessible at all times and in all areas of the country, through local production increases and improvements and commercial purchases in times of need. Food aid comes into the picture only when supply through these two means is inadequate, or in emergency situations caused, for example, by natural disasters. In other words, food aid is accepted as a short-term supplement pending the attainment of permanent food security.

Even here, food aid has been qualified by the move toward monetization. Monetization has replaced food aid handouts and the FFW programme, which had successively been the practice in the country. The move caused a stir at local, national and international levels. It also met with stiff resistance from some international donors to the extent that no significant food aid came into the country, causing shortages, especially in some remote areas.

The controversy around the food aid monetization policy has been briefly discussed in research findings on the topic. The further criticism is made here that the government is imposing harsh measures for causes that can wait. The fight against dependency may be justifiable, but would the government not be well advised, the argument goes, to use all the food aid it can get for the moment and concentrate on projects such as infrastructure, to pave the way for realizing its food security policy? Why purchase food?

Herein lies the crux of the matter. "Can the government really wait?" is the counter-argument. Thirty years of aid and technical assistance have produced mostly negative results. Human suffering in the Third World, especially Africa, is at its shocking worst. Corrupt governments, political parties and pressure groups are thriving on a culture of dependency that has scourged human dignity, self-respect and self-reliance. Should a new nation not learn from this and chart a new course? Should it not seize this opportunity while still largely untainted by the political and social ills that beleaguer most of Africa to score a few strategic victories?

These ideas are at the heart of the food security policy and the prime motive behind the monetization decision. Food aid monetization is meant to help people earn the food that would otherwise be handed to them for not working. However, it has become the object of a controversy over technicalities. Questions concerning who should control the food so acquired, how price mechanisms should be set, and what role the private sector has in actually selling to beneficiaries, obliterate the far-sightedness and level of commitment behind the policy – at least from the government's point of view.

The controversy arises partly from a basic mistrust of government on the part of most of the "donor" community, which tends to put all African governments in one category, distinguished by corruption and inefficiency. The government's food security policy should not be bogged down in this controversy, which as a short-term measure is only incidental to the whole strategy. Food security should instead be analysed in relation to HRD, the infrastructure and social reintegration.

Efforts to increase agricultural productivity and introduce new techniques and improved seed are showing extremely impressive results at the pilot level. Other income-generating activities, such as a flower project near Asmara, are also showing encouraging signs. During the research discussions, concern was voiced on the wisdom of the approach known as the Sasakawa model, which is said to have failed in some countries. The Ministry of Agriculture argues that failures and mistakes do not necessarily repeat themselves in every situation. It all depends on how a model is adapted. There is a lot of optimism in the ministry and the government that a remarkable improvement in production will start to show in a few years' time.

A recurring concern is the possible sidelining of pastoral communities due to the spread of commercial agriculture and returnee and ex-combatant settlement in pastoral areas. This is an age-old issue originating in Italian times. If such displacements have taken place in the rush and confusion of post-Independence, they were not sanctioned by the law. The legal position is that proper readjustments will be made. The Land Proclamation clearly states that grazing areas are to be left to customary use and, unless specifically changed by law, they are also administered in accordance with customary law. The new law, on the other hand, opens up adequate opportunities for pastoralists who wish to settle individually or form co-operative farms. Some have been known to do this (Land Commission, 1995).

The pastoralism issue, along with problems of sedentary agriculture areas, will be settled only when the Land Proclamation is implemented in rural areas. In fact, the Ministry of Agriculture has consistently called for implementation as it sees the delay as a big hurdle to the realization of its food security policy.

Other problems should be taken into account, such as the impact of commercially purchased food and monetization on market prices of locally produced food, and the effects of the massive return of refugees on food availability. One point worth stressing again is that the infrastructure, especially roads, appears to be the most enduring challenge to attaining the food security objective.

The new zonal administration is discussed in detail in the chapter on governance. The pivotal role that administration plays in harnessing resources for national development needs no elaboration. Institutional and labour capacity problems are the main obstacles for effective local government. The chapter also discusses some decline in administrative efficiency and quality of administrators relative to the standards of EPLF days. It appears that, until the zones upgrade the capacity of their own personnel and recruit expertise, their dependence on central government bodies will continue to a large extent. So the need for effective and efficient communication between the two is evident. This factor may slow down the degree of decentralization that zonal administration will need for effective planning and implementation.

The success of the new local administration structure or policy will thus depend heavily on how fast the government's overall HRD strategy progresses. In the meantime, project implementation in the zones is likely to remain a labour-intensive endeavour largely dependent on popular participation. Popular participation in the Eritrean context is, apart from its voluntary aspect, a component of national policy that begins at the village level, where all adult members of both sexes form the *megab'aya* (village session), the lowest level of the legislative ladder. However, the *megab'aya* is more than a legislative body, as it is designed to deliberate on all the affairs of the village and decide and implement projects affecting it. The arrangement does not preclude other forms of participation and organization.

The other major problem facing effective zonal administration is infrastructure. This is more pronounced in the more remote areas of the

Anseba, Gash-Barka, and Southern and Northern Red Sea regions. This is pointed out in the chapter on infrastructure, which establishes that the implications reach well beyond administrative convenience and efficiency and into the very success of the national development strategy.

The question of priorities

We have indicated that it may not be appropriate to talk about priorities at a time when the development strategy is being formulated and areas of priorities identified. To provide food for thought, however, this review will venture to identify "a priority of priorities" – and point to infrastructure as probably the toughest problem facing the nation.

The logic is simple. The other Entry Points discussed, although intricate and complicated, are probably not outside the reach of the national effort if the level of government commitment, rational resource allocation and popular participation anticipated are realized and properly harnessed. These three important components have continued to persist as legacies of the armed struggle and there is no indication that they are likely to betray the nation in its development efforts. They obviously require good and integrated planning and careful handling.

The success of HRD strategy, for example, will greatly depend on how successfully the educational curriculum is reformulated and how effectively the health programme is planned and rehabilitated. It seems that here ideas, proper planning and re-allocation of existing resources – rather than money and equipment – will be decisive. The task involves replacing a system and reorienting policy makers and operatives such as educators and teachers. It is a situation in which huge financial and material expense can conceivably be reduced by dedication, hard work, inventiveness and popular participation. The task also involves changing attitudes and religious and traditional biases. All this requires money, equipment and expertise that local and national resources alone may not be able to cover. With a little, but relevant, outside help and co-operation it is attainable largely through national effort.

With respect to food security, the conviction of the Ministry of Agriculture is that the national objective in this field is also not unattainable. Increasing local productivity builds on traditional agricultural knowledge and expertise, a substantial asset. Water conservation measures and research into seed improvements and diversification show encouraging results. The awakening economy is creating other employment opportunities and further improving prospects, thus raising people's ability to buy food. Here, too, local resources, initiatives, commitment and participation can shoulder most of the responsibility. Relevant and essential foreign co-operation, especially in the research and technical aspects, would greatly benefit and hasten progress.

We conclude that the challenges of the infrastructure are perhaps the most difficult and intricate facing the nation today. If there is a need for foreign co-operation, partnership, grants, loans and expertise, it is probably most visible here. Without overstating the point, and with an eye to the close interaction between all the policies, the emphasis is that infrastructure stands out as the main priority among all the priorities of post-war Eritrea.

Outstanding issues not sufficiently covered by WSP Entry Points were the making of the Constitution, the gender issue, and the question of the environment. The gender question should perhaps have been an Entry Point in itself. The chapter on social reintegration describes the difficulties of reintegrating female ex-combatants, many of whom are in danger of regressing to the traditional secondary position that women hold. This is indicative of the objective problems women face in the present economic situation and in light of societal values that still relegate women to an inferior status.

The government's position on this issue is clear, and it has taken steps with far-reaching consequences. Thus, the Land Proclamation accords women an absolute equal right of access to agricultural and residential land. Women's right to participation in national affairs is established from the *megab'aya* to the National Assembly. In the Zonal *Baito* (Regional Assembly), 30 per cent of the seats are reserved for women, and they have the additional right of competing for the remaining seats. A great deal of attention is given to improving the business capacity of women in rural and urban areas, especially those employed in MSMEs. Finally, in Article 7(2) the Constitution prohibits all practices that deny women fundamental human rights and that limit or impede their role and participation. A woman's equal status with a man in the family unit is also one of the proposals (Article 22(2)).

Obviously, laws and declarations will not be enough. The gains that women made in the armed struggle provide a strong base for further progress in this respect. The government's bold moves on the gender issue are based on foundations laid during the armed struggle. It is hoped that women will be among the chief beneficiaries of the HRD strategy being designed. It is essential for the NUEW and other such organizations to clearly identify and work in ways that lead to solving the gender problem.

The environment was one of the core issues given prominence by the government's macro policy framework. A century of colonial neglect and purposeful misuse coupled with the ravages of war exposed Eritrea to an alarming progress of desertification. The fact that the 30 per cent of land area covered with forests at the turn of the century has dwindled to less than one per cent is illustrative.

The need to protect the environment and raise environmental awareness is not new to the Eritrean population, as traditional methods of environmental conservation abound. The problem is necessity. As the infrastructure research has shown, reliance on fuel wood for the preparation of food and on tree products for housing and shelter are nationwide needs for which adequate replacements have not been found. The matter of soil conservation, including planting trees, on the other hand, is partly obstructed by traditional land tenure arrangements that do not give land-users permanent rights over land that would enable them to make significant improvements on their assigned plots.

This is an issue for which a special agency has been set up. An environmental protection and rehabilitation strategy has already been worked out and an ongoing campaign for environmental awareness has been initiated. This has been recognized as an issue of fundamental importance affecting the activities and programmes of the various bodies and agencies of the government.

The international factor

In *Rebuilding War-torn Societies*, WSP suggests that the intervention of the international community in post-conflict situations has not been integrated into a coherent approach. Humanitarian, developmental, political and military forms of action have been competing with rather than reinforcing each other. What is more, humanitarian assistance is becoming "militarized and politicized", losing its operational space and efficiency. Political assistance, on the other hand, "has often limited itself to the imposition of standard administrative and political formulas and systems ('democratization') – with little regard for local realities and specificity". As a result, international response to conflict and reconstruction has consisted of "short-term and spectacular measures" of a military and humanitarian nature.

The WSP assessment also reveals that international assistance is biased toward humanitarian and military aid. This is rooted in the notion that solutions to the problems of post-conflict societies lie in maintaining peace and in relief operations. As seen in the PROFERI debates of the early 1990s, UNHCR did not perceive its role in the refugee matter as going beyond the repatriation and initial rehabilitation stages of refugee reintegration into society.

When talking in terms of the "policy mix" at international and national levels, however, the question becomes more complex. The tilt toward humanitarian, military and political assistance can only be explained in t he context of the attitude that the so-called "developed" world has adopted toward the so-called "developing", and especially African nations and governments.

Blame for the disaster of war and poverty in most of Africa, more than 30 years after Independence from colonial rule, cannot be imputed only to the governments and people who led the countries concerned. Ever since the Congo crisis of the early 1960s, Western intervention of varying colours – political, military, cultural, humanitarian – has played a significant role in shaping the politics of the continent. African voices of the 1960s demanding that "no strings be attached" to foreign aid and technical assistance were perhaps anticipating and attempting to avert the type of dependency and irretrievable damage to African nationhood that has been caused by the particular routes African governments took. The fact that Western aid, and later Soviet assistance too, helped put in place and maintain repressive and corrupt regimes in power needs no elaboration here.

African governance is now being discredited for the state of affairs in the continent. African governments have been branded, in a dismissive and almost generic way, as corrupt, inefficient, abusive of human rights, not accountable, inclined to massive military spending and, not least significant, "dependent on foreign aid and donations, not just for development purposes, but also for their own existence".

Consequently, as is the case for the rest of the developing world, there is a growing assumption that African governments cannot deliver and must be relegated to a co-ordinating role, while donors and NGOs team up to use assistance from the developed world. The role of the latter would include policy as well as operational functions.

This attitude has been reinforced by the triumph of free market capitalism over the "socialist" camp during the last decade. A new order has been all but officially declared in the world today. Globalization, a much frequented paradigm of the 1990s, is seen as involving strategies of domination and standardization in consumer styles. The notion that the state should limit itself to fixing the framework that permits the market's free play is a basic principle of what is referred to as the one and only way of thinking. A critic of the new thinking defines it thus:

> Private ownership of all the means of production, and thus the privatization of all that belongs to the State, is indispensable. The markets will redistribute better the resources, investment and work: charity and private voluntary services must take the place of all the public programmes for the underprivileged.

It seems that this attitude has determined relations between donors and recipients for some time. Chronic poverty has increasingly forced nations of the Third World to be recipients not only of material aid and grants, but also of ideas and programmes. The African experience has shown that these were not ideas and programmes that alleviated poverty. On the contrary, and good intentions notwithstanding, they reinforced the very dependency that is now deemed to have rendered African governance ineffective and unreliable.

The reasons invented to maintain direct donor intervention in recipient countries are sometimes amazing. In a seminar on food security commissioned by the European Commission, one writer suggested that there may be four institutional combinations that affect the action of the international community. Where there is a strong state, but weak local institutions and markets, he suggests, the international community should strengthen local institutions through NGOs and local authorities, as mediators are necessary between state and local levels. Where the state is weak, but there are strong institutions and markets, co-ordinated action between donors becomes crucial if aid is not to become the hostage of some groups to the exclusion of others. Where the state and local institutions are weak, international aid should certainly intervene at various levels and with various tools. What if the state, local institutions and markets are strong, apparently an ideal mix? The international community should initiate dialogues, in this point of view. A good example is the negotiation of structural adjustment on the question of taxation.

Is there no other way of looking at things? There may be. A recent study by the World Bank's Technical Director for the African Region, Kevin Cleaver, identifies some major weaknesses in donor-supported and financed rural development strategies in Africa. In addition to the often repeated lack of government commitment to rural development and inefficiency, Cleaver criticizes donor and NGO attitudes. Thus, he sees the persistence of both in the employment of expatriate management as by-passing local management and impeding African capacity-building. This in turn leads to conflict and project failures. He sees as erroneous the small-scale projects with autonomous management, resulting in hundreds of projects that are unmanageable and unsustainable without the NGOs. Donor-supported rural projects have been ignoring the poor, whose conditions have not improved. The decline in donor support to rural development projects and integrated commodity projects have led, he claims, to a decline in donor investment in rural health, education, and infrastructure. Natural resource management projects were not sufficiently effective in retarding the high rates of soil, water, forest and wildlife degradation affecting most of Africa (Cleaver, 1996:10–12, 17–20). Cleaver calls for more careful and selective donor involvement and closer co-operation and co-ordination among governments, donors, NGOs and local communities (Cleaver, 1996:20).

Cleaver's critical assessment is refreshing. The international attitude toward aid has reflected and imposed donor assumptions and conclusions about recipient countries. Thirty years of attempts to model African societies on the Western image have resulted in misconstrued development strategies and programmes. Subsequent attempts to redirect donor intervention through NGO activities have also encountered difficulties. It is assumed that governments cannot satisfy the diversified interests and demands of civil society. It is thus incumbent on NGOs to use donor or other funds to fill the perceived gap.

NGO intentions differ and the nobility of the causes for which many of them stand cannot be assailed. In WSP discussions, the tendency of Eritrean officials to fail to see the differences among NGOs, and between NGOs on the one hand and multi- and bilaterals on the other, was pointed out. What is even less understood and appreciated is the Eritrean attitude. The way national and international policies mix in the Eritrean context deserves proper consideration because a different set of perceptions, interactions, attitudes and values are at play here.

A different "policy mix"

Eritrea joined the international community with a pragmatic and flexible approach to most of its affairs, including its policies. At this transitional juncture, the right mix of policies means how well each policy contributes to the underlying principle of laying the foundation of a self-reliant and socially just economy that holds its own competitive position in the world. As mentioned earlier, policies may complement and contradict each other. What stands against the development strategy may be modified or changed, but in a manner consistent with the overall strategy and in answer to local and national demands, not to outside pressure.

This is where national and international policies mix in Eritrea – or perhaps where they do not mix, depending on the perspective. The set of assumptions about post-conflict situations and African governance as generally perceived by the international community do not fit, in whole or in part, Eritrean realities. Standard international solutions to Third World problems are often either inapplicable or unacceptable. Existing Eritrean policies are home-grown, usually carry-overs from the days of the struggle. In fact, the Eritrean government is undertaking its own, not the International Monetary Fund's (IMF) or the World Bank's, structural initiatives and programmes.

Structural adjustment – especially as required by the IMF for eligibility for loans and grants – presses for fiscal, monetary, administrative, taxation and other such major reforms in economic and administrative spheres. It is all meant to solve many of the beneficiary states' structural problems and to provide foreign exchange to pay their inevitably huge national debt. Referring to the African and Latin American experience, Stiefel and Wolfe maintain that the adjustment programmes dictated generally "intensify the fall in employment and incomes and the curtailment of social expenditure, while leaving the future burden of debt intact". Furthermore, the highly visible negotiation with external agents, the deferred hopes of debt reduction, and the frustration of most efforts to exert national policy autonomy, have "contributed to a generalized sentiment that policy decisions have been removed to increasingly distant spheres, unresponsive to the needs of national governments and dominant classes, let alone those of the people" (Stiefel and Wolfe, 1994:162–163).

The Eritrean government has avoided this trap partly because it is in a position to do so. Structural adjustment reform is presumably aimed at curing economies and structures ailing mainly as a result of abuse or neglect by client governments. The Eritrean government had nothing to do with the destroyed economy and administrative apparatus it inherited. The old colonial state infrastructure and system of work had given way to the Derg's war-tuned and dominated provincial bureaucracy and inefficiency. What EPLF brought with it, on the other hand, was a huge army of liberation, whose "civil" section consisted of combatants unfamiliar and uncomfortable with the ways of formal government. There was, in other words, no entrenched bureaucracy to reform and what was left of fiscal, monetary, tax and other policies had gone with the Ethiopians.

Eritrea could thus chart its own course and it has formulated its national policies, no doubt with due regard also to their international implications. Ever since the formulation of the Macro-Policy Document in 1994, a series of economic and structural initiatives have been taken with implications even more far-reaching than any such reform required by the IMF or the World Bank. The Land Proclamation, for example, was proclaimed and the Investment Proclamation issued on the same date. The latter was an improvement on an earlier one issued in 1992. The old Ethiopian taxation system was overhauled and price controls removed to encourage market competition. Houses and property nationalized by the Derg were returned to their rightful owners. The process of privatizing nationalized industries is under way and the government has just announced its intention to allow the opening of private banks. Tied to this is a further Eritrean advantage: its foreign debt is negligible.

An official of the Ministry of Finance said, "Eritrea has been going to all this trouble because that is how it believes its policies should be formulated, not in anticipation of any reward from any angle". In this logical framework, the reward would and should come in the genuine international support and exchange the government feels it should get in its actual developmental efforts. With the time saved in structural adjustment negotiations – and having avoided the humiliating national sentiment that policy decisions have been removed to increasingly distant places – a sigh of relief should resound from an international community frustrated with the way things have gone elsewhere in several assistance-seeking countries.

However, it has not happened. This is where national and international policies are mixing negatively. The difficulties facing the government's policy on reintegrating returnees or PROFERI have already been referred to. Its decision to fight against dependency and complacency by monetizing food aid and pressuring able-bodied people to earn it on the market did not get the expected response. Even in the areas of HRD and infrastructure development, the nation has depended largely on its own resources.

The problem seems to be that international priorities have been pre-set to operate only under certain assumptions and conditions. The tendency to generalize problems and prescribe formulae obliterates the specific needs and demands of individual nations and peoples. Most multilateral organizations have set rules, procedures and models that create problems for the accommodation of different cases – anomalies, if preferred.

The Eritrean context introduces a new element to the general debate. By rejecting the donor/recipient relationship as it is practised in the world today, it accepts, both in theory and practice, a new partnership in development in its international relations. This arrangement is based on the premise that development is "principally a domestic challenge", with external assistance taking "a facilitating and not an initiating role, its main importance being bridging short-term and transitory resource gaps". With the termination of this transitory stage, the long-term strategy is to build up international trade relationships and encourage investment.

Any understanding that will impute into this principle notions that the government is intransigent in its external relations or that it shuns international assistance and co-operation, its officials insist, misinterprets its intentions. The principle is about the right of a nation to make and implement its own plans and policies, not about whether external assistance and co-operation are desirable or not – an issue that has never been seriously challenged. As far as the Eritrean government is concerned, any idea or programme that compromises this principle is unacceptable. That is how Eritrean policies are mixing with international ones.

THE "LEVEL" AND "ACTOR" MIXES

The WSP definitions of the "level mix" and the "actor mix" have been discussed. The former looks into the extent to which local-level actors, initiatives and social dynamics are taken into consideration in the formulation of policy. The latter, on the other hand, deals with the actual interaction between external and internal actors. How can a healthy balance be created between these two so as to make "international aid complementary to natural resources and initiatives"? What is sought here is not only the kind of "actor mix" that will reduce vulnerabilities and promote self-reliance, but also one that looks at internal/external actor relations "not only in terms of aid, but of wider economic, political and social relations of co-operation, with the latter ultimately replacing the former".

The ideas contained in the last sentence seem to coincide with the principle of "partnership in development" as conceived by the Eritrean government. There is, however, more to the matter than meets the eye. For in the "level mix", local-level problems are dealt with in terms of how they are perceived, interpreted, understood and acted on. In the "actor mix", it is the actual human and organizational interaction that is the focal point. Both involve different ways of perceiving problems. Proximity to such problems, cultural traits and biases, political ideology and orientation and local, national and international interests come into play and determine such perception. Thus the declared internal and external aims may look and sound the same, but the means to that end – intentions, agenda and principles involved – may differ.

And they do differ in the Eritrean case. The country's policies have so far been the entire responsibility of the Eritrean government. They represent local-level initiatives, social dynamics and resources the way the government has understood and acted on them. The question of whether the government's perceptions, as reflected in its policies, actually respond to the people's demands and the nation's needs can be answered only with due regard to the long- and short-term implications of the policies. The immediate post-war problems of this country are so numerous and diverse that they defy imagination. Some of the problems – for example hunger and disease – need and get immediate attention and funds otherwise earmarked for long-term development purposes. These are stop-gap measures that do not prevent recurrence of the problems. A million excuses could be provided to give hundreds of other post-conflict problems the prominence needed to be considered essential for project funding.

If projects aiming to solve short-term problems are not controlled and selectively adopted, the government might lose sight of the fact that permanent solutions to post-war problems actually lie in the future, that is in long-term policies or strategies. This has a profound meaning in the Eritrean context, as the underlying principle of all the policies discussed in this research have stressed permanent rather than temporary solutions to problems. Short-term solutions such as food aid and refugee repatriation are adopted as part of long-term policies with a great deal of discomfort and with an effort and determination to drop them from the national agenda as soon as they are overcome.

So it may well be that many post-conflict agendas have been made to wait in Eritrea. The Entry Points studied by WSP are meant to represent the basic and objective needs of the country: the problem of hunger in food security policy; health, education and employment needs in HRD strategy; the bottleneck of communications in the infrastructure; and the self-evident needs of social reintegration and good government. The short-term aspects of these policies are controlled and some details in them may appear as not being sufficiently addressed. From the point of view of some external actors in the WSP Working Groups, issues ranging from "establishment of civil society institutions to find their own solutions to the problems they face" to periodically canvassing public opinion to determine popular demands were raised.

The point that the World Bank's Kevin Cleaver raised is again appropriate here. How many projects would suffice to properly answer Eritrea's immediate problems? Indeed the whole argument against the international NGO solution to the problem of post-conflict societies has been, as Cleaver points out, that they establish hundreds of small-scale projects which are unmanageable and unsustainable without NGO assistance. The Eritrean context does not conceive of post-conflict problem solving in this manner, and if this is what is meant by responding to local demands and resources, then it will probably fail the test. So too will it fail the test of responding to international policies thus formulated and perceived.

This is not to say that the government has not directly or indirectly responded to international policies and agendas. Because one of its national development objectives is to create a modern, technologically advanced and internationally competitive economy, that it is conscious of and responsive to regional and global policies cannot be in doubt. In this respect, its approach has been pragmatic and flexible.

The government's far-reaching measures to streamline its civil service and restructure its administrative apparatus have been discussed. Some of the important legislative and policy decisions, such as the investment policy, that have been taken to position the nation on an advantageous development course have also been noted. These were all wholly its own measures and policies. Some of them, such as the land tenure changes and the new local administrative set-up, were started during the struggle. Although these are national policies designed to answer national needs, they obviously also had international implications. The Macro-Policy Document takes the international context into serious consideration.

The "level mix" is easy to identify here, as it assumes policies of different governments, multilaterals, bilaterals and NGOs interacting on the international scene. National policies hold their own in such a scenario, their point of reference being the "local initiatives, social dynamics and resources" in their respective countries. Any policy adjustments made in response to international requirements will, in this situation, not have been as a result of decisions "removed from national or local spheres".

This line of thinking fairly represents the Eritrean situation: meaningful discussion of international policies building on local-level (Eritrean) actors, initiatives, social dynamics and resources becomes difficult. So far, the international policies and actors that have gained access to Eritrean local levels are those that have been acceptable to or accommodated by national policies and actors. Whenever international policies and actors have found themselves contravening national policies, the government has not hesitated to cancel them or renegotiate their entire content and form.

WSP Working Group discussions never failed to demonstrate the effect of this thinking on the international community in Eritrea, especially NGOs. Roles and mandates are so closely defined here that the kind of leverage external actors probably have in other countries is not available. The idea of NGOs or other external actors by-passing the government – either to help in certain situations or to create their own images in Eritrean civil society – does not seem to have much of a chance in Eritrea. It should be kept in mind that international NGOs have not been operational in Eritrea since the mid-nineties.

This has raised questions and concerns about the future of civil society in Eritrea. The notion that governments cannot adequately respond to the diversity of societal demands and that, therefore, external assistance should be channelled through NGOs to champion the cause, is the main argument presented. Attempts to influence government policies by multi- and bilaterals also follow similar logic. External actors would like to know what mechanisms are available to assure popular participation and communication in policy-making processes. And, of course, "anxieties" about the future of democracy, particularly multi-party politics, are harboured.

The chapter on governance has dealt with this. It may be stressed that political reconstruction in Eritrea is not seen as separate from overall developmental strategy. The task of rebuilding a war-torn economy is regarded as a national political issue that requires harnessing and mobilizing every available national resource. That politics is at the top of this and that it should command and organize toward the realization of the objective and strategy is the underlying logic.

There is much criticism in extant literature about people's participation being made a "component of national policy" (Stiefel and Wolfe, 1994:9-10). The criticism will hold where that policy is not coherent and effective and where there is a lack of leadership and commitment in its implementation. Theories that view popular participation as a weapon opposing rather than co-operating with national policies assume the existence of fundamental conflicts between those policies and popular demands. The argument that sees civil society as organizing to form an alternative to government is based on this premise. There would be, to repeat, as many civil society institutions and NGOs as there would be issues. It is rumoured that some countries are literally run by NGOs.

Eritrea does not allow this. The argument would be that there is a strong government in this country that is determined to make its own policies, commit its own mistakes, correct them in its own way, and run the country according to its perceived needs. The issue of whether its policies reflect those of local-level actors, initiatives and social dynamics, it will be argued, will be resolved in the way the government tackles the people's post-war problems. Whether these will need changes and whether those changes will be effected through the creation of new civil society institutions is a matter for time and the internal interplay of forces to decide. The same apparently holds true for multi-party politics, the desirability of which is not in question, but the advent of which apparently depends on the satisfaction of a set of political, social and economic conditions.

With the institution of constitutional government just around the corner and government restructuring and streamlining coming to its final phase, many of the ambiguities of the transitional period will come to an end. This will further clarify national and local mandates, which are in turn expected to define how national and international policies will interact and work toward not only the disentanglement of Eritrea from its post-war conditions, but also toward aiding it to become a contributor to international political and economic affairs.

Therefore, the level and actor mixes in the Eritrean context offer a new set of national and international relationships. They leave no room for paternalistic, interventionist, and donor-oriented attitudes and approaches that have generally proved to be a waste of international resources and have resulted in disaster in most recipient countries. Instead, Eritrea has charted an independent and basically self-reliant course that invites co-operation and assistance in a "partnership in development" framework.

This may not be the first time that the international community has heard of such a "partnership". The difference is that the Eritreans mean it. To them, development is "a domestic challenge" and, if international co-operation is available only in a way that compromises the charted strategy, all indications suggest that they will proceed on their own.

CONCLUDING REMARKS

WSP Eritrea research into the Entry Points was a stimulating and beneficial exercise that brought to the fore issues and problems in their interaction with each other. The fact that internal and external actors could exchange views, reaffirm similar opinions, overcome differences and compare experiences will stand out as its chief value. In fact the WSP experience was considered so important that concrete moves were taken to establish a successor body after the Project Group meeting of December 1996. A Transitional Committee proposed a Centre for Eritrean Development Studies (CEDS) that would carry on research on dialogue and action initiated by WSP, concentrating mainly on HRD.

In the meantime, the government had finished a broad-based HRD study, carried out at the national level. One of the results of that study was the decision to establish research and HRD units throughout its ministries and other bodies. Because the proposed Centre was, by statute, to draw heavily on the government's human and material resources – and to work closely with it – its perceived relationship with the HRD units still in formation became unclear. There was a feeling in the government that, rather than rushing into the creation of a centre that, in view of the country's strained human resources, could not be adequately staffed, it would be preferable to first empower the units dispersed throughout the government and then form institutions of the type proposed to succeed WSP. This logic prevailed and in spite of the recognized value of the WSP experience the government decided to shut down the Centre, at least for the time being.

This decision notwithstanding, the WSP exercise and its results are still regarded as having contributed to the development debate in Eritrea. This review has attempted to look at the research results from the point of view of the fundamental principles on which the policies of the country are based. The uniqueness of the Eritrean situation has been highlighted. This approach has been chosen as the value of the whole exercise lies in injecting into the general debate the new or original ideas and practice Eritrea has to offer. To date the Eritrean experience has been largely confined to newspaper articles and mission reports and has not really come to the surface where it could be discussed in detail. WSP can take the credit for opening up this forum.

Throughout the research, external actors consistently raised the point that there is a problem of communication on the part of the Eritrean government. Many pointed out that this is a government that says as little as possible – even about its best accomplishments – and this generally gives rise to misunderstandings about plans and intentions. National counterparts have argued that the problem may concern the content and perhaps the manner of what is communicated. Indeed, here is a government that forgoes immediate benefits in preference to long-term results and in a world of lobbies, behind-the-scene dealings, ulterior motives and hidden agendas, the Eritrean approach may appear unconventional. The cultural and historical roots of the Eritrean way of communicating are discussed in the chapter on governance and are mentioned here to point out the need for improvements along these lines. Membership in the international community brings with it interactions that require adjustments in the way governments and peoples communicate and relate, and there are lessons that Eritrea must learn here.

Improving communication, however, does not mean compromising principles or changing policies to suit external demands and pressure. The uniqueness of the Eritrean experience has been that it charted its own course. The challenge to the outside world is to accept the possibility that disadvantaged nations can find their way through the webs and tangles of the development dilemma. In other words, international co-operation should work toward creating equality among states, and free itself from policies and attitudes that categorize the world as either advanced or backward, advantaged or disadvantaged, and as "donor" or "recipient".

REFERENCES

Cleaver, Kevin, *Global 2000 Workshop*, 1996.

Land Commission, *Report on Barka Region*, 1995.

Stiefel, Matthias and Wolfe, Marshall, *A Voice for the Excluded: Popular Participation in Development – Utopia or Necessity?*, Zed Press/UNRISD, London and Geneva, 1994.

WSP, *Rebuilding War-torn Societies: Problems of International Assistance in Conflict and Post-Conflict Situations*, UNRISD, Geneva, 1994.

ANNEX I: BIBLIOGRAPHY

Anderson, D. and Fishwick, R., *Fuelwood Consumption and Deforestation in African Countries,* World Bank, Washington D.C., 1984.

Bridger, G. A. and Winpenny, J. T., *Planning Development Projects: A Practical Guide to the Choices and Appraisal of Public Sector Investments,* HMSO, London, 1983.

Centre for Development Studies, *Eritrea 1991: A Needs Assessment Study,* final report to the Emergency Relief Desk, University of Leeds, Leeds, May 1992.

Cleaver, Kevin, *Global 2000 Workshop,* 1996.

Cliffe, Lionel R., "The Indirect Effects of the War and the Disruption of the Overall Economy", in Resoum Kidane, Lionel Cliffe, June Rock and Philip White, *The Patterns and Socio-economic and Environmental Impacts of Conflict in Eritrea,* Occasional Paper No. 14 in the series Environment and Development in an Age of Transition, University of Leeds, Centre for Development Studies, Leeds, 1996.

CERA, *Evaluation of the Agricultural Component of the Pilot Phase of PROFERI,* Asmara, 1995.

Department of Reintegration of Demobilized Fighters (Mitias), *Annual Report, 1995,* in Tigrinya, Mitias, 1996.

Department of Reintegration of Demobilized Fighters (Mitias), *Survey of the Ex-Combatants,* Mitias, 1993.

EW&FIS, *Rainfall Records,* Asmara, 1996.

ERRA, *Food Needs Assessment Report,* Asmara, 1992.

ERREC, *1995 Annual Report, PROFERI,* Asmara, 1996.

Fatton Jr., Robert, *Predatory Rule: State and Civil Society in Africa,* Lynne Rienner, Boulder and London, 1992.

Firebrace, James and Holland, Stuart, *Never Kneel Down: Drought, Development and Liberation in Eritrea,* Bertrand Russell House,

Nottingham, 1984.

FAO, *Eritrea: Agricultural Sector Review and Project Identification,* Report No. TCP/ERI/2353, 3 Vols., Rome, 1994.

FAO, *Eritrea – National Livestock Development Project Preparation Report,* 2 Vols., Rome, 1995.

FAO, *Food Requirements and Population Growth,* WFS/96/TECH/10, Rome, 1996a.

FAO, *Food Security and Nutrition,* WFS/96/TECH/9, Rome, 1996b.

Gaerke, Inge et al., *Promoting the Reintegration of Former Female and Male Combatants in Eritrea: Possible Contributions of Development Co-operation to the Reintegration Programme,* draft report, German Development Institute, Berlin, May 1995.

GSE, *Basic Education Statistics and Essential Indicators: 1994 – 1995,* GSE Ministry of Education, 1996b.

GSE, *Eritrea: Strategy for Human Resources Development – a Project for Capacity Building,* GSE Office of Human Resource Development, 1996a.

GSE, *Establishment of Local Government Proclamation 26/1992,* 1992a.

GSE, *Investment Proclamation 59/1994,* 1994a.

GSE, *Macro-Policy Document,* Asmara, 1994c.

GSE, *National Environmental Management Plan for Eritrea,* Asmara, 1995.

GSE, *Land Proclamation 58/1994,* 1994b.

GSE, *Study of the Private Sector in Eritrea,* July 1996.

GSE, *Proclamation 23/1992 to Determine Structure and Duties of the Provisional Government of Eritrea,* 1992b.

GSE, *Proclamation 37/1993 to Determine Structure and Duties of the Government of the State of Eritrea,* 1993.

Hyden, Goran, "Reciprocity and Governance in Africa", in James S. Wunsch and Dele Olowu (eds.) *The Failure of the Centralized State,* Westview, Boulder, 1990:245-269.

Immink, M., *Linkages between Integrated Food Security Programmes (IFSP) and National Food Security Policies: The Case of the IFSP/Gash-Setit, Eritrea,* unpublished report for IFSP, Asmara, 1995.

Imperial Ethiopian Government (IEG), *Railway Administration in Eritrea: A Short Description of the System,* IEG, Asmara, 16 November 1965.

Keane, John, *Democracy and Civil Society,* Verso, London, 1988.

Kibreab, Gaim, *Ready and Willing...but Still Waiting,* Life and Peace

Institute, Uppsala, 1996.

Koehn, Peter and Hyden, Goran, *Decentralization for Social Planning in Eritrea,* paper for MLG and UNICEF, January 1996.

Land Commission, *Report on Barka Region,* 1995.

Leach, Gerald and Mearns, Robin, *Beyond the Woodfuel Crisis: People, Land and Trees,* Earthscan, London, 1988.

Mamdani, Mahmoud, *Democratic Theory and Struggles,* in *Democratization Process in Africa: Problems and Prospects,* CODESRIA, 1992.

Ministry of Finance, *Partnership in Development,* January 1995.

Moore, David B., "Development Discourse as Hegemony: Toward an Ideological History, 1945–1995", in David B. Moore and Gerald J. Schmitz (eds.) *Debating Development Discourse: Institutional and Popular Perspectives,* Macmillan and St. Martin, London and New York, 1995:1-53.

Myers, C. and Harbison, F., *Education, Manpower and Economic Growth: Strategies of Human Resource Development,* McGraw-Hill, New York, 1965.

Nader, Leonard and Nader, Zeace, *The Handbook of Human Resources Development,* Wiley and Sons, New York, 1990.

Nauheimer, M., *Animal Health and Livestock Production in Gash and Setit: Assessment of the Sector and Proposal for Improvement,* unpublished report for IFSP, Tessenei, Eritrea, 1995.

Nielsen, Soren Walther, *Capacities and Vulnerabilities in Times of Disaster and Recovery: A Case Study of Eritrea,* Roskilde University Centre, Roskilde, 1995.

PFDJ, *National Charter for Eritrea,* Nacfa, 1994.

Robertson, V., Bristow, S., Oxby, C. and Abu Ahmed, J., *Assessment and Management of Riverine Forests, Western Lowlands, Eritrea,* unpublished report for SOS Sahel, Asmara, 1994.

Schwartz, H. J., *Appraisal of Livestock Production in Gash and Setit Provinces,* unpublished report for IFSP, Asmara, 1994.

Sorenson, Christian, *Alebu: Eritrean returnees restore their livelihoods,* paper presented at the conference Reconstructing Livelihoods: Toward a New Model of Resettlement (9–13 September 1996), Refugee Studies Program, Oxford, 1996.

State of Eritrea, Ministry of Agriculture, *Reports,* Asmara, 1996.

State of Eritrea, Ministry of Industry and Trade, *Reports,* Asmara, 1996.

State of Eritrea, Ministry of Marine Resources, *Reports,* Asmara, 1996.

State of Eritrea, Ministry of Transport, *ETSS: Transport Sector Study,* Transport Survey Report, Vol. 1, Ministry of Transport, 1996.

Stiefel, Matthias and Wolfe, Marshall, *A Voice for the Excluded: Popular Participation in Development – Utopia or Necessity?,* Zed Press/ UNRISD, London and Geneva, 1994.

Telecommunication Services of Eritrea (TSE), *Development of the Telecommunications Network in Eritrea (1994-2008).*

Tseggai, Araia, *Eritrea's Railway and Ropeway System,* Eritrea Profile, 21 May 1994.

UNRISD/PSIS, *Rebuilding War-torn Societies: Problems of International Assistance in Conflict and Post-Conflict Situations,* Geneva, November 1994.

University of Leeds, *Food Needs Assessment Study,* University of Leeds, 1991.

War-torn Societies Project (WSP), *Rebuilding War-torn Societies: Problems of International Assistance in Conflict and Post-Conflict Situations,* UNRISD, Geneva, 1994.

World Bank, *Eritrea: Options and Strategies for Growth,* World Bank Report No. 12930-ER, Vol. 1, Eastern Africa Department, Africa Region, Washington, D.C., 1994a.

World Bank, *Poverty and Hunger: Issues and Options for Food Security in Developing Countries,* World Bank, Washington, D.C., 1986.

World Bank, *Sub-Saharan Africa: From Crisis to Sustainable Growth,* World Bank, Washington, D.C., 1989.

World Bank, *World Development Report 1994: Infrastructure for Development,* Oxford University Press, New York, 1994b.

World Bank, *World Development Report 1996: From Plan to Market,* Oxford University Press, New York, 1996.

ANNEX II: GLOSSARY OF TERMS

adi	village
agnet	makeshift tent
arkobkobai	doum palm tree
awraja	province
baito	district or village-level assembly
bdho	resistance committee
benello	paint brush
birr	Ethiopian monetary unit effective in Eritrea until its replacement by the Eritrean nacfa in November 1997
cambo	camp
Commissario	colonial Italian provincial officer representing the state
dama	Kunama people's village assembly
dehninet	agents of the Derg spy network
demaniale	government land
diglel	feudal lord
Hagerawi Baito	national council
kebabi	a group of villages or settlements
kebele	local political structure imposed by Ethiopia
kentiba	feudal lord
Mahber Fikri Hager	an informal association advocating civil and human rights
megab'aya	village session
meslene	subdistrict head
Mitias	Department of Reintegration of Demobilized Fighters: a semi-autonomous body established within ERRA to deal specifically with the reintegration of demobilized fighters
(food) monetization	raising money by selling donated food

nacfa	Eritrean monetary unit, effective November 1997
shum	feudal lord
sukunda	wise man in the *dama*
swa	local beverage
taita	staple food
wereda	district